THE CIVIL WAR IN MARYLAND

RECONSIDERED

CONFLICTING WORLDS
New Dimensions of the American Civil War
T. Michael Parrish, Series Editor

THE CIVIL WAR IN
MARYLAND
RECONSIDERED

EDITED BY CHARLES W. MITCHELL
AND JEAN H. BAKER

Foreword by Adam Goodheart

LOUISIANA STATE UNIVERSITY PRESS
BATON ROUGE

Published by Louisiana State University Press
lsupress.org

Manufactured in the United States of America
First printing

DESIGNER: Michelle A. Neustrom
TYPEFACE: Adobe Caslon Pro
PRINTER AND BINDER: Sheridan Books, Inc.

JACKET ILLUSTRATION: Belger Barracks, Baltimore, Maryland. Lithograph and
print by E. Sachse & Co., Baltimore, circa 1863. Prints and Photographs Division,
Library of Congress.

LIBRARY OF CONGRESS CATALOGING-IN-PUBLICATION DATA

Names: Mitchell, Charles W., 1954– editor. | Baker, Jean H., editor.
Title: The Civil War in Maryland reconsidered / edited by Charles W. Mitchell,
    and Jean H. Baker.
Description: Baton Rouge : Louisiana State University Press, [2021] | Series:
    Conflicting worlds: new dimensions of the American Civil War | Includes bibli-
    ographical references and index.
Identifiers: LCCN 2021020468 (print) | LCCN 2021020469 (ebook) | ISBN 978-0-
    8071-7289-6 (cloth) | ISBN 978-0-8071-7674-0 (pdf) | ISBN 978-0-8071-7675-7
    (epub)
Subjects: LCSH: Maryland—History—Civil War, 1861–1865.
Classification: LCC E566 .C58 2021 (print) | LCC E566 (ebook) | DDC
    973.709752—dc23
LC record available at https://lccn.loc.gov/2021020468
LC ebook record available at https://lccn.loc.gov/2021020469

For Fergus Fulton MacKinnon and Adele Elizabeth Farha,
the vanguard of the next generation;
and for those Maryland Unionists who wrote, spoke,
fought, convened, nursed, and organized to protect
the nation at its most perilous moment.

CONTENTS

FOREWORD

The Civil War has never quite ended in Maryland. As I write this, 160 years since the first blood was shed, at least one young Confederate still stands unvanquished here on the state's Eastern Shore. Having stood sentry duty for more than a century in front of the Talbot County courthouse, that rebel volunteer—his boyish features molded in copper—continues stoutly to resist all efforts to remove him. Even as dozens of similar monuments have toppled all across the heartland of the former Confederacy, local officials insist that this one serves an essential purpose. It is, in the words of one supporter, "a piece of history and a splendid work of art that tells the story of brother vs. brother where North and South came together, the border state of Maryland."

The lone figure of an infantryman clasping the rebel flag, set on a granite base inscribed with the names of local Confederates, certainly does tell *a* Civil War story—albeit a very partial one. Among many other omissions, it ignores the fact that approximately two-thirds of the men who marched off to war from Talbot County did so wearing the Union blue, including hundreds of African Americans, many of them newly freed from enslavement, who enlisted in the US Colored Troops. Yet its narrative has long been prevalent throughout Maryland, and not only on the rural Eastern Shore: that this was a state kept in the Union only at the point of a bayonet, a place where white supremacy was as intrinsic to regional identity as crab cakes and fried chicken. As late as 1948, citizens of Baltimore gathered to dedicate a massive bronze monument to Robert E. Lee and Stonewall Jackson, with Mayor Thomas D'Alesandro—a staunch New Deal Democrat—urging those in the crowd to let the exemplary lives of the Confederates "remind us to be resolute and determined in preserving our sacred institutions." (The mayor's daughter, Nancy D'Alesandro Pelosi, would grow up to order paintings of Confederates removed from the US Capitol.)

Alternative Civil War stories have always been there, for those who would look and listen. Talbot County—like other communities in even the most "Confederate" parts of Maryland—had an active chapter of the Grand Army of the Republic founded by local Black veterans, who marched in their old uniforms each November to celebrate the state's 1864 passage of emancipation. Some of their descendants continue the tradition to this day.

The Civil War in Maryland Reconsidered, too, is a timely and important corrective to the myth-encrusted narratives that still cling stubbornly to public understanding of our nation's greatest conflict. And while its focus is on Maryland—a state that played an outsize role in the fighting—many of its lessons are larger ones. The scholars represented here, while telling many different stories, together weave a Civil War saga rich in complexities and ambiguities, shredding the familiar dualisms of Union/Confederate, Black/white, North/South, freedom/slavery.

It is, in its own way, a monument.

ADAM GOODHEART
Director of the Starr Center For the Study
of the American Experience, Washington College

ACKNOWLEDGMENTS

The editors wish, foremost, to extend their appreciation to the authors of the chapters in this volume. Their expertise has brought fresh perspectives on topics related to the Maryland Civil War experience that have long required further examination, and they have done so with good cheer while balancing their many professional and personal responsibilities. We have learned a great deal from their insights.

Historians rely on the skills and patience of librarians, archivists, and those who work in special collections. We are particularly grateful to the professionals at the Maryland Center for History and Culture in Baltimore (formerly the Maryland Historical Society) who over the years have made it possible for us, our authors, and countless other researchers to explore the institution's rich collection of materials related to the Civil War in Maryland. We also extend our appreciation to the staffs of other institutions who have helped our work over the years, including those at the Maryland State Archives, the Library of Congress, the Freedmen and Southern Society Project, and the Special Collections Library at the University of Maryland–College Park, Goucher College, Towson University, the Johns Hopkins University (and its archives at the Peabody Library), the Maryland Department of the Enoch Pratt Free Library, the Archives of the Episcopal Diocese of Maryland, and a number of county historical societies in the state.

We also thank Paul Dotson, Editor-in-Chief at the Louisiana State University Press, and Michael Parrish, Professor of History at Baylor University and editor of LSU's Conflicting Worlds series, for their guidance and enthusiasm for this project. We are grateful for the scholars and students of the Maryland Civil War story who will use this work in their own study of a subject that will forever warrant further scrutiny.

THE CIVIL WAR IN MARYLAND

RECONSIDERED

INTRODUCTION

JEAN H. BAKER & CHARLES W. MITCHELL

Maryland's Civil War history—unique, controversial, of enduring interest—has always been a rich vein of state remembrance. In the first phase of this history, Confederate and Union soldiers, often years after the war, published their accounts of what one called "the story of what [soldiers] saw and experienced in the great civil war for the Union," an approach described by historian Carol Reardon as "What Happened to Me."[1] Their memories mirrored the divided allegiances that characterized Maryland's anomaly as a border slave state supporting the Union, a state that contained pockets of opposition to the Lincoln government and that was initially characterized by clamorous minority support for the Confederacy. Most Marylanders endorsed the Union to some degree, but the state's allegiance in the early days of the war became a flash point of historical contention.

Before professional historians began their assessments, Maryland soldiers on both sides provided nostalgic accounts of their wartime service. For example, Frederick Wild, a private in a Baltimore-recruited Union artillery battery, described his enlistment, capture, parole, and the pride he felt when his unit's twelve-pound Napoleons were wheeled into position and started firing. It was like "a tornado howling through the forest."[2] Most firsthand accounts by participants celebrated the fellowship of soldiers and made only passing comments about the enemy and the larger political environment. In 1871 Private Charles Camper of the First Maryland Infantry was an exception, excoriating the Confederates as "base traitors who have attempted to fire this temple of American liberty." At least for the time being "heaven" (and he as well) were "too indignant for forgiveness." Camper expressed his shame that some of his fellow Marylanders had "lifted arms against the glorious Union of these states."[3]

There was little early commentary on the state's emancipation of its enslaved in 1864 or the role of Black soldiers in Maryland forces. Several former Union soldiers, writing at the turn of the century, intended their memoirs to instill patriotism among younger generations. They wrote to educate the state's increasing number of immigrants in what they considered the necessary self-sacrifice required in their new nation.

The accounts by Maryland's Confederate soldiers—numbering about one-third of the state's Union soldiers—became the most popular memoirs. Encouraged by the Maryland Historical Society and written at the turn of the century when state Democrats were attempting to end Black voting and replace slavery with legalized white supremacy, these battleground reminiscences provided support for the state's version of Lost Cause historiography. They accompanied a period, nearly half a century after the war, when Confederate sympathizers throughout the South who had lost the war began to win it in the history books.

For many years they were successful. Henry Kyd Douglas's *I Rode with Stonewall Jackson* later became the most popular of these accounts. (Douglas's self-promotion led one reviewer to comment that a more apt title would have been "Stonewall Rode with Me.") W. W. Goldsborough published *The Maryland Line in the Confederate States Army 1861–1865*, his account of the glory days of the Maryland troops, in 1900, the year that the Poe Amendment disenfranchising Black voters was first introduced into the Maryland legislature and later defeated in a state referendum. During this period statues of Confederate generals and soldiers were placed on public grounds in Baltimore and Annapolis. George Booth's *A Maryland Boy in Lee's Army: Personal Reminiscences of a Maryland Soldier in the War Between the States* appeared in 1898. At the same time in his speeches and writing, former Confederate general Bradley Johnson tried to transform Maryland into what it never had been—a loyal southern state.

By the 1920s most soldiers had died, and Maryland's Civil War experience moved from living memory into written history. By this time the state had developed a Confederate identity, a powerful tool that helped maintain racial segregation and oppression. Events in the Maryland Civil War story, especially in the early days of the war, fit neatly, if inaccurately, into this grand narrative of a noble Confederacy defeated solely because of the Union's greater resources and the tyranny of the Lincoln administration.

In this mythical Maryland version of the Lost Cause, only the detention of members of the state legislature, Lincoln's suspension of the writ of habeas corpus, and the federal army's occupation of Baltimore's Federal Hill by Benjamin Butler's troops in May 1861 kept the state in the Union. Other elements of this false narrative included the response by patriots to the city's "occupation" following the famous Baltimore Riot of April 1861, while the Merryman case revealed the degree to which federal power trampled on the states' rights of Marylanders. The arrest of some Maryland legislators in the fall of 1861 prevented the state from joining the Confederacy, though in fact the legislature, meeting in special session that spring and unimpeded by the federal government, had agreed that it lacked the authority to consider any articles of secession or, indeed, to take any action that could have led to broader public consideration of secession such as a convention.

The autumn arrests of legislators did, however, chart the course for the later neo-Confederate argument that throughout the war the Lincoln government subjected Maryland to unconstitutional and arbitrary actions that kept the state harnessed to the Union. This posture ignored the Baltimore business community's vigorous opposition to secession and overlooked the election of a Unionist governor in November 1861.

This emphasis on federal oppression, so critical to the Lost Cause ideology, had been captured earlier in James Randall's poem, "Maryland, My Maryland," which became the state's official anthem in 1938, with its opening stanza, "The despot's heel is on thy shore/Avenge the patriot gore that flecked the streets of Baltimore." Maryland became a star witness in the so-called "War of Northern Aggression," a view fostered by romantic views of the Old South and promoted by the Sons of Confederate Veterans. Their female counterpart—the United Daughters of the Confederacy—scrutinized the content of schoolbooks well into the twentieth century to ensure that the Lost Cause ideology was perpetuated among Maryland's young people.

For years these views maintained their hold on historical interpretations, and they percolated into state histories as well as general studies of the Civil War. Matthew Page Andrews, writing in 1925 in one of the early and most comprehensive state histories, took the positions that Maryland was part of the antebellum South, that Lincoln's April 1861 suspension of the writ of habeas corpus was illegal, and that Maryland suffered military tyranny throughout the war that reached "Russia-like proportions."[4] Charles Clark, in his 1940 doctoral dissertation at the University of North Carolina, parts of which were excerpted in the *Maryland Historical Magazine*, also exaggerated the state's pro-Confederate sentiment, holding that most Marylanders sided with the South and that only federal military force kept the state tethered to the Union. As late as 1995 a Maryland author argued that the state deserved the Confederacy's twelfth star. But by this time such views collided with the historical evidence developed by university-trained scholars.

Still, preoccupation with the state's allegiance choked off consideration of the kind of examination of state military units, Union and Confederate, that characterized the Civil War history of other states. To this day no comprehensive study of the military operations of the Army of the Potomac's Maryland Brigade and the Maryland Line of the Army of Northern Virginia exists, although Kevin Ruffner's *Maryland's Blue and Gray: A Border State's Union and Confederate Junior Office Corps* explores the experiences, backgrounds, and postwar careers of 365 officers who served in the Virginia theater of operations. Maryland historians did give ample attention to the Battle of Fort Royal, a Confederate victory, when two Maryland regiments, one Confederate, one Union, fought against each other in the brothers' war that romanticized the state's experience.

In time, historical interpretations of Maryland's Civil War shifted, influenced by the civil rights movement of the 1950s–1960s and by new approaches to the discipline of history. These revisions grew out of sophisticated analysis of the state's political history and especially its voting, the latter as accurate an opinion poll as exists for the nineteenth century. During the Civil War the state clearly favored Unionist candidates, and even in the presidential election of 1860, when Lincoln received fewer than three thousand votes and the southern Democratic candidate John Breckinridge won a plurality of votes, nearly 55 percent of the state's ballots were cast for candidates who supported the Union. In the most telling example, the Union Party candidate, former Whig Augustus Bradford, easily defeated the States Rights Party candidate for governor in 1861. Despite the complaint of voter suppression by the military, it was impossible to argue that Union forces had interfered with all the state's wartime elections. In time a broad consensus emerged that Maryland's wartime allegiance throughout the conflict was to the Union.

New analysis of primary materials also helped overturn the increasingly unsustainable Lost Cause narrative. Fresh topics emerged at the end of the twentieth century; women, Blacks and the home front were written into Maryland's wartime experiences and the conflict was no longer confined to the battlefield. In 2003 Edward Longacre published the first account of the state's Black soldiers. His study of the Maryland Fourth Colored Infantry Regiment, part of the all-Black Third Division of the Eighteenth Army Corps, chronicled in detail the transition of former slaves and free Blacks into a fighting unit raised in Baltimore. The unit took part in a series of significant military actions from North Carolina to the famous 1864 battle in Petersburg, Virginia. Earlier Charles Wagandt described the process of emancipation in *The Mighty Revolution: Emancipation in Maryland* (1964), and Barbara Jeanne Fields broke new ground with her 1965 analysis of enslavement in *Slavery and Freedom on the Middle Ground: Maryland during the Nineteenth Century.*

As the pillars of pro-southern arguments began to crumble, historians reevaluated the iconic events in the Maryland story—the 1860 presidential election, the Baltimore Riot, the Merryman case, and the arrest of Maryland legislators and others detained on suspicion of subversive activity. These episodes were now interpreted not as dispositive events forcing the state into support for the Union, but rather as occasional overreaches of federal power that did not affect the state's allegiance. Careful scrutiny of military arrests in Maryland, for example, revealed that most had little to do with suppressing support for the Confederacy, but rather comprised the jailing of a motley band of smugglers, southern refugees, and blockade runners, along with the occasional interrogation of suspected disloyalists. By the twenty-first century the Lost Cause narrative no longer dominated state histories; no longer was Maryland history southernized, as politicians and the press mostly abandoned an ahistorical position that had been useful in efforts to sustain white supremacy and segregation. Meanwhile new avenues for research and writing emerged that went beyond military history.

The essays that follow are intended to bridge the gap between older versions of Maryland's Civil War history and new topics and interpretations. They break fresh ground. Some challenge long-held assumptions, while others provide new perspectives on old debates. All are based on a careful analysis of the records and are enhanced by the use of previously overlooked sources, the illumination of neglected subjects, and new ways of looking at Maryland's Civil War past.

Appropriately, the first three essays in *Maryland's Civil War History Reconsidered* deal with the long-neglected story of the state's enslaved and free Blacks. Given the avoidance of slavery as the cause of the Civil War and years of diversionary explanations—whether those of states' rights, northern aggression, or economic differences between Union and Confederacy—it is fitting that a book based on the latest and best twenty-first-century scholarship begin with three studies of the state's enslaved and freed Black peoples.

In "Border State, Border War: Fighting for Freedom and Slavery in Ante-bellum Maryland," Richard Bell focuses on Maryland's proximity to the free state of Pennsylvania as a determining factor in what he describes as a border war. He uses a variety of new sources including interstate sales, fugitivity, free Black life, and colonization, along with individual stories, to move us away from familiar national flash points. As he does so, the Maryland version of slavery, often obscured in the national story but required for understanding the state's wartime behavior, becomes manifest. Bell moves us beyond the dominant figures of Maryland's Black history—Harriet Tubman and Frederick Douglass. We are introduced instead to Rachel Parker, kidnapped from freedom in Pennsylvania into slavery in Maryland; the slave trader Hope Slatter, whose slave pens in Baltimore were way stations to the South's cotton fields, where so many Maryland slaves ended their lives; and most significantly, to the nameless "oceans" of runaway slaves who found freedom north of the Mason-Dixon line.

Jessica Millward continues this approach of investigating individuals in her study of the remarkable Charity Folks, who was born a slave in Anne Arundel County, later was freed, and whose children were both slave and free, circumstances that affected their relationship with their mother and to each other. Millward's chapter is a cautionary tale that what we sometimes think of as the binary conditions of slavery versus freedom were far more complicated in the realities of family relationships.

After her manumission Folks remained a caregiver in the prominent Ridout family where she had been enslaved. But now she received wages. In time she married, and having been remembered in her employer's will, was able to buy property. Some of her children remained enslaved; others were free. Illustrating the importance of genealogy as a historical tool, Millward follows Folks's children and grandchildren, some of whom became prosperous citizens living in Harlem and Annapolis. Millward displays the power of biography to tell a finely grained tale of a Maryland Black family.

Martha Jones investigates the reaction in Maryland to the infamous 1857 Dred Scott decision that denied all Blacks any rights that whites were bound to respect. Clearly such a bellwether judicial ruling had immense implications for the state's entire Black population. But it held devastating immediate repercussions for the eighty-seven thousand free Blacks who represented nearly half of the state's Black population in 1860. Before Jones's careful analysis no one had looked beyond Dred Scott as an abstraction into its application in state courts, a judicial forum of far more practical importance to Blacks than the federal courts.

Jones covers the reaction to Dred Scott in the *Baltimore Sun,* as well as Baltimore's special connections to the case through its native sons, Roger Taney and Reverdy Johnson. She finds that Maryland's state courts rejected any application of Dred Scott. Thus free Blacks retained their rights as persons of legal standing, and they continued to use the state's judicial system after 1857. Maryland's version of Dred Scott appeared in the little-known *Hughes v. Jackson* case, a complicated judicial proceeding which, under Jones's careful scrutiny, maintained limited state citizenship rights for Blacks. Dred Scott, writes Jones, was merely a "symbolic barrier."

Charles Mitchell puts to rest the question of Maryland's allegiances during the tumultuous period from Lincoln's election in November 1860 to his inauguration in March 1861. In the past, selected instances of support for the South have proved useful props to the Lost Cause argument that only federal military action prevented the state from seceding. Instead, Mitchell's sources indicate that even Marylanders who favored the right to secede and who owned slaves opposed leaving the Union. Sympathy for the South has been mistaken for advocacy of secession, while support for the Union has been overlooked.

Mitchell calibrates public opinion by analyzing several measures of nineteenth-century public opinion. First he turns on their head previous studies that emphasize that Breckinridge, the southern candidate, carried the state, and hence Maryland was for the south. Rather, in Mitchell's view, the critical finding from that election is that 55 percent of Marylanders collectively voted for Bell, Lincoln, and Douglas, all of whom supported the Union. Further, his investigation of newspapers, public meetings, petitions, business sentiment, and pamphlets during the critical secession winter reveals that Unionist voices predominated in the state. Certainly as southern states moved toward the creation of the Confederacy, there was opposition to Lincoln. But few Marylanders went beyond a tepid "Let them go in peace." "Secession," concluded one influential Marylander, "has no more friends than a corporal's guard."

As Mitchell makes clear, one of the flash points in Maryland was the pressure of a minority on Governor Thomas Hicks to convene the legislature in a special session, hopefully to begin the process of leaving the Union. But Hicks resisted for months. When he finally relented, in late April, the lawmakers met but declined to consider passing an article of secession. A telling expression of this Unionist sentiment is that after the attack on Fort Sumter, rather than being energized to support the Confederacy as was the case throughout much of the South, most Marylanders opposed this attack on the United States, a nation they had come to revere. Indeed, the title of Mitchell's article "Maryland is this Day True to the American Union" underscores this sentiment. And so it remained throughout the war.

Frank Towers focuses on what he calls "Baltimore's Secessionist Moment" during the tense period after the Baltimore Riot in April 1861. According to Towers, a group of influential public men "exploited the Riot to push for radical ends that had little popular support." Under the façade of "armed neutrality," they welcomed Confederate arms and communicated their support to leaders of that government. The Baltimore police marshal, rabid secessionist George Kane, even encouraged a group of sympathetic riflemen to come into the city. (Kane, in an example of the overreach of many of these would-be Confederates, issued an order prohibiting the flying of *American* flags in Baltimore.)

Towers looks backward into the city's political life for his explanation of the pro-Confederate behavior of this group of about thirty men. He finds the answer to their Confederate activity in the previous politics of the city. During the 1850s these men had been members of the Reform Association that had battled the Know Nothings in political campaigns notable for election-day brawling that left injured and dead on Baltimore's streets. Emboldened by their success in 1859 when they ousted the Know Nothings from control of the legislature and Baltimore city government, the reformers drew on their ideological, associational, and familial bonds with proslavery conservatives in the South. Additionally, and just as crucially, their previous political enemies, the Know Nothings, tipped toward allegiance with the Union, with Governor Hicks a prime example. In the spirit of their past, the reformers continued to oppose what they considered political fanaticism in the form of Know Nothingism and the Republican Party. They saw in the Baltimore Riot an expression of the disorder and anarchy that led them to offer their loyalty to the Confederacy, a more conservative government than that of the Lincoln administration.

With his focus on Baltimore, Timothy Orr investigates the process of raising Union troops in a city long vilified as a place of limited loyalty. (In a depressing extended expression of this prejudice, Maryland officers were removed from their commands in Gen. Ambrose Burnside's Ninth Corps because they were from suspect Maryland.) Based on archival material, much of it in the adjutant general's papers in the Maryland State Archives, Orr's chapter, "The Fighting Sons of 'My Maryland': The Recruitment of Union Regiments in Baltimore, 1861–1865," indicates that Baltimore supplied its fair share of the state's aggregate forces. Orr notes particularly the heroic effort of the Sixth Maryland Infantry at the Battle of Petersburg in 1865. Two soldiers who had enlisted in Baltimore received the Medal of Honor for their actions there.

But as Orr emphasizes, the process of recruiting in the city was a messy and chaotic one, from its beginnings in May 1861 when men volunteered to serve in the First Maryland Volunteer Infantry (Col. John Kenly's regiment) to, in December 1864, the final fourth federal draft with Baltimore's quota set at 3,700 men. As was the case throughout the United States, few Baltimoreans were ever drafted; generous bounties stimulated volunteering but also led to corrupt bounty jumpers. And there were plenty of exemptions.

Recruited from farms on the Eastern Shore and southern Maryland into the newly formed regiments of the United States Colored Infantry in Baltimore, at least some Black soldiers recently freed from slave jails helped fill the city's quota. One of the contributions of Orr's analysis is his integration of local issues, especially the city council's use of bounties, to address the problem of mobilization in a city that overall fulfilled its manpower responsibilities.

Brian Matthew Jordan illustrates the degree to which, among contemporary scholars, military topics have moved beyond battlefield tactics and a General-centric focus. In "What I Witnessed Would Only Make You Sick: Union Soldiers Confront the Dead," he investigates the reaction of Union troops as they surveyed the dead at Antietam, the first engagement in which Union troops controlled the battlefield after the firing stopped. Antietam was thus soldiers' "first intimate encounter with the grim realities of death on a massive scale." With combined casualties of over twenty-three thousand, the battlefield became a grim laboratory.

Soldiers reported in letters and diaries their efforts to make sense of the carnage—the stench of decaying bodies, the groans of the dying, and the hundreds of circling buzzards amid the searing heat of a Maryland September. Soldiers became statisticians, obsessed with counting the dead. They compared the numbers of Confederate and Union dead. One soldier was convinced that Confederates decomposed more quickly than Union troops because they had no salt in their diet. A few saw the grim death of Confederates as the necessary fate of slave lovers. But rather than causing them to be dispirited or disillusioned, as Jordan writes, "the sights of the battlefield renewed the army's resolve. . . . The dead of Antietam could not be permitted to die in vain."

Working in the established vein of military scholarship, Thomas Clemens scrutinizes the Confederate invasions of Maryland. Three are well known, but Clemens adds a fourth from the early days of the war when Confederates led by Col. Thomas Jackson—before he was Stonewall—occupied a remote portion of the north side of the Potomac River banks. The larger, better-known invasions in 1862, 1863, and 1864, leading to the battles of Antietam, Gettysburg, and Monocacy, indicate just how crucial Maryland was to the success of the Confederacy. Clemens makes clear that the linchpin of Confederate strategy was to control the state and make it more difficult for Union troops to occupy Virginia. To control Maryland was to threaten the Union capital, to create confusion in the north, and to influence its politics and additionally, as a prestige factor, to include another slave state in the Confederacy. Thus Maryland became a crucial military theater with vast armies trooping across its soil, mainly in the western part of the state.

Clemens corrects several faulty interpretations that have become part of the state's military lore. First, Gen. Robert E. Lee did not expect a general uprising of Maryland civilians when he moved north toward what became the Battle of Gettysburg. And while most historians have focused on four days at Gettysburg just across the state line in Pennsylvania, in fact both armies spent more time in Maryland, with a number of skirmishes taking place as Lee's army retreated across the Potomac River during July 6–14. Finally, Clemens emphasizes the threat of Gen. Jubal Early's summer invasion in 1864—the Confederacy's last hurrah. Overall, as Clemens makes clear, the Confederate invasions were costly failures and their lack of success was disastrous in terms of lost manpower and morale. Maryland was the Confederacy's Stalingrad.

In "Achieving Emancipation in Maryland," Jonathan White carefully dissects the complicated process by which emancipation in the state was accomplished—first, the calling of a constitutional convention approved by the state legislature, then the contentious convention in April 1864 that wrote the new constitution, and finally the referendum in November that barely passed, and then only because of the votes of Maryland's soldiers. Even after the referendum a few Marylanders challenged the constitution, arguing that ballots cast outside of Maryland by soldiers should be excluded and that the test oaths of allegiance required of voters were illegal. In most histories only the final, climactic ratification of a new constitution in November 1864, containing an article declaring the enslaved free, is included.

As White makes clear, the critical issues during the year-long process were allowing soldiers to vote outside the state, which angry Democrats noted had occurred *before* the ratification of the new state constitution giving them the right to do so, and the disenfranchising of disloyal Marylanders, again *before* ratification—a kind of post hoc ergo propter hoc inversion. Republican supporters of the constitution took these unusual steps because, according to White, they feared the Constitution would not be approved, and clearly the soldier vote in favor of emancipation was crucial for its approval. Meanwhile several Maryland slaveowners who were about to lose their property went to court to exclude votes from soldiers outside the state and to include those denied because of the test oaths. But their claims were rejected, and the messy process by which Maryland emancipated its enslaved stood as a proud episode in the extension of freedom. But when Democrats returned to power after the war, the Constitution of 1864, in the shortest duration of any state constitution, was quickly replaced by a document that overturned disqualifying test oaths.

Maryland was a flash point for the clash between civilian liberties and wartime necessities. With his emphasis on President Lincoln's actions, Frank Williams explores the conflicts that arose in the state, beginning with the April Riot and Lincoln's conviction that the national peril outweighed any claims that a state could prevent federal military movements. In an action typical of Lincoln's appreciation for the sensitivities of Marylanders, the president deflected, protesting that troops could neither fly over Maryland nor tunnel through its soil, and therefore must march through the state. But after consulting with state leaders, the president ordered troops to travel by ship to Annapolis, from which point they would march through a small sliver of the state to Washington, thus avoiding the risk of further clashes with Baltimore citizens.

Perhaps the most famous confrontation between civilian authorities and the military in Maryland involved the suspension of habeas corpus, the resulting deployment of troops in Baltimore, and the arrest of John Merryman, a supporter of the South who had attempted to recruit a company of Confederate soldiers and who had committed other treasonous acts. In the view of an outraged Chief Justice Roger B. Taney, Lincoln did not have the power to suspend the writ; only Congress did. Again, in Williams's portrayal of Lincoln, the president made the case that the government must resist its destruction: "Are all the laws, *but one,* to go unexecuted and the government go to pieces, lest that one be violated?," Lincoln asked rhetorically. Williams makes the case through other examples—the arrest of Judge Richard Carmichael, the arrest of Maryland legislators, the incarceration of civilians, and the military prisons— that Lincoln's abiding respect for the US Constitution limited these violations of peacetime civil liberties. And when these rights were abused, sometimes by his subordinates, the effect was mitigated by Lincoln's moderation and deep appreciation for these very liberties. In any case, as Williams concludes, Maryland remained a loyal part of the Union.

In recent years historians have moved beyond the battlefield to consider the home front. In the process women have become prime subjects for consideration. In his chapter, "Maryland Women at War," Robert Schoeberlein investigates the activities of Maryland women, who, like the state, were divided in their allegiances. Turning his attention to their organized activities, Schoeberlein goes beyond the stories of the notable few who have made it into the history books, such as the Confederate spy Rose O'Neal Greenhow and the heroine of abolitionist John Greenleaf Whittier's poem, the indomitable Barbara Frietchie. Instead he focuses on the collective activities of organized groups throughout the state such as the Ladies Union Relief Association, whose members visited hospitals, sewed head coverings called havelocks, and gathered food supplies to be delivered to the battle front. Unionist supporters in the Colored Ladies Union Association, organized in Baltimore in 1863, contributed similar aid. Both groups organized patriotic activities such as morale-building flag presentations. The most notable event, the Baltimore Sanitary Fair in 1864, was a large affair that raised money through an auction and was attended by President Lincoln, whose appearance had symbolic meaning for local patriots.

Schoeberlein also covers the activities of Maryland women who provided support for the wounded Confederates in local hospitals and to Confederate prisoners of war held at Point Lookout and Fort McHenry. Some of these women moved beyond the wartime extension of domestic female roles that had led to service as nurses and instead became what Schoeberlein characterizes as a fifth column, carrying messages to Confederate troops, delivering contraband goods, and even storing arms in their homes. Over a hundred secessionist Maryland women were arrested, some charged with disloyal activities and others with more serious charges of treason and violating the rules of war. In a mirror image of the activities of Union women, southern supporters had to wait until 1866 to organize their relief fair.

In her chapter on Reconstruction, Sharita Jacobs-Thompson underscores the precarious position of many enslaved Marylanders following the public announcement of the Emancipation Proclamation. She humanizes this dilemma by telling the story of the Plummer family, with Emily and her children managing to secure their freedom but the husband and father, Adam, remaining enslaved and forced to await Maryland's November 1864 slavery ban. The saga of this family is a lens through which to examine the transition from slavery to freedom in the early stages of Reconstruction in Maryland.

Using Civil War pension files, Freedman's Bureau records, local newspapers, and national and state legislative records, she explores how Maryland emancipated its enslaved population internally, prior to the Thirteenth Amendment, and thus did not enact policies the federal government had prescribed for the former Confederate states. She considers how these dynamics shaped postwar Maryland and their insidious effects on the aspirations of newly freed Blacks to achieve public office, vote, and engage in political and civic life—offering the assertion that many barriers to Black aspirations for full citizenship lasted, to some degree, until the mid-twentieth-century civil rights movement. Maryland's southern planters were not the only ones barring the door; many white Unionists opposed Black suffrage.

She analyzes the Republicans who sought congressional intervention in the state's Reconstruction policies and the Democrats who worked to block such efforts and prevent the Black vote. Maryland Blacks suffered from the limited presence of the Freedmen's Bureau and from barriers to their mobility erected by federal officials (though the latter did try to thwart the insidious apprenticeships that became a de facto continuation of slavery). Blacks suffered both the destruction of their churches and schools and violence at the hands of angry whites who could not abide the prospect of a free Black population and a Democratic Party determined to prevent them from attaining anything resembling the rights of citizenship. Following ratification of the Fifteenth Amendment granting Black men the right to vote, Black support for Republican candidates put Maryland Democrats on notice that a new political opponent was on the horizon. Yet the inability of Black candidates to win public office suggests that the fate of race relations in Maryland, presaging those in the South, was clear by 1866, when Reconstruction in Maryland ground to a halt with the end of both federal protection and Republican rule in the state.

Robert Cook discusses the postwar rejection of Black political empowerment by white Marylanders, Unionists included, who rejected the national Republican Party's Reconstruction-era commitment to political equality. Postwar political realignment in the state, he writes, shifted power back to the Democrats, who, in alliance with conservative Unionists, were able to perpetuate the Confederate "Lost Cause" narrative that went largely unchallenged until the civil rights movement in the mid-twentieth century began to expose the "unfinished racial business" as a residue of the Civil War. Both Union and Confederate veterans sought ways to memorialize their war sacrifices, writing memoirs, erecting monuments, and creating veterans' organizations. Former Confederates such as Bradley T. Johnson portrayed the southern cause as a pursuit of freedom and themselves worthy of honor because they had fought for Confederate independence while natives of a loyal state. By 1890, Cook writes, Johnson and his allies had succeeded in embedding the Lost Cause narrative in Maryland's Civil War mythology.

Cook notes that the Unionist narrative that emerged focused on the successful effort to save the nation while ushering in the destruction of slavery, and that it competed in the post–World War I years with partisans of southern memory who saw the Civil War as a struggle for liberty and self-government. This dual narrative of two sides fighting for noble principles endured well into the twenty-first century, with battle lines drawn during the civil rights movement of the 1950s and 1960s.

Commemorative activities and the construction of monuments to rebel heroes in particular symbolized the repression of the Jim Crow era and helped propel Maryland into a segregationist twentieth century. But in spite of this, Cook tells us, Maryland African Americans, including veterans, refused, in his words, "to relinquish their Civil War memories to their oppressors," even as many whites drew distinctions between emancipation and racial equality—a mindset that continues to bedevil American society today.

Finally, we hope that the fresh scholarship in these thirteen chapters will further illuminate the complexities of Maryland's Civil War story, which remains an important part of our national memory. We hope as well that they will inspire other studies. In the last analysis the racial injustice at the root of that experience, and our ongoing, if flawed, efforts to confront inequality today, continue to define who we are, and aspire to be, as Americans.

NOTES

1. Carol Reardon, "Writing Battle History: The Challenge of Memory," *Civil War History* 53 (2007): 259.

2. Frederick Wild, *Memoirs and History of Captain Frederick W. Alexanders Battery of United States Volunteers* (Baltimore: Press of Maryland School for Boys, 1912), 4.

3. Charles Camper and J. W. Kirkley, *Historical Record of the First Regiment of Maryland Infantry* (Washington, DC: Gibson Brothers, 1871), 96.

4. Matthew Page Andrews, *History of Maryland* (Baltimore: S. J. Clark Publishing, 1925), 865.

BORDER STATE, BORDER WAR

Fighting for Freedom and Slavery in Antebellum Maryland

RICHARD BELL

The farmhouse lay just two miles from the Maryland line, in West Nottingham, Pennsylvania. It belonged to the Millers, Joseph and Rebecca, and it was Rebecca who answered the knock at the back door at eleven in the morning on the very last day of 1851. Through it barged their former postman, Thomas McCreary. A resident of Cecil County, Maryland, on just the other side of the state line, McCreary was notorious in the neighborhood for abducting free people of color to sell as slaves to dealers in Baltimore. Pushing Rebecca aside, he grabbed the Millers' domestic, Rachel Parker, bundled the seventeen-year-old into his buggy, and took off toward the nearest train.

Joseph Miller soon gave chase. By the next morning he had tracked captor and captive to Baltimore and there filed charges of kidnapping to try to prevent his servant from being swiftly sold and shipped out to Natchez or New Orleans as a slave. Rachel would be stashed in the city's jail until the charges could be litigated. But Miller's intervention on her behalf would cost him dearly. On his way home that night, he disappeared. Two days later, locals found his dead body strung up from the branch of a tree by the side of railroad tracks not far from the city.[1]

Investigations followed on both sides of the border. Against all evidence to the contrary, a jury of inquest in Baltimore ruled that Miller had hanged himself. Their decision effectively exonerated Thomas McCreary, the prime suspect in his murder. Months later, the original kidnapping charge finally brought McCreary to court. But at the trial his defense lawyers alleged that Rachel was actually a fugitive slave from Maryland named Eliza Crocus and so, under the terms of the new federal Fugitive Slave Act, the judge barred her testimony. After more twists and turns, McCreary's lawyers succeeded in getting the charges dropped and the case dismissed.

Across the line in Pennsylvania there was disbelief and outrage. Townsfolk in West Nottingham called the decisions preposterous and absurd, and cobbled together a reward of $1,000 for the arrest of Miller's murderer. Others threatened to lynch him. Bowing to extraordinary public pressure, Pennsylvania's governor, William Bigler, eventually requested that Thomas McCreary be extradited to the state to face trial there. But Maryland's governor, Enoch Lowe, refused the application. He was concerned, he claimed, that doing so would ignite sectional feelings.

In truth, that fire was already blazing. Ever since northern states had moved to disentangle themselves from race slavery, Maryland had been a battleground. Slavery's slow death in neighboring Pennsylvania, a process that began with passage of a gradual abolition law there in 1780, had turned the border between these two states into a theater of war in which enslavers, the enslaved, fugitives, freedpeople, and activists all struggled for advantage. Joseph Miller's murder on the first day of 1852 only confirmed what everyone along this stretch of the Mason-Dixon line had known for decades: that opportunistic kidnappers preyed repeatedly upon the fragile liberty of the region's free Black community, producing fierce (sometimes murderous) flare ups of violence in and around the borderland where Pennsylvania and Maryland met.

Thomas McCreary's plan to abduct Rachel Parker should also be situated in a much larger context. As McCreary was well aware, by the 1850s Baltimore had become a major center for slave dealing, a hub for traders who made their living buying enslaved people and then shipping them south to be sold to sugar and cotton planters in Louisiana, Mississippi, and Alabama. This domestic slave trade was big business, turning profits of $50 to $100 per head, and Baltimore's docks had been a primary point of embarkation since the 1820s. Demand for Black bodies to fill departing ships was so high in the second quarter of the century that "legitimate" slave traders sometimes did side deals with criminal traffickers like McCreary if the price was right and no one was looking. Oversight was minimal, and on the rare occasions that they were called to account, men like McCreary would simply hide behind the petticoats of national fugitive slave laws, protected by a political and legal establishment in Maryland that treated enslaved men and women as expendable machines and regarded free Black people as nuisance noncitizens.[2]

This essay argues that Thomas McCreary's Maryland can best be understood as a border slave state engaged in a border war. To do so, it mines a rich vein of recent scholarship on the slave experience, interstate sales, fugitivity, free Black life, colonization, and kidnapping in Maryland in the decades from 1825 to the election of Abraham Lincoln in 1860. It reconstructs several major shifts in power, politics, and population over this critical period as well as the fights and furies that resulted. In so doing, it shifts our attention away from other, more familiar flash points of the sectional crisis—Nat Turner, *Uncle Tom's Cabin*, the Kansas-Nebraska Act, Dred Scott, and John Brown's raid on Harpers Ferry—and toward a new understanding of the war before it unfolded in Maryland, a border slave state that Lincoln and the Union could not afford to lose.[3]

THE WASTING DISEASE:
SLAVERY IN ANTEBELLUM MARYLAND

"It is generally supposed that slavery, in the state of Maryland, exists in its mildest form," Frederick Douglass reported in 1855, "and that it is totally divested of those harsh and terrible peculiarities, which mark and characterize the slave system, in the southern and south-western states of the American union." Born and raised in Talbot County on the Eastern Shore, Douglass knew from personal experience that this was nonsense. But the claim was commonplace nonetheless, turning up in a host of other antebellum sources ranging from reports generated by well-intentioned white anti-slavery activists to novels authored by proslavery propagandists. In John Pendleton Kennedy's *Swallow Barn* (1832), for example, the fictional enslaved Marylanders are carefree, playful people, more than happy to work in the fields from dawn to dusk.[4]

Commentators like Kennedy considered slavery in Maryland both tolerable and humane in comparison to labor regimes further south. They pointed to the fact that the cash crops cultivated in southern Maryland and around the Chesapeake Bay did not require the same grueling, all-consuming toil as cotton and sugar, that slaveholdings there were generally small enough to limit the worst excesses of plantation capitalism, and that there had never been any significant slave rebellions in the state. They argued that the proximity of free soil, just across the line in Pennsylvania, likewise meant that enslavers in Maryland were, in one contemporary's words, "afraid to whip [the slaves], because they knew, if they did, they would run away from them." They noted as well that some enslavers in the state entered into self-purchase agreements with their unfree workers and that many more allowed them to hire themselves out to third parties and to keep a small portion of their earnings for themselves, arrangements that allowed enslaved people considerable personal autonomy and some degree of control over their conditions of work.[5]

Yet the truth was that slavery was slavery whatever the details, and African Americans who later spoke or wrote about their experiences of enslavement in Maryland were anything but nostalgic. One man remembered his former master as "an unfeeling tyrant" who had provided his unfree laborers with "hardly anything to eat" and "no chance to eat it." Douglass himself never shook the memory of Edward Covey, a smallholder on the Eastern Shore who specialized in "breaking young negroes." In 1833, when Douglass was just sixteen years old, Thomas Auld, his owner, had sent him to work for Covey as punishment for trying to start a Sunday School. Covey beat the boy with abandon, lashing him with a cow-skin whip until Douglass eventually snapped.[6]

There was nothing mild and benign about the likes of Edward Covey, and the hundreds of enslaved Marylanders each year who risked everything to try to escape their bondage are the most damning proof of the regime's degradations. As we shall see, in the six counties closest to the Pennsylvania border (Baltimore, Carroll, Cecil, Harford, Frederick, and Washington), so many bondspeople took to their heels in the second quarter of the nineteenth century that slave labor began to lose some of its economic viability. By 1850, the cash value of enslaved people there had fallen to just $177.50 per person; a decade later, in 1860, enslaved people accounted for just 5 percent of these counties' populations.[7]

It was far more difficult, of course, for enslaved people to vote with their feet in the many counties that did not share a border with Pennsylvania, however much they wanted to. They could smell free soil, but never taste it, and their enslavement felt all the more bitter as a result. Slavery in the southern and eastern parts of the state remained robust—not quite thriving, but not quite stagnating either. Tobacco cultivation using slave labor continued apace in Montgomery, Prince George's, Charles, Calvert, and St. Mary's Counties, while on the Eastern Shore planters had recently retooled and retrained their enslaved workers to raise wheat, corn, rye, and oats. By the time Frederick Douglass was born in 1818, that transition was largely complete, and a new equilibrium had emerged on the Delmarva peninsula. Visitors there in the second quarter of the century described it as stuck in time and set in its ways, a place where enslaved laborers continued on as they had for generations, living

TABLE I. African American Population of Maryland Counties, 1820–1860

	Region	Total Population	Enslaved	Free Blacks
1820	Northern	121,575	20,721	6,149
	Baltimore City	62,738	4,357	10,326
	Southern	101,328	47,016	7,555
	Eastern	121,709	35,303	15,700
1840	Northern	147,172	15,951	11,587
	Baltimore City	102,513	3,212	17,980
	Southern	103,003	44,945	11,162
	Eastern	117,331	25,629	21,349
1860	Northern	208,439	11,109	16,201
	Baltimore City	212,418	2,218	25,680
	Southern	121,064	48,905	13,784
	Eastern	145,128	24,957	28,277

Source: US Census; Barbara Jeanne Fields, *Slavery and Freedom on the Middle Ground: Maryland during the Nineteenth Century* (New Haven: Yale University Press, 1985), 62. Northern counties include Allegany, Baltimore County (excl. Baltimore City), Carroll, Frederick, Harford, and Washington. Southern counties include Anne Arundel, Calvert, Charles, Howard, Montgomery, Prince George's, and St. Mary's. Eastern counties include Caroline, Cecil, Dorchester, Kent, Queen Anne's, Somerset, Talbot, and Worcester.

in "rude log-cabins" on scattered smallholdings, their extended families divided across multiple farms.[8]

Visitors to Baltimore, the city rising rapidly across the Chesapeake Bay, sang a very different tune, and the experiences of its small community of enslaved laborers were far more tumultuous and unpredictable. During a stay there in 1835, a New England-born lexicographer named Ethan Allen Andrews concluded that "in this city there appears to be no strong attachment to slavery, and no wish to perpetuate it." That sentiment only grew over time, and in 1845 John Carey, a Baltimore politician, complained that slavery "is a dead weight and worse; it has become a wasting disease."[9]

In a city in which wage labor was the norm, such claims were common. But they obscure the subtle, enduring centrality of slavery to Baltimore's economy in the antebellum era. The city's lawyers and bankers made their money greasing the wheels of the entire southern slave system, and many of the hulls built at the shipyards near the docks were designed to serve the maritime slave trades. Baltimore was also a major processing center for slave-raised cash crops like tobacco and cotton. By 1850, it was home to 120 cigar-making businesses as well as factories that produced finished cotton worth more than a million dollars each year. Its several thousand enslaved workers were an essential element in Baltimore's labor market too, contributing crucial manpower to its manufacturing, commercial, and service sectors. Across the city, enslaved people pressed tobacco leaves, milled wheat, and forged iron. Some worked in construction, shipbuilding, caulking, and sail-making. Many more toiled each day as porters, waiters, servants, cooks, maids, and seamstresses in hotels, restaurants, and private homes.[10]

The nature of the urban labor market was such that Baltimore's enslaved population—many of them hired out by slaveowners living in surrounding counties—often worked side by side with free Black wage earners doing similar tasks. Proximity to that much larger community created all sorts of opportunities. Baltimore was a place where enslaved men and women could seek out and join free Black churches, Sunday schools, and self-improvement societies, and construct all sorts of social ties. When Douglass was dispatched to live with Thomas Auld's brother in Fell's Point, he did all that and more, teaching himself to read, buying books, and meeting his future wife, Anna Murray, at a gathering of the East Baltimore Mental Improvement Society, where he was the only enslaved member.[11]

In his memoirs, Douglass recalled his "ecstasy" when he learned he was to leave the wheat fields of Talbot County and go to work in the big city. But the move brought dilemmas and dangers of its own. When he arrived in Baltimore, the eighteen-year-old lad was confronted by "troops of hostile boys ready to pounce upon me at every street corner. . . . They chased me, and called me 'Eastern Shore man,' till really I almost wished myself back on the Eastern Shore." Worse was to come. Hired out to work in William Gardner's shipyard as a caulker, Douglass was beaten savagely by white journeymen who resented the downward pressure his employment there put on their wages.[12]

In Baltimore, Douglass found himself caught between slavery and freedom, a predicament that embodied the broader contradictions of the slave experience throughout this border state. Legislators in Annapolis reflexively batted down petitions to abolish slavery gradually, even as more and more white Marylanders complained that slavery was a drag on the state's economic fortunes. The size of the overall enslaved population held steady, decreasing by only a few thousand each year between 1830 and 1860, even as conditional manumissions, large numbers of escapes from northern counties, and ever more out-of-state sales frayed slavery's edges.[13]

DEAD, HEAVY FOOTSTEPS: MARYLAND AND
THE DOMESTIC SLAVE TRADE

Those interstate sales propped up the value of slaves in several parts of border-state Maryland, maintaining the institution's viability there against mounting challenges. Most sales were to traders supplying planters setting up along the Gulf Coast. The American settlers crowding into that ever-expanding region demanded a nearly bottomless supply of forced labor to cut sugarcane and pick cotton. They preferred young men, but would take almost anyone, including women and children—and they would pay top dollar, usually $200 more per person than buyers in more settled regions could afford. With the legal supply of slaves limited to domestic sources, Maryland slaveowners struck deal after deal with interstate traders, helping to fuel the rise of the Deep South.[14]

On the face of it, enslaved people were sold away for all sorts of reasons, including debt, downsizing, the death of a slaveholder, or to divest oneself of troublesome individuals. One man sold a woman in his possession because of her "Impertinent Language to her Mistress," while an enslaver in Frederick, Maryland, claimed that he sold a Black family of six for no other reason than that he had "too many." But the main reason was money. Selling slaves raised cash. It turned assets into liquidity. It turned people into profits. When the Jesuit leaders of Georgetown University needed to raise funds quickly to shore up the school's finances in 1838, they did so by selling 272 of the African Americans they owned in Prince George's County to interstate traders who took them to Louisiana. The Jesuits pocketed $115,000 in that single transaction, enough to save the school.[15]

Maryland's slaveowners sold off as many people as they thought could fetch a price. Coffles, as these human convoys were known, were common sights on the roads of the state's six northernmost counties, as owners there tried to sell their slaves south before they could disappear in the direction of the Pennsylvania line. In Hagerstown, George P. Hussy recalled seeing "*hundreds* of colored men and women chained together, two by two, and driven to the south [and] tied up and lashed till the blood ran down to their heels." But the largest number of forced migrants came from southern Maryland and the Eastern Shore. In Talbot County slaveholders sold away one-third of the enslaved population in the 1830s alone; they sold another sixth in the 1840s when a recession briefly depressed cotton prices, and another third in the 1850s. Almost every enslaver made a sale at one time or another, and between 1830 and 1860, owners forced 18,500 enslaved Marylanders to leave the state.[16]

Slave traders were the middlemen who made this happen, and in the second quarter of the century Maryland swarmed with dozens of them. They buzzed around the state's county towns from September to March "watching for chances to buy human flesh," Frederick Douglass recalled, "as buzzards to eat carrion." Because of the small size of most Maryland holdings, it could take weeks to put a coffle of thirty or forty slaves together, and so traders worked an area intensively, like loggers or strip-miners. They took up residence in hotels and taverns and filled local papers like the *Centreville Times,* the *Snow Hill Messenger,* and the *Cambridge Chronicle* with advertisements. Some, like John Denning, promised sellers that they would never separate any family groups "without their consent." Others, like William Harking, pledged to buy "all likely negroes from 8 to 40 years" old and to pay "the highest cash prices" with no questions asked.[17]

Some of these traders worked independently, but many more were agents for firms headquartered in the region's larger urban centers. On his visit to Baltimore in 1835, Ethan Allen Andrews counted "a dozen or more" slave dealers with offices and pens in the city. Each pen could hold "three or four hundred" enslaved captives at once and was usually "strongly built, and well supplied with *iron thumb-screws and gags,* and ornamented with *cowskins and other whips—often times bloody.*" Most were concentrated in a few easy-to-find downtown blocks on Lombard Street, Camden Street, and Pratt Street that were close to onward transportation.[18]

These businesses boomed. By the 1840s, Maryland traders exported huge numbers of enslaved people to the Deep South annually: three thousand over the first six months of 1845 according to a contemporary estimate. One Baltimore-based trader, Walter Campbell, sent fifty-nine shipments of slaves to New Orleans alone between 1844 and 1853, carrying about 120 people out of Maryland each year. Despite occasional bans on printing "Cash for Negroes" ads in city newspapers, and howls of protest from local activists such as Hezekiah Niles, Benjamin Lundy, and William Lloyd Garrison, the domestic slave trade was a major part of Baltimore's economy. When Frederick Douglass lived in the city, he was often woken from sleep by "the dead, heavy footsteps and the piteous cries of the chained gangs" being marched toward the ravenous bellies of the waiting ships at Fell's Point.[19]

The most visible and successful slave dealer in Baltimore in the second quarter of the century was Hope H. Slatter. In the mid-1830s, Slatter set up shop on West Pratt Street, between Sharp and Howard, and did a brisk business there for more than a decade. He specialized in "purchasing for the New Orleans market" and built a state-of-the-art, escape-proof slave pen next to his office that he equipped with separate cellblocks for men and women and an enclosed yard for exercise—facilities, Slatter boasted, that were "not surpassed by any establishment of the kind in the United States." At first, he sent many of his captives to New Orleans by ship, hiring a fleet of omnibuses to carry them to the docks; later, he was one of the first Baltimore dealers to commandeer rail cars to dispatch them to New Orleans via the iron road. Slatter was a well-known man about town. He saw himself as a gentleman providing an essential service, and made a point of giving tours of his facilities and donating ostentatiously to charity.[20]

To the people he bought and sold, however, Slatter was a devil, the stuff of nightmares. Enslaved people were terrified of traders like him, and the constant dread of sale sent some of them mad, like the man Alexis de Tocqueville met during a tour of the Baltimore almshouse in 1831. "The Negro of whom I speak," Tocqueville later wrote, was terrorized by a vision of a slave dealer who "sticks close to him day and night and snatches away bits of his flesh." Enslaved Marylanders did everything in their power to resist these sales or negotiate their terms as best they could. One mother was able to prevent the transport of her son, William, to New Orleans by finding a local farmer who would purchase him instead. Other parents simply fell to their knees to beg their owners not to sell away their children and break up their families.[21]

Occasionally that worked. Most often it did not, and so when an out-of-state sale seemed inevitable, enslaved people sometimes resorted to extreme measures. Some dug in, like the man who shot to death the trader who came to collect his wife and children. A few even turned weapons upon themselves, like the young woman who severed her hand with an axe to make herself unsellable, or the mother from Snow Hill who "first cut the throat of her child,

and then her own" upon learning that the pair were to be sold and forever separated from one another.[22]

Planters and traders used every trick in the book to try to minimize such
losses. Buyers would confer privately with potential sellers, out of sight of
eavesdropping domestics, and return to the premises before dawn the next
day to whisk their new purchases away before anyone was the wiser. "About
six o'clock one morning, I was taken suddenly from my wife," Leonard Har-
rod recalled decades later. "She knew no more where I had gone than the hen
knows where the hawk carries her chicken." Those snatched away did what
they could to escape or resist en route out of state, occasionally succeeding in
overpowering their captors and darting back the way they had come. Lined up
at Baltimore's rail depots and wharves, others could see no way back and cut
their own throats then and there.[23]

The loved ones they had been forced to leave behind were no less desperate,
no less traumatized by these sales. One enslaved man in Washington County
hanged himself after his master sold his wife south. Parents never recovered
from such separations, and children remained scarred for life. Writing in 1836,
nearly fifty years after the fact, Charles Ball admitted that the terrible memory of being ripped from his Maryland mother at the age of four still played
"with painful vividness upon my memory." No enslaved family in the state was
spared. Frederick Douglass lost his sister, two aunts, seven first cousins, and at
least five other near relatives to sales. In Maryland, such fates were facts of life.
"In no state in this confederacy," one beleaguered group of activists reported
in 1826, were slaves "more subject to the painful and distressing evils of family
separation, and the grievous consequences resulting from it."[24]

THE BLACK UNDERGROUND: FUGITIVITY BEFORE
AND AFTER THE FUGITIVE SLAVE LAW

Vowing never to be sold south, enslaved men and women often fled north
instead, turning Maryland into an epicenter of practical abolition. "I did not
intend to go if I could prevent it," recalled Isaac Mason, who took to his heels
when he learned of his master's plan to sell him to a new owner in Louisiana.
Josiah Henson, who later became a leading antislavery orator and the inspiration for the character of Uncle Tom in Harriet Beecher Stowe's novel, escaped
from his Montgomery County enslaver in 1830. Frederick Douglass made his

own attempt to flee Talbot County in 1836, only to be thwarted. When in Baltimore two years later, he tried again, this time making it safely to free soil by posing as a sailor and riding the rails northward toward Philadelphia.[25]

While most enslaved Marylanders found themselves stuck fast in bondage, "the thought of flight," as J. W. C. Pennington, a fugitive from Carroll County, once called it, was never far from their minds. They tried to run whenever they saw an opportunity and did not normally wait for a conductor on the Underground Railroad to come looking for them. Many timed their departures for Saturdays or Sundays, knowing that news of their escape would not appear in the weekly papers until the following Friday. They typically traveled at night, hiding in marshes or woodlands during the day, lacing their tracks with pepper or snuff to thwart bloodhounds who might come sniffing behind them. Some stole boats to cross the Choptank, the Nanticoke, and the Susquehanna Rivers, or hid aboard ships bound for free states. Others stole horses or even carriages to speed their flight. Most headed for Philadelphia, York, Harrisburg, or Pittsburgh, following one of several common freedom routes through this borderland. But the distance to the Pennsylvania line was daunting, especially for people stuck in slavery on the Eastern Shore or in the state's southern counties. Even the journey from Baltimore could take ten days on foot.[26]

On the roads, would-be fugitives had to run the gauntlet, dodging slave patrols and new "vigilance associations" set up across the state to round up runaways and protect the chattel principle. Anticipating that they might have to fight off pursuers, some took guns, Bowie knives, and dirks with them, determined to resist capture with force. In 1845, a constable in Washington County intercepted a group of ten fugitives near Smithsburg. When he and a posse of townspeople confronted them, "the negroes being armed with hatchets, clubs, and pistols, refused to be taken peaceably." In the ensuing brawl, they wounded several white men, giving up only one of their number to the constable's custody. But things did not often go so well. When a group of almost eighty Black men carrying scythe blades and other makeshift weapons marched toward the Pennsylvania line from three of Maryland's southern counties later the same year, hundreds of well-armed white citizens came out to stop them. After a pitched battle, all of the fugitives were dragged back to their masters, who soon sold some of them out of state.[27]

Clashes like these were common across Maryland in the second quarter of the century. Fugitives won some and lost others, but the departures continued. In 1844, William Chaplin, a white antislavery activist, reported that enslaved Marylanders were "escaping in shoals." Two years later, a headline in a Hagerstown newspaper declared that "Oceans of Runaway Negroes" were now leaving Washington County for Pennsylvania, often in small family groups or with friends. Five here, fifteen there. Then seven more, then eleven. The stream never stopped, and only seemed to grow thicker and faster with time. In July 1850, census takers tallied 279 slave escapes from Maryland over the previous twelve months. As historian Barbara Fields has noted, that total was likely a substantial undercount of the number of slaves who had fled over that period. Even so, it was confirmation that Maryland was "the reluctant leader among slave states in this unsought competition."[28]

The Fugitive Slave Law, enacted in September 1850, could not stop this slow-motion migration. That October, a woman and her five children escaped from Middletown in Frederick County. In November, a couple from near Easton walked out of slavery with their five children in tow. In December, a Chestertown woman left with her five offspring. On and on they came. In August 1852, a thirteen-person family fled northwestern Maryland and made it to Harrisburg. That October, more than half of one planter's twenty slaves left his labor camp together and headed for Lancaster. More and more enslaved Marylanders were now setting out in groups, seeking safety in numbers. Toward the end of 1855, twenty-eight enslaved people fled Chestertown en masse. A year later, a group numbering twenty-seven left Cambridge together. Another fifty followed in 1857. According to historian Richard Blackett, by the mid-1850s the volume of fugitive slave escapes from Maryland had reached an all-time high.[29]

The state's slaveholders spent these years in all-out crisis mode, worried that this growing exodus posed an existential threat to their livelihoods, manhood, and way of life. Each new escape was a significant financial loss, and by the 1850s fugitives were costing Maryland slaveholders about $80,000 a year in lost assets, an immense sum equivalent to many millions of dollars today. Anxious and embittered, enslavers lashed out in all directions, convincing themselves that Maryland had been infiltrated by white "abolitionist emissaries" sent there from the free states by kingpins like Horace Greeley, the antislavery editor of the New York *Tribune*.[30]

Under pressure from slaveholders across Maryland, local courts began prosecuting anyone suspected of helping slaves escape. Charles Torrey, a Liberty Party activist from Massachusetts, was arrested and imprisoned in Maryland three times in the 1840s for aiding fugitives and ultimately died in the state penitentiary; in 1844, a Dorchester County court sentenced Hugh Hazlett, a thirty-one-year-old white man, to forty-four years in prison for helping seven slaves escape. Vigilante action against people like Torrey and Hazlett was on the rise as well. At one meeting in Baltimore County, slaveholders openly threatened the lives of any "abolitionists caught in the act . . . of aiding slaves in their flight." Many made good on their word, terrorizing neighbors and strangers they suspected of antislavery sympathies. In 1858, for instance, a band of thugs in Kent County tarred, feathered, and threatened to murder one local man simply because he subscribed to Greeley's newspaper.[31]

To curb their losses, Maryland's slaveholders routinely hired slave catchers to pursue fugitives across state lines into Pennsylvania. They did this time and again in the second quarter of the century, in open defiance of Pennsylvania's 1826 personal liberty law. Enslavers in Maryland detested that law, which decreed that no one could be renditioned out of the state to be held as a slave, regarding it as an affront to their property rights, and in 1842 persuaded the Supreme Court of the United States to strike it down. The case, *Prigg v. Pennsylvania,* turned on the actions of Edward Prigg, a Maryland lawyer turned slave catcher who had crossed into York County, Pennsylvania, to grab a woman named Margaret Morgan and carry her back to her erstwhile owner in Baltimore. It was the first fugitive slave case to reach the highest court in the land, and the justices' ruling was unsparing. In a decision written by Joseph Story, the Supreme Court ruled that any and all state-level personal liberty laws were at odds with the federal 1793 Fugitive Slave Act and thus unconstitutional and invalid.[32]

Northern legislators refused to comply with the court's decision and tried to find loopholes and workarounds to keep Maryland's slave catchers out of their jurisdictions. Their defiance drew yelps of protest from the state's slaveholders and their representatives in Washington, and set in motion the events leading to the passage of the Fugitive Slave Act of 1850, a vastly more muscular revision of the original 1793 statute. It became law on September 18, 1850, and marked a major escalation in the border war between the states. Eight days later, a Black man from Baltimore named James Hamlet became the first person arrested under its powers. Hamlet had fled that city two years earlier and was living in New York when a relative of his former enslaver arrived to drag him back. A porter in Manhattan, Hamlet was apprehended at his place of work and taken before one of the federal commissioners newly appointed under the terms of the act. Hamlet protested, but the new law rendered his testimony as a suspected fugitive inadmissible. He was handcuffed and driven to a pier and stashed on the first steamboat bound for Baltimore.[33]

Fugitive slave renditions like this mushroomed after 1850, and enslavers from Maryland led the charge, crossing state lines in pursuit of runaways and engaging fugitives in violent and explosive confrontations on free soil. For example, on September 11, 1851, Edward Gorsuch, a Baltimore County wheat farmer and slaveholder, arrived outside a house in Christiana, Pennsylvania, intent on dragging the two runaway slaves holed up inside back across the border. Empowered by the new Fugitive Slave Act, Gorsuch was accompanied by a deputy federal marshal and a small posse of armed men. But local opposition proved substantial. The town of Christiana was a Black Underground stronghold, and Gorsuch found the stone house heavily fortified and its occupants— his former slaves and several other Black men and women—entrenched. What began as a tense standoff soon gave way to a full-on firefight, and Gorsuch was shot to death in a hail of gunfire. When his men retreated in panic, the runaways bolted from the house and made their escape north toward Rochester, where Frederick Douglass helped them find their way to Canada.[34]

Douglass later wrote approvingly of those fugitive Marylanders' courage and resolve, declaring that "If it be right for any man to resist those who would enslave them, it was right for the men of color at Christiana to resist."[35]

BLACK CAPITAL: THE EXPERIENCE OF BLACK FREEDOM IN BALTIMORE AND MARYLAND

The Christiana fugitives received vital assistance from free Black Pennsylvanians. But Maryland's Black Underground was no less numerous, and the state's large and rapidly growing community of free people of color went to extraordinary lengths to help, hide, and protect self-liberating slaves who asked them for assistance. Each time Harriet Tubman returned to Maryland from Philadelphia to aid runaways, for instance, she relied upon a network of free Black allies on the Eastern Shore for critical support. No one was more crucial to her operations than Samuel Green, a former slave turned free Black minister, who repeatedly collaborated with Tubman to help enslaved people escape from plantations across Talbot County. When deputies finally raided Green's home in 1858, they found it stocked with train timetables, maps of northern states and of Canada, and a copy of *Uncle Tom's Cabin*—enough evidence of his role as a station agent on the Underground Railroad to earn him ten years in the state penitentiary.[36]

There were men and women like Samuel Green in every county and city in the state. In Hagerstown in western Maryland, for example, a crew of local free Blacks once stormed the jail to liberate the captured fugitives detained inside. Baltimore, too, was home to several leaders of the Black Underground, including Jacob Gibbs, and the city was a haven for fugitives who, in the words of Barbara Fields, "had not waited upon the grace of God, the majesty of the law, or the generosity of their owners to grant them their freedom."[37]

Fugitives who could not make it to free soil in Pennsylvania flocked to Baltimore because of the sheer size of the city's free Black population. Baltimore was the capital of Black America in the second quarter of the nineteenth century, boasting the largest community of free people of color anywhere in the United States. Fifteen thousand strong, according to the 1830 census, their numbers hit twenty-five thousand by 1850, about 15 percent of the city's entire population. Most were fresh from slavery, drawn to Baltimore by its thriving port, which required deep reserves of cheap labor, and by its reputation as the best place in the state, and perhaps the nation, for free Black Americans to seek economic opportunity and carve out a rich family life.[38]

The low-cost, flexible labor of free people of color was the backbone of Baltimore's economy. As the city surged, growing to become the second largest in the country by 1840, free Black men drove its carts, drays, hacks, coaches, and stages. They made Baltimore's nails, bricks, boots, shoes, brushes, combs, glue, cigars, and barrels. They sawed its wood, whitewashed its walls, cut its stone, blacked its shoes, butchered its meat, smithed its horses, and tanned its skins. A few owned and operated their own stores, cookshops, and oyster houses. Others ran basement grogshops or backstreet brothels. Many more worked at the shipyards as caulkers or carpenters, or as mariners on the ocean-going vessels made and maintained there. The pay packets these men took home were usually modest, so their wives also had to work, typically as cooks, domestics, laundresses, and seamstresses.[39]

Beyond their worksites, Black Baltimoreans constructed a vibrant and robust community. Churches served as important building blocks in this effort, and by the eve of the Civil War, the city boasted fifteen free Black meeting-

TABLE 2. African American Population of Baltimore City, 1820–1860

	Total Population	Enslaved	Free Blacks
1820	62,738	4,357	10,326
1830	70,620	4,120	14,790
1840	102,513	3,212	17,980
1850	169,054	2,946	25,442
1860	212,418	2,218	25,680

Source: Fields, *Middle Ground*, 62.

houses representing six denominations. From these houses of worship emerged dozens of mutual aid societies promoting temperance, uplift, charity, and all manner of other social, intellectual, and moral improvements. The city's African Methodist Episcopal church also funded the building and operation of several free Black schools, an abiding financial commitment to the core belief, expressed by Black schoolmaster William Watkins in 1836, that a "good education is the great *sine qua non* as it regards the elevation of our people." By the mid-1840s Baltimore's AME schools enrolled six hundred students. Other denominations had by then begun to follow suit, and by 1860 there were more than a dozen such schools up and running, enrolling 2,600 students across the city.[40]

Free Black Baltimoreans built this thriving, resilient community while living under siege. They had to claw and fight for every advantage, no matter how meager, checked at every turn by the many white residents of the city who resented their presence. Despite (or perhaps because of) their self-evident industriousness and willingness to work for low wages, their white job competitors lobbied the General Assembly in Annapolis to bar them from one occupation after another, bad-mouthing them as indolent, lazy, "more easily influenced by temptations to steal, less influenced by the desire of maintaining an honest reputation, and . . . less fear(ful) of the operations of the law than white people."[41]

Racism on these jobsites spiked each time the economy faltered and whenever European migration to the city climbed. Each time that happened, white employers and workers closed ranks. By the 1850s, Baltimore was buckling under a wave of job-busting riots on the docks, on the railroads, and everywhere else free people of color had the temerity to labor. In 1858, Black bricklayers at one city yard were assaulted by a mob of thirty men calling themselves the White Tigers, who were intent, one witness said, on "driving out the colored employees, and supplanting them in their places." The Black bricklayers had to "run for their lives—pistols, and in several instances guns being fired upon them." The city's free Black workers did their best to hold the line, organizing labor unions to try to boost their wages, insisting that Black foremen keep their jobs, and trying to achieve collective bargaining. But the attacks on their livelihoods were relentless, and by the eve of the Civil War various scare tactics had driven African American caulkers, butchers, carpenters, sawyers, shoemakers, and shopkeepers into retreat and out of occupations they had once dominated. "The white man [now] stands in the Black man's shoes, or else is fast getting into them," one approving local commentator observed.[42]

Black Baltimoreans felt the squeeze wherever they went, and not only at work. White thugs struck at Black churches regularly, "throwing stones and breaking the doors and windows" of the Sharp Street AME Church in west Baltimore during one service in August 1838. The attack caused panic, and many congregants inside were injured "by rushing through the doors, jumping out of the windows, &c." City constables usually turned a blind eye to this sort of racial terrorism and instead embraced the task of enforcing restrictive ordinances that made it illegal for people of color to buy dogs, liquor, tobacco, bacon, or beef without special licenses, and that required them to observe a 10:00 P.M. nightly curfew. Some policemen did far worse, beating legally free Blacks "bloody as a butcher" or throwing them in jail on suspicion of being runaway slaves—as if the fact of their freedom was proof of their criminality. Whatever the alleged crime, the judges and juries of the city's circuit court rarely looked favorably upon defendants of color. As one Baltimore attorney explained, they were "inclined to convict a man merely because he was black," often sentencing those convicted of petty crimes of survival like stealing food or clothes to being transported out of state to be sold into slavery.[43]

The racial climate was no less toxic beyond Baltimore City. The state's breadbasket, the Eastern Shore, was home to more than twenty thousand free Black Marylanders in the century's second quarter. Most worked as artisans of one sort or another, or as seasonal farm hands hired on terms that resembled debt slavery or peonage to do the "heavy, disagreeable, but *indispensable,* duties of 'laborers.'" Because most Black Codes applied statewide, these rural freedpeople lived under the same limits upon their freedom of movement and right to assembly as those in urban areas.[44]

This profusion of anti-Black legal restrictions was difficult to enforce, but the uncertainty, disdain, and hostility that informed them were stark and unambiguous. While white people remained a substantial majority of the state's population throughout the antebellum decades, slaveholders in particular regarded the growing number of free Black people living among them as dangerous sources of disorder, vice, and crime, and despaired that Maryland was "destined to be a free Negro state." The prospect repelled them. As Maryland Senate president Richard Thomas candidly explained in 1838, a man like him would gladly consign "his daughter to the silent tomb than see her led to the hymenial altar by the hand of the colored man." The rest of the state's enslaving class thought much the same. Beginning in the 1840s, they held one panicked convention after another to brainstorm ways to wrestle a different future into being, debating proposals to forbid further manumissions, control or reenslave free people of color, or expel them altogether.[45]

ANY PRACTICAL PLAN: COLONIZATION, OPPOSITION, AND MARYLAND IN LIBERIA

Plans to banish former slaves from Maryland had been on the drawing board for decades, and the state was home to some of the nation's most prominent proponents of colonization. Beginning in 1826, the Maryland Colonization Society (MCS) received a $1,000 annual appropriation from the Annapolis legislature, an extraordinary show of governmental support for its agenda. In the wake of Nat Turner's revolt in nearby Virginia in 1830, the MCS drew new attention and interest from white Marylanders worried that the state was on its own path to racial uprising and who were thus now "favourably disposed to any practical plan to get rid of the Free Blacks." The MCS proposed to do just that, and it soon spawned several county-level subsidiaries, all of them focused on removing newly freed slaves quickly from Maryland to Africa.[46]

It was a Marylander, Robert Goodloe Harper, who coined the name *Liberia*, and in 1831 the MCS sent its first cohort of Black migrants there. Thirty-one made that maiden voyage from Baltimore, and 149 more followed the next year, most of them farmers and their families from Worcester County and Somerset County on the Eastern Shore. In 1834, the MCS established its own resettlement colony independent of Liberia near Cape Palmas, and over the next twenty years about a thousand more voyagers journeyed there through the port of Baltimore, searching for fresh economic opportunities and new lives free from racism.[47]

Looking only at the cumulative number of former slaves who boarded ships in Baltimore, however, obfuscates much more complicated and contested scenes on the docks themselves. Most Black Marylanders vigorously opposed colonization and sometimes followed neighbors who had chosen to emigrate all the way to the gangplanks of these vessels to plead with them to reconsider. Many did, and MCS officers could persuade only fifty people each year, on average, to deport themselves. Most ships leaving Baltimore for Africa left half-empty, usually carrying more migrants from out of state than from Maryland. What's more, those who made these voyages often quickly returned, dismayed by the poor conditions they found in West Africa. In 1857, the MCS colony collapsed and had to be annexed by neighboring Liberia.[48]

Most Black Marylanders were naturally suspicious of any plan that had the support of white enslavers. William Watkins, the leading anticolonization figure in the state, denounced deportation as a brazen villainy pushed by those who "design to make us miserable here, that we may emigrate to Africa *with our own consent.*" Watkins and other antislavery activists refused to participate in any scheme that tied the destruction of slavery to the removal of free people of color. They wanted ardently to build their futures within the United States and within Maryland, where most had been born, and pledged not to be "driven, like cattle, to Liberia."[49]

Black opposition was never monolithic, of course, and MCS officers worked hard to cultivate enthusiasm for colonization whenever they could, especially among the most beleaguered residents of rural counties. Those opposed to deportation had to organize to resist these propaganda efforts. They did so by disrupting MCS meetings and by turning churches and other free Black gathering places in Baltimore, Cambridge, Hagerstown, and Annapolis into what historian Ira Berlin has called "beehives of anticolonizationist activity." Whenever delegates at local and state colored conventions took up the subject of colonization, the debates were often fierce. When a handful of Black delegates spoke up in favor of a move to Liberia at one such meeting in 1852, several hundred anticolonization protestors mobilized to surround the convention site, suspicious that those delegates had been paid off by MCS agents.[50]

REFUGE OF KIDNAPPERS: MARYLAND AND THE REVERSE UNDERGROUND RAILROAD

MCS agents were not the only Marylanders working to siphon off the region's surging free Black population in the second quarter of the century. At the time,

Maryland was well known as a "refuge of kidnappers," a safe haven and rich environment for bands of vicious opportunists who would prowl streets and burst into homes to snatch away anyone they thought they could sell on to interstate slave traders to carry into the Deep South. Kidnapping and human trafficking on this wholly illegal Reverse Underground Railroad carried obvious risks, both legal and physical, but demand for Black bodies in the Cotton Kingdom was such that there was a lot of money to be made selling free people from the Upper South into slavery on the Gulf Coast. "An able-bodied colored man sells in the southern market for from eight hundred to a thousand dollars," a writer for the *Colored American* reminded readers in 1840.[51]

By then, Black Baltimoreans had been fighting off these vultures for decades. Because of the size of the city's free Black community, it had been a "den of man-hunters" since the early 1800s. Over the years, these kidnappers and human traffickers had grown ever more "daring in their depredations," sometimes knocking their targets unconscious on city streets in broad daylight, or enlisting older African Americans to lure youngsters into their clutches. By the second quarter of the century, Black boys and girls under the age of sixteen had become prime targets. Missing persons ads in the city's papers filled with their names—Priscilla Blake, aged 14, Eliza Pisco, aged 11, Jane Harris, aged 10, Henny, aged 6—a roll call for a school of lost children.[52]

Baltimore was a particularly well-stocked hunting ground, but kidnappers operated across the entire state, a fact often remarked upon by visitors from New England and from Europe. Richard Blackett has identified at least one gang based in Hagerstown in western Maryland. Many more operated out of safehouses on the lower reaches of the Eastern Shore, in and around Talbot County, where settlement was thin, slaveholding common, and the politics decidedly conservative. No one knew for sure how many Marylanders made their living on the Reverse Underground Railroad; there was no debate, however, as to its scale. "Kidnapping being a lucrative business it is not strange that it should be extensively practiced," a contributor to the *Colored American* wrote during one survey, but "it is difficult to estimate the extent to which illegal kidnapping is carried [out], since a large number of cases must escape detection."[53]

The concept of free soil meant little to these land-sharks and the most ambitious and predatory among them would launch multiday raids into southern Pennsylvania from their home bases in Maryland. One of these "beasts of prey" was Thomas McCreary, who seized Rachel Parker from the Miller farm in West Nottingham in 1851. As Lucy Maddox, his biographer, has demonstrated, McCreary was a serial kidnapper. From his base in Cecil County in northern Maryland, McCreary had led at least five prior abduction expeditions into southern Pennsylvania and had made off with Rachel's sister, Elizabeth, just two weeks earlier. He was hardly alone. People like McCreary were crouched all along Maryland's northern border throughout the 1840s, ready to dart into Pennsylvania to snatch children, solo adults, and sometimes small family groups whenever they saw an opportunity.[54]

In the 1850s, men and women in McCreary's line of work stepped up their operations. They took ever more free people of color and tried to pass them off as suspected fugitives, a practice made much easier by the terms of the new Fugitive Slave Act of 1850. As Pauli Murray once observed, these people snatchers "cared little whether their victim was a fugitive, a freedman or a free-born person." While some ventured into Pennsylvania clutching warrants naming particular runaways, they often grabbed any person of color they thought could fit those bills and fetch a price when sold to an interstate slave dealer. Traders like Baltimore's Hope Slatter cultivated reputations as respectable businessmen who operated wholly within the law, but as historian Robert Gudmestad has demonstrated, the reality was quite different, and at one time or another every major trader seems to have dabbled in buying people they knew to have been kidnapped.[55]

Monsters like McCreary operated with what historian Stephen Whitman has called "virtual impunity." All too few served prison terms, and Maryland's governors frequently pardoned or commuted the sentences of the few men and women convicted of abduction, human trafficking, or enslavement. Because free people of color had no reliable allies in state government or law enforcement, and only a small core of white activists were willing to lend them any practical aid, they had to defend themselves as best they could. So they did. They organized themselves into protection societies and neighborhood watches, staying "within doors after dark" and hollering, biting, and kicking if a stranger grabbed them. They were dogged and determined, but resistance was often futile and always dangerous. When a Black husband "clambered up to one of the windows" of a rail car to try to stop his legally free wife being sold out of state, Hope Slatter himself "knocked him down from the car, and ordered him away."[56]

* * *

T hings had not always been so dark, lonely, and desperate. In the 1820s, Baltimore had been a hive of antislavery activism and radical, interracial politics. In 1824, Benjamin Lundy had moved his crusading newspaper, the *Genius of Universal Emancipation,* to the city from Tennessee. It was the only explicitly antislavery newspaper published in a border state that decade, and Lundy soon began churning out a mix of polemical reporting and commentary, including his trademark "Black List," which assiduously documented slavery's daily outrages. A year later, in 1825, a group of white city leaders in Lundy's or- bit formed the Maryland Anti-Slavery Society (MAS), a rare accomplishment in a slave state, and over the next three years it attracted about five hundred members and subscribers and spawned eleven county auxiliaries. In 1827, some of the same activists founded a sister organization, the Baltimore Society for the Protection of Free People of Color (BSP). These developments were direct responses to escalating racial oppression. But these were heady days nonethe- less for the state's antislavery activists, and by the end of the decade, Baltimore had twice hosted the American Convention for Promoting the Abolition of Slavery, drawing delegates from organizations in several states to the city for national assemblies and confirming its emerging reputation as "the center of the abolitionist movement."[57]

By the eve of the Civil War, all that was a distant memory. The endur- ing influence of slavery's special interests and the crushing weight of rising "Negrophobia" had long since driven Maryland's white antislavery activists to the point of extinction. Having been slandered, spat at, and physically as- saulted, Lundy had finally fled Baltimore for Washington, DC, in 1830, tak- ing his newspaper with him. By then, both the MAS and BSP had folded too, undone by flagging fund-raising and by a foolhardy decision by MAS officers to put up overtly antislavery candidates in statewide elections. Those who had embraced the cause out of religious obligation were buckling un- der social and political pressure as well. In 1836, the Baltimore Annual Con- ference of the Methodist Episcopal Church announced its absolute opposi- tion to abolition, a striking turnaround for a group that had once contained several notable emancipationists. Two years later, in 1838, Maryland's Hick- site Quakers did the same, declaring that their members should avoid be- coming further entangled in the antislavery cause if they wished to remain in good standing. Stripped of their white allies, the state's African Ameri- can population had to soldier on alone, suffering through decades of humiliation and persecution that had all the trappings of a race war unfolding in slow motion.[58]

A border slave state with an unusually large free Black population, Thomas McCreary's Maryland was, in Barbara Field's famous formulation, "a society divided against itself." By the time Abraham Lincoln was elected president in 1860, those divisions were on full display. Maryland stood at a crossroads, torn between its embrace of northern mercantilism and its heritage of southern cultural affinity and agrarianism. In the state's southern and eastern counties, many Marylanders prized the protection of race slavery and considered Lincoln's antislavery politics anathema. When those voters went to the polls that November, their ballots ensured that Lincoln placed fourth in statewide returns, trailing John Breckenridge, the southern Democrat candidate, by a margin of more than eighteen to one.[59]

Yet most Maryland voters were more pragmatic. The long border with Pennsylvania meant that the state would be difficult to defend in the event of secession and war, something that white residents of the state's northern counties—who had been on the front lines of the fugitive crisis for decades—understood immediately. The same practical considerations produced pro-Union voter turnout in Baltimore, a city that was situated north of Washington, DC, and much closer to Philadelphia than it was to Richmond. Most civic leaders there considered secession a poor choice and worried that a war would lead to a blockade of Baltimore's port and recently extended railroad, strangling trade and endangering fortunes and jobs. While white residents across the state had little love for Lincoln, most rallied around the Unionist cause, pledging a majority of their votes (54.2 percent) to one or another of the three Unionist candidates.[60]

NOTES

1. The best account of this episode, and the source for this selective summary, is Lucy Maddox, *The Parker Sisters: A Border Kidnapping* (Philadelphia: Temple University Press, 2016).

2. Thomas J. Preston, *Young Frederick Douglass: The Maryland Years* (Baltimore: Johns Hopkins University Press, 1980), 79.

3. My conception of antebellum Maryland as a site of intense border conflict owes a debt to Stanley Harrold, *Border War: Fighting over Slavery before the Civil War* (Chapel Hill: University of North Carolina Press, 2010); R. J. M. Blackett, *The Captive's Quest for Freedom: Fugitive Slaves, the 1850 Fugitive Slave Law, and the Politics of Slavery* (New York: Cambridge University Press, 2018);

and Robert H. Churchill, *The Underground Railroad: The Geography of Violence in Antebellum America* (New York: Cambridge University Press, 2020).

4. Frederick Douglass, *My Bondage and My Freedom* (New York: Miller, Orton & Mulligan, 1855), 61; Seth Rockman, *Scraping By: Wage Labor, Slavery, and Survival in Early Baltimore* (Baltimore: Johns Hopkins University Press, 2009), 238; Andrew Delblanco, *The War before the War: Fugitive Slaves and the Struggle for America's Soil from the Revolution to the Civil War* (New York: Penguin, 2018), 147.

5. John W. Blassingame, ed., *Slave Testimony: Two Centuries of Letters, Speeches, Interviews, and Autobiographies* (Baton Rouge: Louisiana State University Press, 1977), 411; Barbara Jeanne Fields, *Slavery and Freedom on the Middle Ground: Maryland during the Nineteenth Century* (New Haven: Yale University Press, 1985), 23, 83.

6. Lewis Charlton, *Sketch of the Life of Mr. Lewis Charlton, and Reminiscences of Slavery* (Portland, ME: Daily Press Print, n. d.), 3, quoted in Damian Alan Pargas, *Slavery and Forced Migration in the Antebellum South* (New York: Cambridge University Press, 2015), 183; Douglass, *My Bondage,* 203; Calvin Schermerhorn, *Money over Mastery, Family over Freedom: Slavery in the Antebellum Upper South* (Baltimore: Johns Hopkins University Press, 2011), 20. Provoked by Covey, Douglass resolved to attack him. According to his often-repeated accounts of that struggle, their fight lasted for the best part of two hours, and left both men bloody and spent. From that day forward, Douglass claimed, Covey never touched him again.

7. Max Grivno, *Gleanings of Freedom: Free and Slave Labor along the Mason-Dixon Line, 1790–1860* (Champaign: University of Illinois Press, 2014), 88–89.

8. Frederick Law Olmsted, *A Journey in the Seaboard Slave States in the Years 1853–1854, with Remarks on Their Economy* (New York: Dix and Edwards, 1856), 11; Pargas, *Forced Migration,* 181, 234–35, 240; Fields, *Middle Ground,* 6–7, 23–24.

9. Ethan Allen Andrews, *Slavery and the Domestic Slave Trade in the United States. In a Series of Letters Addressed to the Executive Committee of the American Union for the Relief and Improvement of the Colored Race* (Boston: Light and Stearns, 1836), 53; John L. Carey, *Slavery in Maryland Briefly Considered* (Baltimore: John Murphy, 1845), 33; Ira Berlin, *Slaves Without Masters: The Free Negro in the Antebellum South* (New York: New Press, 2007), 184.

10. Schermerhorn, *Money Over Mastery,* 86; Fields, *Middle Ground,* 6–8, 47, 62; Rockman, *Scraping By,* 234–35; Berlin, *Slaves Without Masters,* 228–29. Legal bondage also collateralized enslavers' lines of credit and mortgages, and secured the Baltimore city government with a reliable source of tax revenue. For a list of slaveholders in Baltimore in 1840 and 1850, see Ralph Clayton, *Slavery, Slaveholding, and the Free Black Population of Antebellum Baltimore* (Bowie, MD: Heritage Books, 1993), 82–145. For their occupations, see Stephen Whitman, *The Price of Freedom: Slavery and Manumission in Baltimore and Early National Maryland* (New York: Routledge, 2000), 167.

11. Pargas, *Forced Migration,* 36–38, 129, 167–68; Fields, *Middle Ground,* 62, 83–84; Schermerhorn, *Money Over Mastery,* 87.

12. Douglass, *My Bondage,* 134, 141; Pargas, *Forced Migration,* 72; Schermerhorn, *Money Over Mastery,* 82–83, 87–88. On his own first day in Baltimore, Isaac Mason was savagely beaten by two white men for passing between them on the sidewalk—not knowing that custom and law required urban slaves to "take the street to give place to their superiors.'" Pargas, *Forced Migration,* 209.

13. T. Stephen Whitman, *Challenging Slavery in the Chesapeake: Black and White Resistance to Hu-*

man Bondage 1775–1865 (Baltimore: Maryland Center for History and Culture, 2007), 127–28; Calvin Schermerhorn, *Unrequited Toil: A History of United States Slavery* (New York: Cambridge University Press, 2018), 21, 29; Grivno, *Gleanings of Freedom*, 116; Berlin, *Slaves Without Masters*, 199. The enslaved population of Maryland was 102,994 in 1830. In 1860, their numbers stood at 87,189. For more on manumissions in Maryland, see the essay in this volume by Jessica Millward.

14. Steven Deyle, *Carry Me Back: The Domestic Slave Trade in American Life* (New York: Oxford University Press, 2005); Winfield H. Collins, *The Domestic Slave Trade of the Southern States* (New York: Broadway Publishing, 1904); Grivno, *Gleanings of Freedom*, 197; Pargas, *Forced Migration*, 25; Fields, *Middle Ground*, 5.

15. Deyle, *Carry Me Back*, 232, 165, 249, 207; Pargas, *Forced Migration*, 62; Collins, *Domestic Slave Trade*, 47; Delblanco, *War before the War*, 53–54.

16. George P. C. Hussey quoted in Theodore Dwight Weld, *American Slavery As It Is; Testimony of a Thousand Witnesses* (New York: American Anti-Slavery Society, 1839), 76 (emphasis in original); Harrold, *Border War*, 10; Grivno, *Gleanings of Freedom*, 116–17; Fields, *Middle Ground*, 15–17; Schermerhorn, *Money Over Mastery*, 14.

17. Douglass, *My Bondage*, 298; *Baltimore American and Commercial Advertiser*, January 7, 1835; Pargas, *Forced Migration*, 43; *Centreville (MD) Times and Easter-Shore Public Advertiser*, May 4, 1833; Deyle, *Carry Me Back*, 132, 222–23; William Calderhead, "The Role of the Professional Slave Trader in a Slave Economy: Austin Woolfolk, A Case Study," *Civil War History* 23, no. 3 (1977): 197–98, 209. Agents made the rounds of all the county towns on the Eastern Shore. In Dorchester County alone, more than fifteen of them advertised in newspapers between 1831 and 1835, and Charles B. Clark estimated that in all "at least 40 or 50, perhaps 60 or 80, regular traders of various degree" operated there, including dozens of petty traders, some of whom were local residents. Charles B. Clark, *Eastern Shore of Maryland and Virginia*, 3 vols. (New York: Lewis Historical Publishing, 1950), 1:529, 532.

18. Andrews, *Domestic Slave Trade*, 78; Joseph Sturge, A *Visit to the United States in 1841* (London: Hamilton, Adams, 1842), 31; Weld, *Slavery As It Is*, 60 (emphasis in original); Pargas, *Forced Migration*, 42–43, 46–47; Deyle, *Carry Me Back*, 104; Rockman, *Scraping By*, 235.

19. Douglass, *My Bondage*, 448; Harrold, *Border War*, 10; Maddox, *Parker Sisters*, 79; Deyle, *Carry Me Back*, 38, 44, 51, 224; Robert H. Gudmestad, *A Troublesome Commerce: The Transformation of the Interstate Slave Trade* (Baton Rouge: Louisiana State University Press, 2003), 79–80. William Lloyd Garrison, who lived in Baltimore in the early 1830s, prayed that slave traders should be arrested, convicted, and "sentenced to solitary confinement for life" and deserved to spend eternity in "the lowest depths" of hell. Delblanco, *War before the War*, 28–29. On the role of Baltimore (and its most famous trader, Austin Woolfolk) in the domestic slave trade prior to 1825, see Deyle, *Carry Me Back*, 98–100; Calderhead, "Austin Woolfolk." Woolfolk resented activists' attacks on his character and reputation, especially those issuing from Benjamin Lundy, Baltimore's crusading newspaper editor, who decried Woolfolk's business as 'barbarous, inhuman, and unchristian." In January 1827, Woolfolk "beat and stamped upon" Lundy's head, "in a most furious and violent manner, until pulled off by the bystanders." Lundy sued for assault but the judge fined Woolfolk just $1 plus court costs, and noted in his ruling that slave trading was legal and "beneficial to the state." Deyle, *Carry Me Back*, 179–80.

20. *Baltimore Sun*, July 18, 1838; Delblanco, *War before the War*, 28–29; Clayton, *Antebellum Baltimore*, 35; Deyle, *Carry Me Back*, 3, 212; Gudmestad, *Troublesome Commerce*, 163–64. Hope Slatter sold his business to Bernard Campbell in 1848.

21. Alexis de Tocqueville, *Journey to America*, ed. J. P. Mayer, trans. George Lawrence (Westport, CT: Greenwood Press, 1981), 159–60; Rockman, *Scraping By*, 236–27; Pargas, *Forced Migration*, 24, 61, 79; Deyle, *Carry Me Back*, 234. Enslavers exploited slaves' fears of sale without mercy, using the threat of it to deter misbehavior and spur productivity.

22. E. S. Abdy, *Journal of a Residence and Tour in the United States of North America, From April 1833, to October, 1834*, 2 vols. (London: John Murray, 1835), 2:93; Pargas, *Forced Migration*, 76, 81, 83; Grivno, *Gleanings of Freedom*, 75–76. In 1815 a Maryland woman named Anna had jumped from the attic of a tavern in Washington, DC, to try to prevent her sale and the breakup of her family. "I didn't want to go, and I jumped out of the window," she said later, having broken her arms and shattered her spine in this apparent suicide attempt, but still "they have carried my children off with 'em to Carolina." Schermerhorn, *Unrequited Toil*, 151.

23. Benjamin Drew, ed., *A North-Side View of Slavery. The Refugee: or the Narratives of Fugitive Slaves in Canada. Related by Themselves* . . . (Boston: John P. Jewett, 1856), 339; Pargas, *Forced Migration*, 45–46; Deyle, *Carry Me Back*, 255–56; Schermerhorn, *Money Over Mastery*, 16.

24. Charles Ball, *Fifty Years in Chains; or, The Life of an American Slave* (New York: H. Dayton, 1859), 11; *Minutes of an Adjourned Session of the American Convention for Promoting the Abolition of Slavery, and Improving the Condition of the African Race, Convened at Baltimore, on the Twenty-fifth of October 1826* (Baltimore: Benjamin Lundy, 1826), 29; Grivno, *Gleanings of Freedom*, 75–76; Deyle, *Carry Me Back*, 176, 228, 246, 252; Rockman, *Scraping By*, 238; Preston, *Young Frederick Douglass*, 76.

25. Isaac Mason, *Life of Isaac Mason As a Slave* (Worcester, MA, 1893), 35; Pargas, *Forced Migration*, 79–80; Churchill, *Geography of Violence*, 45. "A vicious circle developed as slaveholders sold slaves south to prevent escape and slaves escaped to prevent sale south," explains Stanley Harrold. Harrold, *Border War*, 10.

26. James W. C. Pennington, *The Fugitive Blacksmith; or, Events in the History of James W. C. Pennington, Pastor of a Presbyterian Church, New York, Formerly a Slave in the State of Maryland, United States*, 2nd ed. (London: Charles Gilpin, 1849), 14; Whitman, *Challenging Slavery*, 175–77; Elwood L. Bridner, "The Fugitive Slaves of Maryland," Maryland Historical Magazine 66 (1971): 39, 45; Blackett, *Captive's Quest*, 313; Harrold, *Border War*, 139.

27. (Hagerstown) *Herald of Freedom*, May 8, 1849; Grivno, *Gleanings of Freedom*, 129; Harrold, *Border War*, 14, 127, 129–31, 177.

28. *Albany Weekly Patriot*, January 8, 1845; (Hagerstown) *Herald of Freedom*, September 18, 1846; Fields, *Middle Ground*, 15; Harrold, *Border War*, 103, 106, 139, 148, 153; Grivno, *Gleanings of Freedom*, 128–29. Writing in January 1850, before the passage of the Fugitive Slave Law that fall, a writer in the *Baltimore Sun* told city readers that "Every day but swells the number of absconding slaves from Maryland," *Baltimore Sun*, January 7, 1850; Berlin, *Slaves Without Masters*, 347. Maryland was also a major site of capture for northbound slaves escaping from states further south, like Virginia. When thirteen enslaved people escaped from Loudoun County, Virginia, in June 1858, twelve of them were later recaptured in Maryland, seven of them following a firefight in Boonsboro, a hamlet just south of Hagerstown. Blackett, *Captive's Quest*, 271.

29. Blackett, *Captive's Quest*, 51, 272, 306, 314, 322.

30. *Baltimore Saturday Visiter*, July 19, 1845; Harrold, *Border War*, 139; Blackett, *Captive's Quest*, 4–5, 322–24; Delblanco, *War before the War*, 39.

31. *New York Daily Tribune*, August 18, 1850; Harrold, *Border War*, 127; Sinha, *The Slave's Cause: A*

History of Abolition (New Haven: Yale University Press, 2016), 396–97; Whitman, *Challenging Slavery*, 185–86; Blackett, *Captive's Quest*, 319, 321.

32. H. Robert Baker, *Prigg v. Pennsylvania: Slavery, the Supreme Court, and the Ambivalent Constitution* (Lawrence: University Press of Kansas, 2012); Sinha, *Slave's Cause*, 390; Delblanco, *War before the War*, 178–79; Harrold, *Border War*, 77. In 1842, Maryland state legislators had narrowly failed to pass a law offering "'large rewards for the detection of any person who induces or aids a slave to run away, (to) employ bailiffs to watch the arrival and departure of every steamboat and railroad car," and other similar measures. Two years later, legislators in Annapolis succeeded in setting up a fund that paid out $100 to anyone who could drag back to their Maryland masters any fugitives who had made it to Pennsylvania. Harrold, *Border War*, 127.

33. Blackett, *Captive's Quest*, 3–42; Delblanco, *War before the War*, 264; Sinha, *Slave's Cause*, 504. Hamlet's former owner, Mary Brown, had planned to trade him to slave dealers to raise cash. Ultimately, however, she sold his life and labor to members of the New York's African Methodist Episcopal Zion Church for $800. The AME congregation, who counted Hamlet as one of their own, promptly freed him and by October he had returned to New York, this time with free papers in his pocket.

34. Thomas P. Slaughter, *Bloody Dawn: The Christiana Riot and Racial Violence in the Antebellum North* (New York: Oxford University Press, 1991). See also Delblanco, *War before the War*, 183–85, 286–88; Harrold, *Border War*, 62, 102–3, 108–10, 154–55; Grivno, *Gleanings of Freedom*, 130–31.

35. *Frederick Douglass's Paper* (Rochester, NY), September 25,1851.

36. Blackett, *Captive's Quest*, 315–17. No other slave state had a higher proportion of free people among its Black population or anywhere near the absolute numbers of free people of color as Maryland, though the District of Columbia did. Fields, *Middle Ground*, 1–2. Over the eleven years between 1849 and 1860, Harriet Tubman made thirteen trips back to Maryland and helped dozens of enslaved people liberate themselves. Other lesser known figures, such as Richard Neal (who had escaped from Anne Arundel County), did likewise.

37. Fields, *Middle Ground*, 34; Grivno, *Gleanings of Freedom*, 129; Whitman, *Challenging Slavery*, 180.

38. Thomas W. Griffiths, *Annals of Baltimore* (Baltimore: William Wooddy, 1824), 292; Fields, *Middle Ground*, 62; William S. Neeley, *Frederick Douglass* (New York: Simon and Schuster, 1992), 67; Adam Malka, *Men of Mobtown: Policing Baltimore in the Age of Slavery and Emancipation* (Chapel Hill: University of North Carolina Press, 2018), 22–23. In 1830 nine out of ten free Black Baltimoreans were born elsewhere. Jennifer Hull Dorsey, *Hirelings: African American Workers and Free Labor in Early Maryland* (Ithaca, NY: Cornell University Press, 2011), 58.

39. Bettye Jane Gardner, "Free Blacks in Baltimore, 1800–1860," PhD diss., George Washington University, 1974, 6; Christopher Phillips, *Freedom's Port: The African American Community of Baltimore, 1790–1860* (Urbana: University of Illinois Press, 1997), 76–77; Barbara Elizabeth Wallace, "'Fair Daughters of Africa': African American Women in Baltimore, 1790–1860," PhD diss., University of California Los Angeles, 2001, 81–135.

40. William Watkins, *An Address Delivered before the Moral Reform Society, in Philadelphia, August 8, 1836* (Philadelphia: Merrihew and Gunn, 1836), 13–14; Berlin, *Slaves Without Masters*, 288–89, 296, 304–5; "Condition of the Coloured Population of the City of Baltimore," *Baltimore Literary and Religious Magazine* 4 (1838): 171–75; Wallace, "Fair Daughters of Africa," 169; Malka, *Men of Mobtown*, 162. These sacred sites served functions almost too numerous to name—place of worship, Sunday school, unemployment office, soup kitchen, and fugitive sanctuary, for instance—and

were the central sites of Black community formation. Martha S. Jones, *Birthright Citizens: A History of Race and Rights in Antebellum America* (New York: Cambridge University Press, 2018), 72–73, It was a Baltimorean, Hezekiah Grice, who founded the Black convention movement. Sinha, *Slave's Cause,* 169.

41. *Genius of Universal Emancipation* (Baltimore), January 12, 1828; T. Whitman, *Price of Freedom,* 156. Wages for most Black Baltimoreans were low, barely above survival rates, and by the 1850s less than 1 percent owned any real estate. Malka, *Men of Mobtown,* 108.

42. *Baltimore Sun,* May 18, 1858; John H. B. Latrobe, *Colonization. A Notice of Victor Hugo's Views of Slavery in the United States, in a letter from John H. B. Latrobe, of Baltimore to Thomas Suffern, of New York* (Baltimore: John D. Toy, 1851), 14; Berlin, *Slaves Without Masters,* 231–32, 241, 349–50; Malka, *Men of Mobtown,* 111, 116–21.

43. *Baltimore Sun,* August 28, 1838, May 31, 1837, October 22, 1839; Malka, *Men of Mobtown,* 112, 153–54; Berlin, *Slaves Without Masters,* 158, 232–33, 334–35. People of color boarding northbound trains or steamboats faced ticket checks, inspections of their free papers or passes, and interrogation. William Still called Baltimore "one of the most difficult places in the South for even free colored people to get away from, much more for slaves." Bridner, "Fugitive Slaves of Maryland," 45. In the last two years before the Civil War, eighty-nine Black convicts were sold into term slavery on terms ranging from two years to more than sixty. Fields, *Middle Ground,* 35.

44. *Annapolis Gazette,* December 2, 1858 (emphasis in original); Blackett, *Captive's Quest,* 325–27; Berlin, *Slaves Without Masters,* 192; Clark, *Eastern Shore,* 1:515; Fields, *Middle Ground,* 35; Rockman, *Scraping By,* 250.

45. *Baltimore American,* March 4, 1842; *Maryland Colonization Journal* 1 (1838), 77; Berlin, *Slaves Without Masters,* 199–200, 210–11; Malka, *Men of Mobtown,* 168–69. Slaveholder conventions held in 1858 and 1859 succeeded in lobbying the Maryland legislature to outlaw manumissions, and in 1858 lawmakers also authorized a statewide referendum in which the white population would vote on whether to enslave all free Blacks within its borders. Thanks in part to vigorous "vote no" campaign waged by Black Baltimoreans, the plan was rejected at the ballot box. Whitman, *Challenging Slavery,* 171, 206–8; Berlin, *Slaves Without Masters,* 375, 380.

46. *Baltimore Times,* November 5, 1851; Rockman, *Scraping By,* 249; Sinha, *Slave's Cause,* 212; Berlin, *Slaves Without Masters,* 202, 355; Whitman, *Challenging Slavery,* 128; Clark, *Eastern Shore,* 1:518. On support for colonization among Marylanders prior to 1825, see Jones, *Birthright Citizens,* 37–49. State support for colonization was renewed in 1852, despite protests from Black leaders.

47. Delblanco, *War before the War,* 230; Blackett, *Captive's Quest,* 115; Rockman, *Scraping By,* 249; Berlin, *Slaves Without Masters,* 169–70, 357–59.

48. Blackett, *Captive's Quest,* 126–27, 132; Berlin, *Slaves Without Masters,* 207; Whitman, *Challenging Slavery,* 143–46. The state's small band of white antislavery activists was also dead set against deportation. Benjamin Lundy condemned colonization for its lack of interest in abolishing slavery. He published many Black activists' denunciations of the scheme and was instrumental in convincing a young William Lloyd Garrison to renounce his own early support for it. Sinha, *Slave's Cause,* 170. For a divergent view (and a full list of emigrants to the Maryland in Liberia colony), see Richard Hall, *On Afric's Shore: A History of Maryland in Liberia, 1834–1857* (Baltimore: Maryland Center for History and Culture, 2004).

49. (Boston) *Liberator,* March 23, 1833 (emphasis in original), June 4, 1831; Rockman, *Scraping*

By, 249–50; Whitman, *Challenging Slavery,* 142–43; Sinha, *Slave's Cause,* 243; Berlin, *Slaves Without Masters,* 204–6.

50. Berlin, *Slaves Without Masters,* 204–6; Sinha, *Slave's Cause,* 215–16; Jones, *Birthright Citizens,* 38–39; Whitman, *Challenging Slavery,* 203–4.

51. (Philadelphia) *Pennsylvania Freeman,* April 20, 1854; (New York) *Colored American,* March 21, 1840; Blackett, *Captive's Quest,* 293–94, 305; Clayton, *Antebellum Baltimore,* 53–54; Harrold, *Border War,* 53–54. On the Reverse Underground Railroad, see Richard Bell, *Stolen: Five Free Boys Kidnapped into Slavery and Their Astonishing Odyssey Home* (New York: Simon and Schuster, 2019).

52. John S. Tyson, *Life of Elisha Tyson, the Philanthropist. By a Citizen of Baltimore* (Baltimore: B. Lundy, 1825), 79; *Baltimore Patriot,* July 26, 1817; Ralph Clayton, *Cash for Blood: The Baltimore to New Orleans Slave Trade* (Bowie, MD: Heritage Books, 2002), 39, 49; (New York) *Freedom's Journal,* August 15, 1828. For more on kidnappings in Baltimore see (Washington, DC) *Daily National Intelligencer,* September 26, 1817; (Philadelphia) *Poulson's American Daily Advertiser,* June 12, 1818; (Baltimore) *Niles Weekly Register,* December 12, 1818; *Easton Gazette,* January 11, 1819; *Easton Gazette,* July 23, 1821; (Baltimore) *American and Commercial Daily Advertiser,* August 9, 1822; (Baltimore) *Genius of Universal Emancipation,* July 26, 1826; Dorsey, *Hirelings,* 93–94; Rockman, *Scraping By,* 238–39; Wallace, "Fair Daughters of Africa," 257; Leroy Graham, *Baltimore: The Nineteenth-Century Black Capital* (Washington: University Press of America, 1982), 60; Phillips, *Freedom's Port,* 230–31; Bernard John Medairy Jr., *The Notorious Patty Cannon and Her Gang of Kidnappers on the Eastern Shore: Kidnappers, Robbers and Murderers* (Towson, MD: B. Medairy, 1995), 39–46;. On kidnappers of color, see *Baltimore Patriot & Mercantile Advertiser,* August 13, 1821; (Baltimore) *Genius of Universal Emancipation,* June 9, 1827; Richard Bell, "Counterfeit Kin: Kidnappers of Color, the Reverse Underground Railroad, and the Origins of Practical Abolition," *Journal of the Early Republic* 38, no. 2 (2018): 199–230.

53. (New York) *Colored American,* March 21, 1840; Clayton, *Antebellum Baltimore,* 45–46; E. S. Abdy, *Journal of a Residence and Tour in the United States of North America, From April 1833, to October, 1834,* 2 vols. (New York: Negro Press, 1969), 2:99–100; Blackett, *Captive's Quest,* 302; Bell, *Stolen,* 47–80; Harrold, *Border War,* 53–54.

54. Jesse Torrey, *A Portraiture of Slavery in the United States, Proposing National Measures for the Education and Gradual Emancipation of the Slaves . . .,* 2nd edition (Ballston Spa, NY: 1818), 82; Maddox, *Parker Sisters,* 32–33. For Marylanders abducting free Blacks in Pennsylvania prior to 1850, see Maddox, *Parker Sisters,* 17–18; David G. Smith, *On the Edge of Freedom: The Fugitive Slave Issue in South Central Pennsylvania, 1820–1870* (New York: Fordham University Press, 2013), esp. 97–104; William C. Kashatus, *Just Over the Line: Chester County and the Underground Railroad* (University Park: Penn State University Press, 2002), esp. 29–30.

55. Pauli Murray, *Proud Shoes: The Story of An American Family* (New York: Harper & Brothers, 1956), 97; Maddox, *Parker Sisters,* 17–19, 38–39; Gudmestad, *Troublesome Commerce,* 73–74. For Marylanders abducting free Blacks in Pennsylvania after 1850, see Clayton, *Cash For Blood,* 38–39; Samuel May, *The Fugitive Slave Law and Its Victims,* rev. edition (Freeport, NY: Books for Libraries Press, 1970), 23, 25, 121. The difference between a kidnapper and a slave catcher was often in the eye of the beholder. Blackett, *Captive's Quest,* 302–3.

56. Whitman, *Challenging Slavery,* 169; *Baltimore Patriot,* July 26, 1817; Daniel Drayton, *Personal Memoir of Daniel Drayton, For Four years and Four Months A Prisoner (For Charity's Sake) in Washington Jail, Including a Narrative of the Voyage and Capture of the Schooner Pearl* (Boston: Bela Marsha,

1853), 60; Schermerhorn, *Unrequited Toil,* 147; *Relf's Philadelphia Gazette,* May 22, 1822; Rockman, *Scraping By,* 240; Berlin, *Slaves Without Masters,* 309. On the Baltimore Quaker Elisha Tyson's lonely, unpopular, and dangerous crusade against kidnappers in the 1810s and the short-lived Protection Society of Maryland he founded in 1816, see Tyson, *Life of Elisha Tyson,* 82–87, 101–2, 108–10; Graham, *Black Capital,* 50–51; Whitman, *Challenging Slavery,* 105–6; *Niles Weekly Register,* May 9, 1818.

57. Sinha, *Slave's Cause,* 190, 198–99; Deyle, *Carry Me Back,* 179–80; Whitman, *Challenging Slavery,* 155, 120; Harrold, *Border War,* 118.

58. Phillips, *Freedom's Port,* 231; Gordon E. Finnie, "The Antislavery Movement in the Upper South Before 1840," *Journal of Southern History* 35, no. 3 (1969): 324–25. At a June 1828 monthly meeting, the treasurer of the Baltimore Society for the Protection of Free People of Color reported that society funds amounted to just 37.5 cents. Regular meetings ceased soon thereafter. Baltimore Society for the Protection of Free People of Color. Minutes, 1827–1829. Friends Historical Library, Swarthmore, Pennsylvania.

59. Harrold, *Border War,* 201–2, 204–5; Michael J. Dubin, *United States Presidential Elections, 1788–1860: The Official Results by County and State* (Jefferson, NC: McFarland, 2002), 170–71.

60. Fields, *Middle Ground,* 6; Delblanco, *War before the War,* 28.

CHARITY FOLKS & THE
GHOSTS OF SLAVERY
IN MARYLAND

JESSICA MILLWARD

N arratives of slavery in Maryland exclusively focus on two figures: orator and abolitionist Frederick Douglass; and abolitionist and Civil War scout Harriet Tubman. So large is their presence that they continue in American memory today. During a breakfast with African American supporters in February 2017, Black History Month, for example, Donald Trump noted that "Frederick Douglass is an example of somebody who's done an amazing job and is being recognized more and more, I notice."[1] Then-Press Secretary Sean Spicer did little to rectify that the greatest orator of the nineteenth century is no longer living. According to Spicer, "I think he [President Trump] wants to highlight the contributions that he [Douglass] has made and I think through a lot of the actions and statements that he's going to make, I think the contributions of Frederick Douglass will become more and more."[2] The ahistorical statements of Trump and Spicer were ironically made in Douglass's shadow. In 2013, a seven-foot statue of Frederick Douglass had been unveiled at the US Capitol building to commemorate the Emancipation Proclamation. Whereas the Trump speechwriters or Trump himself made the gaffe, it does not diminish the permanence of Frederick Douglass's presence in Washington, DC, and in American public memory despite being deceased for over a century.

Like Douglass, Harriet Tubman has gained increased notoriety some one hundred years after her death. She is a popular subject of children's and young adult books and appears in school textbooks from elementary school through college. In 2013–14, the National Park Service opened the Harriet Tubman National Underground Railroad Byway on the Eastern Shore of Maryland; and in 2017 it expanded the Harriet Tubman National Historical Park in Auburn, New York.[3] Controversially, in 2016, after considering many nationally known women, the US Treasury announced its decision to place Tubman's image on the twenty-dollar bill, replacing Andrew Jackson's.[4] A year later, Harriet Tubman made a compelling debut on the short-lived WGN television series, *Underground.* Actress Aisha Hinds delivered a riveting, hour-long monologue as Tubman, and the episode won critical acclaim.[5] Finally, in 2019, Harriet Tubman was immortalized in a feature film and accompanying book.[6]

While noting the ways in which Douglass and Tubman shape public memory about slavery and the Civil War in Maryland, this essay focuses on Charity Folks (1757–1834), who lived in Annapolis, Maryland. Formerly enslaved, and manumitted as an adult, Folks lived her entire life in the Chesapeake. Folks did not flee bondage, as did Douglass and Tubman, nor is she as famous. In fact, she has gone largely unknown. Born into slavery in Anne Arundel County, Maryland, Charity Folks was manumitted when she was approximately forty years old. Despite the condition of her birth, she made the most of her remaining years. By the time of her death in the early 1830s, Charity Folks had amassed at least four properties in Annapolis. There are indications that she was able to read; however, she was neither an orator, nor did she pen an autobiography. Folks was also not active in the abolition movement, and she died decades before the Civil War began. For all that she does not represent when compared to Douglass and Tubman, Folks's entire life embodies enslavement and freedom in Maryland. This small geographic region boasted a remarkably fluid population of free, enslaved, and quasi-free Blacks. On the eve of the Civil War, for example, Maryland's enslaved population numbered some 87,189 people, while its free Black population was nearly eighty-four thousand individuals.[7]

This essay historicizes Charity Folks as a manumitted woman, a founding mother, and a ghost of slavery both to account for her personal history as well as to explicate three interrelated points to understanding gendered experiences of freedom in Maryland.[8] First, despite the recent surge in accounts of histories of African American women and their impact on shaping American history and memory, this microhistory illuminates that there is still much to be uncovered about the lives of Black women and their experiences of freedom via manumission. Second, it exposes the limitations in the scholarly measurements of the of Civil War period and emancipation, which account for only the temporal timeline 1860–65. Folks's life exemplifies the African American struggle for freedom. Finally, by exploring her life (and by extension that of her descendants), this chapter suggests that the process of manumission shaped African American concepts of freedom well before the Civil War hastened the demise of slavery. By focusing on Charity Folks's life, we see experiences of freedom in the lives of African Americans in Maryland prior to and during the Civil War. Her life also serves as a representative of slavery's afterlife.[9] By understanding the multifaceted function of "freedom" within the life of this one woman, we can better understand the lives of African Americans in Maryland during the Civil War.

CHARITY FOLKS: A LIFE AND A FAMILY
HISTORY OF MANUMISSION

The invisibility of Black women (particularly enslaved women) in the brick-and-mortar archive has forced scholars to embrace innovative pedagogy in order to document their experiences. Saidiya Hartman suggests that the process of writing about Black women found in the archives of slavery (and by extension its afterlife) is best understood as a form of critical fabulation.[10] By critical fabulation, Hartman refers to how one puts together a history when evidence is elusive. This methodology is particularly helpful when only sparse pieces of evidence exist but nonetheless point to a significant history. Marisa Fuentes takes critical fabulation a step farther by encouraging scholars to read against the binary grain of the archive.[11] This means that scholars should look at Black women (in slavery) as more than the distinct categories of having agency or being passive. Black women occupy a myriad of spaces when one is actively looking for their existence. Despite the paucity of documents from before the Civil War, scholars such as Tera Hunter, Brandi Brimmer, and Sharon Romeo disentangle the preponderance of documents available in government records to distill a history of African American women that is recognizable, though still filtered through the gaze of the state.[12] In all the instances mentioned, power and violence undergird the metanarrative of African American women's history. The archive then is simultaneously a repository of documents, an embodiment of trauma, and a vehicle of state surveillance. And, for better or worse, the archive represents society's informal priorities and values.

The archive on Charity Folks's life is scant but instructive. The brick-and-mortar archive, specifically the Maryland State Archives and the Banneker-Douglass Museum, both in Annapolis, houses key artifacts and documents related to Folks and her family. The life of Charity Folks was also reconstructed using family memories and oral tradition among present community members, as well as critical fabulation.[13] Maryland governor Samuel Ogle owned Belair Plantation, where it is believed that Charity's mother, Rachel Burke, was enslaved. When Ogle passed in 1752, his brother-in-law Col. Benjamin Tasker assumed ownership of Belair and its human property.[14] Despite this commonly held belief, Rachel does not appear on any slave lists for Ogle or Tasker. It is doubtful that Rachel was born in Maryland; she was more likely born in Virginia and moved to the Belair Plantation when Samuel Ogle married Ann Tasker, a member of a prominent Virginia family.[15] Charity's birth is as elusive as Rachel's origin. A freedom certificate suggests she was born in 1757, while a family history lists her birthdate as 1759.[16] One local historian suggests that she was born at Belair Plantation (ten minutes outside of Annapolis), though there is no evidence to support this claim.[17] It is possible that Charity lived the first ten to twelve years of her life in the cellar at Belair with her brother James and their mother. Between 1765 and 1767, Charity became the property of John Ridout when he married Mary Ogle (daughter of Samuel) and moved to Annapolis, some twenty miles away.

Charity Folks lived the majority of her life as someone else's property. Charity gave birth to at least five children: Harriet Jackson, James Jackson, Mary Folks, Hannah Folks, and Charity Folks. The father of her first two children remains unknown. With manumitted slave Thomas Folks she had three daughters: Hannah, Mary, and Charity. Charity Folks enters the historical record through a document granting her freedom in 1797.[18] The public narrative surrounding her manumission is that she gained her freedom as a result of caring for members of the Ridout family, her enslavers in Annapolis. She nursed the Ridout's nephew, Horace Gibson, during a life-threatening illness. In appreciation, John Ridout wrote a codicil to his will awarding Charity her freedom, commencing in 1807.[19] John Ridout died in 1797 and his wife, Mary Ridout, freed Charity for her "faithful services and dutiful behavior."[20] As promised in the last will and testament of John Ridout, three of Charity's children were liberated when they reached specific ages. In his will, he coupled Mary's decision to free Folks with another seemingly benevolent act: liberating three of Charity's five children—eight-year-old James, four-year-old Lil' Charity, and infant Hannah. The elder Charity and Hannah were freed immediately. However, Ridout delayed manumission for James until 1808 and for

Lil' Charity until 1812. It is possible that Hannah was actually Harriet, who was eighteen years old.[21] This would explain why one child was freed, and the other two remained in bondage. Harriet was at an age where she could take care of herself. The immediate liberation of Hannah and Charity and the gradual manumission of James and Lil' Charity exemplify how freedom and enslavement often coexisted within the same family, and how this was particularly challenging for mothers.

Slavery and freedom had an almost simultaneous history in Maryland but never completely eclipsed one another. This overlap was seen in the lives of African Americans. Enslaved women envisioned a freedom that included their families, which is certainly true in the case of Charity Folks. The process of manumission reveals African Americans' complicated Maryland history with freedom. What does it mean when a human becomes "property?" What did it mean to purchase one family member as a commodity? Enslaved women in Maryland addressed these questions and more as they negotiated for their freedom and that of their kin. Slavery and freedom were so intertwined that most free Blacks had a relative or a friend who had been enslaved or who remained in bondage.[22] African American women saw manumission as an attainable goal. They relied on a community ethos as they pressed for self-liberation and the freedom of their family members. At the same time, a number of women were resolved to the reality that freedom had its price. Some women went on to have more children later, and some who never survived the heartbreak forgot how to love altogether.

African American women such as Charity Folks were well versed in the process of manumission. At least five members of Charity's family had preceded her in the transition from slavery to freedom. Her mother, Rachel Burke, had earned her freedom as an adult. Burke later purchased the freedom of her son, Charity's brother James.[23] In 1794, Charity's husband, Thomas Folks, bought his freedom from John Davidson. John Ridout manumitted Charity's eldest daughter Harriet Jackson in 1786, when she was approximately five years old.[24] Five years later, Ridout freed Mary Folks, Charity's third eldest child.[25] During this period, Charity remained enslaved. Rather than stay with their mother at the Ridout house, Charity's daughters lived with Rachel Burke and Thomas Folks. Surely Charity was elated that her children had escaped the cruelties of human bondage, but her separation from them undoubtedly weighed upon her. She must have had moments of anxiety that their freedom might be short-lived.

Charity knew all too well that the path to freedom for African American families via manumission was a narrow one. A caregiver who was skilled in herbal medicine, Charity likely knew that Mary Ridout was terminally ill in 1807. She may have prodded the ailing woman to honor John Ridout's intention to free Hannah, Lil' Charity, and James. It is difficult to determine how much Folks knew about manumission law. But that she knew enough about the law to make certain that the details of her freedom were not only spelled out but were also presented in court says something about her influence on the Ridouts, and her position in their home. Her efforts proved successful. Mary Ridout returned to court in 1807. In exchange for one dollar, Ridout executed a manumission document, freeing James and Lil' Charity and providing gradual manumission for Folks's grandchildren. Ridout also affirmed the legal viability of the previous documents that had freed Harriet, Mary, and the elder Charity.[26] This family shows the complicated legacy of freedom in a slave society. In fact, some forty years passed from the time of the manumission of Charity's first child to the time her grandchildren were freed.

Charity Folks walked into freedom with one of the most tangible expressions of property in African society, her family.[27] According to the 1810 federal census, Charity Folks, Thomas Folks, and three of their children were living in the same house.[28] In time, each of her children married and began families of their own. For the most part, the Folks family appears to be a success story. However, how do we account for her kinfolk who could not be rescued and were lost to slavery? Jennifer Morgan rightfully asserts that scholarship on slavery is in search of metaphor.[29] One cannot accurately describe the lived experiences of the enslaved. An in-depth view of manumission cannot recover the voices of those who were separated from their families as part of a wedding dowry, hiring periods, western migration, or Baltimore's (and increasingly Maryland's) practice of selling slaves to southern plantation owners by means of the domestic slave trade. As the example of Charity's family suggests, freedom allowed African Americans to reestablish their families under one roof. In her study of African Americans and Reconstruction, Heather Williams cautions us to investigate the trauma involved in separation and reunification of Black families.[30] As the next section reveals, though her family was freed decades before the Civil War, Charity and her kin nonetheless exemplify the complications inherent in achieving and maintaining freedom.

FOUNDING MOTHER AND FREEDOM
BEFORE THE CIVIL WAR

Charity Folks began her life as a free woman better off than most manumitted women. Some manumitted women received a small amount of money from their owners at the time of manumission. Others, including Charity, received an allowance that provided a bit of a cushion against financial hardship. John Ridout's will directed his heirs to pay her the sum of twelve silver Spanish dollars and other "aspects of his estate."[31] Ridout also insisted that his heirs care for Charity. Ridout drafted a separate legal document binding his sons, Horatio and Samuel, to respect his wishes to distribute his property as outlined in his will and subsequent codicils.[32] Knowing that many heirs might ignore such a bequest for both financial and social reasons, Ridout made it a point to ask his wife to honor his wishes. In a letter to her mother, Mary Ridout wrote, "He [John Ridout] said Ruth and Charity had been two such faithful servants that he desired more might be done for them than the rest. That if I survived him, he requested me if they were living to leave them a small annuity to maintain them comfortably."[33] Charity received more in 1808 when Mary Ridout died. Mary instructed that Charity should receive her "wearing apparel and feather bed."[34] Ridout also bequeathed Charity one hundred dollars (it is unknown if these were also Spanish dollars or were the US currency of the time).[35] No doubt these funds and material goods served Charity well in freedom.

The majority of manumitted Blacks worked hard but struggled against the barriers of white racism and economic roadblocks. Loren Schweninger notes that a few dozen free Black families were wealthy, but they were exceptions. Most manumitted Blacks entered freedom without the resources to accumulate significant wealth.[36] The occupations of free Blacks often mirrored the work they had performed in slavery. However, working for wages meant competing with whites, who were less than welcoming. Free Blacks were often the target of aggression by whites angry that Blacks were competitors for jobs or were just getting too "uppity" for their race.[37] To counter potential unemployment or the violence resulting from wage competition, many worked as wage laborers for their former owners, as Charity Folks did for the Ridouts after she was manumitted.[38]

Manumitted women entered a society that was quickly producing a class divide. Black women who were not manumitted with a pension or a beneficial relationship with a patron supported themselves in a variety of ways. They rented out rooms to boarders, worked as laundresses, and used their skills as hucksters to provide for their families.[39] A small minority of free Black women also worked as prostitutes, willing to be sexually exploited in order to survive.[40]

Although manumitted Blacks understood themselves to be free, the shadow of their enslaved past was always present. Ironically, manumission produced feelings of resentment among Folks's children. Family members remarked that Charity "appeared to have a greater fondness" for the younger Charity.[41] Charity was the child who spent the most time with her mother and held the greatest influence over her mother in later life. Thomas Folks remarked that his daughter's influence "would carry his wife to hell."[42] The elder Charity's relationship with daughter Mary Folks and son James Jackson, on the other hand, reflected the lasting influence of the violence of slavery; the preference for little Charity also underscores that slavery's impact was not just physical but emotional and psychological. Mary and James felt that they had been unfairly separated from their mother as young children. As these experiences indicate, and despite the desire of Charity Folks to keep her family close, their experiences in slavery continually drove a wedge between them.

Charity's obvious preference for one child over another produced a long-standing rivalry between Mary and Lil' Charity. Their brother, James Jackson, believed that his mother's preference stemmed from "Mary being taken away from her mother when a small child."[43] Mary was manumitted while still a child, while her mother and father still were enslaved. She left the Ridout home (perhaps never in bondage there at all) and lived with free Black family members. Perhaps she lived with her grandmother Rachel Burke. She certainly lived with Thomas after his manumission in 1794, as census records list Thomas as head of household.[44] Freedom should have yielded Mary a happier life; yet for her, manumission drove a wedge through her family and robbed her of her relationship with her mother.

The tension between Lil' Charity and Mary took its toll on their mother. One family member remarked that the sibling rivalry "caused her [Charity] a good deal of trouble."[45] Charity feared that even after her death their hostility toward one another "would bring her grey hairs."[46] The sisters competed for men as well as for their mother's loyalty.[47] Upon their mother's death, the two even fought over eighteen inches of property separating their homes, as evidenced in a court case in 1835.[48] Mary and her husband, Moses Lake, sued the younger Charity and her husband, William Bishop, for erecting a gate in the alley, which prevented Mary and Moses from accessing their home.

Charity's fondness for the younger Charity clearly made her other children uncomfortable, especially as the elder aged. They wondered if the younger Charity held too much influence over their mother. The tension in the family was exacerbated when William and Charity Bishop moved into the Folks home on Church Circle in Annapolis. The younger Charity reorganized the house and ordered her brother James to remove the hogs he kept in their mother's yard. James removed the animals, but a volatile argument ensued . He confronted his mother about siding with his sister. The argument became so heated that James drew "a knife on her [his mother] and called her ill names."[49] Charity never forgave her son. She refused to leave him an inheritance from the considerable fortune she had amassed. After she was manumitted, Charity continued to work for wages in the Ridout home. Additionally, both Charity and Thomas Folks became quite savvy at buying property. Upon her death Charity left property to her daughters Mary, Charity, and Harriet. She also left property for her granddaughter Elizabeth, who is believed to be the daughter of Hannah.[50] James does not appear in Charity's last will and testament.

Charity suffered a paralyzing stroke in early 1834, when she was nearly seventy-five.[51] She regained her ability to walk and some ability to speak, but she died within a year.[52] She was able to leave property to each of her surviving daughters and one granddaughter at a time when only the most privileged used this legal mechanism. She bequeathed to her granddaughter, Elizabeth, "one hundred and eighty dollars due to me from Mr. Samuel Ridout and all the interest thereon at the time of my death."[53] It is not clear whether Elizabeth ever collected the debt, but her grandmother's financial acumen was impressive. Perhaps this was why Charity's success as a free Black property owner overshadows her life in bondage. She had a clear understanding of what it took to succeed in free society and worked hard to become a woman of property and social standing. Though not formally educated, Charity learned legal protocol from life experiences and her exposure to business transactions.

Her last will and testament and its related codicils underscore the importance that she attached to property and kin alike.[54]

FOUNDING MOTHER AND GHOST OF SLAVERY

In an eerie foreshadowing, Charity Folks anticipated being lost from history. In her final years, she often felt displaced and feared being "turned out of doors."[55] She obsessively searched for something lost, and "half of the time she did not know what she was after."[56] Family members and neighbors described her as "deranged."[57] Given her age, her ailing health, and the trauma of her past, it is not surprising that Folks suffered from symptoms likely associated with dementia.

Part of Folks's rootlessness stemmed from a sense that her position as the family's leader was declining in favor of her son-in-law, William Bishop. She lamented being displaced as the "mistress" of the house.[58] Bishop ultimately assumed control of her residence and eventually the deed to the property, substantiating Folks's fear that she was losing power among her kin.[59] A family friend described a fight between William Bishop and Charity, remarking "that there was no other place for her," and she "set off to the graveyard."[60] This was the last public account documenting the life of Charity Folks.

A family genealogical chart notes that Charity Folks, "the wife of Thomas and former servant to the wife of the governor," is buried in St. Anne's Cemetery, which is tucked between the Severn River and Route 150, which connects historic Annapolis and its cobblestone streets with the more modern Annapolis from the world of paved roads and street lights.[61] Markers for notable historic families share the same hallowed ground with people who have passed on recently. No headstone commemorates her existence, so Charity's life appears as a ghost story.[62] She is like the "wandering spirits" who died on board ships during the Middle Passage without a proper burial.[63] Charity Folks has been denied the important process of being remembered and honored by the living. She is forgotten, and because she is forgotten, she is restless. Yet, as in her case, the absence of a body, or even a physical headstone, does not always mean an absence of memory.

Despite being omitted from public memory, Charity Folks is a ghost of slavery who refuses to be silenced. She appears in the company of Margaret Garner's beloved daughter, the young girl known only as "Celia, a slave," Sara Baartman, Sally Hemings, Sojourner Truth, Queen Nannie, and countless unnamed women who haunt historical memory precisely because they carry the weight of the African diaspora's traumatic past. Collectively and individually, their lives are testimony to the multifaceted legacies of enslavement and attempts by its victims to dismantle the slave system without suppressing its most violent and horrific truths.

Despite not being well known, Charity Folks's life clamors for our attention. She is visible to those who choose to see her. The Belair Plantation where she may have been born is part of the city museums of Bowie, Maryland. Tours of Belair have recently incorporated references to the bondspeople who worked there. The John Ridout house at 125 Duke of Gloucester Street in Annapolis, is registered as part of the National Trust for Historic Preservation. Reynolds Tavern, once owned by the Davidson family that enslaved Thomas Folks, is a tourist site popular for its afternoon tea and dinner. However, some of the outlines of Charity's presence are fainter. Her home, on the corner of Duke of Gloucester Street and Church Circle, no longer exists, having been replaced by a Bank of America building—a touch of irony, given her financial success. Properties that Folks and her son-in-law, William Bishop, once owned are sites for archeological digs and continue to yield crucial details about Annapolis. During the late nineteenth century, Folks's property at 84 Franklin Street was sold to the Mount Moriah African Methodist Episcopal Church as the site of their new building. Frederick Douglass delivered the dedication address when the church opened its doors in 1874. Mount Moriah has been converted into the Banneker-Douglass Museum, a repository and exhibition space for Maryland's African American heritage.[64]

Even though she was forgotten, Charity Folks left a legacy greater than her material wealth or the places and spaces that have been commemorated as sites of historical significance. As a founding mother, her influence could be seen in the lives of her family members. Her son-in-law, William Bishop (1802–70), became one of the twelve wealthiest men in Annapolis.[65] The sons of William and Charity Bishop were prominent in their respective fields throughout the Civil War and beyond. James Calder Bishop (1824–93) ran a tobacco shop and built upon William Bishop's considerable property holdings.[66] Moses Lake Bishop (1833–69) was one of the first African American midshipmen at the Naval Academy.[67] Civil War pension records note that Moses Lake Bishop served in this role and that his wife, Joanna, applied for pension benefits upon his death. While Moses Lake Bishop served as a cook on a US naval ship during the Civil War, his brothers Horace Bishop and Nicholas Bishop extended the vision of "freedom" to include settlement in Liberia. Nicholas was appointed as the justice of the peace in Liberia before eventually returning to Annapolis. It is believed that Horace returned to Annapolis at least once before returning to Liberia, where it is believed that he died.[68]

Charity Folks may have thought little about freedom beyond her immediate descendants. Nonetheless, the family's position as free Blacks, and privileged at that, meant that they suffered fewer economic hardships than many other African Americans. Today Charity Folks awaits us in many forms: a manumitted woman, a founding mother, and a ghost of slavery who reveals that freedom had a long history among Maryland's African American families. The archival Charity Folks demonstrates that African American women's quest for freedom prior to the Civil War forces us to rethink how we construct and commemorate public memory surrounding slavery. As a microhistory, Charity Folks demonstrates that the legal categories of slave and free blur when accounting for the long and varied process of manumission in the lives of Black women. Finally, as her life and the lives of her descendants demonstrate, manumission was not simply a rehearsal for Reconstruction; rather, it transformed notions of how freedom was experienced well before the Civil War. The embrace of women such as Charity Folks in the public narratives of slavery in Maryland is long overdue.

NOTES

1. Dan Merica, "Trump: Frederick Douglass 'is being recognized more and more'" CNN, February 2, 2017, www.cnn.com/2017/02/02/politics/donald-trump-frederick-douglass.

2. Merica, "Trump: Frederick Douglass 'is being recognized more and more.'"

3. On Auburn, New York NHP, see www.nps.gov/hart/index.htm and www.nationalparks.org/explore-parks/harriet-tubman-national-historical-park. For eastern Maryland NHP, see www.nps.gov/hatu/index.htm.

4. Martin Crutsinger, "Historic Makeover: Harriet Tubman to be face on $20 bill," April 21, 2016, accessed June 13, 2019, www.apnews.com/cbc61a88b12a41bca0c0a66142c5fee3.

5. "Aisha Hinds on playing Harriet Tubman in a remarkable 'Underground' episode," accessed June 6, 2019, www.nytimes.com/2017/04/12/arts/television/underground-harriet-tubman-aisha-hinds-interview.html.

6. Erica Armstrong Dunbar, *She Came to Slay* (2019); *Harriet,* Kassi Lemmons, Director, Focus Features: 2019.

7. US Federal Census for Maryland, 1860 (Washington, DC); Jennifer Hull Dorsey, *Hirelings: African American Workers and Free Labor in Early Maryland* (Ithaca, NY: Cornell University Press, 2011); Max Grivno, *Gleanings of Freedom: Free and Slave Labor along the Mason-Dixon Line, 1790–1860* (Urbana: University of Illinois Press, 2011); Calvin Schermerhorn, *Money over Mastery, Family over Freedom: Slavery in the Antebellum Upper South* (Baltimore: Johns Hopkins University Press, 2011).

8. Michel-Rolph Trouillot writes, "Slavery is a ghost, both the past and living presence; and the problem of historical representation is how to represent that ghost, something that is and yet is

not"; quoted in Anne Bailey, *African Voices and the Transatlantic Slave Trade* (Boston: Beacon Press, 2005), 25. On ghosts of slavery and the lived experiences of the enslaved women referenced, see Jenny Sharpe, *Ghosts of Slavery: A Literary Anthology of Black Women's Lives* (Minneapolis: University of Minnesota Press, 2003); Henrice Altink, *Representations of Slave Women in Discourses on Slavery and Abolition, 1780–1838* (New York: Routledge, 2007); Joanne M. Braxton, *Monuments of the Black Atlantic: Slavery and Memory* (New Brunswick, NJ: Transaction Publishers, 2004); Daphne Brooks, *Bodies in Dissent: Spectacular Performances of Race and Freedom, 1850–1910* (Durham, NC: Duke University Press, 2006); Clifton C. Crais and Pamela Scully, *Sara Baartman and the Hottentot Venus: A Ghost Story and a Biography* (Princeton, NJ: Princeton University Press, 2009); Annette Gordon-Reed, *The Hemingses of Monticello: An American Family* (New York: W. W. Norton, 2008); Saidiya V. Hartman, *Scenes of Subjection: Terror, Slavery, and Self-Making in Nineteenth-Century America* (New York: Oxford University Press, 1987); Tiya Miles, *The House on Diamond Hill: A Cherokee Plantation Story* (Chapel Hill: University of North Carolina Press, 2010); Toni Morrison, *Beloved: A Novel* (New York: Random House, 1987); Toni Morrison, *Playing in the Dark: Whiteness and the Literary Imagination* (Cambridge, MA: Harvard University Press, 1992); Marie-Elena John, *Unburnable* (New York: Amistad, 2006); Melton Alonza McLaurin, *Celia, a Slave* (Athens: University of Georgia Press, 1991); Lucille Mathurin Mair, *The Rebel Woman in the British West Indies during Slavery* (Kingston, Jamaica: University of the West Indies Press, 2007); Mark Reinhardt, *Who Speaks for Margaret Garner?* (Minneapolis: University of Minnesota Press, 2010); Nell Irvin Painter, *Sojourner Truth: A Life, a Symbol* (New York: W. W. Norton, 1996); Margaret Washington, *Sojourner Truth's America* (Urbana: University of Illinois Press, 2009).

9. Saidiya Hartman, "Venus in Two Acts," *Small Axe: A Journal of Criticism* no. 26 (2008): 1–14.

10. Hartman, "Venus in Two Acts," 1–14.

11. Marisa J. Fuentes, *Dispossessed Lives: Enslaved Women, Violence, and the Archive,* 1st edition (Philadelphia: University of Pennsylvania Press, 2016).

12. Brandi C. Brimmer, "'Her Claim for Pension Is Lawful and Just': Representing Black Union Widows in Late-Nineteenth-Century North Carolina," *Journal of the Civil War Era* 1, no. 2 (2011): 207–36; Brandi C. Brimmer, "Black Women's Politics, Narratives of Sexual Immorality, and Pension Bureaucracy in Mary Lee's North Carolina Neighborhood," *Journal of Southern History* 80, no. 4 (2014): 827–58; Tera W. Hunter, *Bound in Wedlock: Slave and Free Black Marriage in the Nineteenth Century* (Cambridge, MA: The Belknap Press of Harvard University Press, 2017); Sharon Romeo, *Gender and the Jubilee: Black Freedom and the Reconstruction of Citizenship in Civil War Missouri* (Athens: University of Georgia Press, 2016).

13. Saidiya Hartman, "Venus in Two Acts," *Small Axe: A Journal of Criticism* no. 26 (2008): 1–14.

14. Shirley Baltz, *Belair from the Beginning* (Bowie, MD: City of Bowie Museums, 2005). Baltz suggests that Colonel Tasker was Charity's father. This story has crept into local lore and will be used until it's discovered to be untrue. To this date, there is no evidence to support or refute this assumption.

15. The parents of Ann Tasker were among the most prominent members of Chesapeake slaveholding society. Benjamin Tasker Sr. was a founder of the Baltimore County Ironworks, a mayor of Annapolis, and the provincial governor of Maryland from 1752 to 1753, and he actively profited from active participation in the international slave trade. Tasker's mother, Anne Bladen Tasker, was from an equally prominent family. The Bladens included wealthy slaveholders, landowners, court officials,

and governors. The extended branches of the Ogle-Tasker family included the Bladens, the Carrolls, Carters, Dulanys, Ridgelys, and Snowdens, among others. Like most slaveowning families, the Taskers transferred their bondpeople between properties and family members as labor was needed.

16. Joan C. Scurlock, "The Bishop Family of Annapolis," unpublished manuscript, 1999, Banneker-Douglass Museum, Annapolis, Maryland (hereafter BDM); Charity Folks, Certificate of Freedom, April 29, 1811, Anne Arundel County Court Certificates of Freedom, 1810–1831, vol. 823, MdHS, p. 8.

17. Joan C. Scurlock, "The Bishop Family of Annapolis," unpublished manuscript, 1999, 5, Banneker-Douglass Museum. A detailed analysis of the available research can be found in Jessica Millward, *Finding Charity's Folk: Enslaved and Free Black Women in Maryland* (Athens: University of Georgia Press, 2015).

18. Mary Ridout to Charity Folks, Deed of Manumission, December 6, 1797, Anne Arundel County Court, Manumission Record, 1797–1844, Archives of Maryland, 825:17–18, Maryland State Archives, Annapolis, MD (hereafter MdSA).

19. See the lengthy codicil to the 1807 manumission deed for Charity Folks. Mary Ridout to Charity Folks, Manumission Deed 1807, Anne Arundel County Court, Manumission Record, MdSA.

20. Mary Ridout to Charity Folks, Deed of Manumission 1807, Anne Arundel County Court, Manumission Record, MdSA; Mary Ridout to Charity Folks, Deed of Manumission, December 6, 1797, Anne Arundel County Court, Manumission Record, 1797–1844, Archives of Maryland, 825:17–18, MdSA.

21. Mary Ridout to Charity Folks, Deed of Manumission 1807, Anne Arundel County Court, Manumission Record, MdSA. The fact that Hannah was transposed with Harriet is put forward by Joan Scurlock in "The Bishop Family," and in an email conversation with Jean Russo, November 23, 2014.

22. Wilma King, "Out of Bounds: Emancipated and Enslaved Women in Antebellum America," in David Barry Gaspar and Darlene Clark Hine, eds., *Beyond Bondage: Free Women of Color in the Americas* (Urbana: University of Illinois Press, 2004), 127–44; Loren Schweninger, "The Fragile Nature of Freedom: Free Women of Color in the U.S. South," in Gaspar and Hine, *Beyond Bondage,* 106–24.

23. Anne Ogle James, Deed of Manumission 1789, Anne Arundel County Manumission Record, MdSA.

24. John Davidson to Thomas Folks, Manumission Deed 1794, Anne Arundel County Land Records, MdSA.

25. John Ridout to Harriet Jackson, Manumission Deed 1786, Anne Arundel County Manumission Record, MdSA. See the lengthy codicil to the 1807 manumission deed for Charity Folks. Mary Ridout to Charity Folks, Manumission Deed 1807, Anne Arundel County Court, Manumission Record, MdSA.

26. Mary Ridout to Charity Folks, Manumission Deed, 1807.

27. Dylan Penningroth, *The Claims of Kinfolk: African-American Property and Community in the Nineteenth-Century South* (Chapel Hill: University of North Carolina Press, 2003).

28. Federal manuscript census for Washington, DC, 1810; and author's interview with Janice Hayes Williams, November 1, 2009, Annapolis, Maryland.

29. Jennifer L. Morgan, "Gender and Family Life," in Gad Heuman and Trevor Bernard, eds., *The Routledge History of Slavery* (New York: Routledge, 2012), 139.

30. Heather Andrea Williams, *Help Me to Find My People: The African American Search for Family Lost in Slavery* (Chapel Hill: University of North Carolina Press, 2012), 17.

31. Mary Ridout to Anne Ogle, 1797, Ridout Family Papers, MdSA.

32. Horatio Ridout and Samuel Ridout Bond, 1797, Anne Arundel County Chancery Papers, MdSA.

33. Mary Ridout to Anne Ogle, 1797, Ridout Family Papers, MdSA.

34. Mary Ridout to Anne Ogle, December 1807, Ridout Family Papers, MdSA.

35. Mary Ridout to Anne Ogle, December 1807, Ridout Family Papers, MdSA.

36. Schweninger, *Black Property Owners in the South*, 109.

37. Brenda E. Stevenson, *Life in Black and White: Family and Community in the Slave South* (New York: Oxford University Press, 1996), 162. Stevenson's study of Loudoun County, Virginia, reveals that "the County's racial hierarchy placed free persons of color outside sanctioned boundaries of Southern society."

38. Lancaster notes that John Ridgley paid Hercules wages from 1830 to 1851. "Hercules," Kent Lancaster Papers, Hampton National Historic Site, Baltimore, Maryland.

39. "The Estate of Mary Owings, 1835," Dr. John Ridout Account Book, MdSA.

40. Seth Rockman, "Women's Labor, Gender Ideology, and Working-Class Households in Early Republic Baltimore," *Explorations in Early American Culture: A Journal of Mid-Atlantic Studies* 66 (1999): 174–99.

41. Testimony of James Jackson in Moses Lake and wife v. William Bishop and wife, August 6, 1835, Anne Arundel Court, Chancery Papers, MdSA.

42. Testimony of James Jackson in *Moses Lake and wife v. William Bishop and wife.*

43. Testimony of James Jackson in *Moses Lake and wife v. William Bishop and wife.*

44. Federal manuscript census for Anne Arundel County, 1800, National Archives and Records Administration, Washington, DC.

45. Testimony of Hannah Murray in *Moses Lake and wife v. William Bishop and wife.*

46. Testimony of Hannah Murray in *Moses Lake and wife* v. *William Bishop and wife.*

47. See the testimony of Mary Folks Bishop, Hannah Murray, James Jackson, and Stephen Rummels in Moses Lake and Mary Lake v. William Bishop and Charity Bishop, Anne Arundel Court, Chancery Papers, MdSA.

48. *Moses Lake and Mary Lake v. William Bishop and Charity Bishop.*

49. Testimony of Hannah Murray in *Moses Lake and Mary Lake v. William Bishop and Charity Bishop.*

50. Testimony of Hannah Murray in *Moses Lake and Mary Lake v. William Bishop and Charity Bishop.*

51. Testimony of Dr. John Ridout in *Moses Lake and Mary Lake v. William Bishop and Charity Bishop.*

52. Charity Folks Will, 1828, quoted in *Moses Lake and Mary Lake v. William Bishop and Charity Bishop;* Last Will and Testament of Charity Folks, 1828, Anne Arundel County Register of Wills, 1835, MdSA.

53. Dylan Penningroth, *The Claims of Kinfolk: African-American Property and Community in the Nineteenth-Century South* (Chapel Hill: University of North Carolina Press, 2003).

54. Last Will and Testament of Charity Folks, 1828, Anne Arundel County, Register of Wills, 1835, MdSA.

55. Testimony of Hannah Murray, in *Moses Lake and Mary Lake v. William Bishop and Charity Bishop.*

56. Testimony of Hannah Murray in *Moses Lake and Mary Lake v. William Bishop and Charity Bishop.*

57. Testimony of Hannah Murray in *Moses Lake and Mary Lake v. William Bishop and Charity Bishop.*

58. Testimony of Hannah Murray in *Moses Lake and Mary Lake v. William Bishop and Charity Bishop.*

59. Several credit this house as being William Bishop's, when in fact it was the home of Charity Folks (the Younger) and Mary Folks. The sisters bought the property in 1816. See Paul A. Schackel, *Historical Archaeology of the Chesapeake* (Washington, DC: Smithsonian Institution Press, 1994), 201; William L. Calderhead, "Slavery in Maryland in the Age of Revolution, 1775–1790," *Maryland Historical Magazine* (Fall 2003): 308; William L. Calderhead, "Anne Arundel Blacks: Three Centuries of Change," in *Anne Arundel County, Maryland: A Bicentennial History, 1649–1977,* ed. James C. Bradford (Annapolis, MD: Anne Arundel County and Annapolis Bicentennial Committee, 1977), 18; Paul Mullins, *Race and Affluence: An Archaeology of African America and Consumer Culture* (New York: Kluwer Academic/Plenum Publishers, 1999); federal manuscript census of 1830 for Anne Arundel County, Maryland.

60. Testimony of Hannah Murray in *Lake v. Bishop.*

61. Bishop family genealogy chart, William Bishop Papers, MdSA.

62. Annette Gordon-Reed, *The Hemingses of Monticello: An American Family* (New York: W. W. Norton, 2008); Toni Morrison, *Beloved: A Novel;* Saidiya V. Hartman, *Scenes of Subjection: Terror, Slavery, and Self-Making in Nineteenth-Century America* (New York: Oxford University Press, 1987); Elizabeth Fox-Genovese, *Within the Plantation Household: and White Women in the Old South* (Chapel Hill: University of North Carolina Press, 1988); Anne Goodwyn Jones and Susan V. Donaldson, *Haunted Bodies: Gender and Southern Texts* (Charlottesville: University of Virginia Press, 1997).

63. Albert J. Raboteau, *Slave Religion: The "Invisible Institution" in the Antebellum South* (New York: Oxford University Press, 1978).

64. "About BDM," Banneker-Douglass Museum Website, accessed January 31, 2014, http://www.bdmuseum.com/index.html.

65. William L. Calderhead, "Anne Arundel Blacks: Three Centuries of Change," in *Anne Arundel County, Maryland: A Bicentennial History, 1649–1977,* ed. James Bradford (Annapolis, MD: Anne Arundel County and Annapolis Bicentennial Commission, 1977), 18.

66. Calderhead, "Anne Arundel Blacks," 18.

67. Robert J. Schneller Jr., "The First Midshipman at the U.S. Naval Academy," *Journal of Blacks in Higher Education* 48 (Summer 2005): 104–7.

68. Joan C. Scurlock, "The Bishop Family of Annapolis," unpublished manuscript, 1999, Banneker-Douglass Museum, Annapolis, Maryland.

CONFRONTING *DRED SCOTT*

Seeing Citizenship from Baltimore City

MARTHA S. JONES

The *Dred Scott* case was big news in Baltimore. The city's news daily, the *Baltimore Sun,* chronicled the legal wrangling generated by the freedom claims of Scott and his wife and daughters. Commentators parsed the Supreme Court arguments for signs of how Chief Justice Roger Taney's court would rule. When the final decision came down, Baltimoreans quickly learned that the Court had invalidated the Missouri Compromise, making possible the extension of slavery into federal territories. They also learned that the Scott family had no standing, and they were not eligible, as Black people, to bring a suit in federal court. With its words on the page, the Court expanded the rights and expectations of slaveholders, while collapsing the freedom claims of enslaved people.

For Baltimore's free Black community, approaching twenty-five thousand men, women, and children, no dimension of the case was more relevant than that which declared no Black person—enslaved or free—was a citizen of the United States. Taney saw in the original Constitution a color line that meant only white persons had been citizens of the United States at the time of its ratification. Taney did not find the words in the text and so resorted to reasoning by way of a history lesson. There was no evidence, Taney found, that Black people had been regarded as state citizens in 1787. He noted that generally they could not vote, hold public office, or sit on juries. He found no evidence that Black people had possessed rights that whites were obliged to respect—at least they had no rights that could have been enforced through the federal courts. It is worth noting that Taney's rendering of history was flawed if not disingenuous. In his home state of Maryland, for example, free Black men had voted until 1804, when the state required all voters to be free white persons.[1]

Concluding that Black Americans were not citizens, Taney then turned to Article 3 of the Constitution, which restricted the power of federal courts to the hearing of specific types of disputes. Dred Scott and his family had asserted their right to bring a freedom suit in a federal court because the dispute was between citizens of two different states. This was what was commonly termed diversity jurisdiction, as provided for in Article 3 of the Constitution. The Scotts and their adversary, John Sandford, were citizens of different states and could thus be heard by a federal court. But the meaning of the word *citizen,* in Justice Taney's view, mattered. The Scotts, as Black people, were not citizens of the United States and not qualified to bring a freedom suit, or any suit, in federal court under the Constitution's diversity-of-citizenship provision. Not only were Scott and his family barred from bringing a suit before the US Supreme Court, so were all Black Americans, according to Taney.

It is not easy to know precisely what Black Baltimoreans thought about the Dred Scott decision in the weeks and months that followed. They did not leave a record of speeches, memorials, or tracts that commented on the case. The pages of the *Sun* suggest some of what they learned. The Supreme Court was threatening their status, a blow to those among them who had long asserted that they were people with rights like all other citizens. They were discouraged by the *Sun*'s coverage, which endorsed Taney's ideas. The paper, which had previously avoided the subject of slavery, devoted its pages to robust coverage of the subject in the wake of the decision. Reading the *Sun,* Black Baltimoreans with questions about how the decision might affect them found alarming answers.[2]

News watchers widely admired the *Sun* for its editorial vision and skilled reporting.[3] In the 1850s, they recognized the paper for its pioneering, quick, and cooperative news gathering that linked Washington, Baltimore, Philadelphia, and New York. The *Sun*'s Washington correspondent Elias Kingman took the lead in bringing news about *Dred Scott* to Baltimore. He set the paper's tone when recounting the scene as Roger Taney read his opinion: "It was listened to with profound interest, and will be everywhere respected for its wisdom, and acquiesced in as the decision of the constitutional tribunal."[4] Though only a few days had passed since the court released its rulings, the *Sun* went out of its way to declare that "the decision, we are glad to say, seems to be welcomed in most quarters." The paper acknowledged critics, but deemed them without reason and downright lawless: "There are indiscreet and suicidal ravings among some of those who know no law except that of their own violent self-will and passions."[5] The *Sun* also spoke directly to observers in northern cities: "The patriotic and conservative masses at the north receive this judgment as the law of the land and govern their conduct accordingly."[6] This early commentary was little more than boosterism, revealing how the paper *hoped* the decision would be received.

In Baltimore, coverage of *Dred Scott* was an occasion to boast. The paper showcased the city's legal prowess. The team of Henry Geyer and Reverdy Johnson had represented John Sandford before the Supreme Court. The city of Baltimore had long been Johnson's home, even when his professional life took him to Washington. As the nation's foremost constitutional lawyer, he brought prestige to any case he took.[7] He served as a US senator from Maryland and as attorney general under President Zachary Taylor, and he was a slaveholder until at least 1840.[8] Johnson was a friend to Roger Taney, and his legal acumen and intimate esteem shaped Taney's ideas.[9]

Chief Justice Taney loomed larger than any figure in the construction of Baltimore's reputation.[10] Taney began his career practicing law in Frederick, Maryland, and then served as a state legislator and Maryland's attorney general.[11] Throughout his years in Washington, Taney remained a keenly followed and highly regarded figure.[12] In Baltimore, his family home sat just footsteps from Baltimore's courthouse, and Taney sat on the United States Circuit Court for the District of Maryland. Despite the demands of the high court in Washington, he occasionally led public gatherings, including bar proceedings.[13] The *Sun* had long promoted Reverdy and Taney through its coverage, and the men's involvement with *Dred Scott* provided another opportunity to enhance the city's image.

The *Sun* explained the case's implications for the city's free Black community in detail. For lay readers, the paper acted as an interpreter. One editorial set out the "main propositions of constitutional law," two of which concerned the status of Black Americans. The *Sun* left little question about what it believed the case meant. Blackness rendered African Americans noncitizens: "No negro . . . can, even though he be born within the limits of a free State, be recognized by the law as a citizen of the United States." States did not have the power to confer federal citizenship: "Any of the States of this confederacy may, if they see proper, confer upon a free negro the rights of citizenship within that particular State, either by the provision of their organic law or by direct enactment: but the free negro upon whom this right is conferred does not for that reason become a citizen of the United States."[14]

The paper's authoritative tone suggested the Court's reasoning was sound and unassailable. A door opened and claims about Black citizenship became subject to open derision. A commentator in May 1857 mocked the political aspirations of free Black men like Frederick Douglass. The *Sun's* editors pointed out "the impossibility of recognizing negroes as citizens arising from their offence to the olfactories of the white race."[15] It was an old joke, a crude one at that, but one that took on new significance in the wake of *Dred Scott*.

Baltimoreans encountered open defiance of *Dred Scott* when they looked out across the country. Federal courts refused to enforce the case's bar against Black citizenship.[16] Rather than deferring to Justice Taney, lower federal judges leaned toward the dissenting opinions. Justice John McLean, who had disagreed with Taney at the Supreme Court, stayed true to his conclusion that Black Americans were indeed citizens.[17] In July 1857, while sitting on the federal Circuit Court for Illinois, he seriously limited the effect of *Dred Scott* in the case of *Mitchell v. Lamar:* "A negro of the African race born in the United States . . . is a citizen of the United States . . . and entitled as such to sue in its courts."[18] Joseph Mitchell, a free African American from Illinois, had brought suit against Charles Lamar, a white resident of Wisconsin.[19] Lamar had assaulted Mitchell, who sustained significant injuries and thus sought damages.[20]

Could a federal court hear the case as one involving citizens from different states? McLean thought it could and reasoned that Mitchell, a free Black man not descended from slaves, was a citizen in that he was "a freeman, who has a permanent domicile in a State, being subject to its laws in acquiring and holding property, in the payment of taxes, and in the distribution of his estate among creditors, or to his heirs on his decease."[21] McLean conceded that Mitchell did not have rights equivalent to those of white men. Mitchell could not vote. However, "it is not necessary for a man to be an elector in order to enable him to sue in a Federal Court," McLean reasoned.[22] "Such a man is a citizen, so as to enable him to sue, as I think, in the Federal Courts."[23] McLean split hairs, distinguishing Mitchell, a man born of free parents, from Scott, descended from enslaved people, and thereby undermining Taney.

State court judges in Maine and Ohio outright refused to defer to Taney's conclusions in *Dred Scott*.[24] In Ohio, a court examined the phrase, "citizen of the United States," as it was used in its state constitution and concluded that Taney's interpretation did not apply.[25] Justice Taney's opinion was limited to descendants of slaves, while in Ohio a free man of mixed racial descent was a citizen.[26] In Maine, the justices of that state's high court interpreted a key provision of the state constitution that limited an elector to a local male resident, twenty-one years and older, and a "citizen of the United States."[27] The question became whether or not a free man of color could serve as an elector under this provision.[28] Yet Maine's supreme court substituted its reasoning for Taney's: "We are of the opinion that our constitution does not discriminate between the different races of people which constitute the inhabitants of our state; but that the term, 'citizens of the United States,' as used in that instrument, applies as well to free colored persons of African descent as to persons descended from white ancestors."[29] In some nonslaveholding states, Taney's authority was rejected and courts declined to give *Dred Scott* weight, even when US citizenship was at issue.

At least one southern state, Mississippi, confronted the *Dred Scott* question. The high court flip-flopped.[30] In the spring of 1858, it concluded in *Shaw v. Brown* that a free African American had standing to sue in pursuit of his claims as an heir.[31] Writing for the majority, Justice Alexander Handy explained:

> But negroes born in the United States, and free by the laws of the State in which they reside, are in a different condition from aliens. They are natives, and not aliens. Though not *citizens* of the State in which they reside, within the meaning of the Constitution of the United States, they are *inhabitants* and *subjects* of the State, owing allegiance to it, and entitled to protection by its laws and those of the United States; for by the common law, and the law of nations, all persons born within the dominion of the sovereign are his natural born subjects, and owe allegiance to him, and obedience to the laws, and are entitled to protection.[32]

The court acknowledged *Dred Scott* as establishing African Americans as "a subordinate and inferior class of beings" but did not go the next step and deem them without a right to pursue their claims in the State of Mississippi.[33] However, when confronted with a similar set of facts the following spring, the court embraced *Dred Scott* and deemed free Black people "*alien strangers,* of an inferior class, incapable of comity, with which our government has no commercial, social, or diplomatic intercourse."[34] Justice William Harris wrote for the majority while Justice Handy, who had written for the majority in *Shaw* just one year earlier, dissented.[35]

By fall 1858, Roger Taney was uncomfortably aware that his ideas about Black citizenship were being called into question.[36] The ordinarily taciturn Taney wrote to his confidante David Perine: "Have you read the opinion of the court in this case of Scott v. Sanford? I hope you find it all right."[37] Vexed by the "abuse that [had] been lavished" on him, the chief justice took time to privately pen a supplemental opinion to *Dred Scott*.[38] He had one aim: to strengthen his claim that Black Americans were not citizens of the United States at the time of the Constitution's ratification.[39] The chief justice had hoped to publish it "while the question is still exciting attention," but ultimately concluded that "judicial propriety" required that he wait for a relevant case to come before the court. Publishing in pamphlet form was out of the question: "I do not feel willing to write a defense of one of my judicial opinions," Taney explained. The aging jurist suggested that its publication would come only after his death—"My executors must in some form or other bring it before the public"—which is indeed what would happen.[40]

As in *Dred Scott*, Taney's opinion supplement relied on a historical analysis to show that African Americans had enjoyed no rights from 1689, as British colonial subjects, through 1787, when the US Constitution was drafted.[41] The opinion was no mere exercise in argumentation. Taney explained that he stood ready, should the court's docket present him with another opportunity, to clarify and to persuade: "If the questions come before the Court again in my lifetime, it will save the trouble of again investigating and annexing the proofs."[42]

Taney scoffed at all commentary "adverse" to his published opinion. Generally, he deemed a reply not worthwhile, asserting that his critics based their views on mere "misrepresentations and perversions." Privately, the chief justice could not refrain from launching a rebuttal to Horace Gray's 1857 pamphlet, *A Legal Review of the Case of Dred Scott*. Gray was the reporter of decisions for the Massachusetts Supreme Judicial Court, and would be appointed to the Supreme Judicial Court of Massachusetts in 1864 and the United States Supreme Court in 1881.[43] Gray charged that Taney's reasoning had been unsound: "The court have [*sic*] not, and could not have, consistently with sound principles, decided that a free negro could not be a citizen of the United States."[44] He then went further and questioned Taney's character. The chief justice's opinion, according to Gray, was "by no means the ablest or soundest of the opinions" in the case. Its "tone and manner of reasoning, as well as in the positions which it assumes" were "unworthy of the reputation of [Taney] that great magistrate."[45] Taney replied that Gray's volume was "a disingenuous perversion and misrepresentation of . . . what the Court has decided."[46] Taney privately concluded his supplemental opinion on this point, urging that those "in search of truth . . . will read [his original] opinion." Thus, he said, he would not "waste time and throw away arguments" on commentators such as Gray.[47] Contrary to his stated indifference, Taney's tone and the length of his supplemental opinion reveal that he was all too aware of how *Dred Scott* was being called into question by well-informed analysts.

In a formalistic sense, there was no reason to expect a change in Maryland's legal response to a ruling that applied only to federal courts. Still, the Supreme Court's determination invited questions about how other courts—federal and state—would incorporate its conclusions into their deliberations. The Taney court decision may have simply been the latest volley in an ongoing debate over race and citizenship. Or it may have set in motion a series of changes that could reach into local venues.

In Baltimore, free African Americans did comment on how they saw the case, if only by way of their actions. They did not appear in the city's federal courts, but they never had. At least since 1850, Black Baltimoreans had not used the federal courts to make claims. While Taney's opinion appeared to formally bar them, it was a symbolic barrier. Nothing changed in practice after 1857.[48] The city courthouse was a different scene. There, Black Baltimoreans continued to appear, just as they had before *Dred Scott*. They pursued their legal business just as before—applying for permits and licenses, bringing criminal charges, challenging apprenticeship arrangements, and even filing for insolvency. They kept up their steady presence in the Baltimore City courthouse. Their names and the charges against them continued to be marked in the pages of the clerks' dockets.

No one noted their presence as remarkable or out of place. When African Americans initiated proceedings just as they had for years, no one—not clerk, lawyer, or judge—challenged their right to use the city's courts. James Jones filed for insolvency relief for his debts, secured with the sworn support of local magistrate Basil Root and police officer Peter Logue.[49] Joseph Crawford and Edwin Scott challenged their detentions as a deserter from a vessel and a fugitive slave, respectively, using the writ of habeas corpus.[50] Black church leaders continued to wrangle over ownership of property and church governance.[51] Confidence appears to have been high that *Dred Scott* would have no effect.

The story of *Dred Scott* in Maryland was not quite over, however. The next year, 1858, it came before the state's high court—the Court of Appeals—in the case of *Hughes v. Jackson.* Baltimoreans watched from across the Chesapeake Bay as two free Black Eastern Shore men from Dorchester County battled over whether they had the right to bring suit in the state's courts. The Court of Appeals was asked to determine whether the logic of *Dred Scott* should become the law of the state: Should free Black Marylanders be barred from the state courts as noncitizens? No formal principle required the state court to adopt the Supreme Court's reasoning in *Dred Scott.* Maryland's high court had exclusive authority over courts in the state. Thus, in 1858, when the lawyers for Hughes argued that free Black people should be prohibited from suing in Maryland, it was an open question. The state stood at a major crossroads in its regulation of free Black Americans.

Hughes v. Jackson did not pose a wholly new question. Prior cases had examined the extent to which free Black Marylanders possessed rights in the state's courts. The Court of Appeals had from time to time been asked to determine the degree to which Black laws, for example, might conflict with constitutional precepts. Under the leadership of Chief Justice John Carroll Legrand from 1851 to 1861, the court's thinking was murky. It appeared that free African Americans could sue and be sued in Maryland, but actual rulings did not unqualifiedly affirm this in practice. The 1855 case of *Jason v. Henderson,* for example, asked whether a free person could recover damages for being unlawfully detained as a slave. The court said yes, as a general matter. Still, Jason could not recover from Henderson based on the facts because Henderson had not detained Jason "wantonly, and without color of title," but had acted in good faith in that he "supposed the negro to be the property of the estate he represented, and there appears a show of title for such a claim."[52] This sort of conclusion was at best a partial victory for a litigant like Jason: He had a right to sue, but his claim failed.

This muddled state of affairs continued even after *Dred Scott* was decided. Free Black people appeared before the state's highest court, and were never categorically excluded. The Court of Appeals issued rulings that may have pleased advocates for free Black rights but disappointed the actual litigants. In December 1857, nine months after *Dred Scott,* the case of *Atwell v. Miller* probed the rights of free people of color in Maryland. The question: Were free African Americans barred from giving testimony against the interests of white persons?[53] A 1717 statute appeared to govern the question: "No Negro or Mulatto Slave, Free Negro, or Mulatto born of a White Woman, during the Time of Servitude by law, shall be received as Evidence in any Cause wherein any Christian White Person is concerned."[54] The petitioner in *Atwell* nevertheless attempted to introduce the sworn statement of a free Black man, Asbury Johns, at trial. The trial court had refused his testimony categorically, relying on the early eighteenth-century statute.

At the Court of Appeals, the appellant urged that Johns's testimony should have been admitted. The court might have relied on the 1717 law to settle the question, but it did not. Instead, Chief Justice Legrand avoided it. He ruled that the defendants had not established the relevance of Johns's testimony—he was not a principal or agent such that his declarations had bearing on the case. Had his testimony been relevant, might Johns have been able to testify? Legrand did not close off this possibility, remarking: "This view relieves us from all necessity of inquiring, whether the color of the party, whose declarations were proposed to be given in evidence, could have a legal bearing on the question in any event."[55] The court left a door open. Perhaps, under another set of facts, a man of color might be permitted to give testimony against the interests of a white party, notwithstanding the terms of the 1717 law.

Six months later, in *Hughes v. Jackson,* the state's high court confronted *Dred Scott* head on. Dorchester County sat on Maryland's Eastern Shore, a portion of the state where slaveholding remained extensive and proslavery politics dominated.[56] Between 1850 and 1860 the Eastern Shore's free Black population grew by 14 percent, and many landholders in the region depended on free Black laborers.[57] Still, the area's proximity to free soil generated tensions. Rumors of impending slave insurrections and rising numbers of escaped slaves generated a tense solidarity among slaveholders. Harriet Tubman carried out her clandestine raids in Dorchester County, freeing slaves from the county's farms. The escape in 1857 of the Dover Eight, aided by Tubman, had rocked the county courthouse. Former slave Sam Green was arrested for aiding the group and was prosecuted for seditious materials, a copy of Harriet Beecher Stowe's *Uncle Tom's Cabin.*[58] Local slaveholders organized around their fears of the free Black population, which was said to corrupt and demoralize slaves, making men like Hughes and Jackson a troublesome presence.[59]

Hughes v. Jackson grew out of years of stop-and-start litigation between William Hughes and Samuel Jackson that began in 1842 when Hughes purchased two slaves. Hughes was a free Black farmer and landowner who managed his property with the help of four sons: Denwood, William, Josiah, and Robert.[60] He had never before been a slaveholder, though it would not have been out of the ordinary for a farmer like Hughes to hire enslaved people seasonally or for specialized tasks. This changed in the summer of 1842, when he paid Catherine Ray $280 for a woman and her infant daughter.[61] Hughes bargained to hold a temporary title to this "certain Mulatto woman named Mary Teackle and her infant child named Lilly." He agreed that the mother and daughter would be held only for a term of years, after which they would be free. The arrangement was set to begin on August 15, 1840, and terminate eleven years later, in 1851.[62]

Samuel Jackson told a more elaborate version of the bargain between Hughes and Ray. The details he shared were not reflected in the written deed. Yes, Hughes had purchased Mary and Lilly as enslaved people. But Hughes was only a middleman. He had purchased the mother and daughter on Jackson's behalf. The scheme was an effort to unite Jackson's family. Mary Teackle was Jackson's wife. And after 1840, the lives of Samuel and Mary bore this out. Hughes permitted the Jackson family to live together in Dorchester County while Jackson regularly paid Hughes the price for the freedom of Mary and Lilly over time. Jackson later explained that he had, from the outset of the agreement, been in "possession" of Mary and Lilly. Together the three had made a home.[63]

For nearly ten years the bargain between Hughes and Jackson was an easy one, it seems. There were no signs of discord. Samuel and Mary's family grew to include four children: Lilly, the eldest, was followed by siblings Theodore, Dennis, and Ellen.[64] They rented a home from Hughes. Then, sometime in 1850, just one year shy of the end of Mary's and Lilly's formal time enslaved, William Hughes died. His sons Josiah and Denwood took charge of their father's property, and as executors, were charged with distributing the elder Hughes's estate. Jackson and the Hughes brothers were soon at odds.[65] Did the Jackson family belong to William Hughes's estate? The parties did not agree. Jackson, feeling their liberty under threat, gathered his wife and children in an effort to escape the reach of the Hughes family. The Jacksons got as far as the town of Cambridge but were thwarted when they tried to board a ship to cross the Chesapeake Bay to the Western Shore. Denwood Hughes intercepted the family, seizing Mary and her children.[66] It was a vexing circumstance that would take more than a decade to resolve, during which time a local trial court, the state's Court of Appeals, and a constitutional convention would all weigh in. Questions about slavery and freedom were most pressing for the Jackson family. Still, their claims would turn, in part, on whether Samuel Jackson, as a free Black man, had a right to sue in Maryland's courts. This was Maryland's *Dred Scott.*

The Hugheses' intent soon became evident: The Jackson family was an asset. The brothers sold the Jacksons' three youngest children—Ellen, eight; Dennis, seven; and Theodore, four—to a prominent and prosperous white farmer, Alward Johnson, for $460.[67] Johnson purchased the children for cash, and the bill of sale and deed declared them to be the property of widow Mary Ann Hughes, wife of the late William Hughes, and slaves "for life." Johnson's purchase agreement also provided for the children's eventual manumission: Ellen after eighteen years, Dennis after twenty-four years, and Theodore after twenty-seven years. There was, perhaps, some small comfort for Samuel and Mary Jackson in knowing that their children would not be taken far. Johnson's farm was also in Dorchester County.

Samuel Jackson wasted little time before heading to the Dorchester County courthouse. He hired a lawyer and initiated a string of lawsuits aimed at regaining custody of his family and punishing the Hughes brothers. First were five freedom suits filed in April 1851, just weeks after the children's sale to Alward Johnson. Jackson filed these petitions as the so-called next friend of his wife and four children. Second, filed in October 1851, was a claim against Josiah and William Hughes for trespass. Jackson sought damages for the Hughes brothers' unlawful detention of his family. Third, Jackson brought suit against Denwood and Josiah Hughes as executors of the estate of William Hughes, also in October 1851, though the court record does not indicate the specific nature of this claim. Fourth and finally, one year later, in October 1852, Jackson filed suit against Denwood and Josiah Hughes and Alward Johnson. Again, the specific charges are not recorded. These complaints might appear scattershot, but it is more likely that neither Jackson nor his lawyer knew precisely what sort of framework the court was likely to adopt for resolving such a dispute. In this they were not wrong. Very quickly two of the four proceedings came to a conclusion. The freedom suits were marked "off" the court calendar by October 1852, while the case against the Hughes brothers as executors of their father's estate was settled: "Discontinued and Judgment for Defendant Costs." Samuel Jackson paid $19.53⅔ for his trouble.[68]

What followed over the next years was muddled, at least when viewed from the vantage point of the court's docket books. Perhaps a combination of failed attempts at settlement combined with shifts in local political appointments kept the parties from getting to the merits. Hughes and Jackson appeared to be nearing a settlement in the trespass case in the spring of 1852. By the fall of 1853, with no settlement in sight, the court sounded impatient when it noted that if the case were not tried the following spring, it would enter a judgment for the defendants. Another year had passed when a newly appointed trial judge announced that he would disqualify himself; he had been counsel for the Hugheses earlier in the proceeding. A new "special judge" was finally appointed in January 1855. In the spring of 1856, Jackson's lawyers made one more push. A jury sworn in April on the twenty-fifth of that month found in favor of Jackson. The Hugheses were to pay him $750 plus interest and costs for their trespass on his family. Mary and Lilly were granted their liberty, although the three younger children remained in the hands of Alward Johnson.[69]

Samuel Jackson had managed to defeat the Hughes brothers by persuading a jury that he had been wronged. His strongest evidence was likely the array of white witnesses who testified on his behalf. Jackson drew from Dorchester County's associational networks to build his case.[70] Among his witnesses was a Hughes family neighbor, farmer William Corkran. Jackson relied on slaveholders, including the brothers Polish and Banaman Mills. And at least one woman testified, Eliza Hicks, a widow who owned her own farm, which was run by her children and Black laborers. The general climate suggested that free Black men and women in Dorchester County were subject to increasing scrutiny, including in the courthouse. But a modest laborer like Samuel Jackson could still call on the reputations and authority of local whites to substantiate his claim. They knew enough about the bargain between Jackson and Hughes to make them reliable and relevant witnesses. Throughout the proceedings, no one—no lawyer, no witness, no jury member, no judge—questioned Jackson's right to bring suit.

Jackson's victory at trial might have ended the matter, but Josiah Hughes appealed the local court's ruling to the Maryland Court of Appeals, transforming Samuel Jackson's grievances from a local matter into an occasion for testing the reach of *Dred Scott*. Hughes's objections were partly routine. He sought to overturn the verdict or otherwise have it set aside based on technical defects.[71] For example, Jackson had failed to indicate in his initial pleadings that he was a "free" negro, inviting the presumption that he was a slave and thus incapable of bringing suit.[72] Hughes also asserted a novel position. He argued that the Supreme Court's logic in *Dred Scott* should decide the matter. The Hughes family attorney, Elias Griswold, asserted that Samuel Jackson (and, by implication, his own client), as a free Black Marylander, was without standing before the state court, as Dred Scott had been before the federal court.[73] No Black person, Griswold urged, enslaved or free, had standing to sue in the state. Jackson's case, he concluded, must be dismissed.

Hughes provided Maryland's high court its first opportunity to consider the implications of *Dred Scott*. Griswold suggested that in Maryland, legal remedies for Jackson were out of reach. His argument was not tightly woven.[74] Griswold did not rely on specific citizenship language in the Maryland state constitution. Nor did he insist that there was any necessary relationship between federal citizenship, which had been Taney's subject, and the state citizenship that might have been relevant in the *Jackson* case. Instead, Griswold made a vague but cunning argument that might have allowed the court to bend toward the interests of white supremacy.[75] He referred to the "opinion of Chief Justice Taney in *Dred Scott*" to support the view that if Jackson was without standing to sue, the court itself was without jurisdiction. Then, without elaboration, Griswold declared that if no law extended civil rights to Black Marylanders, "the plaintiff in this case had no right to sue."[76]

Jackson's attorneys, James Wallace and Charles Goldsborough, confronted the problem of *Dred Scott* directly, arguing that Maryland should take a distinct position on the question of African Americans' standing to sue and be sued. Their argument relied on an alternative view of history. Since the latter decades of the eighteenth century, Jackson's attorneys explained, African Americans "going at large and acting as free" had been viewed as free men.[77] They had, when the Constitution was ratified, given evidence in court and performed other acts, such as voting, that only subsequently had been reserved to white men. The free African American occupied an "anomalous position, having more rights than a stranger, yet not the same as an heir. He can sue and be sued in our courts, hold property and enjoy the fullest protection of our laws."[78] Jackson's counsel carefully distinguished the US citizenship that was the subject of *Dred Scott* from citizenship in the state of Maryland, arguing that even if Jackson was disqualified under the federal Constitution, "he might still be a citizen of a State, and as such a free man."[79]

Hughes presented a matter of first impression for the Maryland Court of Appeals, while also positioning state court judges to assess Taney's ideas. Had Maryland's high court adopted the chief justice's views on race and rights, it would have been little surprise.[80] Legrand surely understood Taney's position. The two had a great deal in common. Both were raised in slaveholding households.[81] Both had practiced law in Baltimore before entering public service.[82] Taney had served as Maryland's attorney general, and Legrand had held the office of secretary of state.[83] The two were also active lay leaders in the city's Catholic Church.[84] Both men were moderate proslavery voices whose ideas reflected a paternalism that was characteristic of Maryland's pro-colonization white elites.[85]

On the rights of Black people, however, Legrand and Taney parted ways. Despite his general admiration for Taney and their shared cultural sensibilities, Legrand rejected the chief justice's reasoning and unequivocally refused to extend *Dred Scott* into the state of Maryland.[86] Writing for the court, Legrand explained that Samuel Jackson was entitled to bring suit in the state's courts.[87] In Maryland, there were only two instances in which Black people were presumed, by their color, to stand apart from white Americans in legal culture. Blackness barred African Americans from testifying as witnesses against white people, and in freedom suits Blackness raised the rebuttable presumption that they were slaves.[88] Otherwise, Black Marylanders enjoyed a broad right to sue and be sued.[89] The court addressed the relevance of *Dred Scott* through Taney's own approach—a history of race and rights. "From the earliest history of the colony," Legrand explained, "free negroes have been allowed to sue in our courts and to hold property, both real and personal, and at one time, they having the necessary qualifications, were permitted to exercise the elective franchise."[90] In Justice Legrand's view, race had never served as an absolute bar to rights in Maryland. This was consistent, he said, with the state's interests: "To deny to them the right of suing and being sued, would be in point of fact to deprive them of the means of defending their possessions, and this, too, without subserving any good purpose. . . . Neither the policy of our law, nor the well-being of this part of our population, demands the principle of exclusion contended for by the appellant."[91]

Legrand looked ahead and suggested that "so long as free negroes remain in our midst a wholesome system induces incentives to thrift and respectability, and none more effective could be suggested than the protection of their earnings."[92] Maryland's high court rejected Taney's view of both the history and the status of free Black Americans. Legrand laid out for Black Marylanders a bundle of rights.[93] It was an imperfect, partial, but still potent bundle of rights: to sue and be sued, to hold property real and personal, to defend possessions and earnings, and in some cases to vote.[94] Justice Legrand concluded by affirming the lower court judgment, entitling Samuel Jackson to his $750.

In Maryland *Dred Scott* stood for a Supreme Court case that had symbolic meaning but little material effect. The Maryland Court of Appeals rejected the view that the state should bar free Black men and women from its halls of justice. Chief Justice John Carroll Legrand affirmed a set of rights that were not equivalent to citizenship but did include the right to sue and be sued. This possibility alone had long given free Black Marylanders an opening through which to claim their freedom and construct their well-being and belonging. Still, court decisions—even those of high courts, like *Hughes v. Jackson*—did not wholly settle matters in Baltimore City or elsewhere in the state. Lawmakers in Annapolis, the state capital, renewed efforts to set in place some of the most restrictive Black laws the state had ever contemplated. Delegate Curtis Jacobs led a campaign as chair of the Committee on the Colored Population that would have prohibited manumission, imposed a registration requirement on free Black people, and planned for the removal of all free Black Marylanders from the state. Yet Maryland was about to be caught up in an "anti–free Negro" wave that was sweeping much of the South.

NOTES

1. Legal historian David Bogen carefully examines the legal status of Black Marylanders in the early republic and demonstrates that they experienced a decline in their standing at the start of the century. David S. Bogen, "The Maryland Context of 'Dred Scott': The Decline in the Legal Status of Maryland Free Blacks, 1776–1810," *American Journal of Legal History* 34, no. 4 (1990): 396–411, and David S. Bogen, "The Annapolis Poll Books of 1800 and 1804: African American Voting in the Early Republic," *Maryland Historical Magazine* 86, no. 1 (1991): 57–65.

2. Nicholas G. Penniman IV, "Baltimore's Daily Press and Slavery, 1857–1860," *Maryland Historical Magazine* 99, no. 4 (Winter 2004): 491–507.

3. Harold A. Williams, "Light for All: Arunah S. Abell and the Rise of the Baltimore 'Sun,'" *Maryland Historical Magazine* 82, no. 3 (Fall 1987): 197–213.

4. "Washington, March 6," *Sun*, March 7, 1857. Kingman published under the pen name "Ion." Harold A. Williams, *The Baltimore Sun, 1837–1987* (Baltimore: Johns Hopkins University Press, 1987),

269. He is said to have been the first journalist to set up as a permanent correspondent based in Washington. Rufus R. Wilson, *Washington: The Capital City, and Its Part in the History of the Nation,* vol. 1 (New York: J. B. Lippincott, 1902), 219.

5. "The Decision in the Supreme Court.," *Sun,* March 9, 1857.

6. "The Dred Scott Case," *Sun,* March 11, 1857.

7. Don E. Fehrenbacher, *The Dred Scott Case: Its Significance in American Law and Politics* (New York: Oxford University Press, 1978), 155–58.

8. H. L. Mencken, *A Monograph of the New Baltimore Court House: One of the Greatest Examples of American Architecture, and the Foremost Court House of the United States; Including an Historical Sketch of the Early Courts of Maryland* (Baltimore: A. Hoen, 1899), 9–28. Reverdy Johnson would later become a border-state Unionist and support the Thirteenth Amendment. Michael Vorenberg, *Final Freedom: The Civil War, the Abolition of Slavery, and the Thirteenth Amendment* (New York: Cambridge University Press, 2001).

9. Fehrenbacher, *The Dred Scott Case,* 155–58.

10. J. W., "Letter from Old Point Comfort," *Sun,* August 1, 1851 (noting Taney and his family vacationing in Old Point Comfort, VA); "Local Matters," *Sun,* July 16, 1851 (naming Taney as one of the honored guests at the St. Mary's College commencement); "Local Matters," *Sun,* April 28, 1851 (describing how Taney was in attendance at Archbishop Eccleston's funeral); "Married," *Sun,* February 10, 1852 (reporting the marriage of Taney's daughter Maria to Richard T. Allison); "Meeting of the Members of the Baltimore Bar," *Sun,* July 12, 1853, 1 (reporting that Taney was called from his home to preside over a memorial honoring the recently deceased Judge John Glenn).

11. Carl Brent Swisher, *Roger B. Taney* (New York: Macmillan, 1935), 28–37, 114–15.

12. Swisher, *Roger B. Taney,* 469–72.

13. Swisher, *Roger B. Taney,* 353–57.

14. "The Dred Scott Case," *Sun,* March 11, 1857.

15. *Sun,* May 19, 1857, quoted in Penniman, "Baltimore's Daily Press and Slavery."

16. Fehrenbacher discusses these cases in *The Dred Scott Case,* 692, nn. 91 and 92.

17. See Dred Scott v. Sandford, 60 U.S. (19 How.) 393, 529–64 (1857). See Lucas E. Morel, "The Dred Scott Dissents: McLean, Curtis, Lincoln, and the Public Mind," *Journal of Supreme Court History* 32, no. 22 (2007): 133, 134–38.

18. "Decision in the Mitchell Case," *Sun,* July 18, 1857; Roger Brooke Taney, "Supplement to the Dred Scott Opinion" (1858), in Samuel Tyler, *Memoir of Roger Brooke Taney, LL.D., Chief Justice of the Supreme Court of the United States* (Baltimore: J. Murphy, 1876), 578.

19. See "Can Colored Men Sue in the Federal Courts?" *Washington* (PA) *Reporter,* July 22, 1857; "Important Decision in the U.S. Circuit Court: James C. Mitchell vs. Charles Lamar," *Chicago Daily Tribune,* July 15, 1857; *Chicago Democratic Press,* May 15, 1857; *New York Evening Post,* May 20, 1857; and *National Era* (Washington, DC), July 30, 1857.

20. "A Case under the Dred Scott Decision," *New York Herald,* July 13, 1858.

21. "Important Decision in the U.S. Circuit Court."

22. "Can Colored Men Sue in the Federal Courts?"

23. "Important Decision in the U.S. Circuit Court."

24. See, e.g., Opinions of the Justices of the Supreme Judicial Court, on Question Propounded by the Senate, 44 ME. 505, 508 (1857) (declining to apply Dred Scott when interpreting the phrase

"citizen of the United States"); Anderson v. Millikin, 9 Ohio St. 568, 577 (1859) ("The question is not, what the phrase 'citizen of the United States' means in the light of the decision in the case of *Dred Scott v. Sandford,* but what the framers of our [state] constitution intended by the use of that phrase, and what, in the connection in which it is found, and with the light and knowledge possessed when it was used, it was intended to mean"); see also Opinion of the Justices of the Supreme Judicial Court, 41 N.H. 553, 553 (1857) (affirming constitutionality of "[a]n act to secure freedom and the rights of citizenship to persons in this State," which was passed by the NH House of Representatives on June 26, 1857). For an example in which a local court declined to follow the reasoning in *Dred Scott* to bar an African American from suing, see generally Richard F. Nation, "Violence and the Rights of African Americans in Civil War–Era Indiana: The Case of James Hays," *Indiana Magazine of History* 100, no. 32 (2004): 215–30.

25. *Anderson v. Milliken,* 570. The court was required to interpret an 1851 amendment to the state's constitution, changing its requirement for electorship to "white male citizen of the United States" from "white male inhabitants." The latter, originally used in the state's 1802 constitution, had been widely interpreted to include not only white males but also free men of mixed-race descent whose bloodline was less than half Black. *Anderson v. Milliken,* 569–70.

26. *Anderson v. Milliken,* 572, 577

27. Opinions of the Justices of the Supreme Judicial Court, 44 Maine at 507. Fehrenbacher, *The Dred Scott Case,* 688n53.

28. Opinions of the Justices of the Supreme Judicial Court, 507–8.

29. Opinions of the Justices of the Supreme Judicial Court, 515–16.

30. See *Heirn v. Bridault,* 37 Miss. 209, 224–25 (1859); *Shaw v. Brown,* 35 Miss. 246, 315–16 (1858).

31. See *Shaw v. Brown,* 246, 320–21.

32. See *Shaw v. Brown,* 315.

33. For background on Shaw, manumissions, and the right of emancipated Black nonresidents to sue for their inheritance in Mississippi courts, see Paul Finkelman, *An Imperfect Union: Slavery, Federalism, and Comity* (Chapel Hill: University of North Carolina Press, 1981), 287–90; Bernie D. Jones, *Fathers of Conscience: Mixed-Race Inheritance in the Antebellum South* (Athens: University of Georgia Press, 2009), 55–57.

34. *Heirn v. Bridault,* 37 Miss. 209, 224–25 (1859). The majority in *Heirn* rejected *Shaw* and its reliance on comity to hold that a free Black woman from Louisiana had no right to sue for her inheritance in Mississippi, ultimately concluding "free negroes . . . are to be regarded as alien enemies or strangers prohibited, and without the pale of comity, and incapable of acquiring or maintaining property in this State which will be recognized by our courts." See *Shaw v. Brown,* 233. For a detailed analysis of how Mississippi fit into the broader antebellum trend of states "denying blacks' legal citizenship and insisting on their foreignness," see Kunal M. Parker, "Citizenship and Immigration Law, 1800–1924: Resolutions of Membership and Territory," in *The Cambridge History of Law in America,* ed. Michael Grossberg and Christopher Tomlins (Cambridge: Cambridge University Press, 2008), 2:168–203.

35. See *Heirn v. Bridault,* 37 Miss. at 234 (Handy, J., dissenting) (arguing because plaintiff was "alleged to have been a citizen of Louisiana, and the presumption is, that her rights and capabilities as such continue. The question, then, as to her right, as a free person of color of the State of Louisiana, to take a legacy, is the same as that decided in Shaw v. Brown").

36. See Taney, "Supplement to the Dred Scott Opinion," 578–79, 598–608.

37. Roger Brooke Taney to David Perine (June 16, 1857), Box 2, Perine Family Papers, 1783–1941, MS 645, Maryland Historical Society (hereafter MdHS).

38. Fehrenbacher, *The Dred Scott Case,* 687n42, citing Roger Brooke Taney to Caleb Cushing (November 9, 1857), Caleb Cushing Papers, Manuscripts Division, Library of Congress, Washington, DC.

39. Taney, "Supplement to the Dred Scott Opinion," 578–608.

40. Roger B. Taney to J. Mason Campbell, February 19, 1861; and Roger Brooke Taney to James Mason Campbell, February 18, 1861, Box 22, MS 469, John Eager Howard Papers, 1662–1919, 1817–68 (Roger Brooke Taney Correspondence [1817–72]), MdHS. Taney did circulate the supplemental opinion privately, for example to his "friend Mr Stone, one of the Bar of [Washington, DC]." Roger B. Taney to J. Mason Campbell, October 23, 1863 (Washington), Box 22, MS 469, John Eager Howard Papers, 1662–1919, 1817–68 (Roger Brooke Taney Correspondence [1817–72]), MdHS. The supplement would finally be published, but only after a good amount of wrangling between his family, his friends, and his first biographer, Samuel Tyler. Samuel Tyler to J. Mason Campbell, November 20, 1864; Samuel Tyler to F. M. Etting, November 18, 1864; and David M. Perine to F. M. Etting, March 1874, Box 22, MS 469, John Eager Howard Papers, 1662–1919, 1817–68 (Roger Brooke Taney Correspondence [1817–72]), MdHS.

41. Taney, "Supplement to the Dred Scott Opinion," 579–93.

42. Roger B. Taney, "Statement of the Historical Fact in the Opinion of the Supreme Court of the United States in the Dred Scott Case," Box 9, Perine Family Papers, 1783–1941, MS 645, MdHS; Taney, "Supplement to the Dred Scott Opinion," 578. Historian Don Fehrenbacher characterizes Taney's supplemental opinion as a "curious document." Fehrenbacher, *The Dred Scott Case,* 445. The opinion would remain unpublished until nearly a decade after Taney's death. See Tyler, *Memoir of Roger Brooke Taney,* 485–86.

43. Clare Cushman, "The Supreme Court Justices: Illustrated Biographies, 1789–1993" (Washington, DC: Congressional Quarterly, 1993).

44. Horace Gray, "A Legal Review of the Case of Dred Scott, as Decided by the Supreme Court of the United States" 57 (1857), 57. Fehrenbacher cites this as an article by John Lowell and Horace Gray in *The Law Reporter* (June 1857). Theirs was the "aberration" view, which concluded Taney had strayed from his usual style and quality of mind.

45. Gray, *A Legal Review,* 9.

46. Taney, "Supplement to the Dred Scott Opinion," 607.

47. Taney, "Supplement to the Dred Scott Opinion," 608.

48. A review of the docket books of the Federal Circuit Court, Baltimore, for the 1850s evidences no litigants identified as African American. The first Black party to appear in that court after 1850 does so in 1863.

49. *In re* James H. Jones (April 22, 1857), Box 18, T515–21, Insolvency Papers, Court of Common Pleas, Baltimore City, Court of Common Pleas, MSA. On Root, see *Wood's Baltimore Directory, for 1856–57* (Baltimore: John W. Woods, 1856), 289. On Logue, see *Matchett's Baltimore Director, for 1855–56* (Baltimore: B. J. Matchett, 1855), 209.

50. "Proceedings of the Courts," *Sun,* January 6, 1858.

51. African Methodist Bethel Church v. Joel P. Carmack, et al., No. 949, Equity Papers A, Mis-

cellaneous, T53–10, 1857, Baltimore City Circuit Court, Baltimore City, MSA (Circuit Court Order, May 13, 1857).

52. *Jason v. Henderson,* 7 Md. 430 (1855).

53. On restricting Black testimony, see Jeffrey R. Brackett, *The Negro in Maryland: A Study of the Institution of Slavery* (Baltimore: N. Murray, Publication Agent, Johns Hopkins University, 1889), 190–94.

54. Maryland Laws of 1717, chap. 13, § 2. Thomas Bacon, *Laws of Maryland at Large* (Annapolis: Jonas Green, 1765).

55. *Atwell v. Miller,* 11 Md. 348 (1857).

56. See Barbara Jeanne Fields, *Slavery and Freedom on the Middle Ground: Maryland during the Nineteenth Century* (New Haven, CT: Yale University Press, 1985), 66–67.

57. See Fields, *Slavery and Freedom,* 70.

58. On Tubman, see Catherine Clinton, *Harriet Tubman: The Road to Freedom* (Boston: Little, Brown, 2004); Jean M. Humez, *Harriet Tubman: The Life and Life Stories* (Madison: University of Wisconsin Press, 2003); and Kate Clifford Larson, *Bound for the Promised Land: Harriet Tubman, Portrait of an American Hero* (New York: Ballantine, 2004).

59. Fields notes that by 1860 free Blacks made up 19 percent of the Eastern Shore's total population. Fields, *Slavery and Freedom,* 70.

60. Last will and testament of William Hughes, November 25, 1850, MSA. In his will Hughes enumerates in detail the property to be left to his children, including land, cattle, sheep, and cash. No express mention is made of his holding property in persons. However, he provided that the "balance" of his estate was to be inherited by his wife, Mary, and this may well have included enslaved people.

61. Bill of Sale, Catherine S. M. Ray to William Hughes, July 8, 1842, Dorchester County Circuit Court, Chattel Records, 1852–60, 776:195–96, MSA.

62. Dorchester County Circuit Court, Chattel Records, 1852–60, 776:95–96, FJH 2, MSA CM427–2, MSA.

63. Samuel Jackson v. Denwood Hughes, William Hughes, and Alward Johnson, Dorchester County Circuit Court, Equity Papers, T2318–3, MSA.

64. *Samuel Jackson v. Denwood Hughes, William Hughes, and Alward Johnson.*

65. Josiah Hughes in the following year, 1852, served as a representative to the state's "colored" colonization convention, and in the 1860s he would seek ordination to the ministry in the AME Church. C. Christopher Brown, "Maryland's First Political Convention by and for Its Colored People," *Maryland Historical Magazine* 88, no. 5 (Fall 1993): 324–35.

66. *Samuel Jackson v. Denwood Hughes, William Hughes, and Alward Johnson.*

67. Bill of Sale and Deed, Alward Johnson from Josiah Hughes and others, March 15, 1851, MSA.

68. Docket entry (October 1851), Samuel Jackson, negro v. Denwood Hughes and Josiah Hughes exors of William Hughes, MSA.

69. The court would not remark on this turn of events. Only later, during the Civil War, would the family's manumissions be recorded. Mary and daughter Lilly received freedom papers on December 22, 1863, based on the terms of their sale to William Hughes. The three remaining children remained in the possession of Alward Johnson until after Maryland abolished slavery in November 1864. Their manumission was recorded in the state's overall inventory of slaves in 1867. C-690, Certificates of Freedom, 1851–64, Circuit Court, Dorchester County, MSA.

70. Tony Allan Freyer, *Producers versus Capitalists: Constitutional Conflict in Antebellum America* (Charlottesville: University of Virginia Press, 1994).

71. See *Hughes v. Jackson,* 12 Md. 450 (1858), 451, 462–63; "Argument of Appellee," Hughes v. Jackson, S375–21, Briefs, 1857–58, Court of Appeals, MSA.

72. See *Hughes v. Jackson,* 462 (describing the question presented to the court as "whether a negro can maintain an action in this State, without first averring in his pleadings, and establishing by proof, his freedom"). "Argument of Appellee," *Hughes v. Jackson,* MSA.

73. *Hughes v. Jackson,* 450, 451, 452–55; "Argument of Appellee," *Hughes v. Jackson,* MSA.

74. See *Hughes v. Jackson,* 450, 451, 452–55; "Argument of Appellee," *Hughes v. Jackson,* MSA.

75. See *Hughes v. Jackson,* 450, 451, 452–55; "Argument of Appellee," *Hughes v. Jackson,* MSA.

76. *Hughes v. Jackson,* 455; "Argument of Appellee," *Hughes v. Jackson,* MSA.

77. *Hughes v. Jackson,* 459; "Argument of Appellee," *Hughes v. Jackson,* MSA.

78. *Hughes v. Jackson,* 459; "Argument of Appellee," *Hughes v. Jackson,* MSA.

79. *Hughes v. Jackson,* 459; "Argument of Appellee," *Hughes v. Jackson,* MSA.

80. For a history of the Maryland Court of Appeals, see generally Hall Hammond, "Commemoration of the Two Hundredth Anniversary of the Maryland Court of Appeals: A Short History," *Maryland Law Review* 38, no. 2 (1978): 229–41. Notably, the court was restructured pursuant to the state's new 1851 constitution, which provided for, among other innovations, the election of Maryland Court of Appeals justices for ten-year terms. *Hughes v. Jackson,* 459; "Argument of Appellee," *Hughes v. Jackson,* MSA, 235.

81. Tyler, *Memoir of Roger Brooke Taney,* 124–25; Carroll T. Bond, The Court of Appeals of Maryland: A History (Baltimore: J. Murphy, 1928), 153–61.

82. Tyler, *Memoir of Roger Brooke Taney,* 160; see "The Late Hon. John C. Legrand, Chief Justice of the State of Maryland," *Daily Dispatch* (Richmond), January 11, 1862, 2.

83. Tyler, *Memoir of Roger Brooke Taney,* 163; "The Late Hon. John C. Legrand."

84. See Tyler, *Memoir of Roger Brooke Taney,* 475–76; "The Late Chief Justice Legrand: Meeting of the Members of the Bar—Adjournment of the Court—Funeral of the Deceased," *Sun,* December 31, 1861.

85. Regarding Taney, see Swisher, *Roger B. Taney,* 97–99; Timothy S. Huebner, "Roger B. Taney and the Slavery Issue: Looking Beyond—and Before—Dred Scott," *Journal of American History* 97, no. 1 (June 2010): 32–37; John Carroll Legrand, *Letter to Hon. Reverdy Johnson, on the Proceedings at the Meeting, Held at Maryland Institute, January 10th, 1861* (n.p., 1861); and, Eugene S. Vansickle, "A Transnational Vision for African Colonization: John H. B. Latrobe and the Future of Maryland in Liberia," *Journal of Transatlantic Studies* 1, no. 2 (2003): 214–32.

86. *Hughes v. Jackson,* 459.

87. *Hughes v. Jackson,* 464. For an overview of Legrand's tenure on the Maryland Court of Appeals, see Bond, Court of Appeals of Maryland, 153–61.

88. *Hughes v. Jackson,* 463.

89. *Hughes v. Jackson,* 463–64.

90. *Hughes v. Jackson,* 463–64.

91. *Hughes v. Jackson,* 464.

92. *Hughes v. Jackson,* 464.

93. See *Hughes v. Jackson,* 463–64. The "bundle of rights" metaphor is adapted from T. H.

Marshall's view that citizenship cannot be reduced to any specific right and that many Americans throughout time have possessed only a partial version of citizenship. See T. H. Marshall, *Citizenship and Social Class and Other Essays* (Cambridge: Cambridge University Press, 1950), 10–27. While I do not share Marshall's view that citizenship rights can be characterized as progressively amassed, his metaphor displaces the view that citizenship can be reduced to a "yes or no" matter, or that it can be reduced to any one right, such as that of naturalization or the franchise.

94. Legal historian David Bogen carefully examines the legal status of Black Marylanders in the early republic and demonstrates that Black Marylanders experienced a decline in their standing at the start of the century. David S. Bogen, "The Maryland Context of 'Dred Scott': The Decline in the Legal Status of Maryland Free Blacks, 1776–1810," *American Journal of Legal History* 34, no. 4 (1990): 396–411, and David S. Bogen, "The Annapolis Poll Books of 1800 and 1804: African American Voting in the Early Republic," *Maryland Historical Magazine* 86, no. 1 (1991): 57–65.

"MARYLAND IS THIS DAY. . . TRUE TO THE AMERICAN UNION"

The Election of 1860 and a Winter of Discontent

CHARLES W. MITCHELL

T he fall of 1860 to early spring of 1861, a period beginning with Abraham Lincoln's election, confronted Marylanders with the prospect that their state might leave the Union. The plurality of Maryland votes that Vice President John Breckinridge, the Democratic candidate of the Deep South, won that November obscured the reality that the combined number of votes captured by the other three candidates, all Unionists, constituted a majority. For months Governor Thomas H. Hicks refused to summon the Maryland legislature into special session, concerned that their actions might provoke a confrontation with the new Republican administration in Washington.[1] Following an assault on April 19 by a Baltimore mob against northern militia troops passing through Baltimore en route to Washington, Hicks finally relented, by which time Maryland political and business leaders had engaged in national and regional efforts to avert conflict that illuminated for many citizens the catastrophes that awaited a Confederate Maryland. This essay examines a broad swath of public opinion that suggests a sustained Unionist allegiance in Maryland in the period leading up to the outbreak of the Civil War.

Hicks, elected in 1857 as a candidate of the American Party (whose members were known as Know Nothings), was a Unionist who supported slavery and southern rights; he had won election on the strength of the Know Nothing Party's popularity in Maryland and its anti-immigrant, anti-Catholic, though pro-American, platform. The state's legislature was dominated by a planter aristocracy centered in a southern Maryland that enjoyed disproportionally high representation, while a Baltimore City that had seen recent, significant population growth suffered from underrepresentation.

Hicks and other Unionist leaders feared that summoning legislators into special session risked triggering a cascade of events that might lead Maryland into discussions with the southern states that, alarmed at the election of Lincoln, were laying the groundwork to secede from the United States. The pressure on Maryland political leaders to take some sort of action declaring the state's intentions intensified during the autumn of 1860 when embattled federal troops in Charleston Harbor, commanded by Maj. Robert Anderson, became increasingly vulnerable to the predations of an excitable South Carolina militia. There is little evidence that a strategy championed by Hicks and others, that Maryland might navigate any sectional conflict by serving either as a neutral mediator between the northern and southern states or by creating a central confederacy of border states, got much traction.

In the 1860 US presidential election, a coalition of old-line Whigs, Protestants, nativists, and immigrants had carried Republican Abraham Lincoln to a resounding victory in November. Needing 152 electoral votes, he racked up a total of 180. He took every free state but New Jersey (where he still won four electoral votes), an impressive feat considering that voters in many southern states had no Republican/Lincoln ballots to cast (parties at that time printed and distributed their own ballots). Although Lincoln won only 39.8 percent of the popular vote nationally, an impressive tally given that the race featured four candidates, he captured 54 percent of votes cast in the North. Stephen A. Douglas, the candidate of the northern Democrats, placed second in the overall popular vote but won only New Jersey and Missouri and a total of twelve electoral votes, finishing dead last by that essential metric. Vice President Breckinridge of Kentucky, candidate of the southern Democrats (the party had split into northern and southern factions at their April nominating convention in Charleston), finished third in the popular vote and second in the electoral vote, with 72. Lincoln did not receive a single vote in seven of the Deep South states, and he won only two of 996 southern counties. But he won every county in New England, 109 of 147 mid-Atlantic counties, and 252 of 392 counties in Ohio, Michigan, Indiana, and Illinois.

Fifty-eight percent of the national popular vote went for Lincoln and Breckinridge combined, candidates who represented to many voters the two extremes on the issue. John Bell's new Constitutional Union Party, dedicated to little beyond maintaining the Union and Constitution ("The Union as it was, the Constitution as it is," rang their platitudinous anthem), failed to resonate with northern voters; in only three northern states did Bell garner more than 3 percent of the popular vote. Bell did carry the border states of Virginia,

Kentucky, and his home state of Tennessee, and he ran a strong second in Maryland, where he won 45.14 percent of the popular vote, just behind Breckinridge's 45.93 percent. But the election of 1860 meant far more than the end of the Constitutional Unionists; it triggered the final cataclysmic events that, after four years of war, would eventually tear down slavery in the United States. The South had suffered a terrible drought that summer of 1860, a harbinger of the horrors that secession and four years of civil war would inflict on its people, and now a divided nation had essentially decided the slavery issue in favor of the North, with its new president committed to preventing its expansion.

THE ELECTION IN MARYLAND

The nascent Maryland Republican Party, holding few key state offices and lacking significant grassroots support, knew their man would not likely fare well in their state. The party attempted to mobilize German support, hoping to leverage the backing Lincoln enjoyed from former German revolutionaries who had emigrated to the United States and had become important figures in the party, but won the endorsement of only one of the two German newspapers in Baltimore, *Die Wecker*.[2] Maryland Republican leaders such as Montgomery Blair, the patriarch of the distinguished Blair family and its estate, Silver Spring, reminded anxious planters that the noninterference posture of both Lincoln and the party on slavery would ensure its continuity in Maryland. The city's businessmen had reason to worry, though; they had enjoyed a robust business climate in 1860 but feared a Lincoln victory would prompt the southern cotton states to leave the Union with, in the words of one writer, "an attendant disruption of established trade patterns." Reinforcing the angst of the barons of Baltimore business was the collapse of the banking house Samuel Harris & Sons on November 23, showering liabilities of approximately $200,000 on hapless creditors.[3]

Maryland Republicans, heavily concentrated in Baltimore City, confronted physical danger from their better-organized opponents. Lincoln supporters known as Wide-Awakes were pelted with eggs and bricks and suffered the residue of burning cayenne sticks, that nineteenth-century version of tear gas. Eggs, stones, and garbage were hurled at a late-October parade of several hundred Baltimore Republicans. At other Republican demonstrations in Baltimore, reported the *Baltimore Clipper*, "a hostile crowd gathered to hiss, jostle, heave rotten eggs, and force the Lincoln supporters to seek police protection and abandon their gathering."[4]

The Douglas Democrats were unable to shake the yoke of their nominee's doctrine of popular sovereignty, that animating spirit of the 1854 Kansas-Nebraska Act and decidedly unpopular piece of legislation among the southern members of the party. In an almost unprecedented move in an era when candidates left campaigning to surrogates, Douglas gave speeches in September in Frederick, in western Maryland—where he was feted by "roar of cannon"—and in Baltimore, but his campaign's inability to forge an alliance with Bell's Constitutional Unionists doomed any chance of a strong showing in Maryland. The Constitutional Unionist message of fealty to Union and Constitution, all else be damned, resonated well in Maryland—despite the party's trite campaign slogan, "Our Bell rings to the sound of Union. Try it."[5]

The Breckinridge message in Maryland was directed largely to the state's slaveholder constituency. His surrogates in the Democratic Party attacked both Douglas and Bell as untrustworthy on the matter of slavery protection and advocated a "friendly federal attitude toward slavery, especially in the territories," wrote William Evitts. Breckinridge's plurality in the state on election day, however, was not a reliable barometer of Marylanders' sentiments about sectional alignment, for his campaign had successfully appealed to Baltimore voters attracted by allying with state Democratic efforts at municipal reforms of the police and election and judicial procedures.[6]

On election day, Breckinridge captured 42,482 Maryland votes, thereby winning all eight of Maryland's electoral votes. He won 49.1 percent of the vote in Baltimore, representing 35.2 percent of his statewide total. Bell ran a close second with 41,760 votes, while Douglas finished a distant third with 5,996 votes and Lincoln fourth with 2,294 (more than 47 percent of which were from Baltimore City). His national victory was poorly received in counties in southern Maryland and on the lower Eastern Shore, nine of which gave him three votes or less.[7]

The 1860 election results in Maryland reveal the paradox of robust Unionism and distaste for Lincoln's Republican principles: Unionist John Bell won almost as many votes as southern Democrat John Breckinridge, while men in Beantown, in Charles County, passed a resolution demanding that Lincoln voters leave the county by year's end. One striking development was a relatively peaceful Baltimore election, after years of full-on, election-day battles between the city's political gangs: "In the Sixth Ward there were some symptoms of disorder, but the police promptly interfered and suppressed it by carrying the principal actors to the station-house," reported the *Baltimore Sun*. "All the discussions and conversations were carried on in the best feeling and in a moderate tone of voice. The crowds continued throughout the day without the least disorder," related the *Baltimore Daily Exchange* on November 5. The most dramatic incident was the wounding of a policeman in an accidental shooting by a colleague unholstering his revolver after being struck by a spittoon hurled from Bell headquarters.[8]

More than 70 percent of Lincoln's votes in Maryland came from Baltimore City and Allegany County, in the west; in seven counties, he received no votes at all.[9] The state went overwhelmingly for Breckinridge and Bell, who were separated by a mere 522 votes—the Kentuckian the states' rights darling of the Deep South, the Tennessean the patrician of a fledging party spewing pablum about Union and little else. Some Maryland Unionists who backed the right to own slaves were distressed by the refusal of some northern and border states to enforce the Fugitive Slave Law (enacted in 1793 and strengthened in the Compromise of 1850), but they were Unionists nonetheless and cast their ballots accordingly. Breckinridge took sixteen of Maryland's twenty-one counties by a combined margin of only 1,830 votes, winning the state because Bell suffered at the hands of Baltimore voters attracted to the reformist policies of the Democrats. Breckinridge's plurality was more a result of this Democratic alliance than any ideological divisions in the Maryland electorate.[10]

The results of the election in Maryland were striking in one crucial aspect: A clear majority—54.2 percent—of Maryland ballots were collectively cast for the three Unionist candidates, and thus Breckinridge's plurality of just under 46 percent cannot be seen as an endorsement of disunion or secession. In fact, many Marylanders, and especially Baltimoreans, saw no contradiction in the simultaneous embrace of Unionism and slavery, and as would be the case throughout most of the Civil War period, many planters remained loyal as long as their state constitution sanctioned ownership of slaves and, in tandem with the Fugitive Slave Law, thereby offered protection for their business and property interests. The outcome of the 1860 election in Maryland, the antipathy of the state's voters for Abraham Lincoln notwithstanding, would be one of many developments that would gainsay the traditional neo-Confederate narrative of Maryland as a Confederate state-in-waiting. Marylanders remained faithful to their vision of a united nation by casting more than half their ballots for the three men who believed as they did.

Maryland newspapers of the period reveal widespread Unionist sentiment in the autumn of 1860, even from those that advocated a right of secession. Of two papers in Centreville, in Queen Anne's County on the Eastern Shore, one rejected South Carolina's seemingly inexorable march to leave the Union, while the other urged that differences be resolved inside the Union: "We look upon the action of South Carolina as unconstitutional and unworthy of the support or sympathy of Maryland," wrote the *Centreville Advocate* shortly after Lincoln's election. The *Centreville Times* preached the importance of Maryland's resolving any differences inside the Union: "Lincoln is elected, and it becomes us, as law-abiding citizens to submit quietly and await the result . . . should the North attempt to subvert our rights it will be ample time to speak of redress, and even dissolution will be madness. Redress in the Union is possible, and, if rightly sought, certain; out of it, impossible." The *Frederick Herald* exalted in mid-November: "We say hold on to the Union!" Baltimore offered readers nine daily newspapers, some published by political parties, such as the American Party's *Clipper,* and the city's German community enjoyed two papers in their language. The *Baltimore Sun*—critical of Lincoln and supportive of Southern goals—and the *Baltimore American and Commercial Advertiser,* an unabashed backer of Lincoln and Unionist ideology, likely had the widest readership and were thus the most influential.[11]

UNIONISM ASCENDANT

Despite the exit of the Deep South states in December and early 1861, no Maryland leaders emerged to mobilize secession fervor into political and civic action, for many saw that the 1860 election results in the state were no endorsement of southern political goals. "The Breckinridge victory in the State had little significance as an index to the extent of secession sentiment among the people at that time," wrote William Seabrook, the commissioner of Maryland's Land Office. "There were few secessionists per se in the State at that time, the people generally having desired the perpetuity of the Union. I believe that thousands of those who voted for Breckinridge would have done otherwise if they had supposed their ballots in his favor would have been construed as an exhibition of hostility to the Union." Bell, Lincoln, and Douglas men buried the hatchet post-election to back the Union cause: Leading citizens such as author and former congressman, lawyer, and novelist John P. Kennedy; lawyer and state historical society founder Brantz Mayer; Comptroller William Purnell; Governor Hicks; Senator James Pearce; future governor Augustus Bradford; Congressman Henry May; and former US attorney general and senator Reverdy Johnson (the latter two Douglas Democrats) attended meetings of loyal men and lent their voices to efforts to keep their Union intact.[12]

As 1861 dawned, the *Baltimore American and Commercial Advertiser* sounded a strong call for the Union:

> There appears to be a fixed determination, upon the part of some of our sister States, to sever the political bonds of the Union which was formed by the wisdom of our ancestors. Such action threatens to involve our country in that worst of evils, civil war; therefore it is resolved: we do not recognize the success of the Republican party as a cause for dissolution . . . We believe any existing grievance that is or has been inflicted upon the South can be more fully redressed in the Union than out of it . . . We hereby pledge ourselves to maintain our position as citizens of the United States. We furthermore are determined to maintain inviolate the present Constitution and the Union.[13]

And the *Baltimore Daily Exchange*, whose editor, Baltimore lawyer William Wilkins Glenn, was generally sympathetic to the southern political goals, proclaimed its adherence to the Constitution in the days following the election: "though we in common with the South have just reason to feel aggrieved at the treatment we have received from the North, we do unhesitatingly assert that we have not yet been driven to the point at which revolution alone can remedy the wrongs of a people. We do aver, therefore, that Baltimore has not by her vote yesterday sanctioned any disunion scheme or sentiment whatsoever . . . she will only be the ally of the South, so long as the latter seeks to right herself through the laws under the Constitution."[14]

Unionist feelings abounded statewide as meetings of "Workingmen" in Baltimore, Towson, and Annapolis roundly condemned secession. Papers around Maryland voiced similar sentiments: "We all wish that the Union shall be preserved intact," wrote the *Baltimore Sun* in November.[15] The pro-Breckinridge *Kent Conservator* on the Eastern Shore was even more outspoken, proclaiming that, though editors' sympathies were with their "southern brethren," the state was opposed to secession.[16] "Hold on a little longer," the *Frederick Herald* advised its readers.[17]

Unionist sentiment was, of course, not monolithic. Several papers openly backed a right to secede. The Patapsco *Enterprise,* a pro-Breckinridge paper in Baltimore, observed that since secession could be achieved peacefully before Lincoln's inauguration on March 4, Maryland should leave the Union immediately and thereby avoid northern "fanaticism."[18] The weekly *Catholic Mirror* announced on December 1, in comments that would later land its publishers, Michael J. Kelly and John P. Piet, in Fort McHenry for "printing works of a 'treasonable character,'" that the Union should be broken apart rather than allowing the Republicans to "destroy what we believe to be southern State Rights" (an opposite sentiment from its position just prior to the election, when the editors wondered "what true American could be insane and vicious enough to arrest this country's march to greatness by destroying her unity?").[19] The *Baltimore American and Commercial Advertiser* published a petition on New Year's Eve from eleven Maryland state senators urging Governor Hicks to summon the legislature.

Clearly Marylanders were struggling to make sense of the times. "No one who did not live South of the Mason-Dixon Line can comprehend the feeling from the election of Lincoln to the beginning of March," wrote Libertus Van Bokkelen, a Presbyterian minister and educator in Maryland. "The indefinable feeling of uneasiness and alarm which sprang up in the southern states as a result of the election of Lincoln was very noticeable in Maryland," noted Hicks's biographer, while another historian described the state's mood as "gloomy . . . and dumb silence . . . followed by a gradual reawakening of public sentiment to the seriousness of the situation."[20]

Hicks himself would recite his ambiguous position in testimony in February 1861 before a congressional committee investigating plots against the national government. "I am a slaveholder, and have been the owner of slaves since I was 21 years old; and my sympathies are with the south," he testified. "That I say to the world. But I am a Union man, and would live and die in the Union." J. Hanson Thomas, a physician, banker, and state legislator, saw a struggle between good and evil: "I have just returned from Washington. There seems to be no chance for an honorable adjustment of our present difficulties. God help us!—for we seem to be possessed of the devil; and nothing but Divine interposition can save us from total disruption to civil war."[21]

Union meetings occurred in December and January in Baltimore and in the western Maryland cities of Frederick and Cumberland. A petition from Unionist leaders in Anne Arundel County endorsed Hicks's refusal to call the legislature into special session: "The undersigned, citizens of Anne Arundel county, beg leave to express to your Excellency their full approval of the course you have pursued on the subject of calling an Extra Session of the Legislature," read their entreaty. "And they assure your Excellency that they confide in your patriotism and discretion to preserve for us and our children . . . the integrity of our glorious and happy Union."[22] In November Hicks had explained his posture on such a legislative assembly: "I cannot but believe that the convening of the Legislature in extra session at this time would only have the effect of increasing and reviving the excitement now pervading the country. . . . it would at once be heralded by the sensitive newspapers and alarmists throughout the country as evidence that Maryland had abandoned all hope of the Union and was preparing to join the traitors to destroy it." Hicks cited conversations with fellow citizens that gave him "no hesitation in declaring it as my opinion that an immense majority, of all parties, are decidedly opposed to the assembling of the Legislature at this time."[23]

That Maryland had plenty of Unionists who either owned slaves or supported a right of secession illustrated the complexity of slavery as a defining matter. Many Marylanders associated themselves with both constituencies. The institution enjoyed federal and state constitutional protection. Considering the long and essentially indefensible northern border with Pennsylvania, a Union naval blockade of the growing port of Baltimore (simultaneously applying a chokehold on other segments of the economy such as financial services that had evolved to support the city's maritime commerce) and a Union army interdicting movement of goods toward the Ohio Valley via the Baltimore & Ohio Railroad and the Chesapeake & Ohio Canal, many believed continued prosperity rested with the Union.

Lincoln's friend Joseph Medill underscored the importance of Maryland to the Union cause in a December 26 letter to the president-elect, less than a week following South Carolina's secession: "The secession epidemic is spreading with fearful rapidity and violence thro' the Slave States, and if Maryland gives way your friends will have to fight their way with the sword from the Pa. line to the Capitol. And rather than let the rebels hold possession of Washington and exclude the rightful Administration, it were better to lay wast [*sic*] Maryland to reach here." Medill concluded with comments about "the vicious rabble" in Baltimore and that "a reign of terror will domineer over the city."[24]

A commercial alliance between Marylanders and South Carolinians was sown in the aftermath of Lincoln's election. The latter began arming themselves, to the delight of Baltimore hardware firm Magruder, Taylor & Roberts— "a Dirk knife with six-inch blade & belt & scabbard," and "six Colts Repeaters six shooters at as low figgers as you can," read one order. Another customer sought fortification of a different nature: "You will please send us one Pound strong essence Jamaica Rum by Adams Express Co. as we . . . can not get it in Charleston nor Columbia." Some Marylanders rushed to show solidarity with the Carolinians. "We desire to have some Palmetto flags made here. Please send us immediately a copy of one drawn in colors, or a small flag. We appreciate the pluck of the gallant little South Carolina. Send us her flag—*we are ready to defend it!*" extolled some Baltimoreans in mid-November.[25]

The commercial overtones of this partnership acquired a political dimension, as South Carolina tried to lure an Upper South slave state from the Union. The *Charleston Courier* announced that "a Palmetto tree, drawn in colors by Col. E. B. White, was sent to Baltimore on Thursday . . . this handsome token of amity and friendship . . . will be placed, as we understand, alongside the Colonial flag of Maryland." Further Carolinian gratitude came by way of praise for Maryland footwear: "Baltimore made boots and shoes are noted in the Charleston papers as superceding similar Northern manufactures." Marylanders reciprocated by offering at least a thousand soldiers from their National Volunteers, whose members were loyal to the Union but believed that others had a right to leave it, while Philip Harry Lee, who claimed descent from Light Horse Harry Lee of "revolutionary memory," offered 1,300 Light Horse National Volunteers from Baltimore.[26]

Another contribution from Maryland appeared in mid-December by way of a pamphlet by John Pendleton Kennedy that outlined a scheme by which the border states could present their own set of grievances while opposing Union attempts to coerce any seceded states. This plan would create a central confederacy that could serve as an engine of unity between the sections: "Supposing a disintegration of the Union. . . . The Border States, in that event, would form, in self-defense, a Confederacy of their own, which would serve as a centre of reinforcement for the reconstruction of the Union." Kennedy envisioned that New York and states as far west as Illinois, and perhaps further, "would be unable to resist the tendency toward this centre." Though this plan may have been part of the rationale for the Washington Peace Conference that would convene in February, this writer has found no evidence that this plan was ever realized, perhaps because no leaders emerged to oversee its implementation, it failed to attract sufficient support from those in government who held political power and, once war erupted in the spring of 1861, its adherents (especially in Maryland) may have recognized the center's vulnerable position between the warring sections. Hicks's biographer asserts that he corresponded with the governors of Virginia, Tennessee, Kentucky, and Missouri about "some manner of cooperation among the border slave states which would have for its object, the bringing about of a compromise between the parties of the North and South," but he was criticized both for the idea and for refusing to consult the legislature about it.[27]

"MARYLAND IS THIS DAY . . . TRUE TO THE AMERICAN UNION"

The departure of South Carolina in December 1860 and other Deep South states early in 1861 (Florida, Mississippi, Alabama, Louisiana, Texas, and Georgia) did not go unnoticed by Maryland leaders in politics, business, and civic life. Governor Hicks, having made clear his disapproval of secession in principle, opposed South Carolina's. "Should I be compelled to witness the downfall of that Government inherited from our fathers, established, as it were, by the special favor of God?" he thundered. "I will at least have the consolation, in my dying hour, that I neither by word nor deed assisted in hastening its disruption."[28] The governor's posture was endorsed in January by the Episcopal bishop of Maryland, William Whittingham, who recounted his recent meeting with leaders of ten Maryland counties: "Without any exception, I have found convictions of the present duty and policy of Maryland, in the main agreeing with those expressed by your address," he wrote to Hicks. "May I be allowed to say that in my own opinion your forcible, frank, manly and true-hearted statement of your policy, and the grounds on which it has been adopted and will be maintained, cannot but be attended (under the Divine blessing) with the happiest results?"[29] The Baltimore business community, with some dissenters, supported the governor's refusal to convene the legislature, as 1,300 businessmen and others signed a petition to that effect in December and another 5,000-plus followed suit in January.[30]

Further pleas came from Anna Ella Carroll, a prominent Eastern Shore

CHARLES W. MITCHELL

Know Nothing who reminded Hicks that "although you were opposed to the election of Mr. Lincoln, you are for maintaining this Union," and a letter in the *Baltimore Sun* that applauded the governor's position, lest convening the lawmakers "bring ruin upon us all."[31]

Though the legislative corridors in Annapolis were quiet, much was stirring in Washington, where committees from the House and Senate were devising strategies to prevent other Deep South and Upper South border states from severing ties with the Union. An ad hoc group of congressmen from the latter constituency—including Congressman J. Morrison Harris of Baltimore, a member of the Know Nothing Party, lawyer, and leading southern Unionist who served as secretary and kept rough notes of the proceedings—met three times, on December 28, 1860, and January 3 and 4, 1861. This "Border State Plan" attempted to reassure the South on the sanctity of slavery by strengthening the Fugitive Slave Law and protecting it in Washington, DC; prohibiting Congress from interfering with the return of slaves, as Lincoln had promised during his presidential campaign (rather than proposing a slave code ensuring congressional protection); amending the Missouri Compromise line of 36°30′ to extend through existing territories; and allowing people living in territories acquired after the Mexican War to choose how they would deal with slavery as they organized to join the United States—this latter proposal a nod to the doctrine of popular sovereignty that Illinois senator Stephen Douglas had enshrined in the Kansas-Nebraska Act in 1854.[32]

Though the Border State Plan temporarily tantalized the delegates as a means of averting separation, it went too far in appeasing the South. The Republicans therefore rejected it. North Carolinian John Gilmer, serving on the Border State Committee, described the grim mood in Washington to a friend: "Northern extreme men are working night and day to defeat all Compromises. Southern extreme men do the same thing, and send telegraph dispatches out South to excite and inflame our people to the utmost tension. The fury and madness of the South hourly becomes more and more aggravated. . . . We are in real trouble. There is real danger at hand. . . . I often shed tears in silence."[33]

As calendars turned to 1861, tempers were on edge: Fisticuffs erupted between a US senator from Georgia and the nation's top military official. "Mr [Robert] Toombs & Genl [Winfield] Scott had a bout at No. 4 (John R's)," recounted Elizabeth Blair Lee, daughter of Montgomery Blair. "The first called

94

the Old Hero a liar—whereupon the Genl rushed into him—Civil War seems inevitable—even at friendly dinner parties" (fortunately for the good senator, the dispute went no further, for General Scott then tipped the scales at close to three hundred pounds).[34]

Signs of Maryland Unionism were prevalent. A resolution emanating from an early January meeting of all Maryland counties declared that "Maryland is this day, as she ever had been, true to the American Union; that she will exert all her influence for its peaceful preservation."[35] Irrepressible Frederick Unionists resolved to prevent an effort "to commit 'noble old Maryland' to any sectional issue" that would expel the state from the "broad aegis of the Constitution and the laws."[36] Congressman J. Morrison Harris announced that "the movement in some of the southern States . . . has none of my sympathy, and no particle of my approval." Addressing the US House of Representatives, he allied himself with the southern Unionists whose voices were increasingly influential in the border states such as Maryland, and he took direct aim at South Carolina: "I stand here as a southern man; and my State, a southern State, hangs upon the brink of a precipice," he thundered, "because of the intemperate, the unnecessary action of an extreme southern State, that has chosen to realize her dream of thirty years in this matter of secession." Harris's retort to a challenge from his Maryland colleague, Congressman George W. Hughes, drew applause from the galleries: "At this moment, according to my honest, and I believe well-informed judgment upon the subject, the doctrine of secession cannot, in the State of Maryland, to-day raise more friends than would make up a corporal's guard."[37]

Though Governor Hicks's ongoing refusal to align his state with either side still brought forth a chorus of cries that he allow the Maryland General Assembly (a divisive body whose 1860 session had been chaotic and violent) to deliberate, he had plenty of support as the new year dawned. "Public property and even private is in danger, and personal safety is at a discount should the legislature of this state be brought together," wrote a friend of the governor, who feared that the legislature would send emissaries to the seceded states and thereby legitimize them. Hicks found further support from the endorsements of President James Buchanan, US senator John Crittenden of Kentucky, and former president Franklin Pierce.[38]

The Washington Peace Conference, convened by Virginia, opened in the nation's capital on February 4, 1861—"thus was born the last, sad effort to avert war," wrote historian Allan Nevins. Amid rumors of plots to seize the capital, 132 men crammed into Willard's Concert Hall, adjacent to the Willard Hotel, though the Deep South states, busy organizing their new government in Montgomery, refused to attend. The Pacific states of California and Oregon abstained, citing the distances their representatives would have to travel. In the chair was former president John Tyler, still a slaveowner; on the floor were seven Maryland delegates appointed by Governor Hicks to represent their state, some still harboring grandiose ambitions that Maryland could play a role as crisis mediator: Reverdy Johnson, Augustus Bradford, William Goldsborough, John Crisfield, J. Dixon Roman, John Dent, and Benjamin Howard—distinguished men who overall gave the state's presence a Unionist mien.[39]

Reverdy Johnson, former US senator and US attorney general and no secessionist, cautioned against any efforts by the federal government to coerce states. John Crisfield, a moderate Eastern Shore congressman and railroad president from Somers Cove, proclaimed that Maryland wished to "stand by the Union."[40] (Maryland would convene its own peace conference on February 18, though following a brief session it adjourned until March 12, to meet earlier only if Virginia were to secede. Though the conference did reconvene on March 12 to pass a handful of resolutions—one of which pronounced that any attempts by the Union to "retake any forts seized by the Confederacy would in itself be an entire dissolution of the compact of the Constitution"—it accomplished little other than an agreement to monitor Virginia's action.)[41]

The environment was hardly conducive to a search for peace. Chairman Tyler was elected a delegate to Virginia's Secession Convention the same day the Peace Conference opened and would ultimately vote to support Virginia's secession. Winfield Scott, the aged general-in-chief of the army, deployed 700 troops around the Capitol and fretted that more were needed. Tyler bickered with President Buchanan over a parade announced in the Washington papers for February 21, Tyler opposing its militaristic trappings and the indecisive, pro-southern Buchanan prodded by fiery New York congressman Daniel Sickles to let it go forward. Horace Greeley, the unctuous editor of the New York *Tribune*, was "unimpressed by this array of great and onetime great, (and) damned the gathering as an 'Old Gentlemen's Convention' of 'political fossils' disinterred only because of the shock of the secession movement." Governor Hicks told Lincoln friend William H. L. Wallace that "if the conference adjourned without doing anything . . . he should immediately call the Legislature of his state together & the state would at once secede." This attempt to forestall conflict failed as well, as compromise appeared increasingly impossible—and five Virginia congressmen, whose state had convened the meeting, opposed its proposals.[42]

Entreaties from the South urged Maryland to collaborate with the new Confederacy, or at least with Virginia. "Can there not be found men bold and brave enough in Maryland to unite with Virginians in seizing the Capitol at Washington?" snorted the *Richmond Enquirer,* a cannon of Confederate propaganda often aimed at the loyal border states. At a celebration of Washington's birthday in the southern county of St. Mary's, Thomas Gough proclaimed that "Maryland and Virginia having grown together in prosperity, they should cling together in adversity," while Maj. John Milburn expressed the sentiment of a southern-rights Marylander: "Our rights in the Union, if we can, but our rights in or out of the Union." A doctor in Bladensburg, Maryland, bloviated that "noble South Carolina has done her duty bravely. Now Virginia and Maryland must immediately raise an armed force sufficient to control the district, and never allow Abe Lincoln to set foot on its soil."[43] Confederate emissaries were enticing border states to join their new venture, and the president-elect's choice for secretary of state, William Seward, was quietly making it known that he, rather than the unpolished Illinois prairie lawyer, was the man to talk with on the topic of relations with the Confederacy.

Earlier, Illinois congressman Elihu Washburne expressed worry over matters in Maryland. "To my observation things look more threatening to-day than ever," he had written to Lincoln on January 10. "I believe Va. and Maryland men are both rotten to the core. We have had one of our friends from N.Y. (the kind I wrote about) in Baltimore, sounding matters there, and he gives most unfavorable reports. *Great danger is to be apprehended from that quarter.* The very worst secessionists and traitors at heart, are *pretended Union* men." At Fort McHenry in February, Capt. John C. Robinson recalled how "the officers at the post were on friendly and visiting terms with some of the leading families of Baltimore, but when secession became the harbinger of war, they found many of these acquaintances were intensely Southern in their feelings, and ready to unite with the seceding States in their efforts to destroy the Union." On the fifteenth of that month, Worthington Snethen, a leading Republican in Baltimore, urged caution in a letter to Lincoln: "it has been deemed unadvisable, in the present state of things, to attempt any organized display on our part, as Republicans, on the occasion of your approach to, and perhaps through, Baltimore, on your way to the Capitol." A member of the Shriver family of Union Mills, Christopher Columbus Shriver, reminded his cousin, Frederick, that "self preservation is the first law of the land," and that "the Stars and Stripes ain't doing their duty and we must disown them."[44]

Others despaired over what they saw as a leadership void in Maryland on the direction the state should take. William Wilkins Glenn, whose criticisms earned several visits with federal authorities at Fort McHenry, complained that "every one saw that matters were getting worse daily and still nobody in Maryland at least dreamed of the terrible revolution into which we were drifting," he wrote in early February. "What astonished me most was that there were no leaders in Maryland who were willing to take a prominent part or act independently. There was but one opinion. Everyone said 'Wait for Virginia. See what she does.'" Edward Spencer, a farmer near Randallstown in Baltimore County, wrote to Anna Bradford Harrison of Easton, whom he was courting, of his frustration at what he saw as an inevitable Civil War.[45]

As Lincoln was completing his rail journey east from Springfield, Illinois, to Washington in early February to be inaugurated, his advisors caught wind of a plot to assassinate him upon arrival in Baltimore as he changed rail stations in the city, again placing Maryland at the center of national affairs. When first informed, the president-elect insisted on meeting his remaining commitments—speeches at a flag-raising ceremony at Independence Hall in Philadelphia and to the Pennsylvania General Assembly at Harrisburg—but agreed to alter his itinerary by passing through Baltimore on an overnight train. He may have been unaware of General Scott's bravado in the face of threats against the inauguration: "Present my compliments to Mr. Lincoln when you return to Springfield, and tell him I expect him to come on to Washington as soon as he is ready," he told Lincoln's emissary, Thomas Mather, the adjutant general of Illinois. "Say to him that I'll look after those Maryland and Virginia rangers myself; I'll plant cannon at both ends of Pennsylvania Avenue, and if any of them show their heads or raise a finger I'll blow them to hell."[46]

Though Lincoln arrived safely in Washington, he had handed his enemies an opportunity to parody him as a coward—in a nineteenth-century version of "fake news," one reporter falsely accused Lincoln of disguising himself in a "Scotch kilt" during the journey. Further ridicule spewed forth when a Chicago railroad detective, Allan Pinkerton, later spun a fanciful tale of a plot orchestrated by an Italian barber, Cypriano Ferrandina, who plied his tonsorial trade in Baltimore's fancy Barnum's Hotel, and that he, Pinkerton, set up shop as a "Stock Broker" and claimed that one of his operatives infiltrated the plotters. Newspapers were then as scathing as tabloids of any era; one described the episode as "More Ass-ass-in-nation." Pinkerton would write three versions of his adventures with the "Baltimore plot," each more grandiose than the last, and his inflated opinion of himself would continue to balloon when he became the self-appointed chief of the fledgling US Secret Service during the Civil War and intelligence-gatherer for the Army of the Potomac.[47]

Compounding the rising tensions was a deteriorating national economic climate that did not spare the state. The prior fall, Baltimore banks had suspended specie payment, and two had suspended business. Activity in the city's port was contracting. Companies manufacturing and selling firearms were an exception, as orders flooded in from throughout the South: "those of our merchants who are engaged in the sale of fire-arms have their hands full of orders. Not a mail arrives from the South but comes charged with orders from all sections of that country for guns and pistols."[48] Elizabeth Patterson Bonaparte, the wife of Napoleon Bonaparte's younger brother, Jerome, received a letter in Paris from William Mentzel, the manager of her properties in Baltimore, describing difficulties collecting her rents: "Our Country is in such a state that it is almost impossible to get money, owing to the fact that no business is doing," he wrote in early March 1861. "I have been compelled to take dribs on account running daily after them, and in some instances to take Virginia money which is at 6 per cent discount, for fear I should get none if I refused."[49]

Baltimore County farmer Edward Spencer lashed out at Lincoln about economic conditions: "No one has any idea of the distress in Baltimore. There are 8000 persons unemployed, and as many more working on half-time. If there should occur any disturbance it will be awful, for men become fiends when bread is lacking," he wrote to Anna Harrison on March 28, barely three weeks after Lincoln had been inaugurated. Referring to the new president as "that infamous clown in the White House," Spencer made no effort to mask his sentiments, telling Anna that "it makes me savage when I think we have fallen so low as to have such a man for President." A desperate woman wrote to Baltimore mayor George Brown, begging for employment for her husband: "I am compelled from poverty to be separated from husband & child, weighed down with troubles & misfortunes," wrote Mrs. Henry Cox in February. "Can you not give my husband some employment. If so, oh how happy I should be & the prayers of a grateful heart would ever be offered up for your happiness & prosperity. My heart is too full to say more."[50]

Marylanders—few of whom had voted for Lincoln—were keen to see what the new president would say in his March 4 inaugural address. John Pendleton Kennedy was impressed: "In the evening we get Lincoln's inaugural. It is conciliatory and firm—promising peace, but brooking no purpose to visit aggression against the Government." He seconded his observation the following day, March 5: "I read the Inaugural again and like it better. I think its tone is dignified and truthful, and its spirit for promotion of concord."[51]

Though Maryland congressmen voted unanimously for a proposed Thirteenth Amendment to the Constitution that would have permanently left the matter of slavery to the states, this last effort at sectional compromise was left writhing in defeat on the floor of the US Senate, in a vote taken in the early dawn of March 4, the day of Lincoln's inauguration. Loyal Marylanders awaited events with anxiety and foreboding, and none crystallized the dangers facing a Confederate Maryland more succinctly than John Pendleton Kennedy, whose contemplation of the situation poured out of a pamphlet published in May: "Out of this Union, there is nothing but ruin for [Maryland],"wrote the ardent Unionist. "If Maryland should be a member of that Confederacy, then the North, in time of war, may also shut up the Chesapeake against us; and not only that, but may also shut up our Western and Northern railroads. It may deny us the Ohio River; it may deny us access to Philadelphia, to New York & utterly obliterate our trade, but cut off our provisions."[52] Kennedy's recitation of the Union's punitive action against a seceded Maryland would find little rebuttal, even from the most enthusiastic advocates of secession who, as they paid homage to the chimera of "states' rights," acknowledged the accuracy of his analysis.

Newspaper editorial boards, prominent citizens, and even Governor Hicks advocated a posture of neutrality that would see Maryland either as an arbiter between North and South or simply sitting out any conflict. "As far as we have been able to gather the sentiment of the people of Maryland," the *Frederick Herald* had editorialized in November, "we think one thing is manifest, that while they do not think that the election of Lincoln to the Presidency is sufficient cause for any Southern State to secede, they will oppose the use of measures to coerce a State into the Union . . . though Maryland should assume a position of neutrality, it should be one of *armed neutrality*." Allan Bowie Davis, a prominent Montgomery County planter, wrote to his son, William Wilkins Davis, a student at St. James Academy in Hagerstown: "It is a great misfortune that we have at such a time a President for whom we cannot entertain political sympathy & hardly personal respect—it greatly weakens the chance of sustaining the government," he wrote in mid-April. "I think as Marylanders we should if possible keep out of the contest—but this may not be practicable." Leonidas Dodson, an Eastern Shore Unionist, believed that Governor Hicks should call up Maryland militia only with a promise from Lincoln that "these troops shall be held only to preserve the peace of Md and protect the District of Columbia. This is in my view the course of prudence, and will have the effect to make Md a sort of armed neutrality," read an April diary entry. Hicks had indicated his interest in mediating any conflict, in a January 1861 letter to the Rev. William Whittingham: "It is my purpose, so far as I am able to do so, to keep Maryland out of strife that now seems to be inevitable; not only, that she may be free from the horrors of civil war; but also that she may continue to be, in a position to mediate between the hostile sections. I have lost almost all faith in the disposition of Congress to settle our troubles."[53]

Emissaries of the Confederate states dispatched to inveigle Maryland leaders to join their cause included A. H. Handy of Mississippi and Alabama's commissioner for Maryland, Ambrose Wright. Wright's report on his visit to Governor Hicks in March revealed the latter's predilection for some sort of neutral position that would keep Maryland out of any conflict: "I regret to say that I found him not only opposed to the secession of Maryland from the Federal Union, but that if she should withdraw from the Union he advised and would urge her to confederate with the Middle States in the formation of a central confederacy," Wright told his government in Montgomery. Hicks himself stated that "we have violated no rights of either section. We have been loyal to the Union. The unhappy contest between the two sections has not been tormented or encouraged by us, although we have suffered from it in the past," he would pronounce at the special legislative session in Frederick in the spring of 1861, which he had called on April 22. "The impending war has not come by any act or wish of ours. We have done all we could to avert it. We have hoped that Maryland . . . might have acted as mediator between the extremes of both sections and thus have prevented the terrible evils of a prolonged civil war."[54]

On the evening of April 12, 1860, with the bombardment of Fort Sumter in Charleston Harbor under way, English journalist William Howard Russell arrived in Baltimore, and took a room at the Eutaw House. "After breakfast I was visited by some gentlemen of Baltimore, who were highly delighted with the news," he wrote, "and I learned from them that there was a high probability of their State joining those which had seceded. The whole feeling of the landed and respectable classes is with the South. The dislike to the federal government at Washington is largely spiced with personal ridicule and contempt of Mr. Lincoln."[55] That morning, as the Baltimoreans conversed with the visiting newspaperman, a large Union meeting was preparing to convene in Carroll County "without distinction of party," to pass resolutions declaring South Carolina's secession "premature," approving of Hicks's course, supporting the Union and opposing a Maryland secession.[56]

The Confederate attack on Fort Sumter and Maj. Robert Anderson's heroic defensive stand breathed new life into Union sentiment in Maryland: "There was great excitement in Baltimore [and] the general feeling was against the action of South Carolina," recorded William Wilkins Glenn, who noted that William T. Walters, a Baltimore liquor dealer, marked the moment by "collecting subscriptions for the purpose of firing a salute in honor of the occasion." John Pendleton Kennedy wrote that "Maryland . . . must soon become a Free State, and she will then be found to be wholly ungenial to the principle upon which the Southern Confederacy is established." Primary source materials, such as letters, diaries, and period newspapers—and the fact that three times as many Maryland men would fight for the Union as for the Confederacy— suggest that such sentiment, though by no means universal, was the prevailing one in Maryland.[57]

Southern bravado was, however, the animating spirit at the Maryland Club in Baltimore, whose members were said to be "elated at the news" of Sumter's fall at an April 14 dinner at the club that Russell described as a "secessionist evening." Citizens of St. Mary's County, in the labor-intensive land of tobacco in southern Maryland, rejoiced at the fort's surrender, as "the wildest enthusiasm broke forth among our people . . . the bells rang out a merry peal and [Riley's] 'Rifles' fired several volleys in honor of the event," related the *St. Mary's Beacon*. "We have never witnessed an excitement more general and intense . . . it indicates in the most unmistakable manner that the sympathies of our people are exclusively with the South."[58]

Despite the traditional dominance of the planter aristocracy over Maryland's mid-century politics, structural and institutional obstacles thwarted any serious move toward Maryland secession. Members of the state's congressional delegation were integral players in efforts at compromise designed to avoid war, as they—along with leaders in state politics and the business and civic communities—recognized both the advantages to remaining in the Union and the destructive forces poised to rain down upon a Confederate Maryland. Over the course of the war, the evolution of the state's progressive political dynamics would reach a point where emancipation, enacted by the legislature, would take effect on November 1, 1864. A week later, Abraham Lincoln would win reelection with 55.1 percent of the popular vote in Maryland and nationally—as Marylanders, ever practical, realized their fortunes envisioned in the nation's founding principles.

NOTES

1. The legislature was in session only during the early months of even-numbered years and could not otherwise convene legally unless the governor called a special session.

2. *Baltimore Wecker*, October 13 and 16, 1860; *Der Deutsche Correspondent*, April 15, December 15, and December 22, 1860, in Jean H. Baker, *The Politics of Continuity* (Baltimore: Johns Hopkins University Press, 1973), 35, 38.

3. Board of Trade, Annual Report, 1860, 5; Corn and Flour Exchange Annual Report, 1860, 5, in William B. Catton, "The Baltimore Business Community and the Secession Crisis, 1860–1861." M.A. thesis, University of Maryland, College Park, MD, 1952, 44; *Baltimore Clipper*, November 24, 1860, in Catton, "Baltimore Business Community," 56.

4. *Baltimore American and Commercial Advertiser*, November 2, 1860, and *Baltimore Wecker*, November 1, 1860, in Baker, *The Politics of Continuity* (Baltimore: Johns Hopkins University Press, 1973), 36 (cayenne sticks); *Baltimore American and Commercial Advertiser*, November 1, 1860, in William J. Evitts, *A Matter of Allegiances: Maryland from 1850 to 1861*, 142 (October parade); *Baltimore Clipper*, October 30 and November 2, 1860, in Catton, "Baltimore Business Community," 49. See Catton, 49–50, for mention of several early Republican backers in Baltimore, including lumber and coal dealer Francis S. Corkran, cabinetmaker Philip Hiss, lumber merchant A. J. Randolph, and marine underwriter and Quaker James Carey Cole.

5. *Baltimore American and Commercial Advertiser*, May 15, 1860, in Baker, *Politics of Continuity*, 41.

6. Evitts, *Matter of Allegiances*, 145; Baker, *Politics of Continuity*, 27. Baker implies on page 43 that Democratic reform efforts in Baltimore may have been somewhat disingenuous, as they were "under the guise of a nonpartisan reform party first organized in 1857."

7. Of Lincoln's votes, 1,083 came from Baltimore City and 522 from Allegany County. In the Eastern Shore and Southern Maryland counties of Howard, Prince George's, Worcester, Somerset, Kent, Queen Anne's, and Calvert, Lincoln received no votes. See *Baltimore Sun*, November 12, 1860,

for contemporaneous county totals in Maryland, and the discussion of the campaigns and results in Evitts, *Matter of Allegiances,* 139–53.

8. *Baltimore Sun,* December 3, 1860 (Beantown resolution); *Baltimore Daily Exchange,* November 5, 1860, in Catton, "Baltimore Business Community," 52; *Baltimore Sun,* November 7, 1860 (spittoon).

9. Evitts, *Matter of Allegiances,* 150 (calculated from Table 2).

10. Evitts, *Matter of Allegiances,* 168, 149. Evitts points out (149–53) that while the Democrats allied themselves with the forces of reform, Bell's Constitutional Unionists remained mired in Know Nothing mud.

11. *Centreville Advocate* in *American,* November 14, 1860; *Centreville Times* in *American,* November 14, 1860; *Frederick Herald* in *American,* November 14, 1860.

12. William L. W. Seabrook, *Maryland's Great Part in Saving the Union* (Westminster, MD: n.p., 1913), 3; Evitts, *Matter of Allegiances,* 168.

13. *Baltimore American,* January 4, 1861. See also William C. Harris, *Lincoln and the Border States: Preserving the Union* (Lawrence: University Press of Kansas, 2011), 20, for passages from other Maryland newspapers.

14. *Baltimore Daily Exchange,* November 7, 1860, in Catton, "Baltimore Business Community," 53–54.

15. *Baltimore Sun,* November 16, 1860; *Baltimore Sun,* January 10, January 19, March 3, 1861, in Evitts, *Matter of Allegiances,* 171 ("Workingmen's meetings").

16. *Kent Conservator* in *Baltimore American,* November 19, 1860.

17. *Frederick Herald* in *Baltimore American,* November 14, 1860.

18. *Patapsco Enterprise* in *Baltimore American,* November 14, 1860.

19. *Catholic Mirror,* November 3 and December 1, 1860, in Thomas W. Spalding, *The Premier See: A History of the Archdiocese of Baltimore, 1789–1989* (Baltimore: Johns Hopkins University Press, 1989), 175; *Baltimore American,* December 31, 1860.

20. Libertus Van Bokkelen, "Memorandum on the Civil War," Van Bokkelen Papers, MS 1451, Manuscripts Division, Maryland Center for History and Culture Library. This document is a chronological list of phrases describing events during the spring of 1861 and includes these entries: "Union feeling increased," "*All for the Union now*" (emphasis his), and "Union feeling strong in Md. and Va." George L. Radcliffe, *Governor Thomas H. Hicks of Maryland and the Civil War* (Baltimore: Johns Hopkins University Press, 1902), 19.

21. Carl M. Frasure, "Union Sentiment in Maryland, 1859–1861," *Maryland Historical Magazine* 24, no. 3 (1929): 212–13 ("gloomy . . . and dumb"); *Report of the Select Committee,* "Alleged Hostile Organizations Against the Government within the District of Columbia," US House of Representatives, 36th Congress, Report 79, January 26, 1861, 1–2 (Hicks testimony 166–78; quotes on 171–72 [No. 28]); J. Hanson Thomas to John L. Manning, November 23, 1860, MS 1860, Manuscripts Division, Maryland Center for History and Culture Library (Thomas would spend several months in Union prisons early in the war).

22. *Baltimore Sun,* December 7, 1860, in Evitts, *Matter of Allegiances,* 157; Citizens of Anne Arundel County to Thomas H. Hicks, 1861, MS 1860, Maryland Center for History and Culture Library.

23. Thomas H. Hicks to Thomas G. Pratt, Sprigg Harwood, J. S. Frankin, Llewellyn Boyle, and J. Pinckney, in *Baltimore American,* November 29, 1860.

24. [Joseph] Medill to Abraham Lincoln, December 26, 1860, Abraham Lincoln Papers, Series 1. General Correspondence, Manuscript/Mixed Material, 1833–1916, Library of Congress.

25. C. T. Mason, Sumter, South Carolina, November 3, 13, and 21, 1861; Thomas Steed (or Steen), Greenville, South Carolina, November 20 and December 27, 1860; Joel Smith, Brewerton, South Carolina, December 29, 1860; Steele & Co., Rock Hill, South Carolina, December 2, 1860; Moores & Major, Anderson Courthouse, South Carolina, October 4 (emphasis theirs) and December 4, 1860, all to Magruder, Taylor & Roberts, Magruder, Taylor & Roberts Papers, MS 553, Manuscripts Division, Maryland Center for History and Culture Library; *Baltimore Sun,* November 16, 1860 ("defend it"). For additional transactions between Magruder, Taylor & Roberts and southern customers, see Catton, "Baltimore Business Community," 57–58.

26. *Baltimore Sun,* November 16, 1860 ("a thousand volunteers"), November 19, 1860 ("Palmetto tree"), November 22, 1860 ("boots and shoes") and December 5, 1860 ("1,300 Volunteers").

27. John P. Kennedy, "The Border States: Their Power and Duty in the Present Disordered Condition of the Country" (Philadelphia: n.p., 1861), 35; Radcliffe, *Governor Hicks,* 36. See the discussion of Maryland's role in Kennedy's plan in William C. Wright, *The Secession Movement in the Middle Atlantic States* (Cranbury, NJ: Associated University Presses, 1973), 21–73.

28. Frank Moore, ed., *The Rebellion Record: A Diary of American Events,* 12 vols. (G. P. Putman, 1861), vol. 1, diary 9, document 16, "Extract from Governor Hicks' Address," 18.

29. Wm Whittingham to T. H. Hicks, January 9, 1861, in William Francis Brand, *Life of William Rollinson Whittingham II* (New York: E. & J. B. Young, 1883), 10. For a discussion of tensions in the congregations of religious denominations in Maryland at this time, see Richard R. Duncan, "The Social and Economic Impact of the Civil War on Maryland," PhD diss., Ohio State University, Columbus), 168–95.

30. *Washington National Intelligencer,* January 1, 1861, in Frasure, "Union Sentiment in Maryland," 214–15 ("1,300 businessmen"); *Baltimore American,* January 1, 1861 ("5,000 businessmen"), in Catton, "Baltimore Business Community," 62.

31. A. E. Carroll to T. H. Hicks, November 1860, Carroll Papers, in Janet L. Coryell, *Neither Heroine Nor Fool: Anna Ella Carroll of Maryland* (Kent, OH: Kent State University Press, 1990), 47; John G. Stone in *Baltimore American,* January 8, 1861 ("firmness in not").

32. J. Morrison Harris Papers, December 27, 1860, and January 3–4, 1861, MS 2739, Manuscripts Division, Maryland Center for History and Culture Library, and appendix therein for his delegate list. Harris's notes include—as far as this writer is aware—the only list of delegates to this meeting of border-state representatives. See Daniel Crofts, *Reluctant Confederates: Upper South Unionists in the Secession Crisis* (Chapel Hill: University of North Carolina Press, 1989), 195–214, for a succinct account of the work of the Senate Crittenden Committee, the House Committee of 33, the Border State Plan, and the Washington Peace Conference—all compromise efforts designed to defuse the crisis by coaxing back the seceded states or, failing that, forestalling secessions by the Upper South states—and *Congressional Globe* 36: 2, 279–82, in Crofts, 200. See the discussions of these plans in Harris, *Lincoln and the Border States,* 31–35; and Allan Nevins, *The Emergence of Lincoln: Prologue to Civil War, 1859–1861,* vol. 2 (New York, Charles Scribner's Sons, 1950), 401–13.

33. John A. Gilmer to Dr. D. H. Albright, January 8, 1861, Gilmer Papers, North Carolina Department of Archives and History, in Crofts, *Reluctant Confederates,* 201, 128–29.

34. Virginia Jeans Laas, *Wartime Washington: The Civil War Letters of Elizabeth Blair Lee* (Urbana: University of Illinois Press, 1991), 23 (entry of January 12, 1861). "John R." was John R. Thompson, a Democratic US senator from New Jersey.

35. John Fulton, "The 'Southern Rights' and 'Union' Parties Contrasted" (Baltimore, 1863), 15–16.

36. *Baltimore American and Commercial Advertiser,* January 10, 1861.

37. "State of the Union," Speech of Hon. J. Morrison Harris of Maryland, US House of Representatives, January 29, 1861, J. Morrison Harris Papers, MS 2739, Manuscripts Division, Maryland Center for History and Culture Library.

38. Louis Schley to Thomas H. Hicks, January 16, 1861, Hicks Papers, MS 1313, Maryland Center for History and Culture Library, quoted in Evitts, *Matter of Allegiances,* 161; Rev. William Hamilton to Thomas Hicks, January 27, 1861, cited in Radcliffe, *Governor Hicks,* 25 (endorsements).

39. Nevins, *The Emergence of Lincoln,* 411; see Robert Gray Gunderson, *Old Gentlemen's Convention: The Washington Peace Conference of 1861* (Madison: University of Wisconsin Press, 1961), 105–6, for a detailed discussion of the Washington Peace Conference and its list of delegates.

40. Lucius E. Chittenden, "A Report of the Debates and Proceedings in Secret Sessions of the Conference Convention, for Proposing Amendments to the Constitution of the United States," held at Washington, DC, A.D. 1861 (New York, 1864), 449 (Johnson), 295 (Crisfield), 385–87.

41. Radcliffe, *Governor Hicks,* 41–42.

42. Parade in W. L. Swanberg, *First Blood: The Story of Fort Sumter* (New York: Penguin, 1990), 201; Greeley in Gunderson, *Old Gentlemen's Convention,* 7–9; W. H. L. Wallace to Ann Wallace, Washington, February 27, 1861, Wallace-Dickey Papers, Abraham Lincoln Library and Museum, Springfield, IL, in Michael Burlingame, *Abraham Lincoln: A Life,* 2 vols. (Baltimore: Johns Hopkins University Press, 2008), 42–43. For succinct discussions of the Peace Conference's failure, see Crofts, *Reluctant Confederates,* 248–53; Radcliffe, *Governor Hicks,* 37–42; and Nevins, *The Emergence of Lincoln,* 412.

43. *Richmond Enquirer,* December 25, 1860, in James Ford Rhodes, *History of the United States, 1850–1877* (New York: MacMillan, 1910), 3:300; Gough and Milburn in *St. Mary's Beacon,* March 7, 1861, in Edwin W. Beitzell, *Point Lookout Prison Camp for Confederates* (Leonardtown, MD: n.p., 1983), 5; Bladensburg man in Benson J. Lossing, *Pictorial History of the Civil War* (Philadelphia: George Childs, 1866), 1:142.

44. E. B. Washburne to Abraham Lincoln, January 10, 1861, Abraham Lincoln Papers, Series I, General Correspondence, 1833 to 1916, Manuscript/Mixed Material, Library of Congress (emphases Washburne's); John C. Robinson, "Baltimore in 1861," *The Magazine of American History* 14 (September 1885): 260; Worthington G. Snethen to Abraham Lincoln, February 15, 1861, Abraham Lincoln Papers, Series I, General Correspondence, 1833–1916, Library of Congress; C. C.]Shriver] to F[rederick] A. Shriver, February 2, 1861, MS 2085, Manuscripts Division, Maryland Center for History and Culture Library.

45. Bayley Ellen Marks and Mark Norton Schatz, eds., *Between North and South: A Maryland Journalist Views the Civil War: The Narrative of Williams Wilkins Glenn, 1861–1869* (Rutherford, NJ: Fairleigh Dickinson University Press, 1976), 25 (entry of February 3, 1861); Edward Spencer to Anna Catherine Bradford Harrison, March 3, 1861, in Anna Bradford Agle and Sidney Hovey Wanzer, "Dearest Braddie: Love and War in Maryland, 1860–1861," pt. 1, *Maryland Historical Magazine* 88, no. 1 (Spring 1993), 78. Glenn would be interrogated and briefly detained several times by the Union authorities for his southern sympathies before eventually fleeing to England to wait out the war.

46. Douglas L. Wilson and Rodney O. Davis, *Herndon's Informants: Letters, Interviews, and Statements about Abraham Lincoln* (Urbana: University of Illinois Press, 1998), 709.

47. *Albany Atlas and Argus,* February 28 and March 5, 1861, in Gunderson, *Old Gentlemen's Con-*

vention, 83. For accounts of Pinkerton's role, see Norman Cuthbert, *Lincoln and the Baltimore Plot* (San Marino, CA: Huntington Library, 1949), a comprehensive work that contains Pinkerton's original notes of his investigation ("The Record Book of 1861"), two 1866 letters he wrote to William Herndon, Lincoln's law partner, and versions from Lincoln advisers Howard Judd and Ward H. Lamon. See also Allan Pinkerton, *Spy of the Rebellion: Being a True History of the Spy System of the United States during the Late Rebellion* (1883; reprinted Lincoln: University of Nebraska Press, 1989), chaps. 3–7.

48. *Baltimore Clipper,* November 1, 1860, and *Baltimore Daily Exchange,* November 22, 1860, in Catton, "Baltimore Business Community," 55–56 (banks and port), 57 ("those of our merchants"). See Catton 55–58 for some discussion on the business climate in Baltimore at this time.

49. [William] Mentzel to Madame [Elizabeth Patterson] Bonaparte, March 6, 1861, Elizabeth Patterson Bonaparte Papers, 1802–1879, MS 142, Maryland Center for History and Culture Library.

50. Edward Spencer to Anna Catherine Bradford Harrison, March 28, 1861, Anna Bradford Agle and Sidney Hovey Wanzer, "Dearest Braddie: Love and War in Maryland, 1860–1861," pt. 1, *Maryland Historical Magazine* 88, no. 1 (Spring 1993); Mrs. Henry Cox to Mr. [George W.] Brown, February 11, 1861, RG9 S2 Box 31, Baltimore City Archives.

51. Diary of John Pendleton Kennedy, March–April 1861 (March 4 and March 5), John Pendleton Kennedy papers, PIMS.0058, Arthur Friedheim Library Special Collections, Peabody Institute, Johns Hopkins University.

52. John Pendleton Kennedy, "The Great Drama: An Appeal to Maryland," in "Political and Official Papers by John P. Kennedy" (New York, 1872), 592, 598 (pamphlet published May 9, 1861).

53. *Frederick Herald* in *Baltimore Sun,* November 28, 1860 (emphasis theirs); Allan Bowie Davis to William W. Davis, April 16, 1861, Allan Bowie Davis Letters, 1855–1904, MS 1511, Maryland Center for History and Culture Library; Papers of Leonidas Dodson, Series I, April 19, 1861, University of Maryland Library; Thomas H. Hicks to the Right Rev. William Whittingham, January 11, 1861, Maryland State Archives (Hicks finally summoned the legislature into Special Session on April 22, 1861; the members assembled in Frederick, where the session opened on April 26).

54. A. R. Wright to G. W. Crawford, March 13, 1861, *The War of the Rebellion: A Compilation of the Official Records of the Union and Confederate Armies,* Washington, DC: Government Printing Office, 1880–1901, 4:1 (pt.1), 152; "Message of the Governor of Maryland to the General Assembly in Extra Session, 1861" (Frederick, 1861), 13–14.

55. William Howard Russell, *My Diary North and South,* ed. Eugene H. Berwanger (Baton Rouge: Louisiana State University Press, 2001), 71 (entry of April 12, 1861).

56. *Baltimore American and Commercial Advertiser,* April 13, 1861.

57. Marks & Schatz, *Between North and South,* 27; Kennedy, "The Great Drama," 7.

58. Russell, *Diary,* 1:114, in Robert J. Brugger, *The Maryland Club: A History of Food and Friendship in Baltimore, 1857–1997* (Baltimore: The Maryland Club, 1998), 17 ("elated at"), and Martin Crawford, *William Howard Russell's Civil War: Private Diary and Letters, 1861–1862* (Athens, GA, 1992), in Brugger, 21 ("secessionist evening"); *St. Mary's Beacon,* April 18, 1861, in Beitzell, *Point Lookout Prison Camp,* 5.

BALTIMORE'S SECESSIONIST MOMENT

Conservatism and Political Networks in the
Pratt Street Riot and Its Aftermath

FRANK TOWERS

This essay looks back to Baltimore's Pratt Street Riot of April 19, 1861, and its aftermath to better understand the political context in which Baltimore's elected leadership—most of them members of the recently organized City Reform Association, also known as Reformers—became identified with secession. In doing so, Reformers made a grand political miscalculation that landed them in federal prison and returned their enemies to power for the duration of the Civil War. Because secession had little objective chance of success in Maryland, much less Baltimore, the behavior of these municipal leaders warrants investigation. This essay argues that the actions of the Reformers can be understood as the product of their local and national connections, which caused them to lump local political rivals, abolitionists, and the Lincoln administration into one common, existential threat to the established civic order.

Although the essay's goal is to illuminate the political world in which Reformers lived, to get there it must first engage the impressive body of scholarship that already exists on the Pratt Street Riot.[1] Historians have mostly studied this event for what it reveals about popular support for secession in Maryland and the state's decision to remain in the Union. Early histories tended toward a Lost Cause explanation of the riot as a manifestation of widespread support for the South.[2] Since the 1970s, most historians have agreed with William Evitts's assessment that "Unionism was dominant in Maryland except during that one brief, inflammatory encounter. . . . Furthermore, the riot itself was not entirely attributable to offended Southern sympathies."[3] In this interpretation, the violence on April 19 was a spontaneous, short-lived reaction to the presence of northern militia on city streets, and, just as importantly, city government did its best to prevent bloodshed and keep Maryland in the Union. This historiography often uses the Reformers' own memoirs to argue that secession found little support in Baltimore, even during the riot, and that the city's elected leadership worked to save the Union.

It is on this last point, the Unionism of the city's elected leaders and their delegates during the tumultuous weeks of late April and early May of 1861, where this essay parts company with the dominant interpretation of the event, but it does not argue that secessionism had the weight of public opinion behind it in Baltimore, nor statewide for that matter. The Reform leadership was a small group of wealthy, politically prominent men with family and professional ties to proslavery conservatives across the country. They and their political network not only loathed the Republican Party to the point of contemplating secession, but also mistakenly believed enough Border South whites shared their views to give secession a chance in Maryland. As evidenced by Baltimoreans' quick rejection of their extreme measures, the Reformers stood for no one but themselves in a state where, in the words of wartime governor Augustus Bradford, "the masses were from the first born onward" by "a strong patriotic undercurrent."[4]

Once it became clear that Unionism was dominant in Maryland and especially in its largest city, Reformers began writing histories of the riot to rebut the accusations of secessionism that led to their arrest. Their efforts continued long after the war ended and, along with Maryland Confederate veterans such as J. Thomas Scharf, some of these men were instrumental in developing the professional study of Maryland history.[5] Thereafter, the first generation of professional historians helped to make the Reformers' memoirs canonical sources for the study of Baltimore during the Civil War.[6] Thus, it is no easy task to decouple the Reformers of 1861 from the larger pro-Union movement in Maryland.

This essay begins with a summary of the events of late April and early May and the ensuing federal reaction. From there it examines accounts from the spring and summer of 1861 to show how Reformers were perceived in the aftermath of the riot. Although observers on opposing sides of the sectional conflict thought the Reformers' post-riot actions aided secession, Reformers themselves denied the charge. A key point in their defense was to distinguish their opposition to federal coercion of the seceding states from secession itself. After reviewing the differences between this policy's operation in Baltimore versus the rest of the Border South, the essay closes by exploring the ideas and relationships of the Reformers to shed new light on their motives and worldview.

A BRIEF NARRATIVE OF THE PRATT STREET RIOT AND ITS AFTERMATH

Occurring on April 19, 1861, in downtown Baltimore, the Pratt Street Riot was a violent attack by a large crowd on soldiers of the Sixth Regiment Massachusetts Volunteer Militia and five companies of Pennsylvania militia volunteers that were known as the Washington Brigade. These units, comprising approximately two thousand men, had been ordered by their respective state governors to travel to Washington, DC, in response to President Abraham Lincoln's April 15 call "to all loyal citizens to favor, facilitate, and aid this effort to maintain the honor, the integrity, and the existence of our National Union."[7]

Lincoln mobilized these troops after the Confederate military attacked US forces at Fort Sumter, South Carolina, on April 12. The Confederacy had been formed two months earlier out of seven slave states in the Lower South that seceded in reaction to Lincoln's victory in the 1860 presidential election. In the eight slave states that remained in the Union, Lincoln's call for volunteers galvanized Southern radicals who insisted that any effort to coerce the seceded states violated the Constitution. On April 17, the Virginia legislature voted to secede. In Maryland, Confederate sympathizers responded by increasing their calls for Governor Thomas H. Hicks to convene the legislature so that it could vote on secession. The next day, a contingent of Pennsylvania volunteer militia arrived in Baltimore via the Northern Central Railway, which terminated at Bolton Street Station. From there they marched southward to Camden Street Station, where they boarded a Baltimore and Ohio Railroad train for Washington.[8] A crowd gathered to insult the troops and throw rocks at them, but city police headed by Marshal George P. Kane preserved order, and the troops left with only a few injuries from objects thrown by the mob.[9] Later that day a "State Rights Convention" met to protest the Lincoln administration and issued resolutions against the deployment of northern state militia in the South, including a vow to "to repel, if need be, any invader who may come to establish a military despotism over us."[10]

Then, on a rainy Friday morning, a trainload of Massachusetts and Pennsylvania militia arrived at President Station, terminus of the Philadelphia, Wilmington, and Baltimore Railroad (PW&B) located on the eastern side of the Basin (today known as the Inner Harbor) and prepared to traverse roughly one and one-half miles of city streets to Camden Station, just west of the Basin, for the last leg of their trip to Washington. Blocking their way was an angry crowd that, according to both pro-Union and secessionist newspapers, numbered in the thousands and "vociferously cheered for Jefferson Davis and the Confederacy" while displaying a South Carolina state flag.[11]

City police were not present at President Station, leaving the northern militia volunteers to fend for themselves as rioters tore up the tracks for horse-drawn streetcars that an initial contingent of the Sixth Massachusetts had used to reach Camden Station. The absence of local law enforcement remains a puzzle given the events of the prior week, and the gathering of a noisy crowd at President Station as well as over thirty horse-drawn street cars loudly assembling to move the troops.[12] City officials deflected blame onto the PW&B for failing to notify them that soldiers would be on the Friday morning train.[13] Left on his own, Colonel Edward F. Jones, commander of the Massachusetts volunteers, ordered the remaining 220 men in his unit to march their way to the southbound cars. However, when the Sixth Massachusetts encountered violence in their march down Pratt Street, Marshal Kane, Mayor George William Brown, and fifty police officers put themselves between the mob and the militia volunteers to bring the soldiers to Camden Station, where they departed for Washington.[14]

Meanwhile back at President Station, rioters attacked the Pennsylvania volunteers, most whom were unarmed and not in uniform. After a lopsided two-hour battle police finally showed up to help the Pennsylvanians get back onto their cars for a return trip to Philadelphia. Routed by the mob, some volunteers were killed, others captured, and still others who had been separated from their unit fled north through the Maryland countryside where they were pursued by secessionist militia.[15] At the end of the day, the northern volunteers had left the city and at least nineteen people had been killed in the riot—seven of them soldiers defending the Union—and scores more suffered injuries.[16]

Coming one week after Fort Sumter and two days after Virginia's secession, the Pratt Street Riot precipitated a standoff between the United States and Baltimore's municipal government, which initiated a policy that came to be known as "armed neutrality."[17] Given the city's key position at the junction of railroads and telegraph lines connecting the North to Washington, DC, and the absence of any similar strategic importance to the Confederacy, municipal officials' decision to prevent access through Baltimore applied in only one direction, northward, and practically meant defending the city against federal incursions.

Those defensive actions began the night of the riot when city officials ordered that the telegraph line to Washington be cut and sent local militia volunteers to destroy railroad bridges north of city. In the following days, municipal authorities burned more railroad bridges; embargoed commerce out of the port; appropriated $500,000 for defense; raised 15,000 militia volunteers; procured weapons to arm them, including the seizure of a federal arsenal in Baltimore County; and used the police to disarm and arrest pro-Union paramilitaries while allowing Southern sympathizers to attack outspoken Unionists and their businesses.[18] On April 24, an unopposed States and Southern Rights ticket won a low-turnout election to fill the city's seats in the Maryland House of Delegates, where they advocated for secession.[19]

Meanwhile, after meeting with Governor Hicks, Mayor Brown, and other Baltimore officials, Lincoln agreed to keep troops out of Baltimore, but continued to insist on the necessity of transit across Maryland, which, following the secession of Virginia, provided the only passage from the rest of the Union to the federal capital. Therefore, state militias pledged to serve the federal government began moving around Baltimore via sea landings at Annapolis and a land route to the west of the city. These troops quickly isolated Baltimore's secessionists from potential allies in Confederate Virginia.[20]

Although armed neutrality continued, within a week of the riot Unionists, who initially kept a low profile, reemerged to oppose secession. On April 29, their allies in the state legislature defeated a bill to create a "Committee of Public Safety" staffed by Southern sympathizers and empowered to control the Maryland militia and ally with the Confederacy. Baltimore's delegation supported the bill, which had been drafted by one of its members, state Senator Coleman Yellott. By May 1 the US flag flew over the federal Customs House (the mayor had earlier banned flag displays), and the next day a pro-Union convention met in the city. In the following week Mayor Brown urged Baltimoreans to support the federal government and allow its soldiers to pass through the city, which a contingent did on May 9. The last traces of armed neutrality ended on May 13 when one thousand troops from the Sixth Massachusetts and the Boston Light Artillery peacefully entered Baltimore and set up cannons on Federal Hill overlooking downtown.[21]

Federal commanders initially left the existing city administration in place, but they grew frustrated with police who refused to cooperate with weapons searches and who had purged pro-Union officers for actions such as testifying to a grand jury about the riot or refusing to lower a US flag.[22] On June 27, Nathaniel P. Banks, military commander of the city, arrested Marshal Kane. Four days later, after discovering sizeable caches of weapons and ammunition hidden at the City Collector's office and the Middle District police station,[23] he imprisoned the board of police commissioners and installed a federal provost marshal to oversee the police. In July and August, this new, federally directed police force arrested individuals for aiding the Confederacy and suppressed public displays in favor of secession. In mid-September another round of high-profile arrests took in Mayor Brown, eight of the ten members of the House of Delegates elected on the States' and Southern Rights ticket, editors of two pro-southern newspapers, and US Representative Henry May. Although charges were never formally filed, federal authorities stated that these men helped secessionists in late April and were still plotting to bring Maryland out of the Union. By the fall of 1861 approximately thirty Baltimore city officials and prominent allies had been arrested on charges related to secessionist activity in the aftermath of the Pratt Street Riot.[24]

Because it gave Lincoln an excuse to act, the Pratt Street Riot and its aftermath effectively ended the possibility of Maryland's secession from the Union. The Lincoln administration used the very real danger that the riot and armed neutrality posed to Washington, DC, as the pretext for establishing military control over the state. With the immediate threat quieted, Unionists gained time to organize and consolidate public support, especially among Southern sympathizers who nonetheless worried about living in a war zone.[25]

Although Democrats held their own in June elections for the US Congress, they were routed in Baltimore at the November contests for state and federal offices. Democrats cried foul when US troops monitored the polls to, in Banks's words, "protect Union voters and see that no disunionists are allowed to intimidate them or interfere with their rights."[26] Following victories at these elections, the newly organized Union Party—an organization that drew most of its support from adherents of the American Party (a.k.a. Know Nothings) who had governed Baltimore from 1854 until Reformers defeated them in 1860—went on to win reelection in city and state contests for the duration of the war.[27]

The removal of the Reform administration and its allies silenced what had been a formidable block of political leaders aligned with the Democratic Party. Although the Reform Association was officially nonpartisan and included some supporters from the defunct Whig Party, such as Mayor Brown, its followers overlapped with the pro-Southern, proslavery wing of the Democrats.[28] Similarly, the Reform Association shared supporters with the city's smaller, less well-organized constituency of secessionists.

To identify the core of secession's Baltimore support, historians often cite a rally held on February 1, 1861, as the start of a more aggressive movement to sever Maryland's ties to the Union. From its speeches and resolutions, the meeting committed to the policy that "if a settlement could not be reached, Maryland should act in concert with Virginia, which was expected to secede."[29] A search through the available newspaper and manuscript sources found that one-half of the eighty-four officers of that meeting were also involved in the Reform Association. Of the remainder, twenty-one were Democratic Party activists.[30]

Reformers also attracted a few outspoken Unionists to their cause, such as wartime emancipation advocate Henry Stockbridge, who ran on the Reform ticket for the House of Delegates in 1859, but Reformers had no commensurate level of support from the men who went on to lead the wartime Union Party.[31] A more significant exception was Mayor Brown, who voted for Constitutional Unionist John C. Bell in the 1860 presidential election and opposed secession thereafter.[32] Brown's moderation was such a notable contrast from some of his secessionist colleagues that one Unionist said Brown "was as honest, courageous, and true-minded a man as ever presided over the affairs of this city, but he was totally unaware of the purposes of the people who surrounded him."[33] Albeit with a different emphasis, secessionist editor William W. Glenn shared these views. "Brown has always had his head filled with a parcel of Yankee ideas about the progress of civilization and such like sentiment," he wrote in 1867. "The really able men I know think that slavery is an essential part of democratic institutions." In short, although Brown was a leading Reformer he was considered an outlier in regard to his views on the sectional conflict.[34]

The Reform Association drew on a much broader constituency than did the secession campaign, but the overlap between the two groups was sufficient to make for close connections between some of their leaders. Six of the ten men running on the States' and Southern Rights ticket were also members of the Reform Association. Among the remaining four, three were Democratic Party activists. Of those three, T. Parkin Scott watched the Tenth Ward polls for the Reformers and testified in their behalf when they challenged the results of the 1859 elections, and John C. Brune was Mayor Brown's brother-in-law.[35] For these reasons, the imprisonment of Reform and States' Rights officials severely weakened the leadership of the wartime opposition to the Maryland Union Party. Thus, in addition to giving Lincoln an opening to occupy Maryland, Reformers' handling of the riot and its aftermath produced what one historian terms an "irreversible defeat" that put their enemies in charge of state and local affairs for years to come.[36]

ARRESTING THE REFORMERS:
PERCEPTIONS OF BALTIMORE'S ARMED NEUTRALITY
IN THE SPRING AND SUMMER OF 1861

Reformers' version of the Pratt Street Riot is addressed in later pages of this essay. That makes sense chronologically because they wrote their most influential accounts long after 1861. Here, the real-time observations about the intentions of city officials during and after the Pratt Street Riot are considered.

The federal officials who ordered the arrests of the Reform leadership believed that their targets were, as Lincoln said, "in unmistakable complicity with those in armed rebellion against the Government of the United States."[37] General Banks described police chief Kane as "the head of an armed force, hostile to [the US government's] authority and acting in concert with its avowed enemies."[38] State Department records called Baltimore lawyer and Reform Association leader Severn Wallis "the leader of the band of conspirators, who were known to be plotting to pass an act of secession."[39] And, according to US Senator John Sherman of Ohio,

the Mayor and Board of Police Commissioners took military control of the city, the port and telegraph lines to Washington and Harper's Ferry while they cut those to the North [and] the running of trains to Washington was arrested. . . . The attempt [that] has occasionally been made to explain those acts as precautions for the preservation of the internal peace of the State, or to repel lawless incursions of armed men from the North, is unworthy of further notice. I cannot see how a candid man can be misled by them."[40]

Baltimore Unionists felt the same about municipal authorities. In February 1861, Henry Winter Davis, an outspoken Unionist and American Party Congressman, had warned Lincoln that "the *reformers* . . . are the most mischievous enemies you have in Baltimore." Shortly after the Pratt Street Riot, Davis said, "The Union men are down and the secessionists . . . are now our Masters."[41] Writing to a friend five weeks later, David Creamer, foreman of a grand jury investigating the riot, said "Again—I repeat the fact,—our 'Authorities' are *disloyal* and in almost open collusion with our enemies."[42] In late June, a local Unionist warned Governor Hicks that "the military of this city are almost unanimous for secession, therefore it would strengthen the rebel element of this city by re-arming these men."[43]

The northern press shared these perceptions. In a warning to Maryland, the *New York Times* editorialized, "Some claiming to represent you talk of an 'armed neutrality.' We spit upon the term! There is no 'armed neutrality' written on our programme." As for Mayor Brown, the *Times* called him "Magistrate of the rascally crew who have been murdering our soldiers, and who seek now to cut us off from saving Washington." At the *New York Tribune*, editor Horace Greeley said Baltimore's "government was in the hands of the Breckinridge Democracy . . . and the leaders of the Democracy were deep in the counsels of treasons." Although it did not equate the Democratic Party with secession, the *New York Herald*, a leading Democratic newspaper, shared the criticism of Baltimore city government expressed by the Republican-aligned *Times* and *Tribune*. Commenting on armed neutrality, the *Herald* warned merchants that "there is no room now for doubt as to the political affinities of the people of Maryland—or at all events Baltimore. . . . So long as the war lasts Baltimore must be classed among the doubtful ports . . . Property sent to Baltimore may any day be seized by the rebels." It also announced "terrorism reigns in Baltimore . . ."[44]

Another group of northerners, the state militia volunteers who traveled through Baltimore in May, had a close-up view of the city. They believed armed neutrality measures such as the burning of the railroad bridges had been done "by the Secessionists." The captain of a Pennsylvania regiment said "the population of Baltimore received us with a sullen silence that indicated anything but a friendly feeling. There was neither a display of flags nor cheers. Crowds gathered in the streets and both men and women heaped curses and imprecations upon us, and threatened us." These impressions persisted through the summer. In August, an Indiana soldier wrote, "There are more secesh than union in Baltimore now[;] that is certain."[45]

Although Reformers dismissed accusations from these pro-Union voices as partisan attacks, avowed Baltimore secessionists also equated armed neutrality with disunion. Two days after the riot, Joseph Booth, a long-time Democratic activist, compared Governor Hicks to Pontius Pilate for having "handed our beloved state, over to blustering Abe to be crucified." Booth told a relative, "Our City councils have appropriated five hundred thousand dollars, for defense. Ten thousand men are already enrolled, and ere ten days rolls round thirty thousand of us will be in arms." These men were "determined to fight . . . the barbarian hordes."[46] According to a September statement by a member of the armed neutrality militia, Charles C. Egerton, commander of the First Light Division of Maryland Volunteers, "said we'll let the troops pass through now but when they come back we will play into them. The officers generally spoke constantly of their expectation that the Virginians would come to aid them. . . . Kane told me this was slow work—if he had been our Major Genl [sic] we would have been fighting long ago."[47] On the day of the riot another Baltimore Confederate sympathizer put things more succinctly: "Our marshal is a secessionist which aided the affray today. . . . We are on armed neutrality and I think we will remain so."[48]

To fire-eating secessionists in the Lower South, Baltimore's armed neutrality militia seemed like an ally in their plans to bring Maryland into the Confederacy. Writing in her diary a week after the riot, Mary Chesnut, a wealthy South Carolinian whose husband James was a prominent Confederate politician, wrote "Baltimore in a blaze. Ben Huger commanding there. Robert E. Lee in Virginia—son of Light Horse Harry Lee. Won't we show them a brave fight with such commanders." She referred to Benjamin Huger, who resigned his commission in the US Army on April 22 to take command of the Fifty-Third Maryland Infantry, part of the armed neutrality force. Although Huger quickly left Maryland for the Confederate military, his presence gave confidence to Confederate insiders such as Chesnut that the city was on their side. Chesnut's views were reinforced by her hometown newspaper, the *Charleston Mercury*, owned by arch fire-eater Robert Barnwell Rhett. A week after the riot its Richmond correspondent said, "Maryland's daring stand, right in front of the invading hordes of the North, thrills every heart. [Confederate] Vice President [Alexander] Stephens . . . said the cause of Baltimore should be the cause of all, and so, please God it shall be." Boasting of aid to the armed neutrality militia, the reporter said, "already as many muskets as we can spare are on the way to Baltimore, and I trust that Virginia soldiers will follow them."[49]

These impressions, including the claim that Virginia secessionists sent weapons to Baltimore, reflected the reality of armed neutrality officials' contact and cooperation with high-ranking Confederates. In late April Isaac Trimble, commander of the post-riot volunteer militia, gave detailed instructions to a South Carolina military commander on how to clandestinely send arms to Baltimore. "Most of the transportation will be supplied by Virginia. For special purposes, and personal expenses, you will draw through me, or Marshall of Police, George P. Kane, for such funds as you may need." The correspondence listed at least forty-eight pieces of artillery and discussed using arms Confederates had seized from the US navy yard at Hampton Roads. Those cannons formed part of an arsenal that included weapons confiscated from US military stores at President Street Station.[50] Funds came from the half-million-dollar defense appropriation made by city government. When Trimble and an estimated five thousand other Baltimoreans made their way into Confederate ranks, they brought along as much of this weaponry as they could.[51]

Trimble was not the only Baltimore secessionist asking Confederates for military assistance. Other city officials, including police board commissioner Charles Howard,[52] made such requests, as did private citizens. Five days after the riot, merchant George Harrison wrote to Confederate President Jefferson Davis to say, "Baltimore is in a blaze," and to ask for troops to march from Virginia.[53] Samuel Wethered, a textile maker whose brothers were active Reformers and secessionists, urged Daniel Barringer, a leading North Carolina politician, to send "arms and men" to stop the approaching "hordes from the North."[54] The most infamous of these pleas came from Marshal Kane, who telegraphed secessionist Bradley Johnson in Frederick, Maryland, to "send expresses over the mountains of Maryland and Virginia for riflemen to come without delay. Fresh hordes will be down on us to-morrow. We will fight them and whip them, or die." Kane and Johnson, who showed up the next day with a group of volunteers, later fought for the Confederacy.[55]

In addition to arming Baltimore militia, Confederates also consulted with the Southern Rights delegates who were trying to bring about secession in the late April special legislative session. James Murray Mason, formerly a US senator from Virginia known for drafting the Fugitive Slave Law of 1850, arrived in Maryland four days after the riot on a Confederate government-appointed mission to "ascertain from her prominent men, the condition of public sentiment there; & how far the state could be relied on to unite her destinies with the south." Mason attended the legislature, which had moved to Frederick to avoid federal troops in Annapolis, and "was in free communication with the principal men with us in sentiment in both houses." He reported to Davis that "from every quarter I was beset with applications for arms from Virginia, to be used by volunteers, collected under officers ready and willing to lead them." In the event of federal occupation of Baltimore, Mason believed "the unquelled spirit of masses of people in that city, will not yield it without a struggle."[56] Earlier in the year, representatives from Alabama, Georgia, and Mississippi tried and failed to persuade Governor Hicks to join them in secession,[57] but in April Confederate officials found allies in Baltimore whom they encouraged to bring about Maryland's secession.

This review of contemporary opinions about Baltimore's elected officials in the aftermath of the Pratt Street Riot reveals the widespread perception that city leaders had aligned themselves with secession. This testimony from the spring and summer of 1861 cannot disprove that Reformers such as Brown wanted to preserve the peace and opposed secession, but it does confirm that outside Reformers' own circle armed neutrality was understood as help for secession and looked upon favorably by the Confederate high command.

ARMED NEUTRALITY IN BALTIMORE AND
CONDITIONAL UNIONISM IN THE BORDER SOUTH

Establishing the state of public opinion on the riot in late April and in the months that followed challenges the later claims made by Reformers that their actions had nothing to do with secession. When they looked back, Reformers relied on a careful distinction between their vocal opposition to the Lincoln administration and an outright call for secession. In speeches and editorials produced between April 19 and the arrival of Butler's troops on May 13, Reformers said plenty about their support for the South, the wrongs committed by the North, and their bellicose opposition to the presence of federal forces on Maryland soil. Although *The South*, a newspaper started three days after the riot, declared secession "a righteous and holy cause," most of these speakers avoided explicitly calling on Maryland to leave the Union.[58]

At a rally held at Monument Square shortly after the violence ended on Pratt Street, Reform Association leader Severn T. Wallis asked that "the blood which has been spilt, this day, among us, be the seal of the covenant of our re-union in the holy cause of the South."[59] On April 20, the *Daily Exchange*, a strongly pro-Reform newspaper edited by Frank Key Howard, son of the head of the board of police commissioners, said "to invade seven States which have declared themselves independent . . . is a usurpation, which may be rightfully treated as such, and to which resistance is a holy obligation."[60] The same day, the *Daily Baltimore Republican*, a Democratic newspaper that backed the Reform administration, stated, "the Old Union, for which our fathers fought and bled, has been sacrificed by a Black Republican despot, and he now seeks to wrench from us our Liberty and independence." Yet for all of their bluster, the speakers usually stopped short of expressly demanding that Maryland secede. For example, in an April 26, 1861, editorial the *Daily Exchange* said: "The people of Maryland are at this moment in a state of *quasi* rebellion against the Federal government," but then closed the piece by promising that they would "wait until the popular will can be known."

After it became clear that Baltimore was under Union control, Reformers backtracked. In mid-May William Louis Winans, son of Southern Rights delegate Ross Winans, warned his brother Thomas, who had been "appointed a secession member of a Defense Committee," that he and his father ran against the current of public opinion and should be on guard to not "compromise" themselves.[61] In June Reform activists denied that the riot and city government had anything to do with disunion. According to Reform attorney George M. Gill, who also represented John Merryman in his habeas corpus case, "the events arose from a sudden impulse which seized many of our people," and Baltimore police were committed to preventing violence even if Marshal Kane "and his whole force lost their lives."[62]

After their arrests, Reformers began a decades-long campaign to rebut charges that they had acted in any way that might be construed as aiding secession. During their incarceration, Reformers penned public letters and memoirs of prison life. Those texts took aim at federal violations of civil liberties, joining the chorus of dissent over Lincoln's suspension of habeas corpus. Writing from prison to Ohio US Senator John Sherman in 1862, Severn T. Wallis first refuted the allegation of secessionism and then challenged the constitutionality of his arrest, denying that Lincoln "had the shadow of a lawful right to break up the Maryland Legislature."[63]

Above these rebuttals of the arrests stood Reformers' insistence that secessionism was not the same thing as opposing coercion of the seceding states, including armed resistance to federal troops trying to move through Baltimore. For example, imprisoned Southern Rights delegate Laurence Sangston said that he and his colleagues

> sympathized with the South in her efforts to resist the aggressions of the North against her domestic Institutions, at the same time they recognized the fact that Maryland was a State in the Union, and while such, bound by all her Constitutional obligations to the Union—they were opposed to coercion and war because they believed Disunion would be the inevitable result, and they were not disposed to take any active part in measures that, in their judgment, would certainly destroy the Union, and with it all hopes of a re-construction.[64]

Or, as George William Brown wrote in his influential memoir of the riot published in 1887, "The house of every man is his castle and he may defend it to the death against all aggressors.... And where constitutional rights of a people are in jeopardy, a kindred right of self defense belongs to them. Although revolutionary in its character, it is not the less a right." Brown balanced this endorsement of armed resistance to federal troops with the assertion that he "did not believe in secession as a constitutional right, and in Maryland there was no sufficient ground for revolution. It was clearly for her interest to remain in the Union and to free her slaves."[65]

In arguing for city government's Unionism in late April 1861, historians often cite Brown's memoir and incorporate Reformers' anti-coercionism into the broader conditional Unionism that prevailed among whites in the eight slave states that had remained in the Union through Fort Sumter. In response to Lincoln's call for volunteers, four of these states (Arkansas, North Carolina, Tennessee, and Virginia) seceded whereas the other four (Delaware, Kentucky, Maryland, and Missouri) did not. In all eight, voters' opinions about secession ranged from unconditional Unionism at one extreme to unapologetic secessionism at the other, with most standing somewhere between these poles. In the four states that left the Union, secessionists used the anti-coercionist argument to their advantage to push conditional Unionists into becoming what historian Daniel Crofts has termed "reluctant Confederates." In the loyal Border South states, as Michael Robinson has recently argued, the approach that triumphed was proslavery Unionism, an outlook inherited from the region's political past "where moderation had overawed extremism from either quarter."[66]

In these states some anti-coercionists turned to armed neutrality as a way to maintain their principles without leaving the Union. This policy mattered most in Kentucky, the largest border slave state by population and area. There, the government refused to allow either US or rebel forces to operate within its boundaries, and it held to the policy through the summer until after Unionists had triumphed in local elections. Furthermore, Kentucky secessionists initially held the upper hand, making armed neutrality "a defensive measure for Unionists" seeking to buy time.[67]

In Maryland, the phrase "armed neutrality" had been discussed as an option by Governor Hicks and other leading moderate Unionists, such as John Pendleton Kennedy, who sought to leverage the influence of the Border States to resolve the sectional standoff. Fort Sumter and the Pratt Street Riot convinced moderates that neutrality was a dead end, and by early May they had dropped any pretense of supporting it. In this respect Maryland's neutrality resembled a shorter, more informal version of Kentucky's experience. Referring to the statewide significance of the policy, William Harris argues that "the chimera of neutrality had a large following and contributed to keeping Maryland safely in the Union when the state was most susceptible to secession."[68]

It was only in Baltimore where the circumstances surrounding armed neutrality differed dramatically from elsewhere in the Border South. Because of Baltimore's strategic importance as the communications and transportation junction connecting the rest of the Union to Washington, DC, its leaders' commitment to armed neutrality created an immediate threat to the federal capital. As Lincoln said to a request that he keep troops out of Maryland, "Our men are not moles, and cannot dig under the earth; they are not birds and cannot fly through the air. There is no other way but to march across, and that they must do."[69] In the post-riot context of an isolated federal capital, accurate reports of communication between Virginia Confederates and the armed neutrality militia, and a movement by pro-southern legislators, led by Baltimore's delegates, to seize power via the Committee of Public Safety, city leaders' actions looked to most observers, especially the decision makers in Washington, like active assistance to secession.

To their mutual credit, President Lincoln avoided a direct assault on the city and Mayor Brown worked to tamp down secessionism, making the arrival of Butler's troops on May 13 an anticlimax for those expecting another confla-gration. However, all of this happened while other key figures in the city and the legislature worked toward a full-fledged alliance with the Confederacy. When it came to the threat posed by these actions, Lincoln lost patience with Baltimore's version of armed neutrality, and most Marylanders agreed.[70]

THE REFORM NETWORK: PROSLAVERY CONSERVATISM ON THE OUTER REACHES OF THE SECESSION MOVEMENT

Having delved into the details of conditional Unionism and how the Reform-ers got themselves close enough to secession to end up in federal prisons, it is worth thinking more about why they did so. Although Reformers protested to the end of their days that accusations of aiding secession were lies propagated by zealous partisans, had they acted more moderately they likely would have avoided arrest. Defending the city from a rumored invasion was a valid con-cern, but why seek arms from Virginia? If maintaining order was essential why arrest only Unionists, and not their foes, and why fire those police who tried to protect Unionists? Even if burning bridges on the night of the riot can be written off to the heat of the moment, why burn more? Why run down and harass the unarmed Pennsylvania volunteers who fled the city? Why permit Confederate recruiting and removals South? Why raid armories? Why inter-fere with federal provost marshals? Why continue to push for disunion in the legislature? Refraining from any or all of these choices would not have risked public order, but it might have won the goodwill of the city's Unionists and the federal government, which in hindsight held all the cards as far as Bal-timore was concerned. By comparison, major cities elsewhere in the Border South avoided the kind of standoff with federal authorities experienced in Baltimore.[71] Why, then, did the Reformers act in ways that, intended or not, aided secession after the riot? The answer goes to the Reformers' relationship to local and national politics.

Locally, Reformers' experience in city politics had accustomed them to regard their American Party opponents as enemies worthy of all-out war. After winning a polarizing fight that left each side deeply suspicious of the other, Reformers had only been in power for six months before the Pratt Street Riot occurred. In this sense, the riot was merely one more step on the road to a local civil war, and Know Nothings' enthusiastic Unionism made secession seem a more tempting option for Reformers determined to keep them from regaining power. Exemplifying this outlook, imprisoned States' Rights delegate Laurence Sangston said "a class of people, generically known as 'PLUG UGLIES,' who had for years, by violence and fraud ruled the city of Baltimore, and had finally been put down, after a long struggle by the reform party, suddenly became 'loyal' men, devoted to the Union."[72]

The American Party came to power in 1854 by winning over native-born white workers upset by foreign immigration and economic hard times. Baltimore Know Nothings also shared in a nationwide "antiparty" reaction against the dominant Whigs and Democrats who seemed like two sides of the same corrupt establishment coin. One manifestation of Know Nothings' antipartyism was their belief that Democrats stole elections via fraudulent immigrant votes. This conspiratorial narrative motivated election rioting wherever Know Nothings contended for power, with nativists attacking foreign-born voters at the polls and rioting in immigrant neighborhoods. Democrats, especially foreign-born workers, fought back, often giving as good as they got. For example, at Baltimore's 1856 municipal and federal elections, seventeen people were killed and over 250 injured in violence at the polls and at the headquarters of partisan fire companies, often instigated by gangs affiliated with the parties. Continuing violence in 1857 and 1858 convinced Democrats they could not win back the city without help from state government and from upper-class ex-Whigs within the city, which led to the formation of the City Reform Association in 1859.[73]

Emerging from this context, Reform campaigns took on an emotional and physical intensity similar to the rhetoric of wartime partisanship after 1861. At the 1859 elections, Know Nothing rowdies affiliated with south Baltimore's infamous Tiger Club murdered Adam B. Kyle, Jr., son of a prominent Irish-born merchant, while he tried to distribute Reform ballots at the Fifteenth Ward polls. Reformers staged a public funeral for Kyle featuring a procession of "an unusual number of private carriages followed by hundreds of gentlemen arm in arm, four by four." His pallbearers included two critical players in the Pratt Street Riot's aftermath: George William Brown and Henry Warfield. The pro-Reform *Daily Exchange* said, "It has been a long time since the people of Baltimore displayed so general a feeling of sympathy at the loss of one of her citizens," and praised "the universal and spontaneous response of those respectable citizens who paid the last tribute." In the run-up to the 1860 municipal elections, a Reform editorial declared "the blood of the Kyles cries from the ground." After the Pratt Street Riot, McHenry Howard, son of the police board commissioner and brother of the *Daily Exchange*'s editor, told a northern friend that Baltimore's Unionists "were the same lot of Roughs whose killing of Adam Kyle was the reason for the formation of the Maryland Guard," a volunteer militia comprised of young merchants and professionals, almost half of whom later fought for the Confederacy as did McHenry Howard.[74]

The emphasis on "respectable citizens" in the report on Kyle's funeral fit with Reformers' self identification as defenders of what they regarded as the rightful order of the city: an honest government led by men from prominent families and dedicated to the protection of property rights and white supremacy, including slavery. Describing a contingent of militia stationed at Monument Square on April 19, 1861, a pro-Reform newspaper said, "Many of our most wealthy and well respectable citizens were among the volunteers." A secessionist editor described the Southern Rights candidates as "well known citizens—men of character, and substance—enjoying and deserving the respect and confidence of the community." Similarly, Frank Key Howard said of his fellow prisoners, "They were all gentlemen of high social position and unimpeachable character."[75]

Along with respectability, Reformers also used the word "conservative" to define themselves in opposition to "radical" enemies such as working-class gangs, corrupt Know Nothing politicians, and northern abolitionists. For example, in their 1859 campaign, ward associations "earnestly appeal[ed] to every conservative and order-loving citizen in the Ward to come out and support the Reform movement." Three days before that election, Samuel K. George, a Reform Association vice president who later backed secession and whose son went from the Maryland Guard to the Confederate military, described the Reformers as a "movement of citizens to crush out the rowdy elements of the population and to establish the freedom and purity of the ballot box. . . . Conservative citizens are determined to accomplish this purpose or die."[76]

After Democrats won control of the legislature in November 1859, they passed the Baltimore Bills, a series of measures drafted by the City Reform Association that circumvented the municipal Know Nothing regime's control over elections by putting state government in charge of its police and courts. In appreciation of these laws, Wallis praised the legislature's Democratic majority for "that conservative action of theirs on your behalf and mine, that red-handed murder no longer writes election returns among us." Following the Pratt Street Riot Frederick Brune, Mayor Brown's business partner and brother-in-law, said that Know Nothing Governor Hicks and Congressman Davis "were elected by *fraudulent majorities in the city—and to such an extent did the corruption of this party proceed that it aroused the opposition of all conservative men in the city.*"[77]

Recent scholarship on Civil War era conservatism helps to contextualize this rhetoric. Unlike today, when the term *conservative* evokes a particular partisan allegiance, policy agenda, and constituency, in the mid-1800s the term stood for a "disposition," or sensibility, that signaled "a measured, mature approach to the problems of the world," and an "ethic of self-discipline and self-restraint" about politics. Conservatives valued orderly progress worked out through established institutions in opposition to rash action from momentary passions or the will of the mob. Although rarely used in the early years of the Republic, "conservative" became an ever more popular self-descriptor as upheavals at home and abroad beginning in the 1840s put the standing order in jeopardy.[78]

Malleable enough to be championed by opposing parties—in the 1860 presidential election, for example, all four candidates claimed to be the conservative choice—conservatism was used as an explanatory framework for northern Republican arguments in favor of free soil in the territories, and as a defense of the Buchanan administration, which advocated the protection of slavery throughout federally administered lands. This pattern could also be seen in Baltimore, where American Party leaders claimed to speak for the "conservative sentiment of the state" in opposing secession while their critics at the *Daily Exchange* advertised themselves as "INDEPENDENT and CONSERVATIVE, sympathizing with and watchful over the true interest of the South and West."[79]

Conservatism mattered most for Reformers as a political marker that differentiated their cause from that of their foes whom they often called "rowdies," "mobs," and "fanatics." Reformers employed this contrast to defend the Pratt Street Riot when they said, "It was the merchants and all the best citizens (not the rowdies) who armed themselves to prevent more troops passing through our city."[80] In addition, Reformers' identification with the politics of conservative respectability built an ideological bridge between their local battle with working-class Know Nothings and the sectional conflict raging across the country. Their proslavery Democratic allies in other states also defined themselves as conservatives representing the respectable classes in opposition to radical demagogues, in their case the Republican Party, who spoke for the unruly mob.

Some of those allies initially assumed that Know Nothing gangs perpetrated the Pratt Street Riot. According to Supreme Court Associate Justice John A. Campbell, who later held Confederate office, this "startling insurrection . . . was a wild spontaneous uprising and the clubs and associations that had paralyzed every one, as the tools of Hicks & Davis were foremost in it."[81] Although Campbell had the facts wrong, his description of the Know Nothings as puppeteers of the mob rang true to conservative Democratic opinion on urban violence. As Edmund Ruffin, Virginia's arch secessionist, put it, "Baltimore has long been under the rule of law breakers—of organized rioters, robbers, and murderers."[82]

Recently, historian Joshua Lynn has shown how 1850s Democrats adopted the conservative label but gave it a specific meaning as the antithesis of "fanaticism." Conservative Democrats applied fanaticism to an array of ills that went well beyond antislavery to encompass the many "isms" of the day that together used "the state to impose restrictive moral codes on independent white men, degrading their democratic autonomy and mastery."[83] The capture of municipal governments by working-class rowdies and the federal government by northern Republicans easily fit Democratic conservatism's larger political narrative.

Reinforcing the ideological bond of proslavery conservatism, Baltimore Reformers shared personal and professional relationships with many of the same influential politicians whose views they echoed. Of the prominent conservative Democrats connected to Reformers and secession activists, the one with the most ties was James A. Bayard Jr., a US senator from neighboring Delaware. Bayard's son and political advisor, Thomas, married Louisa Lee, the daughter of a wealthy Baltimore banker who was a member of northern Virginia's Lee dynasty, a family that included the famed Confederate general. Another, more circuitous family connection to Baltimore ran through the Chew family, one of Philadelphia's oldest and wealthiest family lines, with extensive real estate and mercantile investments, including land and slaves in Maryland. James Bayard's brother married into the Chews, as had John Eager Howard, Maryland's late eighteenth-century governor and the father of police board commissioner Charles Howard.[84]

Working through these prominent Baltimore relatives, the Bayards developed business relationships with Reform leaders George M. Gill, an attorney who lived next door to Thomas Bayard's mother-in-law, and E. Wyatt Blanchard, a Reform City Council member who, on April 19, 1861, encouraged armed resistance to the militia passing through Baltimore. Richard Snowden Andrews, the militia commander in charge of burning the northbound railroad bridges the night of the riot, was Thomas Bayard's brother-in-law and looked after one of Thomas's children who attended school in Baltimore. Finally, Charles Pitts, a Reformer and member of the Southern Rights delegation, counted the Bayards as friends and exchanged visits with them.[85]

Unlike the Reformers, James Bayard managed to avoid federal prison, but behind the scenes he frequently expressed his opinion that "the South is in the right," and schemed "to act with discretion so as to give time for such a concentration of the Southern Confederacy that we shall be supported efficiently if the people of Del[aware] determine to go with the South."[86] Although this statement remained private, pro-Union activists in Bayard's hometown of Wilmington knew enough of his secessionist leanings to call for his arrest. Bayard's son warned him of "the strange wild savage spirit of man that has arisen in the North, and cowed men either into compliance or silence" and had spurred on an attempt "to array Mob Law against you." Aware that "I may be mobbed in my native town," James Bayard worried that "we are near the *reign of terror,* and the law abiding portion of the Northern Cities will find to their cost that the wild spirit of lawlessness aroused for one purpose will not easily be allayed." In this exchange, the Bayards echoed their Baltimore allies in portraying themselves as conservative men of "firmness and moderation" fighting fanatical enemies bent on mob rule.[87]

The fact that the Bayards only managed to get their correspondence past federal monitors with the help of John and Frederick Brune suggests how dense personal ties between Baltimore Reformers and conservative Democrats outside the city reinforced their shared outlook on the politics of secession. These contacts also helped Bayard during the critical days of late April 1861. He traveled to Baltimore to "see the most intelligent men" from whom he sought advice on secession's popularity on Maryland's Eastern Shore, which bordered Delaware and would be an essential part of any attempt at bringing Bayard's home state out of the Union.[88]

Although the Bayards had the thickest network of Reform allies, several prominent Southern Democrats-turned-Confederates shared similar connections to the city officials of April 1861. For instance, the Howards were long-time friends of and occasional hosts to Jefferson Davis, which helps explain why Charles Howard felt comfortable lobbying Davis to give his sons Confederate military commissions. Howard was also related to James Murray Mason, another in-law of the Chew family. Late in 1862, the two had an odd reunion when they met as federal prisoners in Fort Warren, Massachusetts, after Mason was seized by the US Navy while trying to reach Britain on a diplomatic mission.[89]

Militia commander Isaac Trimble also counted Davis as a friend and hosted him after the war. Before 1861, Trimble, an engineer, had a successful career building railroads for slaveholder investors such as Richmond industrialist Joseph Anderson.[90] Baltimore's Samuel Wethered asked his brother-in-law, North Carolina secessionist Daniel Barringer, to send arms. Charles Gwinn, state's attorney for Baltimore in 1861 and a secession campaigner, had lobbied on behalf of a railroad interest for his friend Robert M. T. Hunter, a fire-eating US senator from Virginia who resigned his office to serve in the Confederate Senate. In 1860, Gwinn had collaborated with Hunter and the friends of President James Buchanan to fight Stephen Douglas's bid for the Democratic presidential nomination.[91]

Hunter was a business partner of John Kettlewell, a Baltimore guano merchant, whose high-powered endorsements included Georgia's Howell Cobb, "a personal friend . . . of many years standing," who was Buchanan's treasury secretary and later a Confederate senator. In an account of the Pratt Street Riot published in the *Charleston Mercury*, Kettlewell said, "We fought the enemy in our streets, for a mile and a half, with stones, bricks, pistols, hammers and *fists . . . Maryland is not subjugated!"*[92] Finally, James Chesnut Jr., Mary Chesnut's husband and a US senator from South Carolina who helped write the Confederate Constitution, was friends with William Preston, a Reform candidate for a Baltimore US House district in 1859 and a secession advocate two years later. Chesnut also helped Baltimore merchant Gustav Lurman distribute German translations of secessionist pamphlets.[93]

This is by no means an exhaustive list of Reformers' personal and professional relationships to prominent Southern secessionists, but it does indicate the depth of such ties and suggests how they reinforced Reformers' ideological affinities with proslavery conservatives. When Bayard, Mason, Davis, Hunter, Chesnut, and Barringer spoke to Baltimore Reformers about the dangers of northern fanaticism and the merits of the southern cause, they did so as long-time friends, business partners, and family members. Ideas and information circulated through this network via correspondence, friendly newspapers, and personal visits. Immersed in these circuits, Reformers operated in something like today's information bubbles, in which news consumers seek out like-minded sources and discount or ignore those that contradict their worldview. Reformers had far fewer ties to northern Republicans, and they shunned local Know Nothing leaders, such as Henry Winter Davis.[94] Illustrating this point, Nathaniel Banks, US military commander in Baltimore in July 1861, said that Charles Howard and men like him "do not comprehend the condition of things at all—They read nothing but their own papers. . . . They live and move in small coteries into which no ideas can penetrate except their own distorting medium . . ."[95]

Bolstering these personal and ideological affinities with secessionists, Baltimore Reformers' decision to take extralegal action in pursuit of their political objectives had plenty of practical precedents. Reformers had come to power only after changing the state's laws governing local police and courts. Moreover, the policy of armed neutrality and the legislative call for a "Committee of Public Safety" hearkened back to the numerous vigilante movements of the 1850s, which were concentrated in cities undergoing intense partisan political conflict. From California to New York, self-styled law-and-order conservatives tried to change the rules of city politics through intervention by allies in state government and the creation of nonpartisan vigilance committees.[96] Furthermore, secession itself unfolded not as an orderly constitutional process but instead as a series of dramatic steps taken by individual states, and often accompanied by paramilitary actions such as the seizure of federal arms, coercion of local Unionists, and embargoes of vital commodities, most notably cotton.[97] Those tactics failed miserably in Baltimore, but the men who employed them were operating in a political world that gave them plenty of reasons to think they would succeed.

Although armed neutrality amounted to little more than a brief secessionist moment in an otherwise staunchly pro-Union city, the example of Baltimore's Reformers offers insights into the fate of the Confederacy. Like the Baltimore leadership, most of the political leaders in the South's secession movement were ardent proslavery Democrats in the late 1850s.[98] They had been in communication for decades and often shared ties of family and work that reinforced ideological agreement.

Secession failed in short order in Maryland and it also failed nationally in the longer term, and for similar reasons. Overall the federal government and the free states had far more power than secessionists wanted to believe. The rush to secede through special legislative sessions and hastily called conventions left dissenters unreconciled and ripe for recruitment to the Union cause. And, even if secessionists had spent more time accommodating southern Unionists, it is doubtful they could have won them over given that their core purpose was to defend slavery even at the cost of disunion. In this respect, the proslavery conservatism that Baltimore Reformers shared with Southern secessionists, and which they used to wrap their support for slavery into a more generic claim to defend society against fanaticism and mob rule, failed to break the majority of Americans' deep attachment to the Union.

NOTES

1. The author thanks Charles Mitchell, Jean Baker, Jewel Spangler, and John Quist for their helpful comments on earlier drafts.

The scholarship on the Pratt Street Riot is too vast to fully catalogue here. For studies published in the twenty-first century see Charles W. Mitchell, "The Whirlwind Now Gathering: Baltimore's Pratt Street Riot and the End of Maryland Secession," *Maryland Historical Magazine* 97, no. 2 (2002): 203–32; Robert F. Bailey, "The Pratt Street Riots Reconsidered: A Case of Overstated Significance?," *Maryland Historical Magazine* 98, no. 2 (2003): 153–72; Frank Towers, *The Urban South and the Coming of the Civil War* (Charlottesville: University of Virginia Press, 2004), 149–82; David Detzer, *Dissonance: The Turbulent Days between Fort Sumter and Bull Run* (Orlando, FL: Harcourt, 2006), 104–66; Charles W. Mitchell, ed., *Maryland Voices of the Civil War* (Baltimore: Johns Hopkins University Press, 2007), 48–123; Nelson Lankford, *Cry Havoc: The Crooked Road to Civil War, 1861* (New York: Viking, 2007); Harry A. Ezratty, *Baltimore in the Civil War: The Pratt Street Riot and a City Occupied* (Charleston, SC: The History Press, 2010); William C. Harris, *Lincoln and the Border States: Preserving the Union* (Lawrence: University Press of Kansas, 2011), 42–79; Jonathan W. White, "Forty-Seven Eyewitness Accounts of the Pratt Street Riot and Its Aftermath," *Maryland Historical Magazine* 106, no. 1 (2011), 70–93; Jonathan W. White, *Abraham Lincoln and Treason in the Civil War: The Trials of John Merryman* (Baton Rouge: Louisiana State University Press, 2011), 10–24.

2. Matthew Page Andrews, "Passage of the 6th Massachusetts Regiment through Baltimore, April 19, 1861," *Maryland Historical Magazine* 41, no. 1 (1919), 60–76. An even earlier version of this perspective is in J. Thomas Scharf, *The Chronicles of Baltimore: Being a Complete History of "Baltimore Town" and Baltimore City from the Earliest Period to the Present Time* (Baltimore: Turnbull Brothers, 1874), 598–99, 605.

3. William J. Evitts, *A Matter of Allegiances: Maryland from 1850 to 1861* (Baltimore: Johns Hopkins University Press, 1974), 184. Also see Jean H. Baker, *The Politics of Continuity: Maryland Political Parties from 1858 to 1890* (Baltimore: Johns Hopkins University Press, 1973), 54; Robert Brugger, *Maryland: A Middle Temperament, 1634–1980* (Baltimore: Johns Hopkins University Press, 1988), 277; Mitchell, ed., *Maryland Voices of the Civil War*, 4; Harris, *Lincoln and the Border States*, 64; Michael D. Robinson, *A Union Indivisible: Secession and the Politics of Slavery in the Border South* (Chapel Hill: University of North Carolina Press, 2017), 179.

4. *History of Antietam National Cemetery, including a descriptive list of all the loyal soldiers buried therein: together with the ceremonies and address on the occasion of the dedication of the grounds, September, 17th, 1867* (Baltimore: J. W. Woods, 1869), 36.

5. *History of Antietam National Cemetery, including a descriptive list of all the loyal soldiers buried therein: together with the ceremonies and address on the occasion of the dedication of the grounds, September, 17th, 1867* (Baltimore: J. W. Woods, 1869), 36.

Patricia Dockman Anderson, ed., "A History of the Maryland Historical Society," special issue, *Maryland Historical Magazine* 101, no. 4 (Winter 2006), 431–34; Patricia Dockman Anderson, "Laying the Foundations: Herbert Baxter Adams, John Thomas Scharf, and Early Maryland Historical Scholarship," *Maryland Historical Magazine* 89 (Summer 1994), 170–83; Wendell H. Stephenson, "Herbert Baxter Adams and Southern Historical Scholarship at the Johns Hopkins University," *Maryland Historical Magazine* 47, no. 1 (1947), 1–20.

6. Andrews, "Passage of the 6th Massachusetts." At the turn of the twentieth century, Andrews, who was active in the Sons of Confederate Veterans, and Richard D. Fisher, a Reformer and volunteer in the secession-sympathizing Maryland Guard, gathered testimony from surviving eyewitnesses to the riot. Their social contacts with Lost Cause sympathizers may explain the pro-southern tilt to many of these accounts. For Fisher's biography see the *Sun* (Baltimore), August 18, 1910. For Andrews see Paul A. Shackel, *Memory in Black and White: Race, Commemoration, and the Post-Bellum Landscape* (Lanham, MD: Rowman and Littlefield, 2003), 71.

7. Series 1. General Correspondence. 1833–1916. Abraham Lincoln, Monday, April 15, 1861 (Proclamation on State Militia). Available at *Abraham Lincoln Papers at the Library of Congress*, Manuscript Division (Washington, DC: *American Memory Project*, 2000–02).

8. The separation of the railroad stations was an artifact of early railroad building when companies ran separate lines, and because of public opposition to allowing steam trains into the central business district. See Mary P. Ryan, *Taking the Land to Make the City: A Bicoastal History of North America* (Austin: University of Texas Press, 2019), 325.

9. Scott Sumpter Sheads and Daniel Carroll Toomey, *Baltimore during the Civil War* (Linthicum, MD: Toomey Press, 1997), 13–14.

10. *Daily Exchange* (Baltimore), April 20, 1861.

11. Quotation is in *The South* (Baltimore), April 22, 1861. Also see the *Baltimore American*, April 20, 1861. My first published article addressed the question of crowd size. Frank Towers, "'A Vociferous

Army of Howling Wolves': Baltimore's Civil War Riot of April 19, 1861," *The Maryland Historian* 23 (Fall/Winter 1992): 1–27.

12. Ezratty, *Baltimore in the Civil War,* 53.

13. Charles B. Clark, "Baltimore and the Attack on Sixth Massachusetts Regiment, April 19, 1861," *Maryland Historical Magazine* 56, no. 1 (1961), 41–42. Clark points out that Kane, in fact, had notice and time to prepare. See page 52.

14. *Baltimore American,* April 20, 1861.

15. *Public Ledger* (Philadelphia, PA), April 23, 1861; Edward G. Everett, "The Baltimore Riots," *Pennsylvania History: A Journal of Mid-Atlantic Studies* 24, no. 4 (1957): 331–42, 335. For the pursuit of the volunteers see Richard Snowden Andrews, *A Memoir,* ed. by Tunstall Smith (Baltimore: Sun Printing Office, 1910), 32.

16. Casualty numbers for the riot have been the subject of debate. Although most histories say rioters only killed four soldiers, all members of the Sixth Massachusetts Regiment, credible evidence indicates that they killed at least three and possibly five unarmed volunteers of the Washington Brigade at President Station. My earlier research argued for a higher Union death count based on accounts of soldiers who died from their wounds later or those Pennsylvanians who scattered after the riot and were never heard from again. Without better confirmation of those deaths, however, it is more accurate to talk about minimum numbers rather than conjecture about additional ones.

For the most frequently cited firsthand sources on casualties see George William Brown, *Baltimore and the 19th of April: A Study of the War* (Baltimore: N. Murray, 1887); the documents collected under the heading "Riot in Baltimore" in US War Department, *The War of the Rebellion: A Compilation of the Official Records of the Union and Confederate Armies* (Washington, DC: Government Printing Office, 1880–1901), ser. 1, 2:7–21; John W. Hanson, *Historical Sketch of the Old Sixth Regiment of Massachusetts Volunteers during Its Three Campaigns* (Boston: Lee and Shepard, 1866); and the *Sun* (Baltimore) and *Baltimore American* for the days immediately following the riot.

Primary source accounts of the Pennsylvania volunteers include the *Public Ledger* (Philadelphia), April 20 and 23, 1861. Also see Everett, "The Baltimore Riots," 334; Jacques Kelly, "2nd Civil War Riot, Rivalling Pratt Street, Is Unearthed," *Baltimore Sun,* March 18, 1992; Detzer, *Dissonance,* 139; Sheads and Toomey, *Baltimore during the Civil War,* 153–54.

17. Local newspapers do not mention the term immediately after the riot, but it appears in private correspondence as early as April 19 and by the following Monday was circulating in the press and correspondence as the policy of municipal government. See Henry Lowe to John Judge, April 19, 1861, John Judge Papers, Southern Historical Collection, Wilson Library, University of North Carolina, Chapel Hill (hereinafter cited as UNCSC); *New York Times,* April 22, 1861. Mayor Brown devoted an entire chapter of his memoir to "Armed Neutrality."

18. These measures are listed in almost every account of the riot. In addition to the sources in note 1, see Clark, "Baltimore and the Attack on Sixth Massachusetts Regiment," 55–61, 65. For more on the seizure of arms and documents from the Pikesville Arsenal see Andrews, *A Memoir,* 34.

Police actions against Unionists are described in David Creamer, "Notes of Evidence before the U.S. Grand Jury, June Term, 1861," Manuscript Division, Library of Congress (hereinafter LC), 3-5, 7, 17-18, 22-24, 27, 33-34, 36; and William Bowly Wilson, Reminiscences of the Nineteenth of April 1861, Civil War File, Special Collections, Maryland Historical Society (hereinafter MdHS).

For anti-Union mob violence see the *Baltimore American,* April 22, 1861, and *Sun* (Baltimore),

April 22, 1861; David Einhorn, "A Farewell to Baltimore," *American Jewish Archives* 13 (November 1961): 150–54; Catherine Smith to "Ellen," April 20, 1861, vertical file, MdHS.

19. *Baltimore American,* April 25, 1861. In 1860, the Democratic Party majority in the state legislature removed the Know Nothings elected from Baltimore on the grounds that they obtained their seats through force and fraud. The April 24, 1861, elections filled those vacated seats. See Matthew A. Crenson, *Baltimore: A Political History* (Baltimore: Johns Hopkins University Press, 2017), 230.

20. Recent reviews of these events are in Robinson, *A Union Indivisible,* 164, and Harris, *Lincoln and the Border States,* 57–59.

21. For an especially vivid account see Mitchell, *Maryland Voices of the Civil War,* 48–123. Also see Sheads and Toomey, *Baltimore during the Civil War,* 30. The Committee of Public Safety is described in Robinson, *A Union Indivisible,* 167.

22. Firing of pro-Union officers is described in the *Baltimore American,* May 1, 1861.

23. Federal provost Marshal Kenly found over 400 muskets and pistols, thousands of rounds of ammunition, and four cannons in city offices. See the *Baltimore American,* June 29, 1861.

24. In addition to the sources in note 1, see Harold R. Manakee, *Maryland in the Civil War* (Baltimore: Maryland Historical Society, 1961), 52–55; and Frank Towers, "Strange Bedfellows: The Union Party and the Federal Government in Civil War Baltimore," *Maryland Historical Magazine* 106, no. 1 (2011): 11–13. For newspapers see Sidney T. Mathews, "Control of the Baltimore Press during the Civil War," *Maryland Historical Magazine* 46, no. 2 (1941): 150–70.

25. Evitts, *Matter of Allegiances,* 186–87; Mitchell, "The Whirlwind Now Gathering"; Harris, *Lincoln and the Border States,* 57; Robinson *A Union Indivisible,* 165–71.

26. Banks quoted in Bernard C. Steiner, *Citizenship and Suffrage in Maryland* (Baltimore: Cushing, 1895), 41.

27. The leading work on Maryland's Civil War politics remains Baker, *The Politics of Continuity.* For Baltimore see Crenson, *Baltimore: A Political History,* chap. 20.

28. For the close connection between the Reform Association and Democrats see Baker, *Politics of Continuity,* 27.

29. Timothy Snyder, "The Susquehanna Will Run Red with Blood: The Secession Movement in Maryland," *Maryland Historical Magazine* 108, no. 1 (2013), 57–78. Quote is on page 37. Also see Evitts, *Matter of Allegiances,* 67.

30. The list of officers published in the *Sun* (Baltimore), February 2, 1861, was checked against an array of primary sources. The most useful were the Baltimore newspapers the *Sun, Daily Exchange, Daily Baltimore Republican,* and *Baltimore American.*

31. *Baltimore American,* November 3, 1859.

32. George Brown to Frederick Brune, July 13, 1860, Brune-Randall Collection, box 6, MdHS.

33. Hugh Lennox Bond, Recollections of April 19, 1861, n.d., in J. Morrison Harris Papers, box 5, MdHS.

34. W. W. Glenn, *Between North and South: A Maryland Journalist Views the Civil War. The Narrative of William Wilkins Glenn, 1861–1869,* ed. by Bayly Ellen Marks and Mark Norton Schatz (Rutherford, NJ: Farleigh-Dickinson University Press, 1976), 290.

35. Reform Association members on the States' and Southern Rights ticket were William G. Harrison, Charles Pitts, Lawrence Sangston, J. Hanson Thomas, Severn T. Wallis, and Henry M. Warfield. In 1859 Harrison ran as the Independent/Reform nominee for the Fourth Congressional

District against American Party incumbent Henry Winter Davis (*Baltimore American,* November 3, 1859). In 1859 and 1860 Pitts spoke at Reform Association rallies and was a member (*Baltimore American,* October 29 and 31, 1859, and the *Daily Exchange,* October 4, 1860). Sangston was the Eighteenth Ward delegate on a Reform committee contesting the results of the 1859 elections (*Sun,* November 18, 1859). Thomas was a Reform ward leader and election judge (*Baltimore American,* October 8 and November 1 and 3, 1859). Wallis helped found the Reform Association was a featured speaker at its rallies (e.g., *Daily Exchange,* October 4, 1860). Finally, Warfield's Reform involvement included serving as a pallbearer for Adam Kyle Jr., whose murder by Know Nothing gang members became a celebrated cause for the Reform Association. Kyle's murder is discussed below. For Scott see US House of Representatives, "Evidence in the Case of William G. Harrison, Contesting the Seat of Henry Winter Davis," from the Fourth District of Maryland. House Miscellaneous Document 4, 169–70, in US House of Representatives, *The Miscellaneous Documents of the House of Representatives printed during the First Session of Thirty-Sixth Congress, 1859–60* (Washington, DC: Thomas H. Ford, 1860).

36. Robinson, *A Union Indivisible,* 199.

37. Abraham Lincoln, "Statement Concerning the Arrests in Maryland," September 15, 1861, in Roy P. Basler et al., *The Collected Works of Abraham Lincoln,* vol. 4 (1953, rpr. University of Michigan Digital Library Production Services: Ann Arbor, Michigan, 2001), https://quod.lib.umich.edu/l/lincoln/lincoln4/1:976?rgn=div1;view=fulltext;q1=July+4%2C+1861#.

38. Nathaniel P. Banks, Major General Commanding the Department of Annapolis, "Proclamation to the People of the City of Baltimore, June 27, 1861," in the *Sun* (Baltimore), June 28, 1861.

39. Bernard C. Steiner, "Severn Teackle Wallis: First Paper," *The Sewanee Review,* 15, no. 1 (1907), 72.

40. Severn T. Wallis and John Sherman, *Correspondence between S. T. Wallis, Esq. and the Hon. John Sherman, of the U.S. Senate, Concerning the Arrest of Members of the Maryland Legislature, and the Mayor and Police Commissioners of Baltimore in 1861* (Baltimore: Kelly, Hedian, and Piet, 1863), 10.

41. Henry Winter Davis to Abraham Lincoln, n.d. [February 1861], Abraham Lincoln Papers, LC; Gerald S. Henig, *Henry Winter Davis: Antebellum and Civil War Congressman from Maryland* (New York: Twayne, 1973), 155 (2nd quote).

42. Thomas L. Shanklin, "David Creamer and the Baltimore Mob Riot, April 19, 1861," *Methodist History* 13, no. 4 (1975), 63.

43. "Old Guard" to Thomas Hicks, June 25, 1861, Thomas Hicks Papers, MdHS.

44. *New York Times,* April 22 and 25, 1861; Marc Egnal, *Clash of Extremes: The Economic Origins of the Civil War* (New York: Hill and Wang, 2009), 303 (Greeley quoted); *New York Daily Herald,* April 22 and 23, 1861.

45. Ira F. Gensil, entry for May 15, 1861, "Journal of the Doylestown Guards, 1861," William W. H. Davis Papers, Spruance Library, Bucks County Historical Society, Doylestown, Pennsylvania; William Watts Hart Davis, to Anna Davis, May 16, 1861, W. W. H. Davis Papers, Beinecke Rare Book and Manuscript Depository, Yale University, New Haven, Connecticut; Robert H. Crist to his father, August 26, 1861, in Robert H. Crist, Letters, 1860–1861, Filson Historical Society, Louisville, Kentucky.

46. Joseph C. Booth to Phebe Daugherty, April 21, 1861, in the Phebe Wood Coburn Daugherty Papers, Filson Historical Society. To the best of this author's knowledge Joseph C. Booth was not related President Lincoln's assassin, John Wilkes Booth.

47. Testimony of Robert H. Walker in White, "Forty-Seven Eyewitness Accounts," 92.

48. Lowe to Judge, April 19, 1861.

49. Mary Chesnut, *The Private Mary Chesnut: The Unpublished Civil War Diaries,* ed. by C. Vann Woodward and Elisabeth Muhlenfeld (New York: Oxford University Press, 1984), 62–63. For more on Huger see *The South* (Baltimore), April 22, 1861, and Mitchell, ed., *Maryland Voices of the Civil War,* 79; *Charleston Mercury,* April 26, 1861.

50. Isaac Trimble to Morris A. Moore, Adjutant to Gov. Pickens, April 30, 1861, Isaac Trimble Papers, MdHS. In the Trimble Papers also see I. Thomas to Isaac Trimble, May 5, 1861. Charles Howard to Major M. M. Clark (USA), May 1, 1861, and Charles Howard to George P. Kane, May 2, 1861, in Letters Sent by the Baltimore Board of Police, 1861, Military Records, Middle Department, RG 393, part 4, National Archives and Records Administration, College Park, Maryland.

51. City spending charges are in Wallis and Sherman, *Correspondence,* 10. For Confederate volunteer estimates see Daniel D. Hartzler, *Marylanders in the Confederacy* (Westminster, Maryland: Family Line Publications, 1986), 1.

52. Wallis and Sherman, *Correspondence,* 10; Charles Howard to "General Mason" (CSA), April 30, 1861, and Howard to Col. Benjamin F. Huger, May 3, 1861, in Letters Sent by the Baltimore Board of Police, 1861.

53. G. D. Harrison to Jefferson Davis, April 24, 1861, in *The Papers of Jefferson Davis,* vol. 7, Spring 1861, eds. Lynda Laswell Crist and Mary Seaton Dix (Baton Rouge: Louisiana State University Press, 1992), 121.

54. Samuel Wethered to Daniel M. Barringer, April 19, 1861, Daniel Moreau Barringer Papers, box 3, UNCSC. For the secessionist activities of Charles and John Wethered see *The South* (Baltimore), April 22, 1861 and the *Sun* (Baltimore), April 20, 1861.

55. Kane quoted in Sheads and Toomey, *Baltimore during the Civil War,* 19–20. For Kane's Confederate activities see George P. Kane, *To All the Marylanders in the Confederate States* (n.p., 1864), https://www.loc.gov/item/rbpe.03101700/.

56. James M. Mason to Jefferson Davis, May 6, 1861, in *The Papers of Jefferson Davis,* 7: 148–151. Also see Robert W. Young, *James Murray Mason: Defender of the Old South* (Knoxville: University of Tennessee Press, 1998), 18.

57. George L. P. Radcliffe, *Governor Thomas H. Hicks of Maryland and the Civil War* (Baltimore: Johns Hopkins University Press, 1901), 33–35; Evitts, *Matter of Allegiances,* 164.

58. *The South* (Baltimore), April 22, 1861.

59. *The South* (Baltimore), April 22, 1861.

60. For the *Daily Exchange* in 1861 see Glenn, *Between North and South,* 18–19.

61. William Louis Winans to Thomas Winans, May 17, 1861, Ross Winans Papers, MdHS.

62. William Louis Winans to Thomas Winans, May 17, 1861, Ross Winans Papers, MdHS. George M. Gill to George W. Brown, July 12, 1861, in *War of the Rebellion,* ser. 1, 2:21–22.

63. Wallis and Sherman, *Correspondence,* 6.

64. Lawrence Sangston, *The Bastilles of the North, by a Member of the Maryland Legislature* (Baltimore: Kelly, Hedian and Piet, 1863), 4.

65. Brown, *Baltimore and the 19th of April,* 26, 115.

66. Robinson, *A Union Indivisible,* 5. Also see Daniel W. Crofts, *Reluctant Confederates: Upper South Unionists in the Secession Crisis* (Chapel Hill: University of North Carolina Press, 1989); Ed-

ward L. Ayers, *In the Presence of Mine Enemies: The Civil War in the Heart of America, 1859–1863* (New York: Norton, 2003); and Christopher Phillips, *The Rivers Ran Backwards: The Civil War and the Remaking of the American Middle Border* (New York: Oxford University Press, 2016).

67. Aaron Astor, *Rebels on the Border: Civil War, Emancipation and the Reconstruction of Kentucky and Missouri* (Baton Rouge: Louisiana State University Press, 2012), 84 (quotation); Anne E. Marshall, *Creating a Confederate Kentucky: The Lost Cause and Civil War Memory in a Border State* (Chapel Hill: University of North Carolina Press, 2010), 17; Phillips, *The Rivers Ran Backwards*, 125–26.

68. Harris, *Lincoln and the Border States*, 72. Also see Evitts, *Matter of Allegiances*, 186–87; Baker, *Politics of Continuity*, 53; Lankford, *Cry Havoc*, 148–49; and Robinson, *A Union Indivisible*, 90–91, 177.

69. *Sun* (Baltimore), April 23, 1861.

70. Baker, *Politics of Continuity*, 50–53; Evitts, *Matter of Allegiances*, 184.

71. Towers, *Urban South*, 189–92, 210–11.

72. Towers, *Urban South*, chap. 5; Sangston, *Bastilles of the North*, 5.

73. Towers, *Urban South*, 119–20. On antipartyism see Mark Voss-Hubbard, *Beyond Party: Cultures of Antipartisanship in Northern Politics before the Civil War* (Baltimore: Johns Hopkins University Press, 2002) and Ronald P. Formisano, *For the People: American Populist Movements from the Revolution to the 1850s* (Chapel Hill: University of North Carolina Press, 2008).

74. For Kyle's pallbearers and first quotation see *Daily Exchange* (Baltimore), November 5, 1859. Other quotes and larger context are presented in Towers, *Urban South*, 149–51, 171–72, 174.

75. *The Daily Baltimore Republican*, April 20, 1861; *The South* (Baltimore), April 23, 1861; Frank Key Howard, *Fourteen Months in American Bastilles* (Baltimore: Kelly, Hedian, and Piet, 1865), 9.

76. *Daily Exchange* (Baltimore), October 11, 1859, and February 4, 1861 (Wallis quoted); Samuel K. George to Thomas H. Seymour, October 13, 1859, Thomas H. Seymour Papers, Connecticut Historical Society, Hartford.

77. Frederick W. Brune to "Forbes," June 21, 1861, Brune-Randall Collection. For the Baltimore Bills see Evitts, *Matter of Allegiances*, 132.

78. Adam I. P. Smith, *The Stormy Present: Conservatism and the Problem of Slavery in Northern Politics, 1846–1865* (Chapel Hill: University of North Carolina Press, 2017), 5 (quotation), 135–64; Adam I. P. Smith, "The Emergence of Conservatism as a Political Concept in the United States before the Civil War," *Civil War History* 66, no. 3 (2020), 231–55; Matthew Mason, *Apostle of Union: A Political Biography of Edward Everett* (Chapel Hill: University of North Carolina Press, 2016); Michael F. Conlin, "The Dangerous *Isms* and the Fanatical *Ists:* Antebellum Conservatives in the South and the North Confront the Modernity Conspiracy," *Journal of the Civil War Era* 4, no. 2 (2014): 205–33.

79. J. Morrison Harris, *State of the Union. Speech of Hon. J. Morrison Harris, of Maryland, Delivered in the House of Representatives, January 29, 1861* (Washington: H. Polkinhorn, 1861), 5; *Daily Exchange* (Baltimore), May 11, 1861.

80. Jabez D. Pratt to John C. Pratt, April 27, 1861, Civil War File, MS#1860, Special Collections, MdHS.

81. John A. Campbell to Jefferson Davis, April 23, 1861, in *The Papers of Jefferson Davis*, 7: 117.

82. William K. Scarborough, ed., *The Diary of Edmund Ruffin*, 2 vols. (Baton Rouge: Louisiana State University Press, 1972–76), 1:294.

83. Joshua A. Lynn, *Preserving the White Man's Republic: Jacksonian Democracy, Race, and the Transformation of American Conservatism* (Charlottesville: University of Virginia Press, 2019), 36.

84. Scharf, *History of Baltimore City and County,* 67; John L. Jordan, ed., *Colonial Families of Philadelphia,* vol. 2 (New York: Lewis Publishing, 1911), 1,702.

85. Bayard's contacts with Baltimore Reformers are documented in the Thomas F. Bayard Papers, LC. See the following correspondence: George M. Gill to Thomas Bayard, August 8, 1859; E. Wyatt Blanchard to Thomas Bayard, February 24, 1860; Charles Pitts to Thomas Bayard, July 3, 1860; and R. Snowden Andrews to Thomas Bayard, January 24, 1861. Andrews, *A Memoir,* 32.

For Blanchard's Reform activism see the *Baltimore American,* November 3, 1859; *Daily Exchange* (Baltimore), October 11, 1860; Bond, Recollections of April 19, 1861.

86. James Bayard to Thomas Bayard, April 26, 1861, Bayard Papers. Also see Robinson, *A Union Indivisible,* 160.

87. In the Bayard Papers see James Bayard to Thomas Bayard, April 26 and May 1, 1861, and Thomas Bayard to James Bayard, April 29, 1861.

88. James Bayard to Thomas Bayard, April 26, 1861, Bayard Papers.

89. Jefferson Davis to Benjamin Chew Howard, August 1, 1858, Howard Family Papers, Special Collections, MdHS; Charles Howard to Jefferson Davis, April 4, 1861, in *The Papers of Jefferson Davis,* 7:91; James Murray Mason to Eliza Murray, December 3, 1861, in Virginia Mason, *The Public Life and Diplomatic Correspondence of James M. Mason with Some Personal History,* 2nd edition (New York: Neale Publishing, 1906), 207.

90. "Postwar Life and Career," *The Papers of Jefferson Davis,* Rice University, https://jeffersondavis .rice.edu/about-jefferson-davis/chronology/postwar-life-and-career. For Trimble's engineering work see Daniel B. Rood, *The Reinvention of Atlantic Slavery: Technology, Labor, Race, and Capitalism in the Greater Caribbean* (New York: Oxford University Press, 2017), 107, 110.

91. Charles J. M. Gwinn to Robert M. T. Hunter, June 20, 1860, Robert M. T. Hunter Papers, Library of Virginia, Richmond.

92. John Kettlewell to Robert M. T. Hunter, July 30, 1852, Hunter Papers; Augusta, Georgia, *Daily Constitutionalist and Republic,* December 13, 1859; *Charleston Mercury,* April 26, 1861.

93. William P. Preston to James Chesnut, April 28, 1860, and Gustav W. Lurman to James Chesnut, July 2, 1860, in the James Chesnut Papers, South Carolina Historical Society, Charleston.

94. Henig, *Henry Winter Davis,* 118–19; Frederick W. Brune to Emily Brune, October 27, 1860, Brune-Randall Collection, box 14.

95. Nathaniel Banks to William H. Seward, July 9, 1861, quoted in Harris, *Lincoln and the Border States,* 67.

96. See especially Mary P. Ryan, *Civic Wars: Democracy and Public Life in the American City during the Nineteenth Century* (Berkeley: University of California Press, 1997). Also see Louis S. Gerteis, *Civil War St. Louis* (Lawrence: University Press of Kansas, 2001), 111–12; John Mack Faragher, *Eternity Street: Violence and Justice in Frontier Los Angeles* (New York: W. W. Norton, 2016), 389–96.

97. A comprehensive history of these steps is presented in William W. Freehling, *The Road to Disunion, Volume 2. Secessionists Triumphant* (New York: Oxford University, 2007).

98. Of course, not all of the South's proslavery Democrats became secessionists. The point is simply that these leaders shared prior political ties.

ABRAHAM LINCOLN, CIVIL LIBERTIES, & MARYLAND

FRANK J. WILLIAMS

Much like the United States itself, Maryland was a state divided during the antebellum period and the Civil War. During the antebellum era, most Marylanders accepted slavery, while a few either opposed slavery or were vehement abolitionists. During the Civil War, these same divisions persisted. Most Marylanders supported military force to remain in the Union, while a significant portion of the population wanted to create a Border State confederacy to broker a peace between North and South. On the other hand, a minority of Marylanders wanted the state to secede and join the Confederacy.[1] These tensions caused President Abraham Lincoln to take extraordinary steps after his inauguration as president to ensure that the state stayed under the control of the United States government.[2] These steps may have crossed peacetime constitutional bounds, but in the end, they helped to keep Maryland in the Union, preserving the nation as unified.

VOLATILITY IN MARYLAND BEFORE AND DURING THE CIVIL WAR

Maryland was a center of volatility throughout much of the beginning of the Civil War. On November 6, 1860, Republican Abraham Lincoln from Illinois was elected the sixteenth president of the United States, receiving 39 percent of the votes cast in a four-candidate race. While not a majority, it was proof positive of the strength of the new Republican Party, which would dominate national elections until just before World War I. Even before his election, southern states had threatened secession if he was elected.[3] In an effort to encourage unity, despite the secession of seven states, Lincoln decided to travel from his home in Springfield to Washington, DC, on a whistle-stop tour that took him along 1,904 miles of railroad tracks. He traveled on eighteen different trains and made brief appearances along the way to speak to crowds. He stopped in the cities of Indianapolis, Cincinnati, Columbus, Pittsburgh, Cleveland, Buffalo, Albany, New York, Philadelphia, and Harrisburg. In doing so, Lincoln believed that he could reach out to the people and unite them behind his presidency.[4]

To provide security, the railroad hired Allan Pinkerton to protect the president while traveling.[5] Pinkerton, head of the Pinkerton Detective Agency, alleged that there was a plot to ambush the president-elect in Baltimore, believing that assassins would be among the crowds greeting Lincoln when he left the train.[6] Accordingly Pinkerton pleaded with the president-elect to avoid Baltimore after his stop at Harrisburg and instead go directly to Washington. But Lincoln insisted going through to Baltimore after stopping in Philadelphia. In his remarks at Independence Hall, after he raised the American flag, he stated, "If it can, I will consider myself one of the happiest men in the world if I can help to save it. If it can't be saved upon that principle, it will be truly awful. But, if this country [the United States] cannot be saved without giving up that principle—-I was about to say I would rather be assassinated on this spot than to surrender it."[7] Was the president-elect thinking of the danger to him of the Baltimore plot? Pinkerton especially feared Baltimore because it required switching trains by walking or riding between two stations. Pinkerton believed that he had, at the time, intelligence that the president-elect would be killed during this transfer.

On the evening of February 22, 1861, eleven days after the start of Lincoln's trip, in an extraordinary extension of his authority, Pinkerton ordered the telegraph lines into Baltimore cut as a security measure. Lincoln then boarded a secret train to travel through Baltimore in the middle of the night.[8] As was often the case in Baltimore when switching between President Street and Camden Stations, Lincoln's train car was drawn by horses.[9] The *New York Times* reported that Lincoln, while traveling through Baltimore, wore "'a Scotch plaid cap and very long military cloak.'"[10] Despite this report, Lincoln did not adopt such a disguise; instead, he wore "a soft, low-crowned hat, a muffler around his neck, and a short bob-tailed overcoat."[11] But the caricature of Lincoln in a plaid cap and overcoat persisted in negative cartoons of the president. And "[t]he Baltimore newspapers portrayed a cowardly president elect sneaking into the capital afraid for his life."[12] This ridicule of the president-elect did much to diminish the seriousness of future threats in Lincoln's mind. There was no mention of anyone believed to be in a conspiracy to assassinate Lincoln. This and lack of evidence makes one believe that the attempt on Lincoln's life to be unsubstantiated.

Ten days later Abraham Lincoln was sworn in as the nation's sixteenth president. He concluded his inaugural speech by imploring:

> We are not enemies, but friends. We must not be enemies. Though passion may have strained it must not break our bonds of affection. The mystic chords of memory, stretching from every battlefield and patriot grave to every living heart and hearthstone all over this broad land, will yet swell the chorus of the Union, when again touched, as surely they will be, by the better angels of our nature.[13]

The new president's plea for unity and peace was genuine, but it did not accomplish his goal. The secession of southern states continued, and the Civil War rapidly became the most violent confrontation on our soil that this country has ever seen. It brought with it continuing challenges to civil liberties that were especially notable in Maryland in the early days of the war.

Maryland was an essential link between Washington, DC, and Union states in the North. The state, with Virginia, surrounded the capital. The only railroad connections to Washington, via several rail lines, ran through the state, with stops in Baltimore to switch trains. Critical telegraph lines and bridges connected the federal government with northern states.

Maryland, as a Border State, was home to both slaveholders and antislavery supporters as well as secessionists and Unionists. "[Maryland] had voted for the southern Democrat, [John C.] Breckinridge, in the 1860 presidential election, and its legislature was controlled by Democrats sympathetic to the South." The eastern side of the state, according to one authority, "was slave-dependent and drawn to the Confederacy" while "[t]he northern and western sections of the state, where there were virtually no slaves, were loyal to the Union." Meanwhile Baltimore, which contained one-third of the state's population, held an appreciable number of southern sympathizers.[14] Troops, intended for service to the Confederate states, were already being recruited in Maryland before Lincoln's inauguration.

With a population of more than two hundred thousand, Baltimore was nearly twice the size of Chicago, and was, at the beginning of the Civil War, the nation's fourth largest city, after New York, Philadelphia, and Brooklyn. It was a major shipping hub and also served as a port of arrival for immigrants from both Ireland and Germany.

These factors made Maryland a hotbed of problems for President Lincoln's administration. He needed desperately to maintain Maryland as a Union state, in part to keep Washington, DC's, physical connection with the North.

SUSPENSION OF HABEAS CORPUS
AND *Ex Parte Merryman*

The first challenge to civil liberties involved the suspension of the ancient protection of habeas corpus allowing citizens to be arrested and detained without a hearing for cause before a magistrate. On April 27, 1861, Lincoln initially suspended the writ of habeas corpus along the rail lines through Maryland with a letter to Lieut. Gen. Winfield Scott, General-in-Chief of the US Army. This was meant as a military order to cover the areas near and on rail lines to keep troops moving through the state.[15] Lincoln's letter suspending the writ made clear the narrow parameters for such suspension:

To the Commanding General of the Army of the United States:

You are engaged in repressing an insurrection against the laws of the United States. If at any point on or in the vicinity of the [any] military line, which is now [or which shall be] used between the City of Philadelphia and the City of Washington, via Perryville, Annapolis City, and Annapolis Junction, you find resistance which renders it necessary to suspend the writ of Habeas Corpus for the public safety, you, personally or through the officer in command at the point where the [at which] resistance occurs, are authorized to suspend that writ.

ABRAHAM LINCOLN.[16]

Lincoln believed that the right of habeas corpus was so important that the president considered the bombardment of Maryland cities as preferable to the suspension of the writ, having authorized Gen. Scott to bombard the cities, but only "in the extremest necessity" was Scott to suspend the writ of habeas corpus.[17] Gen. Benjamin F. Butler, who was stationed "at a point called Relay

House, on the Baltimore and Ohio Railway, eight miles south of Baltimore" decided, on the basis of "suppress[ing] a rumored riot," to enter Baltimore itself.[18] His troops took possession of Federal Hill and trained guns and cannon on the city.[19] Butler sent a letter to Fort McHenry's commander, Maj. William Morris, stating, "I have taken possession of Baltimore. My troops are on Federal Hill, which I can hold with the aid of my artillery. If I am attacked tonight, please open upon Monument Square with your mortars."[20] However, "[t]he people of Baltimore were justly incensed at this insult, so Scott quickly sent Butler a message of rebuke and acted to remove him from direct command of his brigade."[21] Lincoln, acknowledging that Butler was a pro-Union Democrat and himself furious with Butler's actions, instead proposed he be sent to command Fortress Monroe in Virginia to get him out of the way.[22]

The Union command began arresting suspected southern sympathizers and conspirators.[23] These arrests arguably violated the civil liberties as civilian defendants were held without being charged with any crime. A court, state or federal, "can use the writ of habeas corpus to determine if a state's detention of a prisoner is valid."[24] Further, "[a] writ of habeas corpus is used to bring a prisoner or other detainee . . . before the court to determine if the person's imprisonment or detention is lawful."[25] It was through this legal vehicle that President Lincoln first tested his wartime authority.[26]

After the Confederates bombarded Fort Sumter in Charleston Harbor in April 1861, Lincoln acted. He federalized seventy-five thousand state militia to suppress "combinations in seven states too powerful to be suppressed by the ordinary course of judicial proceedings." In one of the first of several constitutional anomalies, there was no declaration of war by the US Congress, as it was not in session during this time.[27] In fact, the Union government did not regard the Civil War as similar to a conflict between independent nations; thus it did not fall under the requirement in Article 1, Section 8 of the US Constitution that required a congressional declaration of war. Rather it was a war of rebellion.

Confederate troops visible from the White House placed the capital in jeopardy, given that it was bordered by Virginia, a state that would soon secede, and Maryland, where there were southern sympathizers and an undercurrent of secession.[28] At the urging of his secretary of state, William H. Seward, Lincoln concluded that it was necessary to suspend the "Great Writ" of habeas corpus.[29] Although Congress was in recess, Lincoln, relying on the constitutional authorization that the framers had perceptively included years before, authorized General Scott to suspend the writ, believing that his duty to protect the capital and the Union during a rebellion required such an action.[30] The president would explain his actions in his special message to Congress on July 4, 1861, and in his 1863 letter to Erastus Corning.[31]

> Ours is a case of Rebellion—so called by the resolutions before me—in fact, a clear, flagrant, and gigantic case of Rebellion; and the provision of the constitution that "the privilege of the writ of Habeas Corpus shall not be suspended, unless when in cases of Rebellion or Invasion, the public Safety may require it" is the provision which specially applies to our present case. This provision plainly attests the understanding of those who made the constitution that ordinary courts of justice are inadequate to "cases of Rebellion"—attests their purpose that in such cases, men may be held in custody whom the courts acting on ordinary rules, would discharge. Habeas Corpus, does not discharge men who are proved to be guilty of defined crime; and its suspension is allowed by the constitution on purpose that, men may be arrested and held, who can not be proved to be guilty of defined crime, "when, in cases of Rebellion or Invasion the public Safety may require it." This is precisely our present case—a case of Rebellion, wherein the public Safety does require the suspension.[32]

The effect was to enable military commanders to arrest and detain citizens indefinitely when it was believed their words and acts were disloyal.[33] Lincoln saw the need for immediate action, though he was often unaware of the extent of this arrests. He and some of his advisors believed that it was necessary to divest these civil liberties from those who were believed to be treasonous and whose overt acts against the United States threatened its survival.[34]

A month after the proclamation, Capt. Samuel Yohe, empowered by Lincoln's suspension of habeas, entered the Baltimore County home of John Merryman, a Baltimore County farmer who had spoken out vigorously against President Lincoln and who had been complicit in destroying bridges and telegraph lines necessary to travel through Maryland to Washington.[35] He arrested Merryman for various acts of treason, including his leadership of the secessionist group that had destroyed railroad bridges after the Baltimore riots in April

1861 when troops of the Sixth Massachusetts were attacked as they made their way between train stations on their way to defend Washington.[36]

Merryman's attorney sought a writ of habeas corpus, directing his petition to US Supreme Court Chief Justice Roger Brooke Taney, at the time sitting as a judge of the United States Circuit Court for the District of Maryland. Taney granted the writ.[37]

Taney, who grew up in a slaveholding family, but did not own slaves himself, had been a strong supporter of Andrew Jackson in 1828. When Jackson was elected, Taney was appointed United States attorney general, and following that post, he became the secretary of the treasury. Taney was President Jackson's choice to serve as chief justice of the United States Supreme Court after Chief Justice John Marshall's death in 1835.

Chief Justice Taney, according to one authority, "steered the Court away from expansive decisions when slavery was an issue, insisting that the relevant state law governed." Taney, however, became infamous for an exception: his holding in the 1857 *Dred Scott* decision, in which he and a majority of the Supreme Court held that Blacks could not be citizens and they had "no rights which the white men were bound to respect." He and President Lincoln disagreed over whether the South had a legal right to secede from the Union. In fact, Chief Justice Taney believed that "not only . . . that secession was legal, but also that a peaceful separation of North and South, with each forming an independent republic, was preferable to civil war."[38]

On Sunday, May 26, 1861, Taney issued a writ to Gen. George Cadwalader, who was military commander in Baltimore, but not in command at Fort McHenry, directing him to produce Merryman before the court the next day. A lawyer himself, Cadwalader respectfully refused on the ground that Lincoln had authorized the suspension of the writ of *habeas corpus*.[39]

Cadwalader's actions were constitutional blasphemy to Taney, who immediately issued an attachment for Cadwalader for contempt.[40] But the marshal could not gain entrance to the fort to serve the attachment, so Taney, recognizing the impossibility of enforcing his order, wrote his now famous opinion, *Ex Parte Merryman*.[41] The chief justice conducted a hearing, at which "[h]e appeared to be marking time, impatiently, until he could bring the session to a close."[42] When the hearing concluded, Chief Justice Taney announced his decision:

General Cadwalader was by that writ commanded to produce the body of Mr. Merryman before me this morning . . . that the case might be heard, and the petitioner be either remanded to his custody or set at liberty if held on insufficient grounds. But he has acted in disobedience to that high writ.[43]

He then issued a second writ addressed to General Cadwalader, directing him to appear before the chief justice at noon the following day to show cause why he should not be held in contempt of court.[44] Outraged, Taney pointed out that Congress alone had the power to suspend the writ of habeas corpus.[45] Yet Taney's opinion, captioned "Before the Chief Justice of the Supreme Court of the United States at Chambers," carried no precedential value as an "in chambers opinion" without the full Supreme Court hearing the case.[46] Chief Justice Taney "was acting in his capacity as a circuit court judge" and not in his capacity as the chief justice of the United States Supreme Court, with the full members of the Supreme Court sitting in session.[47] It appears that Taney had no appreciation a civil war had begun and that there were significant challenges to the United States government. Moreover he gave no deference to Lincoln, as president, whom he had previously sworn into office.

Notwithstanding that he was in his eighty-fifth year, the chief justice vigorously defended the power of Congress alone to suspend the writ of habeas corpus.[48] He took this position, in part, because permissible suspension was in Article I § 9 of the Constitution, the section describing congressional duties.[49] He ignored the fact that it was placed there by the Committee on Drafting at the Constitutional Convention in 1787 as a matter of form, not substance, which Lincoln believed justified his decision.[50] Lincoln also relied on the fact that Congress was out of session and would take weeks to reconvene if called to return. There were also several state elections for congressional seats during that spring that made it difficult for Congress to convene.

Disregarding this "in chambers opinion," Lincoln boldly broadened the scope of the suspension of the writ on July 2, 1861, moving the authorization as far north as New York City.[51] In his report to Congress on July 4, Lincoln passionately defended his position:

The whole of the laws which were required to be faithfully executed, were being resisted, and failing of execution, in nearly one-third of the States. Must they be allowed to finally fail of execution? . . . [A]re all the laws, *but one,* to go unexecuted, and the government itself go to pieces, lest that one be violated?[52]

Of the military arrests of civilians before February 1862, nearly one-third were Maryland citizens.[53] Of these arrests, however, Lincoln "often learned about such cases only after the fact, if at all, and he usually regretted their occurrence."[54]

Lincoln explained that the outbreak of the Civil War made it necessary "to call out the war power of the government and so to resist force employed for the destruction by force for its preservation."[55] Lincoln further professed that his actions, "whether strictly legal or not, were ventured upon under what appeared to be a popular demand and a public necessity, trusting then, as now, that Congress would readily ratify them."[56] And indeed, in the Habeas Corpus Act of 1863, Congress authorized the president to suspend the privilege whenever in his judgment the public safety required it.

JUDGE RICHARD B. CARMICHAEL

Judge Richard B. Carmichael served as a judge of the circuit court for several Maryland counties on the Eastern Shore. He was generally considered one of the principal leaders of the secessionist movement in that part of Maryland, and he openly opposed the war. After the November 1861 arrest of three men for heckling Unionists at a political rally, Carmichael sought to stop the practice of arrests without legitimate charges and asked a grand jury to indict anyone who had been part of these arrests.[57] Secretary of State Seward found such a brazen move a local overreach that would undermine the authority of the president to run the government.

In response, Seward ordered Carmichael arrested. In May 1862 Gen. John Adams Dix, the Union commander in Maryland, issued an arrest order on the grounds that Judge Carmichael was a southern sympathizer.[58] Soldiers entered Carmichael's courtroom and, when he refused to leave, dragged him out of the room.[59] He was taken to Fort McHenry and kept there for six months, without charges, until his eventual release.[60] The government's handling of the incident provided fodder for critics of the Lincoln administration who charged that the rights of even a Maryland judge were being violated by the government.

Lincoln's words reflected his own belief that he had exercised a power that required at least some cooperation and approval from Congress. Whatever confusion remained regarding the legality of Lincoln's unilateral suspension of habeas was quelled two years later when Congress enacted legislation empowering the president to suspend the writ nationwide while rebellion continued.

MOVEMENT OF UNION TROOPS

Even as opinion in Maryland shifted to strong support of the Union, due to the shift in the policies of elected officials, the number of slaves in the state, and the Civil War itself—many citizens continued to oppose Union troops crossing their state.[61] Earlier such sentiments had led to another of the state's confrontations with the federal government over civil liberties. In April 1861, "[t]he first large contingent of Union soldiers, about two thousand men from Massachusetts and Pennsylvania, entered Baltimore by Train on April 19 and encountered a large, hostile crowd."[62] One regiment, the Sixth Massachusetts, was "attacked by howling mobs."[63]

The mob attempted "to prevent [the Massachusetts] from reaching Washington, D.C." by "throwing stones and sticks and breaking store windows."[64] Because of these attacks, the soldiers were forced to march through the streets to connect to their second train.[65] When the crowd continued to attack, the soldiers opened fire.[66] Baltimore police were called to assist, and the troops were able to escape.[67] However, twelve civilians and four soldiers were killed.[68]

On April 21, a delegation from the Young Men's Christian Associations of Baltimore met with President Lincoln regarding the troop movements.[69] This group, also known as the "Baltimore Committee," complained about the troop movements as a violation of the sovereignty of a free state, but Lincoln responded that Union troops were "surrounded by the soil of Maryland; and mathematically the necessity exists that they should come over her territory. Our men are not moles, and can't dig under the earth; they are not birds, and can't fly through the air. There is no way but to march across, and that they must do."[70] Clearly the national peril outweighed any claims that a state could prevent military movements. But the president quietly made plans that future troop movements avoid Baltimore and arrive in Annapolis before marching on to Washington, DC.

* * *

ASSURING UNION ALLEGIANCES

While most Marylanders favored the Union, there were pockets of disloyalty in this slave Border State. This dichotomy was on full display in the Maryland legislature.

On April 22, Governor Thomas Holliday Hicks called for the legislature to meet on April 26, 1861, in Frederick, rather than the capital of Annapolis "to deliberate and consider the condition of the State, and take such measures in their wisdom they may deem fit to maintain peace, order, and security within our limits."[71]

On the second day of the session, the Maryland Senate stated that "[i]t is . . . our duty to declare that all such fears [of secession] are without just foundation. We know that we have no constitutional authority to take such action."[72] Three days later, the House of Delegates voted fifty-three to twelve to declare that they had no such authority to secede.[73]

Nevertheless, two committees were appointed to visit both the president of the United States and the president of the Confederacy.[74] The committees reported back to the legislature but no action was taken before September 1861 to approve of secession or to remain in the United States.[75]

In September 1861, President Lincoln "remained worried about the intent of the Maryland legislature when it met in Frederick in special session"[76] and acknowledged:

The Secessionists had by no means given up the hope of dragging Maryland into the Confederacy. The Legislature was to meet at Frederick City on the 17th of September. There was believed to be a disunion majority, and they expected and intended to pass an ordinance of secession.[77]

According to Frederick Seward, Secretary of State Seward's son and an assistant to his father, "[t]he administration believed . . . that 'a disunion majority' in the Maryland state house would then pass an ordinance to secede."[78] Frederick Seward recalled President Lincoln stating that disloyal legislatures "would be quietly turned back toward their homes, and would not reach Frederick City at all."[79]

Gen. George B. McClellan recalled the event differently, stating that Secretary of War Simon Cameron had "instructed Gen. Banks to prevent the passage of any act of secession by the Maryland legislature, directing him to arrest all or any numbers of the members, if necessary, but in any event to do the work effectively."[80] Secretary Cameron wrote "[t]he passage of any act of secession by the legislature of Maryland must be prevented. If necessary, all or any part of the members must be arrested. Exercise your own judgment as to the time and manner, but do the work effectively."[81]

The twenty-six legislators arrested included the Speaker of the Maryland House of Delegates, Elbridge George Kilbourn, Ross Winans, and Severn Teackle Wallis, based on their southern sympathies.[82] Lincoln justified the arrests as necessary and legitimate, stating:

> The public safety renders it necessary that the ground of these arrests should at present be withheld, but at the proper time they will be made public. Of one thing the people of Maryland may rest assured: that no arrest has been made, or will be made, not based on substantial and un-mistakable complicity with those in armed rebellion against the Government of the United States. In no case has an arrest been made on mere suspicion, or through personal or partisan animosities, but in all cases the Government is in possession of tangible and unmistakable evidence, which will, when made public, be satisfactory to every loyal citizen.[83]

The results of the arrests remains debated to this day. "Some, like Lawrence Denton, argue that only the union Army prevented Maryland from seceding. He claims that 'if free to choose, Maryland would have opted to join the Southern Confederacy.'"[84] However, "historian Jean Baker debunks such arguments, quoting William Schley, a prominent contemporary Baltimore attorney, who wrote, '[t]here has never been a moment when Maryland could have been forced into secession.'"[85]

Exercising their First Amendment right of free speech, Maryland legislators were arrested because of their political beliefs. This action by the Lincoln government arguably deprived them of their civil rights and denied their constituents their right to representation. President Lincoln believed that, under his wartime powers, the arrests were a necessary avenue for keeping Maryland in the Union, and, in the end, keeping the United States one nation, consistent with the oath he had taken at his inauguration.

PRISONERS OF WAR

Maryland was home to several wartime prisons where Confederate soldiers, along with civilians, were held for various periods of time during the Civil War.[86] Lincoln had signed General Order 100, now known as the Lieber Code, which provided for the ethical treatment of those in occupied areas, prisoners of war and those on the battlefield. Often in both the Union and the Confederacy it was impossible to provide suitable conditions.

In 1863, Lincoln issued General Order Number 100 (the "Lieber Code"— named for its author, Professor Francis Lieber, who taught at Columbia College), which covered an "array of topics: from martial law to the protection of persons, religion and the arts and sciences; from the treatment of deserters, women, prisoners of war, partisans, scouts, spies and captured messengers to prisoner exchanges and flags of truce; from battlefield booty to the parole, armistice and assassinations."[87] General Order Number 100 was the first attempt to establish humanitarian rules regarding the conduct of war by the US government.

One such prison was located at Point Lookout in St. Mary's County, at the junction of the Potomac River and the Chesapeake Bay, where thousands of Confederate soldiers died. Another, Fort McHenry, was situated on the banks of the Patapsco River in Baltimore to protect the city from attack from the bay. Soldiers and citizens were held in both places, with some 240 citizens in Point Lookout by 1864.[88] Poor sanitation and general conditions of overcrowding killed both citizens and soldiers; men were more likely to die in prisons than on the battlefield.

Confederate soldier James E. Hall recounted his time at Point Look, stating "that there was 'nothing that a man can eat. The crackers are as hard as flint stone, and full of worms. I don't believe God ever intended for one man to pen another up and keep him in this manner. We ought to have enough to eat, anyhow.'"[89] The imprisonment of opposition troops in such poor conditions can only be considered cruel and unusual punishment and a violation of their civil rights.

Even during the war, prisoner-of-war camps became propaganda tools used by both Confederates and Yankees. While the status of a prisoner of war was covered by the Lieber Code, it was the incarceration of civilians that became one of the prime examples of the Lincoln administration's purported arbitrary violation of civil liberties—in this case, arrests of civilians undertaken for political reasons. Yet, according to historian Mark Neely, most civilians were not incarcerated for disloyalty—that is, treasonous expressions of speech, press, and assembly. Rather they were imprisoned for more mundane reasons: defrauding the government, swindling recruits, and smuggling. Thus civilian arrests, with some exceptions, had little significance as instances of violations of civil liberty, although in Maryland they became very much a part of the critique of Lincoln.[90] Nevertheless, Neely quotes Lincoln as saying "that during the existing insurrection and as a necessary measure for suppressing the same, all Rebels and Insurgents . . . shall be subject to martial law and liable to trial and punishment by Courts Martial or Military Commission."[91] Neely also added that there is little known about the number of trials that occurred, when they occurred, and whether they occurred for some or all.[92]

Certainly the American Civil War had international implications and was one factor in the organization of the First Geneva Convention in 1863.[93] The United States was invited but did not attend. The Geneva Conventions sought to address war issues that both the Civil War and European wars of the nineteenth century had made apparent, and the international agreements were to ease the horrors of war.[94] These conventions still remain an important touchstone in international law and provide a certain level of rights to all combatants.

ABOLITION OF SLAVERY

Abraham Lincoln is often proclaimed as the president who ended slavery in the United States. His first step toward this advance was the Emancipation Proclamation, a military order, made under what the president believed to be the constitutionally granted war powers of the executive branch.[95] Lincoln's reasoning was not accepted by all—North as well as South—because the president, the opposition claimed, was seizing property [the slaves] in violation of Article 5 of the Bill of Rights, which prohibited such taking without compensation. Yet this decision by the president was not one that he made lightly. He insisted on gathering the opinions of each member of his cabinet. It was here that Abraham Lincoln showed his leadership and persuasive ability.

In the summer of 1862, the Confederacy had made many advances in northern Virginia. During this time the slaves of the Confederacy replaced white men on southern farms and plantations. They also helped the Confederate army perform labor, like digging trenches and building fortifications that would normally be done by Confederate army soldiers.[96] Clearly liberating slaves would deny the Confederacy an important labor force as well as a source of recruitment of freed African Americans to serve in the Union army and navy.[97] There were many, from the North and South, who believed the Emancipation Proclamation violated the right to property guaranteed by the Constitution by taking property from private citizens without adequate compensation.[98]

The Emancipation Proclamation itself was a legal document that cited the president's war power as the justification for freeing slaves in rebellious states.[99] The order would not affect the loyal Border States and areas of rebellious states occupied by the Union army but would apply only to the states, or parts of states, currently in rebellion.[100] Because of this military application, President Lincoln could not free the slaves in the Union slaveholding states of Missouri, Kentucky, Maryland, and Delaware as the Constitution still protected slavery in occupied areas and in the Border States.[101]

This led Maryland to face the issue of slavery on its own.[102] Even before the war, slavery had been slowing in Maryland through self-emancipation, the end of the international slave trade, and sales of Maryland slaves to cotton states. The war only decreased the number of slaves with the passage of the Emancipation Act in 1862 by Congress, which compensated loyalist slave holders for each slave in the District of Columbia. In 1864, Maryland adopted a new state constitution, which was supported by Maryland's Unionists and opposed by the state's Democrats. Article 24 of the new state constitution outlawed slavery.[103] The constitution narrowly passed, with Democrats raising the fear of federal interference with a local institution as well as insisting on federal compensation for the taking of private property.[104]

The Emancipation Proclamation led Lincoln to work vigorously in the later months of his presidency to encourage Congress to pass the Thirteenth Amendment that would grant final freedom.[105] Lincoln's zeal for the amendment rested on his fear that the Emancipation Proclamation, a military measure, would likely terminate at the end of the war. He stated in his December 6, 1864, address to Congress that "there is only a question of time as to when the proposed amendment will go to the States for their action. And as it is to so go, at all events, may we not agree that the sooner the better?"[106] The Senate passed the amendment easily in 1864, but in the House of Representatives the vote was much closer.[107] In fact, the Speaker of the House, Schuyler Colfax, postponed the vote, fearing defeat.[108] When the vote was called in 1865, it passed 119 to 56, just two votes more than necessary.[109]

THE ASSASSINATION OF ABRAHAM LINCOLN

Five days after Lee surrendered, President Lincoln was assassinated by John Wilkes Booth. Booth, a Marylander and born into a well-known family of actors, fled first to southern Maryland and then to northern Virginia.

Booth had initially entered into a conspiracy to kidnap President Lincoln, but when that plan failed and the South was about to lose the war, Booth changed the plan to assassination.[110] It took twelve days for the military to hunt down John Wilkes Booth and his companion, David Herold—who had attacked Secretary of State Seward—to a barn in Virginia.[111] Herold surrendered, but Booth was shot and killed.[112] Booth and Herold had escaped by following a route through southern Maryland used by Confederate agents to bring contraband and intelligence into the Confederacy. Both men were aided by Maryland citizens, including Dr. Samuel A. Mudd, who set Booth's broken leg and denied knowing him. But he had met Booth, and Mudd was charged and convicted before the military tribunal. He was sentenced to imprisonment at Fort Jefferson in the Dry Tortugas at the very end of Key West.

Eight conspirators were charged during the investigation.[113] Again confronting a familiar problem during the Civil War, President Andrew Johnson and his Secretary of War Edwin Stanton debated whether to try the conspirators in a civilian or military court.[114] Attorney General James Speed wrote an opinion saying that a military tribunal was appropriate.[115]

On May 15, the conspirators, including Mudd, were tried before a nine-member military panel.[116] After seven weeks of trial, the military panel deliberated in private, but with Judge Advocate General Joseph Holt present.[117] Only a majority of the panel was required to find the defendants guilty.[118] The panel sentenced four prisoners to be hanged, three to "hard labor for life," and one to six years in prison.[119] President Johnson approved the sentences and they were carried out.[120]

Clearly the conspirators' civil rights had been violated. While a military tribunal for civilians may have been lawful, the judges had a bias against them and denied their right to due process. Questions remain as to the fairness of a military tribunal trying civilian noncombatants. The issue is still contested in our courts to this day.

CONCLUSION

Mark E. Neely writes in the conclusion of his book *The Fate of Liberty* that "[w]ar and its effect on civil liberties remain a frightening unknown."[121] He states that "Lincoln's steadily growing confidence [during the war] or decisiveness was as much a function of his indifference to constitutional scruple as anything else—except his sure sense of the purpose of the government to win the war and keep the country whole so that democracy could not be said to have failed."[122]

Lincoln was many things, but he respected the Constitution. It is unlikely that he meant simply to avoid the constraints of the Constitution, but attempted to work, in his own way, within the system.

Neely is correct to say that war's effect on civil liberties "remains [a frightful] unknown," as we battle to this day with similar issues. This is the benefit of hindsight in many ways. Maryland seems to have hosted a variety of civil rights abuses during the Civil War. But, in the end, Lincoln held true to his oath: the United States remained one nation and Marylanders did not secede.

NOTES

1. William Worthington Goldsborough, *The Maryland Line in the Confederate States Army, 1861–1865* (Charleston, SC: Nabu Press, 2010).

2. Mark E. Neely, *The Fate of Liberty: Abraham Lincoln and Civil Liberties* (New York: Oxford University Press, 1992).

3. William R. Nester, *The Age of Lincoln and the Art of American Power, 1848–1876* (Lincoln, NE: Potomac Books, an imprint of the University of Nebraska Press, 2013).

4. William R. Nester, *The Age of Lincoln and the Art of American Power.*

5. Jay Bonansinga, *Pinkerton's War: The Civil War's Greatest Spy and the Birth of the U.S. Secret Service* (Landham, MD: Lyons Press, 2014).

6. Bonansinga, *Pinkerton's War.*

7. Abraham Lincoln et al., *The Collected Works of Abraham Lincoln* (Brunswick, NJ: Rutgers University Press, 1990), 4:240–41.

8. Lincoln et al., *Collected Works of Abraham Lincoln,* 4:240–41.

9. Lincoln et al., *Collected Works of Abraham Lincoln,* 4:240–41.

10. Edward Steers, *Blood on the Moon: The Assassination of Abraham Lincoln* (Lexington: University Press of Kentucky, 2005).

11. Steers, *Blood on the Moon.*

12. Steers, *Blood on the Moon.*

13. John Channing Briggs, *Lincoln's Speeches Reconsidered* (Baltimore: Johns Hopkins University Press, 2005), 299.

14. James F. Simon, *Lincoln and Chief Justice Taney: Slavery, Secession, and the President's War Powers* (New York: Simon & Schuster, 2006), 184.

15. Lincoln et al., *Collected Works of Abraham Lincoln,* 4:347.

16. Lincoln et al., *Collected Works of Abraham Lincoln,* 4:347.

17. Frank J. Williams, *Judging Lincoln* (Carbondale: Southern Illinois University Press, 2007), 63.

18. John Eisenhower, *Agent of Destiny* (Norman: University of Oklahoma Press, 1999), 384.

19. Eisenhower, *Agent of Destiny,* 384.

20. Mark Andrew Swank and Dreama J. Swank, *Maryland in the Civil War* (Mt. Pleasant, SC: Arcadia Publishing, 2013), 20.

21. Eisenhower, *Agent of Destiny,* 384.

22. Eisenhower, *Agent of Destiny,* 384.

23. William H. Rehnquist, *All the Laws but One: Civil Liberties in Wartime* (New York: Knopf, 2001).

24. LII Staff, "Habeas Corpus," *LII / Legal Information Institute,* Legal Information Institute, June 11, 2017, www.law.cornell.edu/wex/habeas_corpus.

25. LII Staff, "Habeas Corpus."

26. *Ex parte Merryman,* 17 F. Cas. 144, 147 (C.C.D. Md.1861).

27. Lincoln et al., *Collected Works of Abraham Lincoln,* 4:430; Abraham Lincoln and Don E. Fehrenbacher, *Abraham Lincoln: A Documentary Portrait through His Speeches and Writings* (Palo Alto, CA: Stanford University Press, 1977), 160–62.

28. Daniel A. Farber, *Lincoln's Constitution* (Chicago: University of Chicago Press, 2004), 16.

29. Rehnquist, *All the Laws but One,* 23.

30. Lincoln et al., *Collected Works of Abraham Lincoln,* 4:344.

31. Lincoln et al., *Collected Works of Abraham Lincoln,* 4:421–41.

32. Lincoln et al., *Collected Works of Abraham Lincoln,* 6:264.

33. Michael Lind, *What Lincoln Believed: The Values and Convictions of America's Greatest President* (New York: Anchor Books, 2006), 174.

34. Richard A. Posner, *Not a Suicide Pact: The Constitution in a Time of National Emergency* (New York: Oxford University Press, 2006), 45.

35. William F. Duker, *A Constitutional History of Habeas Corpus* (Westport, CT: Greenwood Press, 1980), 147.

36. Duker, *Constitutional History of Habeas Corpus,* 147. *See* the previous chapter for a more thorough analysis of the April 1861 Baltimore riot.

37. *Merryman,* 17 F. Cas. at 145, 147.

38. Simon, *Lincoln and Chief Justice Taney,* 2, 194.

39. Simon, *Lincoln and Chief Justice Taney,* 2, 194.

40. Arthur T. Downey, "The Conflict between the Chief Justice and the Chief Executive: *Ex parte Merryman,*" *Journal of Supreme Court History* 31, no. 3 (2006): 262–78, https://doi.org/10.1111/j.1540-5818.2006.00142.x.

41. Downey, "Conflict between the Chief Justice and the Chief Executive."

42. Downey, "Conflict between the Chief Justice and the Chief Executive."

43. Brian McGinty, *The Body of John Merryman: Abraham Lincoln and the Suspension of Habeas Corpus* (Cambridge, MA: Harvard University Press, 2011), 12.

44. McGinty, *Body of John Merryman*, 12.

45. *Merryman*, 17 F. Cas. at 147.

46. Carl B. Swisher, *The Oliver Wendell Holmes Devise History of the Supreme Court of the United States* (New York: Macmillan, 1974), 848.

47. Simon, *Lincoln and Chief Justice Taney*, 2, 191.

48. Williams, *Judging Lincoln*, 64.

49. Williams, *Judging Lincoln*, 64.

50. Williams, *Judging Lincoln*, 64.

51. Lincoln et al., *Collected Works of Abraham Lincoln*, 4:419; Abraham Lincoln et al., *The Collected Works of Abraham Lincoln*, vol. 5 (Rutgers University Press, 1990), 35, 436–37; Lincoln et al., *Collected Works of Abraham Lincoln*, 6:451–52.

52. Lincoln et al., *Collected Works of Abraham Lincoln*, 4:430.

53. Neely, *Fate of Liberty*, 26.

54. Neely, *Fate of Liberty*, 26.

55. Lincoln et al., *Collected Works of Abraham Lincoln*, 4:426.

56. Lincoln et al., *Collected Works of Abraham Lincoln*, 4:429.

57. John A. Marshall, *American Bastile: A History of the Arbitrary Arrests and Imprisonment of American Citizens in the Northern and Border States, on Account of Their Political Opinions, during the Late Civil War, Together with a Full Report of the Illegal Trial and Execution of Mrs. Mary E. Surratt, by a Military Commission, and a Review of the Testimony, Showing Her Entire Innocence* (Philadelphia: T. W. Hartley, 1885), 428–48.

58. Marshall, *American Bastile*, 428–48.

59. Marshall, *American Bastile*, 428–48.

60. Marshall, *American Bastile*, 428–48.

61. Michael Burlingame, ed., *Abraham Lincoln: The Observations of John G. Nicolay and John Hay* (Carbondale: Southern Illinois University Press, 2014), 55.

62. Kevin Conley Ruffner, *Maryland's Blue & Gray: A Border State's Union and Confederate Junior Officer Corps* (Baton Rouge: Louisiana State University Press, 1997), 34.

63. Ruffner, *Maryland's Blue & Gray*, 34.

64. Spencer C. Tucker, ed., *American Civil War: The Definitive Encyclopedia and Document Collection* (ABC-CLIO, 2013), 125.

65. Tucker, *American Civil War*, 125.

66. Tucker, *American Civil War*, 125.

67. Tucker, *American Civil War*, 125.

68. Tucker, *American Civil War*, 125.

69. Norman Hapgood, *Abraham Lincoln: The Man of the People* (Charleston, SC: Nabu Press, 2010), 209.

70. Charles W. Mitchell, *Maryland Voices of the Civil War* (Baltimore: Johns Hopkins University Press, 2007).

71. John Thomas Scharf, *History of Western Maryland* (Baltimore: Genealogical Publishing, 1968), 202.

72. Scharf, *History of Western Maryland*, 202.

73. Scharf, *History of Western Maryland*, 202.

74. Scharf, *History of Western Maryland*, 202.

75. Scharf, *History of Western Maryland*, 203–5.

76. Mitchell, *Maryland Voices of the Civil War*, 234.

77. Mitchell, *Maryland Voices of the Civil War*, 235.

78. Neely, *Fate of Liberty*, 15.

79. Neely, *Fate of Liberty*, 15.

80. Neely, *Fate of Liberty*, 16.

81. Neely, *Fate of Liberty*, 16.

82. Robert J. Brugger, *Maryland, A Middle Temperament: 1634–1980* (Baltimore: Johns Hopkins University Press, 1996), 281.

83. Lincoln et al., *Collected Works of Abraham Lincoln*, 4:523.

84. Herbert Charles Smith, and John T. Willis, *Maryland Politics and Government: Democratic Dominance* (Lawrence: University of Nebraska Press, 2012), 326n71 (quoting Lawrence M. Denton, *A Southern Star for Maryland: Maryland and the Secession Crisis* [Baltimore: Baltimore Publishing Concepts, 1995], 127).

85. Smith and Willis, *Maryland Politics and Government* (citing Jean H. Baker, *The Politics of Continuity: Maryland Political Parties from 1858 to 1890* [Baltimore: Johns Hopkins University Press, 1973], 54).

86. Richard H. Triebe, *Point Lookout Prison Camp and Hospital: The North's Largest Civil War Prison* (Dorset, UK: Coastal Books, 2014).

87. Rick Beard, "The Lieber Codes," *New York Times*, April 24, 2013, https://opinionator.blogs.nytimes.com/2013/04/24/the-lieber-codes/.

88. USwars.com, "Point Lookout Prisoner of War Camp," https://www.mycivilwar.com/pow/md-point-lookout.html.

89. Benjamin G. Cloyd, *Haunted by Atrocity: Civil War Prisons in American Memory* (Baton Rouge: Louisiana State University Press, 2010), 15.

90. Neely, *Fate of Liberty*, 127–38.

91. Neely, *Fate of Liberty*, 161.

92. Neely, *Fate of Liberty*, 161.

93. Triebe, *Point Lookout Prison Camp and Hospital*.

94. Angela Bennett, *The Geneva Convention: The Hidden Origins of the Red Cross* (Gloucestershire, UK: Sutton, 2006).

95. Doris Kearns Goodwin, *Team of Rivals: The Political Genius of Abraham Lincoln* (New York: Penguin, 2013), 452–67.

96. Goodwin, *Team of Rivals*, 452–67.

97. Goodwin, *Team of Rivals*, 452–67.

98. *US Constitution*, Fifth Amendment.

99. *US Constitution*, Fifth Amendment, 464.

100. *US Constitution*, Fifth Amendment, 464.

101. *US Constitution,* Fifth Amendment, 464.

102. Barbara Jeanne Fields, *Slavery and Freedom on the Middle Ground: Maryland during the Nineteenth Century* (New Haven, CT: Yale University Press, 1985), 131–67.

103. Fields, *Slavery and Freedom on the Middle Ground,* 131–67.

104. Fields, *Slavery and Freedom on the Middle Ground,* 131–67.

105. Harold Holzer and Sara Vaughn Gabbard, eds., *Lincoln and Freedom: Slavery, Emancipation, and the Thirteenth Amendment* (Carbondale: Southern Illinois University Press, 2007).

106. Holzer and Gabbard, *Lincoln and Freedom.*

107. Holzer and Gabbard, *Lincoln and Freedom.*

108. Holzer and Gabbard, *Lincoln and Freedom.*

109. Holzer and Gabbard, *Lincoln and Freedom.*

110. Holzer and Gabbard, *Lincoln and Freedom.*

111. Douglas O. Linder, "The Trial of the Lincoln Assassination Conspirators: An Account," *Famous Trials,* famous-trials.com/lincoln/2163-home.

112. Linder, "Trial of the Lincoln Assassination Conspirators."

113. Linder, "Trial of the Lincoln Assassination Conspirators."

114. Linder, "Trial of the Lincoln Assassination Conspirators."

115. Linder, "Trial of the Lincoln Assassination Conspirators."

116. Linder, "Trial of the Lincoln Assassination Conspirators."

117. Linder, "Trial of the Lincoln Assassination Conspirators."

118. Linder, "Trial of the Lincoln Assassination Conspirators."

119. Linder, "Trial of the Lincoln Assassination Conspirators."

120. Linder, "Trial of the Lincoln Assassination Conspirators."

121. Neely, *Fate of Liberty,* 235.

122. Neely, *Fate of Liberty,* 235.

"THE FIGHTING SONS OF 'MY MARYLAND'"

*The Recruitment of Union Regiments
in Baltimore, 1861–1865*

TIMOTHY J. ORR

O
n April 14, 1865, Surgeon Edwin K. Foreman wrote to one of Baltimore's newspapers, taking pride in the fact that his regiment, the Sixth Maryland Infantry, had played a significant role in the collapse of the Confederacy. Two weeks earlier, on April 2, the Army of the Potomac had executed a dramatic attack against Confederate earthworks southwest of Petersburg. As part of the Second Brigade, Third Division, Sixth Corps, the Sixth Maryland participated in the army's grand offensive. In the aftermath, Maj. Gen. Horatio Wright singled out this particular Maryland regiment as having been the first unit to breach Confederate lines. The distinction was important, mainly because it came with prize money. For months, Lieut. Gen. Ulysses S. Grant had been holding $460, donated by several wealthy northerners, to be given to the first US soldier to raise an American flag over Richmond. Since Richmond did not fall by frontal attack, Grant determined the money should be dispersed among the "three soldiers most conspicuous for gallantry in the final and successful assault on Petersburg." Accordingly, two of the awards went to soldiers who had enlisted in Baltimore. Cpl. Jacob Tucker of the Fourth Maryland received one-third of the money (he having been singled out by his own corps commander), and Col. J. Warren Keifer recommended Sgt. John Ezra Buffington of Surgeon Foreman's regiment to receive the share allotted to the Sixth Corps. Years after the war, both men received the Medal of Honor.[1]

"Prouder than all" because of the part that Baltimore played in the war's final act, Foreman wrote, "We are the *loyal* descendants and *fighting sons* of '*My Maryland.*'" Readers likely understood Foreman's reference. *My Maryland* referred to the controversial Confederate poem, "Maryland, My Maryland," penned by Baltimorean James Ryder Randall. By referencing the Baltimore Riot of April 1861, the poem claimed that Baltimore (and all of Maryland with it) stood firmly on the side of the rebellion. For the next four years, Baltimore's Unionists had to grit their teeth and plug their ears when they heard their secessionist neighbors sing Randall's obnoxious lyrics, which encouraged Marylanders to "spurn the Northern scum." At last, Foreman pointed out, the nation could see Baltimore's true contribution to Union victory. The city had supplied a wealth of muscle to the Army of the Potomac. The loyal sons of Baltimore had turned out in appreciable numbers, and those Marylanders were willing to keep fighting until the last vestige of secession had been destroyed. Foreman continued, "Our service expires on the 2d of the coming of September, but should the government require our services for a longer period, we are ready and willing, with our hearts and hands and, if need be, our lives to aid in wiping out every vestige of treason and sedition which now desecrates our land."[2]

Since 1865, historians have rarely told the story that Surgeon Foreman wanted them to tell, that Baltimore's "fighting sons" generally wore blue, not gray. For a full century, Maryland's Confederate history dominated the publishing world, and only in the 1970s did authors begin to address the state's contributions to the Union's war effort in any sophisticated way. (Recently, David K. Graham contended that mass culture of the twentieth century overwhelmingly "southernized" Maryland in the nation's popular memory of the war.)[3] And yet Union Baltimore is still largely unappreciated. In his Pulitzer Prize-winning tome, *Battle Cry of Freedom,* James McPherson depicted Baltimore as a city that mainly allied with the Confederate cause. He wrote, "The loyalty of Baltimore, with a third of the state's population, was suspect. The mayor's Unionism was barely tepid, and the police chief sympathized with the South. Confederate flags appeared on many city homes and buildings during the tense days after Sumter."[4] In his survey of the Union home front, *A People's Contest,* Phillip Shaw Paludan did not mention Baltimore at all.[5]

The bulk of the literature has largely mirrored those examples, casting Baltimore as a "border city"—a population defined solely by its mixed loyalty. But despite these depictions, the US War Department did not treat Baltimore as a special case. When it came to recruiting soldiers, US Army officers extracted recruits from Baltimore the same way as they had in other areas of the North. The War Department asked for volunteers in 1861, and when that method of recruiting dried up in 1862, it forced Baltimoreans to execute other methods to meet the manpower quotas: the raising of bounties, the enforcement of conscription, and the recruitment of United States Colored Infantry (U.S.C.I.) regiments. For four years, the federal government relied on Baltimore as a pool from which military manpower could be drained.

But Baltimore's manpower mobilization was far from perfect. The federal, state, and city governments attempted to share the responsibility of recruitment but rarely coordinated their efforts. Mob violence defined Baltimore's mobilization, as did fraud, kidnapping, desertion, and bounty jumping. Almost never did Baltimore's effort to raise soldiers for the Union army follow an orderly trajectory; but in the end, the city may have contributed 36 percent of Maryland's 46,638 Union military personnel, a statistic that was slightly higher than the city's overall percentage of the state's population. Perhaps, then, Baltimore's role in the nation's four-year quest for manpower may have outweighed the significance of the impulsive four-week period in the spring of 1861 when the city's treasonous whims were at their worst.[6]

Baltimore's war began on April 15, 1861, when President Abraham Lincoln called up seventy-five thousand state militia to serve for three months under federal command. Secretary of War Simon Cameron promptly contacted Maryland's governor, Thomas H. Hicks, instructing him to provide four regiments to fill this demand. Worried that outfitting federal troops in Maryland might spark a riot, or worse, instigate civil war within the state, Hicks replied that he would organize no such regiments unless they operated only within Maryland's boundaries and only under the guise of home defense. A member of the anti-immigrant American (or Know Nothing) Party, Hicks had weathered the secession crisis by hedging his bets, refusing pleas from southern sympathizers to call a secession convention, but at the same time denouncing the supposed fanaticism of the Republican Party.[7] In part, Hicks's prediction held true. On April 18, five companies of Pennsylvania militia passed through Baltimore, and a hostile secessionist crowd chucked bricks at them. The next day, three more northern militia regiments arrived in the city and the mob again assaulted them, this time with bricks *and* firearms. A Massachusetts regiment returned fire, and the ensuing tussle resulted in the deaths of five Union soldiers and twelve civilians.[8]

Believing the April 19 riot indicated the city's general support for the rebellion, Mayor George William Brown encouraged citizens to commence recruiting troops for the Confederacy—or at least troops who might resist the federal army. On April 20, apparently believing he had the consent of the governor, he ordered one of the city militia companies, the Baltimore City Guard, to destroy the railroad bridges north of town and thus prevent northern troops from reaching Baltimore by rail.[9] Meanwhile, the chief of police, Marshal George P. Kane, issued an order prohibiting the exhibition of any American flags. The next day, a battalion of Confederate soldiers led by Col. Bradley Johnson entered the city from Frederick and began confiscating the militia's weapons stockpile.[10] Members of the city's militia division—called the Light Division—put up no resistance, allowing their weapons to be taken. Perturbed by what he had seen, one of the Light Division's few Unionist officers wrote to Governor Hicks, advising him not to trust the division and never to give it weapons "unless the members thereof *individually & collectively swear allegiance to the Government of the United States, the State of Maryland, & the Star Spangled Banner.*"[11]

As dangerous as these days were for Baltimore, the Confederate force forming there failed to reach completion because Union troops from outside Maryland speedily reopened Baltimore's "closed gate." When it became clear that no Confederate reinforcements were on the way from Virginia, Johnson's battalion departed, having spent only one week inside the city. In the meantime, four of the city's militia regiments—the Baltimore City Guard, the Independent Greys, the Law Greys, and the Maryland Guards Battalion—began holding secret meetings to deduce who among their membership wished to fight for the Confederacy. Once those militiamen identified themselves, they secured their belongings and began an uneasy transit to Virginia, ultimately assembling new units in Richmond or Winchester. The secessionist members of the Maryland Guards Battalion—a unit of wealthy southern sympathizers who formed in the aftermath of John Brown's raid—began safeguarding all remaining uniforms and weapons from their regimental armory and concealed them in their homes. (One large stockpile was even hidden in the home of the archbishop.) McHenry Howard of the Guards Battalion took three muskets with him and concealed them in his father's house. After his father, the president of the Board of Police, was arrested by Union authorities later that year, federal soldiers uncovered these errant weapons, still in their hiding place. Of course, by that point, Howard was long gone, unable to be prosecuted. On June 1, with two friends in tow and his militia uniform hidden in his baggage, Howard traveled to St. Mary's County under the flimsy pretense of going sightseeing.

There, he borrowed a canoe and paddled his way to Virginia. By June 14, he was mustered into service of the First Maryland (Confederate) Infantry.[12]

During the night of May 13, Union troops marched into Baltimore. Their commander, Brig. Gen. Benjamin Butler, wisely ordered his men to seize as many weapons owned by the Light Division as could be found.[13] The same day that Butler's troops arrived, Governor Hicks—now ardently supportive of the federal government—opened the city's first US recruiting office at 112 West Baltimore Street. He appointed John Reese Kenly, a lawyer and veteran of the Mexican-American War, to raise the first regiment. On the first night of recruiting, a gang of secessionists fired at the building and hurled bricks at the windows. Some of the recruits came armed and returned fire. After a few minutes, the secessionists scattered. The incident left no casualties on either side.[14]

This moment of violence proved to be a parting shot by disgruntled southern sympathizers. Without the Light Division to molest them and two brigades of US infantry occupying the city, Union army recruiters continued their mission without obstacle. As it was, Lincoln's administration wanted more men who could serve for longer terms. On May 3, the President had called up an additional forty-two thousand volunteers to serve for three years. Colonel Kenly's regiment, now designated the First Maryland (Union) Volunteer Infantry, helped fill Maryland's quota under this call. By the end of May, his regiment reached capacity with at least 670 Baltimoreans on its roster.[15] Spurred by the First Maryland's success, two additional regiments formed in Baltimore later that summer—the First Maryland Volunteer Cavalry, which opened an office on Greene Street, and the Second Maryland Volunteer Infantry, which recruited at the 112 West Baltimore Street office.[16]

Over time, Baltimore's secessionist element gradually lost power. On June 27, Baltimore's new federal commander, Maj. Gen. Nathaniel P. Banks, ordered the arrest of Marshal Kane, as well as Baltimore's four police commissioners. After Banks transferred to a new command, his replacement, Maj. Gen. John Adams Dix, continued making arrests. On September 12–13, Dix's provost marshal arrested eighteen suspected Confederate sympathizers, including Mayor Brown.[17] Politically, the Unionist tide kept rising all summer, culminating on August 15 when the state's Union convention met at Baltimore's Law Buildings and overwhelmingly nominated Augustus W. Bradford, an ex-Whig, for governor.[18] The Union Party—composed of War Democrats and Republicans—passed eight resolutions, one of which denounced secession as a "fatal heresy" and entreated all loyal Marylanders to come forward and join the army being raised in Baltimore to suppress the rebellion.[19]

Baltimore's voters upheld Maryland's increasing Unionism during the autumn elections, supporting twenty Union Party candidates for the First Branch of the City Council (although all ran unopposed) and giving Bradford a 14,400 vote majority over his "Peace Party" opponent.[20] As Baltimore underwent this political facelift, the recruitment of the volunteer regiments sputtered along. The new regiments were beset with disciplinary complications arising from idleness. By the dozens, Union soldiers wandered the streets drunk, often in broad daylight. For instance, on June 24, a police officer charged Pvt. Peter Streetzer of the First Maryland with disorderly conduct, at which point Streetzer— who was intoxicated—tried to stab him with his bayonet. Other officers intervened and carted off the inebriated private in a paddy wagon. At the same time, a new private in the Second Maryland told his company commander that he wished to visit friends in the city. His captain informed him that any visit required a written pass signed by the colonel, and until he procured that, the soldier could not leave. The unruly private swore, declaring that he had yet to take the oath of allegiance, so the captain had no authority to order him to do anything. Angry at having his power flouted, the captain roused the other soldiers in his company, who drove the disobedient recruit out of camp, beating him with sticks along the way.[21]

As autumn continued, the line officers attempted to keep the peace by enforcing tighter discipline, but this only led to more serious injuries, and even death. In November, a private in the Second Maryland named Gardner made his third attempt to run the guard, and his platoon commander, Second Lieut. David E. Whitson Jr., shot him dead. One of Gardner's friends, Pvt. Joseph H. Kuhnes—another frequent guard-runner—vowed to avenge his death. On December 10, Kuhnes shot Whitson in the chest, killing him. A court-martial found Kuhnes guilty of murder, and the US Army hanged him on March 7, 1862. The *Baltimore American* reflected on Whitson's murder: "In this connection it is proper to add that the discipline of some of the regiments stationed near the city is far from approximating to the standard of army regulations. Already the most pernicious consequences have ensued, and if permitted to continue will produce still more injurious results."[22] However, the reporter added, "In justice to the men, it should be stated that they are really tired of the long period of inaction, and long for a brush with the enemy."[23]

Despite these problems, more regiments began organizing in Baltimore during the autumn. First came the Third Maryland, authorized in August 1861, followed by the "German Rifles" and the "Dix Light Infantry." (These latter regiments never reached completion, and under Bradford's direction, they had to be folded into the Third Maryland for lack of men.) In October, Postmaster William H. Purnell began raising a nine-company battalion of infantry augmented with two batteries of artillery and three companies of cavalry to be known as the "Purnell Legion." In September, Baltimore lawyer William Louis Schley began raising the "Public Guard Regiment" (eventually designated the Fifth Maryland Infantry), "to remain as a local regiment for home and city defence." Schley appealed to married men and fathers, promising $23 per month in bonus pay for each dependent child in their family.[24] By winter, Baltimore was hosting six different regiments, totaling about 6,600 men.

In the spring of 1862, once they had been properly armed and equipped, Baltimore's regiments left for the front amid spectacular fanfare. Before departure, each unit held an elaborate flag ceremony to assuage national fears about Baltimoreans, pledging their willingness to die for the Union and not to betray its honor. At the Second Maryland's flag presentation, the keynote speaker, Baltimore lawyer John L. Thomas, reminded the soldiers of their sacred duty. He explained:

> Soldiers, Maryland soldiers! You are about to leave your peaceful, quiet happy homes for the dread, terrible stern realities of war. . . . You are not called upon to wage an "unholy war" upon friends and kinsman. You are asked to defend your country—to protect this flag—to wipe out the foul stigma that has attempted to be put upon it by its foes—. . . In a word, [you are] to ferret out *treason,* and to put down *traitors*—to protect the right and crush the wrong. This, then, is no cause of which you need be ashamed. It is not the war of Lincoln. It is the war of Jeff Davis and his Confederate traitors upon the Great American people and the Great American Republic.[25]

But not everyone in the Union army accepted the Marylanders' promise. As soon as the Second Maryland Infantry landed in Newbern, North Carolina, the officers of the Maj. Gen. Ambrose Burnside's "Coastal Division" (later the Ninth Corps) began removing Maryland-born officers from regimental and company command. Apparently unconcerned about terminating promising military careers, the Coastal Division officers saw to it that a small New York-born faction controlled the regiment instead. The Maryland officer purge began in earnest as soon as the regiment arrived at the front. In the midst of the Camden expedition, Brig. Gen. Jesse L. Reno placed the Second Maryland's colonel under arrest for "disobedience of orders." Rather than offer him a chance to defend himself at court-martial, Reno locked him away, and under duress, forced him to resign his commission. Next, a lieutenant and a captain were removed for public intoxication, which was certainly justified under orders, but highly unusual given that public drunkenness abounded in Union-occupied Newbern without any legal action taken. It was, at least, a selective prosecution.

One by one, other Maryland officers began disappearing, harassed out of their positions. The captain of Company D resigned, led away under a corporal's guard, then the captain of Company G resigned, and then the captain of Company I. When a new colonel arrived from Baltimore to replace the one arrested by Reno, he was immediately summoned by Burnside's officer examination board, found wanting, and sent back to Baltimore. He had been in camp less than three hours. By the end of the purge, eight Maryland officers had left Newbern, and a ninth, the regimental major, endured the same campaign of harassment. Evidence suggests that the April 1862 purge originated from the mind of Lieut. Col. Jacob Eugene Duryée, a New Yorker who wanted the Marylanders gone so he could command the regiment with a staff of loyal line officers. One Maryland officer complained to the governor that Duryée's cabal "will oust every one of us [Marylanders] if possible."[26]

Duryée's motives were not entirely clear. The son of a Union general, he came from a prominent New York family, and at the war's outset, he accompanied the Seventh New York State Militia (the so-called "Dandy Seventh") during its bloodless, thirty-day service protecting Washington, DC.[27] Most likely, Duryée used his political connections to convince the Coastal Division staff to remove any Marylanders who threatened his bid for command. But those Marylanders who resisted his harassment believed that a general anti-Maryland bias existed in the army. One Marylander overheard a New York officer damn the whole State of Maryland while Duryée laughed approvingly. Another was even choked by an angry New Yorker and called "a damn negro" in front of his company. He implored Governor Bradford, "Sir, if we had a Marylander for our commander we would be treated as soldiers and gentlemen[.] . . . All I want is justice and I hope the day is not far distant."[28]

The Second Maryland's problems were not unusual. Without exception, every Maryland regiment contained bickering factions that schemed for promotion. Even before the First Maryland Cavalry saw combat, its officer corps unified against its regimental commander, Col. Andrew G. Miller, because of his chronic alcoholism. The First Maryland Cavalry's junior officers placed him under arrest and forced him to resign. Unfortunately, the junior officers could not settle on a suitable replacement. Gen. James Cooper, the state's ranking officer, received multiple petitions from the regiment discrediting the various contenders. He moaned to Governor Bradford, "The means taken to procure the signatures of officers to these papers are discreditable, and obnoxious to the severest censure. Promises and threats have both been used, and officers utterly opposed to both projects have called on me to explain the circumstances under which their signatures were obtained." Cooper had to conclude that he knew "of no officer in the regiment, in all respects, suited to command it." Eventually, much to the displeasure of every officer in the regiment, Cooper and Bradford appointed an outsider to command it.[29]

Union Marylanders' lackluster reputation in the army stemmed from a real problem, the refusal of some Maryland soldiers to pass over the state's borders. When they enlisted in 1861, some Baltimoreans did so under the assumption they would be retained for state defense only. When these same soldiers resisted orders to march into Virginia in 1862, the scenes became ugly. On March 2, 1862, as the First Maryland prepared to cross the Potomac, First Sgt. John H. Shaw adamantly declined to leave the state. On the spot, Colonel Kenly organized a drumhead court-martial, paraded Shaw before the regiment, and expelled him, with the drummer boys cutting off his buttons.[30] Two months later, one hundred men belonging to the Third Maryland likewise refused to cross the river. This contingent, led by Capt. Thomas McGowan, had once been part of an independent company called the Patapsco Guards. As a unit, it swore into the service of the federal government, but only under the condition that it never leave the state. Now, as the Third Maryland rushed to join the fighting in the Shenandoah Valley, McGowan's men refused to get into a canal boat. After a heated argument with the regimental commander, McGowan's company was detached and sent to York, Pennsylvania, even though it, too, was outside the state border. The regimental chaplain later mocked these men: "There [in York], they were sure of good quarters, no fighting, but to guard hospitals and graveyards *to keep the dead from rising.*"[31]

Major General Dix faced similar trouble with the Fifth Maryland when he attempted to order it to Fort Monroe. Like McGowan's company, the Fifth Maryland enlisted under the condition that it remain in Maryland as home guards. Dix addressed the soldiers personally, telling them that he intended to order them to Hampton Roads, but if any felt reluctance to leave the state, he would grant them an immediate discharge. Three soldiers availed themselves of this option, but fourteen others wrote to Governor Bradford, complaining of Dix's order. They wrote:

> we was rased to stay in Md to gard rail Roads[,] . . . that the ridgment has got more then thirds of men of familys forsed to go from home contrary to thair espectation and we beg of you as Governor of MD to interseed in our behalf[.] . . . we are forced out the state from home while other solders is doing what we whare raised to do[.] . . . our wifes is riting to us with a vengents against the the [sic] officers for Deceiven their husbans.

Bradford looked into the matter, but the officers of the Fifth Maryland told him that the men had no right to complain. One officer declared, "[T]he whole Reg. before leaving Balto. were interrogated by Genl. Dix and all professed themselves willing to leave the State." When the Fifth Maryland finally left, eight men deserted.[32]

Whatever the capabilities of their leaders or the homesickness of their rank and file, Unionist Baltimoreans first experienced combat in the spring of 1862, and the news that reached the city was not good. On May 23, 1862, Confederate forces under Stonewall Jackson assaulted a one-thousand-man garrison at Front Royal, Virginia. After a fierce, all-day engagement, Jackson's men swept the bluecoats from the field, inflicting 773 casualties. The First Maryland suffered more than the other regiments, losing 592 men, including 535 taken prisoner. Near the end of the fight, Colonel Kenly fell wounded, struck by a saber blow to the back of the head.[33] This news blindsided Baltimore's Unionists. The city's premier regiment had fallen in its first major engagement, and the bulk of the prisoners were bound for the horrid confines of Belle Isle in Richmond. For two days, gangs of Unionists roamed the city streets, bludgeoning anyone who ridiculed the First Maryland's demise.[34]

With newspapers crying for a prompt response, Governor Bradford took action. Contacting Lincoln's new secretary of war, Edwin Stanton, he requested authority to commence a new wave of recruiting. Although Stanton had officially halted recruiting everywhere, he agreed to Bradford's demand, allowing Maryland to make use of the rage produced by the defeat of Kenly's regiment. Wasting little time, Bradford ordered Col. William L. Schley to take command of Camp Hoffman, a barracks at Lafayette Square in Baltimore City. Making sure that Baltimore's Unionists understood the gravity of the situation, Schley implored them to join up, if for no other reason than to exact vengeance for the defeat of Kenly's men: "Marylanders! Recollect the brave men, under the gallant Colonel Kenly, who fell in the field of battle, and their duty to their State, and their memories, to avenge the cold bloody murder perpetrated." When Camp Hoffman opened on June 10, a line of new recruits stood at the door, ready to enlist. In a few days, Schley reported that recruitment was going on at "full blast."[35]

The season of crisis did not abate. On July 2, after news reached Washington that the Army of the Potomac had been stalemated on the peninsula, the War Department issued a call for three hundred thousand more three-year volunteers. Then, on July 17, Congress passed a new militia act allowing the president to draft state militia into federal service for up to nine months. Under the law's guidelines, if any state failed to meet the manpower quota set by the War Department, the governor of that state was required to conscript the remainder (or "deficiency," to use the terminology of the era) from their militia regiments. With this new law in place, on August 4, the War Department called up an additional three hundred thousand men. Under these two back-to-back requisitions, Baltimore City had to provide 2,646 recruits.[36]

The threat of a draft forced Baltimoreans to redouble their efforts. No one wanted the city to suffer the ignominy of conscription. One teenaged recruit, eighteen-year-old Edward Schilling of Frostburg, used this news as his excuse to enlist. "More men were called for," he reminisced. "From the first I had a strong desire to enlist, but my dear parents would not hear of my going, therefore would not give their consent. Finally, a draft was spoken of, and asking my parents if they would not prefer that I should go of my own accord, rather than be drafted and forced away, they, with this powerful argument in my favor, consented." With that, he left home and traveled by rail to Baltimore. When he arrived at Camden Station, a helpful citizen pointed him to the nearest recruiting office.[37]

Despite Schley's optimism, none of the new regiments were full by the end of the summer. New recruits noticed how Baltimore's mustering officers appeared desperate to fill their quotas. Frederick W. Wild enlisted underage (but with his father's permission), and, surprisingly, the examining surgeon raised no concerns. He merely had Wild strip, saying quickly, "You will do. You have never been seriously ill in your life." Wild further remembered that dozens of men who joined his artillery battery were not from Baltimore, but the adjoining countryside. "What a motley looking crowd we were, without uniforms," he recalled. "The country boys in their home-spun clothes, others in their working clothes, the dude in patent leather shoes and Piccadilly collar, the farmer and blacksmith, altogether it was typical of the make-up of that great Union Army."[38]

Rural recruits often traveled to Baltimore to enlist because they received more money than in their hometowns. To spur recruiting, the First Branch of Baltimore's City Council drew up Ordinance Number 74, appropriating $300,000 to fund a city bounty, whereby each Baltimore volunteer received $50 at enlistment and $10 each month for the next five months. This bounty ordinance passed only after violence compelled the city council to act upon it. In mid-July, the Second Branch voted against Ordinance 74, a foreseeable decision since nine of the ten were widely supposed to be sympathetic with the Confederacy.[39] The day after the vote, a raucous crowd stormed into City Hall, brandishing nooses and threatening summary hangings if the Second Branch did not reconsider its vote. At the day's end, four Second Branch councilmen had to flee City Hall under police escort. Two others were chased by a mob and attacked as they entered their carriages. Frightened for their lives, the Second Branch members sought the protection of Maj. Gen. John Ellis Wool, the federal commander of the Middle Department, the unified command that supervised Baltimore. Wool—an aging Democrat—sympathized with the councilmen's plight but advised them to resign if they could not, in good conscience, pass the bounty ordinance. Taking Wool's advice, nine of them resigned en masse the very next day.[40]

The mob's threat of violence produced the desired effect. On July 28, ex officio Mayor John Lee Chapman ordered a special election to replace the nine Second Branch councilmen. That election filled the Second Branch with nine Union Party candidates. On August 5, at their first meeting, they passed the city bounty ordinance, even raising the total to $350,000.[41] The new funds went a long way in assisting the state's new regiments, unofficially called the "Maryland Brigade." In addition to taking the First Maryland back to full strength, Maryland now raised four new infantry regiments—the Fourth, Sixth, Seventh, and Eighth Maryland Volunteer Infantry regiments—and a light artillery battery known as Alexander's Baltimore Battery. Baltimoreans enlisted in all of these, although they were most represented in the Fourth and Eighth Regiments and the artillery battery. By best estimates, the brigade contained about 1,030 Baltimoreans.[42]

The Maryland Brigade did not wait long for its first deployment. On September 18, word reached the city that a costly battle had been fought on the banks of Antietam Creek in Washington County. Without parade or fanfare, or sufficient rations, or even a complete roster of troops, the officers of the five infantry regiments roused their men late at night and put them on cars to Hagerstown. Once there, the brigade, along with Alexander's Battery and the recently exchanged and promoted Brigadier General Kenly, made a forced march to Williamsport, where it discovered that the Confederate army had recrossed the river in retreat. Governor Bradford met the brigade at Williamsport and inspected it, and despite its speedy deployment and incomplete equipage, he declared it ready for service.[43]

As the Maryland Brigade departed for the front, Baltimore braced for the draft. Despite the city's best efforts, it came up short of its quota. Awkward phraseology of the new bounty ordinance limited its influence. That law did not make clear that anyone who received a bounty had to be credited against the city's quota. The surrounding counties took advantage of this nebulous provision by sending men to the city to collect the bounty but then credited them against their own quotas. Angrily, Baltimore's city council amended the bounty ordinance, but too late to have any statistical effect.[44]

Under Maryland's existing draft law, all white male citizens, ages eighteen to forty-five, had to enroll. The state law allowed exemptions, primarily based on occupation, including—but not limited to—clerks, postmasters, ferrymen, stage drivers, state officers, teachers, physicians, ministers, marines, and pilots. Physical disability, alienage (the nineteenth-century term to describe US residency, but with foreign citizenship), and conscientious objection also warranted exemption, but, so wrote newspaper editor Charles Fulton, the state law stood in "such a confused state" that no reasonable Marylander could accurately interpret it.[45]

As a result, hundreds of citizens arrived at the draft commissioners' headquarters to apply for exemptions. On the first day of the hearings, Commissioner John B. Seidenstricker adjudicated fifty cases in the First Ward. Most applicants in this ward claimed physical disability, but, noted a reporter, "Unseemly as it would appear, they each evidenced the possession of considerable muscle, as they eagerly pressed forward to get into the room in which the commissioner was seated, in order to procure the desired exemption." In five days, the First Ward received four hundred applicants, and Seidenstricker granted 294 exemptions, 154 of them for disability.[46]

Exemptions based on noncitizenship angered Baltimoreans who did not want immigrants avoiding the draft. None of Baltimore's three draft commissioners expressed sympathy for foreigners, and one of them, Seidenstricker, attempted to trick them into admitting to US citizenship. In the Third Ward, he encountered a forty-year-old Irishman who applied for exemption. "So," the Seidenstricker asked, "you prefer to remain a subject of Queen Victoria?" Indignantly, the Irishman answered, "No," stating that he preferred the government of the United States. Later, Seidenstricker faced a twenty-four-year-old unnaturalized Prussian who had immigrated to Baltimore ten years earlier. The commissioner asked him if he still considered himself a subject of the King of Prussia. Emphatically, the man answered, "No." Rather than approve their exemptions, Seidenstricker laid over both cases for further contemplation.[47]

After two months of bureaucratic preparation, on October 15 the Superintendent of Enrollment in Baltimore, Col. John Angel James Creswell, put the draft into effect. His clerks poured 20,621 slips with names into a large box, three feet wide and two feet deep. For over an hour, they stirred the slips, and then, while blindfolded, one of them drew out forty-six names and another read them aloud. According to Creswell's questionable arithmetic, Baltimore had almost met the governor's quota. On the appointed day, only nineteen of the drafted men arrived. Of the absentees, five reported themselves ill, one had died since the draft, and the rest simply failed to appear.[48] In all, the result was abysmal.

Though Baltimore provided only nineteen draftees, it still had to accommodate those from Maryland's countryside, as eighteen counties had also enforced the draft. Within days, 460 drafted men and substitutes arrived. They encamped at Camp Bradford, formerly the city's cattle showgrounds. Nearly every day in November, the guards called out an alarm as one or more of these recruits tried to flee their confines. On November 7, a Carroll County substitute was shot through the cheek as he tried to scale the camp's fence.[49] A few days later, November 11, forty-one men managed to escape in a single day.

Three were caught when they used their substitute bonuses to buy new clothes and change their appearance. Arrested, the men confessed they had escaped by bribing the sergeant of the guard. Upon learning this news, Camp Bradford's commander, Brig. Gen. Edward Shriver, ordered all substitute bounties placed in banks and held until muster. This reduced the rate of desertion, but the damage had already been done. By the end of the winter, 421 men had deserted the showgrounds, 91 percent of the original contingent.[50] Others deserted on their way to the front. Col. Joseph M. Sudsburg expressed anger when two hundred substitutes from Camp Bradford deserted as soon as they reached the Third Maryland's camp at Aquia Creek, Virginia. "Devoid alike of patriotic sentiment, religious faith, or manliness," he wrote, "these scoundrels entered the service only in order to make money; they made it and deserted. The example is demoralizing in the extreme." Likewise, the First Maryland Cavalry lost about 160 men. Col. Eugene Von Kielmansegge complained, "A part of those substitutes being apparently men . . . [whose] intention is not to serve the country, but merely to obtain a certain sum of money."[51]

The Republicans in the US Congress were displeased with the outcome of state drafts, generally. Not only had Baltimore put only nineteen drafted men into service, but also two cities—New York City and Philadelphia—had failed to draft anyone, fictitiously declaring their quotas filled by volunteering. During the lame-duck session of 1863, the lawmakers passed a rigorous conscription bill, allowing the US War Department to enforce a nationwide draft. Expanding the powers of the federal government, this piece of legislation—the "Act For Enrolling and Calling Out the National Forces"—wrested control of conscription from the hands of the governors. Now, the War Department's Provost Marshal Bureau was responsible for filling any deficiencies incurred by a presidential call-up. Provost Marshal General James B. Fry possessed sole authority to calculate how each quota was to be divided. Further, he possessed the power to appoint assistant provost marshals to each congressional district, officers who could enforce enrollment and the drawing of names. Although any drafted person could avoid military service through legal exemptions, state power had greatly diminished. Within weeks of the new law, two provost marshals, Capts. Robert Cathcart and Leopold Blumenberg, arrived in Baltimore and commenced redrafting the city's rolls for the planned conscription.

But before a federal draft could be implemented, Baltimore faced a different manpower crisis. On June 15, 1863, President Lincoln called up one hundred thousand six-month Emergency Militia in response to the Army of Northern Virginia's attack on the Union garrison at Winchester, Virginia. Under Lincoln's call, Maryland was to provide ten thousand men.[52] Within twenty-four hours, the city council passed a $400,000 ordinance offering a $100 bounty to each volunteer who joined the Emergency Militia.[53] By July 1, one newspaper speculated that 1,300 Emergency Militiamen had been raised in the city.[54]

Despite this turnout, Governor Bradford was not pleased. On June 21, he reprimanded Baltimoreans for not mobilizing with sufficient speed. He complained that the president's call (which Bradford had seconded), "has not met with that prompt and practical response which I thought I had a right to expect." Admonishing his fellow citizens, he implored, "Are you willing to leave the metropolis of the state undefended because they [your neighbors] may fold their arms and offer no assistance? God forbid!"[55] As Bradford pleaded, the new commander of the Middle Department, Maj. Gen. Robert Schenck, took action. He ordered city police to go door to door, dragooning free Black people into the street and forcing them to erect barricades around the city.[56]

Schenck's "recruitment" of Black laborers shocked Baltimore's residents, but he believed it was necessary to stave off a Confederate invasion. By that time, Baltimoreans had learned that the Army of Northern Virginia had crossed the Potomac River on its way to what became the crucial battle at Gettysburg. If the Confederate army had turned toward Baltimore, street barricades would have been the city's only means of defense from the north and west. (Unlike Washington, Baltimore was not surrounded by a ring of forts.)

Pleased with the process begun by Schenck, Bradford asked the War Department if he could reinforce his militia with Black recruits.[57] Schenck asked permission as well, even though he had already put men into uniform without departmental approval. A timely letter written to Lincoln on July 4 greased the wheels, and the next day Secretary Stanton directed Brig. Gen. William Birney to proceed to Baltimore and organize a regiment of U.S.C.I. By then, most of Schenck's laborers had been paid and dismissed, but Birney appealed to them to return to duty, this time as armed infantry. On July 9, thirty-four Black Baltimoreans followed a recruiting officer to Birney's office and were sworn into the service of the US volunteers, the first Black troops sworn into US service in Maryland.[58]

Maryland's first Black regiment, the Fourth U.S.C.I., filled quickly, reaching 898 enlisted men by mid-September.[59] However, the next authorized regiment, the Seventh U.S.C.I., struggled to reach minimum strength. Noticing the slow pace of recruiting, General Birney requested authority to send his officers to recruit among Maryland's enslaved population. On October 3, the War Department assisted him by authorizing General Orders 329, enabling federal officers in Maryland, Missouri, and occupied Tennessee to enlist enslaved men into federal service. Specifically, this order established that enslaved men who were offered by their owners could be enlisted, so long as those owners received compensation not exceeding $300. Additionally, "slaves belonging to those who have been engaged in or given aid and comfort to the rebellion" could be enlisted into the Union army without compensation. Most importantly—for the enslaved—"All persons enlisted into the military service shall forever thereafter be FREE."[60]

Baltimore became a nerve center for the U.S.C.I. recruiting drive. Throughout the summer and autumn, Birney's officers set sail from the Inner Harbor and cruised down the Chesapeake Bay, seeking out coastal stopping points to enlist enslaved Marylanders. Invariably, Maryland slaveowners saw these Union officers as willful thieves who brazenly disobeyed state law that entitled slaveholders to their "property." Of course, the Union officers who set out from Baltimore cared little about their opinions. They were under pressure to fill the city's quota before another draft came along. One enterprising army officer who sailed from Baltimore asked enslaved men at an Eastern Shore plantation if they preferred to join the Union army. In unison, the enslaved men answered, "yes." Quietly, the officer told them that if they desired to enlist, they should meet him at the wharf at sundown, where he had anchored his steamship. Forty recruits showed up, but a county constable also arrived, forbidding their departure, calling it theft. The Union officer curtly replied, "I have orders from the Secretary of War to do what I am doing, and if you wish any redress go to him." Turning to the recruits, he said, "Boys, go aboard." As the steamer floated away from its moorings, the newly freed recruits sang jubilantly, mocking the enraged constable: "Fare you well, fare you well, I am going away to leave you, fare you well."[61]

In a remarkably similar incident, Maj. Samuel Kramer, a Baltimorean from the Third Maryland, landed a steamboat just outside of Easton. Some hours later, his recruiting detail came back with fifty Black recruits and a crowd of angry slaveowners hot on their heels. When one of them accosted Major Kramer, claiming that the recruits were his servants, Kramer replied, "But, sir, they are free, by act of the Government, and hereby are free to enlist in its service, and I shall take them to Baltimore." Placing guards at the gangway, Kramer held off the angry slaveowners until the ship was loaded. Kramer recalled, "We were soon steaming away, while the chagrined and mortified rebels stood gazing in mute astonishment at the receding boat, bearing off 'their servants,' as they called them."[62]

Not all recruiting officers got away unscathed. On October 20, Lt. Eben White lost his life recruiting Black soldiers. White's detail disembarked at Benedict, Maryland, a small crossroads at the eastern border of Charles County and the Patuxent River. Taking along two privates, he reached the plantation of John H. Sothoron. There, he asked two enslaved Marylanders if they wanted to enlist in the Union army. One answered "yes," and it seemed that the other intended to answer affirmatively also but then demurred when he saw Sothoron and his son, Webster, approaching with pistols drawn. One of the privates asked permission to shoot the plantation owners, but White ordered him to hold his fire. With little ado, John Sothoron called Lieutenant White a "damned nigger-stealing son of a bitch" and Webster Sothoron spat in his face. White attempted to defend his actions by explaining how he had been ordered to recruit for the Union army. John Sothoron interrupted, "Hell and damnation! I know right from wrong as well as you do. . . . Don't you talk to me about business, you damned son of a bitch." Convinced he should defend himself, White grabbed a rifle from one of his men and cocked it, but the two slaveowners opened fire, shooting him in the head and breast. The two soldiers who had accompanied White beat a hasty retreat to their boat, and the last image they saw of their commander as they drew out of sight was that of Webster Sothoron beating White's corpse with the butt of a pistol. Knowing they might face arrest for murdering a Union officer, the two Sothorons abandoned their plantation and fled to Richmond. In November, Union forces occupied their property, recovering White's body and turning over the land to the Freedman's Bureau.[63]

As dangerous as these recruiting drives could be, they tended to be successful, and even in a Border State where slave ownership was supposed to be respected by the federal government, the recruiting officers prioritized their mission above Maryland slaveowners' property rights. It is important to note that, in part, these liberations arose from a genuine concern for human dignity. On March 9, 1864, a recruiting detachment for the Nineteenth U.S.C.I.

discovered twenty enslaved men and women held in Upper Marlboro's "slave jail." One room contained twelve women and children who had been placed there in 1861 for "safe keeping." The second room contained eight adult men, all chained to a single staple in the middle of the floor. The detachment's junior officer, Lieut. David B. Holmes, described the slave jail as "horribly filthy." He explained, "Tubs at the sides and corners of the room were used for the necessities of nature and other filth. They had the appearance of being emptied but seldom. The atmosphere of the room was exceedingly offensive, and so much of the jail as was seen by me was disgraceful to any country." While there, Holmes shouted an imprecation at the local sheriff, "expressive of my abhorrence of the administration of laws which would confine in such a manner human beings called slaves, for trying to run away from such a country."

The detachment's commander, Lieut. Col. Joseph G. Perkins, determined that the eight adult men should be *"liberated by Military authority."* Hiring a blacksmith, he ordered the chain cut, declaring, "I will not have any man enlisted into the military service of the United States with *irons* on." As Perkins swore the eight men into the service of the Nineteenth U.S.C.I., he purposefully left the cell door ajar, allowing the twelve women and children to flee into the countryside. Perkins admitted this was technically illegal, but in this case, he felt it necessary to uphold a semblance of human decency by releasing them from bondage. When the local sheriff later arrived at the Nineteenth U.S.C.I.'s bivouac demanding that Perkins send a patrol to catch the twelve runaways, Perkins told him to get lost. He said that the Confiscation Act of 1862 prohibited Union officers from participating in the re-enslavement of any freed person.[64]

However, US recruiters in Maryland did not always treat African Americans with dignity and respect. By the following year, the new commander of the Middle Department, Maj. Gen. Lew Wallace, and the officer in charge of Black recruitment, Col. Samuel Bowman, sent squads into the homes of Black Baltimoreans, dragooning military-capable men into the U.S.C.I. Writing to Lincoln, a group of frustrated Black Baltimoreans complained, "Squads of colard soaldiers accompaned som times by white men come to our houses demand admitance under the authoritey of Col. Bowman. Surtches the house Curses our wives our sisters or mothers or if the man be found he is made to fall in and martch to the drilling room and thare give his name thare is one instance of a man being Shot at while trying to escape thare are others whare our white inemies go with thoas soaldiers for the purpos of Maltreating us."

Another Black Marylander, William Jackson of Anne Arundel County, was cajoled into the army by a recruiting officer who came into his home, saying that he could volunteer now and receive $400, or "be forced to go and get nothing." Jackson pointed out that he could not serve, as he suffered from epileptic fits. As he later explained, "I was totally unfit for military duty and could only expect to drag out a few months of a miserable existanse—an incubus upon the United States Government If I was forced to enter its servise." Jackson dutifully provided certificates from two physicians to prove his disability, but the recruiting officer would not accept them. Instead, he dragged Jackson to Baltimore, where an army surgeon declared him fit for service, and then mustered him into the ranks of the Thirty-Ninth U.S.C.I. Jackson eventually petitioned Lincoln for an investigation into his case. Ever sympathetic to the plight of victims of injustice, Lincoln ordered his immediate discharge.[65]

Although General Orders 329 promised compensation to slaveowners who lost property to Union recruiting drives, most Maryland slaveholders had little expectation of going through proper channels to acquire their remuneration. Instead, they appealed to Democratic politicians to bring an end to Black recruiting. In January 1864, when the new legislature met in Annapolis, Democrats demanded the assembly petition Lincoln to rescind General Orders 329. The Union Party did not agree. Although the Confederate invasion had long since ended, the demands of the federal draft law now weighed so heavily upon the state that federal recruiters could no longer do without African American recruits. The *Baltimore American* argued that the same politicians who complained about the injudiciousness of recruiting enslaved Marylanders into the army were the same people who rejoiced when the draft did not fall heavily upon their rural counties. These men ought to support the recruitment of the enslaved, the newspaper argued, just as their nonslaveholding neighbors did, for "they are well satisfied to see the negro—'the poor man's substitute'—taken instead of themselves, and all rejoice that their counties are saved from the draft."[66] In the end, the Union Party prevailed. In late January, the legislature passed a state bounty to supplement the federal compensation fee. Maryland would now pay $100 to each enslaved person who enlisted and $100 to his owner, provided the owner showed a deed of manumission. In no sense, then, did the Union Party oppose the process of emancipation already unfolding. In short, the recruitment of African Americans soldiers undermined the peculiar institution in Maryland.[67]

With the legislature and Middle Department in agreement, Baltimore's Black mobilization continued unobstructed. Recruits trained at Camp Belger, a segregated camp along Madison Avenue in the northwest corner of Baltimore. Generally, the training of these soldiers occurred without incident, but when traveling inside the city, the soldiers often faced harassment.[68] The situation grew tenser in the winter of 1864 when white Union veterans began arriving in the city on their thirty-day reenlistment furloughs. In early April 1864, four white veterans fired at a party of Black soldiers. When city police questioned the four furloughed men and not the Black soldiers, they tried to flee; one of them jumped into the Jones Falls to escape arrest. After a donnybrook, the police apprehended all four suspects.[69]

The War Department confiscated John Sothoron's plantation and converted it into a training facility called Camp Stanton. It continued to operate Camp Belger—later renamed Camp Birney—into 1865, so, despite protests by white residents, the city retained its Black military presence throughout the war.[70] Indeed, when President Lincoln visited Baltimore in April 1864 to speak at the city's Sanitary Fair, soldiers quartered there—the Thirty-Ninth U.S.C.I.—stood watch, at parade rest, at the edge of the crowd.[71] As Lincoln spoke about the tragic news of the Fort Pillow Massacre, he gestured toward the men of the Thirty-Ninth, saying, "If there has been the massacre . . . there . . ., it will be conclusively proved; and being so proved, the retribution shall as surely come. It will be matter of grave consideration in what exact course to apply the retribution; but in the supposed case, it must come." Baltimore's Union Party paper agreed with Lincoln's optimistic sentiment, arguing, perhaps too hopefully, "To see black men in uniform, bearing arms, is quite common of late. There are now two full regiments at Birney Barracks, and the third is rapidly filling up. . . . Under these circumstances the prejudices against colored troops is fast giving way."[72]

Not every Baltimorean supported the recruitment of the U.S.C.I. When the Nineteenth U.S.C.I. marched down the main thoroughfares for its farewell parade, some Baltimoreans uttered "curses not loud but deep." A newspaper correspondent witnessed one woman who "thought it had come to a pretty pass when she had to stand [aside] to allow 'niggers' to pass." And yet, Baltimore's Unionists reminded their neighbors that despite their dyspeptic exclamations, they could do nothing to disparage the importance of this moment as a slice of the city's history. The *American*—a stalwart defender of the U.S.C.I.—pronounced, "A few years ago the man who would have said that the negro would have marched through the streets of Baltimore in military equipments . . . without being assaulted, would have been considered a fit case for a lunatic asylum." None could deny that the sight of Black men marching under the nation's banner, wearing suits of blue, brass buttons glinting, and carrying rifles on their shoulders, amounted to a world-shattering tableau. "They were lustily cheered," commented a reporter. "In many places along the route of march, flags were waved from the stateliest or from the humblest dwellings. . . . May we have many more such regiments to credit to the quota of Maryland, as those that passed the *American* office this morning." Years later, one of the white officers involved in the Nineteenth U.S.C.I.'s parade, Capt. James H. Rickard, declared himself impressed by the whole spectacle. With pride, he professed that the recruitment of African American soldiers was "perhaps the most important event that hastened the success of the Union cause."[73]

The rising number of Black recruits reduced Baltimore's quota for the anticipated federal draft, but it did not stop its imposition. As the threat of conscription loomed, Baltimoreans did anything they could to diminish the quota, even offering Confederate prisoners of war incarcerated at Fort Delaware a chance to enlist. After lively debate, the War Department authorized Col. Charles Carroll Tevis, a graduate of West Point, to raise the Third Maryland Cavalry from prisoners who had taken loyalty oaths. By the end of the month, 422 Confederate prisoners had availed themselves of this opportunity and joined the Baltimore cavalry regiment. All of them quartered in the city until the regiment filled.[74]

Baltimoreans also turned to substitute brokers to meet the city's manpower quota. These businessmen purchased the services of potential recruits and took a cut of their bounty, only to sell them back to drafted Baltimoreans after skimming off a profit. In an ideal situation, substitute brokerage operated under the premise that a broker could offer substitutes a maximum bounty while sparing unwilling citizens from the possibility of going into the service. In reality, Baltimore's substitute brokerage businesses became a racket. They operated gangs who kidnapped recruits—not merely to steal a portion of their bounty— but to run them to other cities where the bounties proved more expensive, thus denying Baltimore its much-needed manpower credits.[75]

Although a substitute could, theoretically, enlist in any city or town of his choice, the War Department considered it illegal for anyone to participate in

"substitute running," that is, the act of bullying, bribing, or kidnapping a potential substitute with the intent to take a cut of the bounty. General Schenck
tried to address the crimes committed by substitute brokers by drafting several
orders, making it illegal to "entice" recruits out of their congressional districts
or to sell liquor to men intending to enlist. Schenck's soldiers arrested criminal
brokers every week, but most of their illicit activity undoubtedly went un-
checked. One victim, Gerhardt Schloss, was rescued only because he shouted
loud enough for police to come to his assistance. Schloss had been given alco-
hol by a substitute broker who kidnapped him, intending to take him to Philadelphia to get the bounty there. Schloss tried to escape by jumping from a
train at President Street Station, but the broker, George Garlin, recaptured him
and beat him severely. Garlin took his captive back to his business on Thames
Street, tore off his clothes, and dressed him in a stolen sailor's uniform so he
might be dragooned into the US Navy. Policemen, alerted by Schloss's cries for
help, arrived and arrested Garlin.[76]

As brokerage-related crime rose, Baltimore's first federal draft began in
November. After haggling with federal authorities, the city government convinced Provost Marshal General James B. Fry to place the quota at 3,097. The
draft began simultaneously at the Second and Third District draft offices on
November 23 and continued each weekday until December 5. On the first
day of drawing, at his office (3 South Exeter Street), Captain Cathcart pulled
names from the First Ward. His clerks had poured 871 names—all written on
strips of heavy cardboard, one inch wide and two inches long—into a large re-
volving wheel. Commissioner L. M. Haverstick gave the wheel five or six turns.
Then, while blindfolded, Capt. W. P. Brightman pulled the requisite number, taking sixty-five minutes to draw and read them. According to a reporter,
"everything passed off harmoniously, the only interruption being the occasional
laughter and jocose remarks of some of the drafted ones who were present in
the room." Meanwhile at the other office (the Third District office at 26 Holliday Street), Captain Blumenberg hired Samuel Stewart, a graduate of the
Maryland Institute for the Blind, to pull the names so that no one could complain that the process was rigged. Notwithstanding his loss of sight, Stewart
wore a blindfold while he drew the names from the Eighth Ward.[77]

As had occurred after the state draft of 1862, Baltimore's citizens crowded
the provost marshal offices, producing proof of ailments, commutation fees,
and doctors' affidavits. For the next eighteen weeks, the two federal offices

in Baltimore each adjudicated roughly fifty cases per day. After all had been tallied, the federal draft produced few soldiers. For instance, by the end of December, the Third District—which comprised thirteen of the city's twenty wards—issued 2,720 exemptions (64 percent of the number drafted), most based on physical disability. Another 108 (2.5 percent) purchased substitutes, 719 (17 percent) paid for commutations, and 561 (13.2 percent) failed to report. Only fifty-five (1.3 percent) made it to the draft rendezvous at Mason's Island in the Potomac River.[78] These statistics compared closely with the national trend for the first federal draft: 56 percent acquired exemptions, 9 percent purchased substitutes, 18 percent paid for commutations, 13 percent failed to report, and 3 percent (292,441) were held to service.[79]

When the first federal draft concluded, the War Department announced a second one, initially scheduled for February 1864. To reduce the state's quota, Governor Bradford called on Maryland's soldiers who were then serving in the field to reenlist for three more years, or until the end of the war. Under War Department guidelines, if any regiment reenlisted half its numbers, it could "veteranize," that is, retain its old numerical designation and its officer corps, and its men would receive a thirty-day furlough.[80]

Although the federal government offered reenlisted veterans a $402 bounty, Maryland soldiers demanded a state bounty as well. They pledged to reenlist only if Maryland showed its appreciation by paying into the veteran volunteer program. A soldier in the First Maryland explained, "Our regiment, or a majority of them, whose service expires in two or three months from now, have not reenlisted as veterans. What is the reason? will be asked. It can be summed up in a few words. The men do not care to reenlist in Maryland, because they can go to other states and get a large state bounty. . . . [W]e do not care to fight for the state if our services are not considered as much as that of other states."[81] Lawmakers responded. On February 8, the legislature passed a state bounty ordinance, providing $325 to all reenlisted veterans. One week later, Baltimore's city council followed suit, passing an ordinance that paid an additional $200. Any veteran reenlisting in Baltimore stood to receive $927 in combined bounties.[82]

This increase in Baltimore's bounties seemed to have had the desired effect. Several of Maryland's regiments achieved "veteran volunteer" status. The First Maryland Cavalry, veterans of nineteen battles, returned to the city on February 3, having reenlisted 280 out of 300. The First Maryland Infantry reenlisted

300 of 380 who were eligible, and the Second Maryland, fresh from victories near Knoxville, Tennessee, reenlisted 197, of whom 157 resided in Baltimore.[83]

The return of the veteran volunteers to the city brought a measure of violence. Many of the reenlisted Marylanders detested rubbing elbows with the provost guards who had been quartered in their city for months. Maryland veterans especially despised the First Connecticut Cavalry. That regiment had an agent who paid Connecticut's bounty to any Baltimorean who enlisted. Perturbed by this poaching, the Maryland veterans heckled the Connecticut cavalrymen, mocking them for their lack of combat experience. Eventually, this mean-spirited banter led to a March 8 gunfight between the First Maryland Cavalry and the First Connecticut. A reporter commented, "At one time, regular volleys were fired, and the hooting and yelling of the contestants kept the residents of the vicinity of West Baltimore Street in constant alarm."[84]

Violence also accompanied the presence of the Third Maryland Cavalry, the unit full of ex-Confederates. Not only did the ex-Confederates clash with the U.S.C.I. and the furloughed veterans, but they also regularly attacked citizens on the streets. In October 1863, two drunk ex-Confederates randomly began attacking pedestrians with their sabers. Another Third Maryland cavalryman grabbed a young boy and ordered him to cheer for Jeff Davis. The boy refused, grabbed a brick, and smashed the ex-Confederate in the face, knocking out several teeth. In each of these cases, police arrested the ex-Confederate in question and charged him with assault or attempted murder.[85]

Despite the successful recruiting drive among the veteran volunteers, Baltimore endured a second federal draft. In May 1864, Provost Marshal General Fry determined that the city's deficiency stood at 1,879 men. On May 13, Provost Marshals Cathcart and Blumenberg began drawing out 2,811 names, arbitrarily increasing Fry's number by 33 percent to account for the predictable surge of post-draft exemptions.[86]

Even before this draft had finished, Baltimore suffered another alongside it. On May 4, Governor Bradford—alarmed by reports from Virginia—ordered a state draft in the event of a Confederate invasion. A month later, on June 6, this 100-day militia draft drew an additional 721 names from Baltimore.[87] This draft helped fill two regiments—the Eleventh and Twelfth Maryland—that were called out in response to Lieut. Gen. Jubal Early's short-lived invasion of the state, but the emergency did nothing to halt the continuous manpower demands of the federal government. As the uproar over this invasion subsided,

Cathcart and Blumenberg enforced a "deficiency draft," an unplanned drawing to make up for the exemptions they had already granted. On July 23, they drew another 956 names from fifteen of the city's wards, and then almost immediately announced that Lincoln had issued yet another call for men, asking for the equivalent of five hundred thousand one-year volunteers.[88] Provost Marshal General Fry placed Baltimore's new quota at 3,718, and the city worked hard to reduce this quota by raising another set of bounties. The city council's summer of 1864 bounty promised $150 to all one-year volunteers, $225 to all two-year volunteers, and $300 to all three-year volunteers. When that draft went into effect in October and November, only five of the city's twenty wards were deficient. The provost marshals drew 1,120 names from them.[89]

On December 19, Lincoln called for a fourth, and final, federal draft. The nation once again had to come up with three hundred thousand one-, two-, or three-year volunteers. Provost Marshals Cathcart and Blumenberg estimated that Baltimore's quota would likely stand at 3,700. By this point, many Baltimoreans had run out of patriotic spirit. Believing the end of the war finally in sight, they felt no need to raise money to fund another city bounty. In March 1865, when the city council proposed to pay $300 to all new volunteers, Mayor Chapman vetoed the measure. By adding the army's wage, the state relief bounty, and other funds, Chapman calculated that each Baltimore draftee now stood to make $1.60 for each working day. "This amount," he argued, "is more than our laboring men can earn independent of their own support." Although he had been in favor of high bounties throughout the war, Mayor Chapman now argued it was time to cut back:

> The city has up to this time paid over two millions of dollars for bounties. Her finances were in the best condition at the beginning of these levies, or our taxes would have been burdensome in the extreme. It must be remembered that extravagant taxes weigh heavily upon the poor and middling classes of society and will drive away the energetic class who desire to take their place among us. It must also be remembered that a continuance of these levies impairs the city's credit, and makes it impossible to obtain loans except at advanced rates of interest.[90]

The city council did not heed the mayor's warning. In a nearly unanimous decision, it overrode his veto. Unfortunately, most Baltimoreans did not see the problem associated with these high bounties. Few of the recruits lured into the service ever reached the front. Each week, dozens of "bounty jumpers" took the city bounty and deserted. Quite often, these same men returned to the city to take another bounty, repeating their fraud over and over. For instance, Thomas Coy entered as a substitute from the Ninth Ward on May 28, 1864, receiving $250 for his services. After three days at Lafayette Square Barracks, he deserted. On July 2, he reentered service as a substitute, but this time in Baltimore's other congressional district. Coy was apprehended because an agent from Cathcart's office happened to be present in Blumenberg's office when Coy attempted to muster in. Another bounty jumper, Samuel W. Downing, had deserted from multiple commands no less than twelve times, earning over $7,750 in bounties in less than a year. Downing had originally enlisted in the 110th Pennsylvania but had deserted after the Battle of Gettysburg. Since then, he had traveled across the nation, taking bounties from Philadelphia; New York City; Cincinnati; Columbus, Ohio; and Columbus, Indiana, until provost marshals arrested him on July 9, 1864, when he came to Baltimore to take a substitute bounty of $500. Downing was found guilty of desertion and executed by firing squad on September 16.[91]

Bounty jumpers in Baltimore became successful whenever they received help from dishonest substitute brokers who facilitated their escape from the city's barracks. For instance, Edward R. Hubbard owned a restaurant on Baltimore Street that he moonlighted as a brokerage business. One of his accomplices, Abel Tyson, received $550 for going as a substitute, of which Hubbard received $100. On August 30, 1864, Tyson went to Lafayette Square Barracks and deserted. He returned to Hubbard's restaurant, where Hubbard furnished him with a new set of clothes for disguise. Then Hubbard paid for Tyson's ticket to another city, where Tyson planned to take a new bounty and escape. Unhappily for both of them, Union guards arrested Tyson at President Street Station and arrested Hubbard shortly thereafter. Tyson and Hubbard, of course, represented the unlucky few who were caught. Hundreds of others performed similar feats without punishment.[92]

But even if a bounty jumper did not escape from the barracks, he could just as easily slip away while traveling to the front. In November 1864, Lieut. Col. Benjamin Franklin Taylor, commander of the Second Maryland, asked Governor Bradford for 600 new recruits. In December, Lieut. Col. G. A. Washburne, commander of the draft rendezvous at Baltimore, forwarded a detachment of forty-six draftees to City Point, Virginia. The detachment never arrived. Enraged at what he dubbed gross mismanagement in transportation affairs, Taylor fired off an angry letter to Adjt. Gen. Seth Williams, demanding an investigation. Taylor's letter bounced from headquarters to headquarters, referred to no fewer than five senior brigade or divisional commanders. Brig. Gen. Simon Griffin, Taylor's division commander, blamed the disappearance on "the general carelessness, inefficiency, or criminal neglect of duty on the part of officers through whose hands recruits for the various regiments of this command pass, between the North and the front. Not only are numbers lost en route to City Point, but after reaching that post many still fail to reach the command."[93]

Faced with a dwindling number of recruits, Baltimore residents hoped the war would end before the new draft would take effect. As of February 14, 1865, only one ward had met its quota. A writer for the *American* guessed that, if the war did not reach its conclusion, the draft would "fall like a thunderclap very soon."[94] On March 15, Provost Marshals Cathcart and Henry Clayton (who had replaced Blumenberg) began spinning the draft wheels and drawing out the names. But two weeks later, the situation in Virginia changed dramatically, as Union forces occupied Petersburg and Richmond. On April 13, four days after Robert E. Lee surrendered the Army of Northern Virginia at Appomattox, Baltimore's drawings came to a halt. Secretary Stanton announced that the draft should cease everywhere and that all draftees held at any military rendezvous should be dismissed. Baltimore's last official acts of mobilization came on April 14, when Captain Clayton dismissed a squad of drafted men from the Eighteenth Ward who had arrived at his office to seek exemptions. No longer needed, these men sauntered home.[95]

It is difficult to determine the exact number of soldiers and sailors from Baltimore who served. Records did not always distinguish between *residents* of Baltimore and men *credited* to the city. Further, in 1864, the office of the provost marshal counted each three-year volunteer as the numerical equivalent of three one-year volunteers, complicating the already confusing arithmetic. Based on a close reading of the surviving muster rolls in the Maryland State Archives and the published provost marshal reports in the *Baltimore American,* approximately seventeen thousand Baltimoreans served in the North's armed forces during the Civil War.[96] To put this in perspective, in 1860, Baltimore contained

30.8 percent of the state's population, and during the war, it supplied 36.4 percent of the state's aggregate forces.[97] In short, Baltimore provided slightly more than its fair share.

But this is not to say that the city's manpower mobilization was to be admired. It suffered from serious flaws that no agent or institution ever corrected. Certainly, Baltimore could have done even better had state or federal authorities quelled the profusion of bounty fraud, desertion, and violence that plagued Baltimore during the second half of the war. But notwithstanding these defects, by the end of the war's first year, Baltimore had thrown off the constraints of its mixed loyalty and began providing soldiers to the US Army at an appreciable rate. In many ways, Baltimore's experience mirrored that of other cities. In other urban centers, US recruiters mobilized tens of thousands of men, even as mobilization stumbled forward awkwardly. In 1990, Ernest McKay remarked on the two-faced story of New York City's Civil War. He concluded, "In the end, the city that continually badgered the president and enraged the administration became a disappointment to the South and rallied around the Union. The city answered the reveille, but it was a strange reveille."[98] The same could be said of Baltimore.

The story of Baltimore's recruitment of Union regiments also represented a vital piece of Maryland's history. It proved how some citizens took especial pride in national service. As Surgeon Foreman explained, Baltimore's Union volunteers were the true "fighting sons" of *his* Maryland. Maryland's postwar governor, Thomas Swann, echoed the same sentiment. On April 27, 1866, during a ceremony at the state house, Swann received the colors of the First Maryland from Brigadier General Kenly. While addressing Kenly, Swann reflected on the important role played by Union Marylanders. He concluded, "Amidst the sneers and reproaches of that class of our fellow-citizens—your property destroyed, your person insulted—you went forth, sir, in the great march of human freedom to battle for the liberties of our common country, and, sir, your record is before the world; we all know it and glory in it. . . . Maryland has done her part."[99]

In the years following the Civil War, some Marylanders worried that Baltimore's manpower contribution would be forgotten, that future generations would remember only that Baltimoreans had killed some of the Union's first volunteers, and that the city had once been home to Lincoln's assassin. In 1898, as another war approached, Maryland's general assembly commissioned a two-volume survey of the state's contribution to the Union war effort. On the first page, the commissioners concluded, "The sacrifices made by the people of Maryland for the preservation of the Union have never been properly understood or appreciated."[100]

Today, these same words might aptly describe Baltimore's, and Maryland's, contribution to Union victory.

NOTES

1. A. Wilson Greene, *The Final Battles of the Petersburg Campaign: Breaking the Backbone of the Rebellion,* 2nd edition (Knoxville: University of Tennessee Press, 2008), 249–50; John Thomas Scharf, *The Chronicles of Baltimore: Being a Complete History of "Baltimore Town" and Baltimore City from the Earliest Period to the Present Time* (Baltimore: Turnbull Brothers, 1874), 646. In the final verdict, another Sixth Corps soldier, Sgt. David Wilson Young (139th Pennsylvania), received the Sixth Corps prize money. Although several officers advanced Buffington's claim, for an unknown reason, Maj. Gen. Horatio Wright selected Sergeant Young instead. To complicate matters, after the war, rumors circulated that Buffington had, in fact, received the money. In April 1908, when reporting the War Department's decision to award Buffington with the Medal of Honor, his hometown newspaper, the *American Sentinel,* stated that General Grant had selected him as the recipient of the prize money, even reproducing an order from his divisional commander to prove it.

2. *Baltimore American and Commercial Advertiser,* April, 22, 1865 (hereafter *Baltimore American*).

3. Jean H. Baker, *Ambivalent Americans: The Know-Nothing Party in Maryland* (Baltimore: Johns Hopkins University Press, 1977); Barbara Jeanne Fields, *Slavery and Freedom on the Middle Ground: Maryland during the Nineteenth Century* (New Haven, CT: Yale University Press, 1985); Charles W. Mitchell, ed., *Maryland Voices of the Civil War* (Baltimore: Johns Hopkins University Press, 2007); Frank Towers, "Strange Bedfellows: The Union Party and the Federal Government in Civil War Baltimore," *Maryland Historical Magazine* 106 (Spring 2011), 7–36; David K. Graham, *Loyalty on the Line: Civil War Maryland in American Memory* (Athens: University of Georgia Press, 2018), 75–77.

4. James McPherson, *Battle Cry of Freedom: The Civil War Era* (New York: Oxford University Press, 1988), 285.

5. Phillip Shaw Paludan, *A People's Contest: The Union and Civil War, 1861–1865* (Lawrence: University Press of Kansas, 1988).

6. *The War of the Rebellion: A Compilation of the Official Records of the Union and Confederate Armies Official Records of the War of the Rebellion,* ser. 3 (Washington, DC: Government Printing Office, 1880–1901), 4:72–74, 1,264, 1,269; 5:730–745.

7. Jonathan W. White, *Abraham Lincoln and Treason in the Civil War: The Trials of John Merryman* (Baton Rouge: Louisiana State University Press, 2011), 10–11.

8. George Whitmarsh diary, April 19, 1861, Maryland Center for History and Culture Library, Baltimore, Maryland; John Wesley Hanson, *Historical Sketch of the Old Sixth Regiment of Massachusetts Volunteers during its Three Campaigns in 1861, 1862, 1863, and 1864 Containing the History of Several Companies Previous to 1861, and the Name and Military Record of Each Man Connected with*

the Regiment during the War (Boston: Lee and Shepard, 1866), 46–56; Scott Sumpter Sheads and Daniel Carroll Toomey, *Baltimore during the Civil War* (Linthicum, MD: Toomey Press, 1997), 19–20; Frank H. Taylor, *Philadelphia in the Civil War, 1861–1865* (Philadelphia: Published by the City, 1913), 29. The Union dead included: Corporal Sumner Henry Needham, Private Luther Ladd, Private Charles Taylor, and Private Addison Whitney (all of the Sixth Massachusetts), and Private George Leisenring of Colonel William F. Small's Pennsylvania Regiment.

9. White, *Abraham Lincoln and Treason in the Civil War,* 15–16; Mitchell, ed., *Maryland Voices of the Civil War,* 61–63. Considerable controversy exists concerning the origins of the order to destroy the railroad bridges. After his arrest, Mayor Brown vehemently denied concocting the order, although without a doubt, the order originated from a meeting held at his home on the evening of April 19. Possibly, Governor Hicks crafted the order, as he was the most senior politician present. However, more likely, Brown bullied Hicks into giving the order. One journalist explained that Brown followed Hicks into a bedroom, demanding orders for the city militia. With a sheet over his face, said the journalist, Hicks, "rolled and groaned. Brown insisted and declared he would not act without explicit orders from him. Hicks twisted the sheet over his head rolled over against the wall and moaned rather than exclaimed, 'Oh! Yes. Go and do it.'" After receiving Hicks's approval, Brown contacted a state militia officer (and future Confederate general) Col. Isaac R. Trimble, transmitting the orders to him.

10. *Baltimore American,* April 22, 23, 27, and 29, 1861.

11. "One of the Old Guard," to Thomas H. Hicks, June 25, 1861, Hicks Papers, Maryland Historical Society (hereafter MdHS).

12. Joseph M. Balkoski, *The Maryland National Guard: A History of Maryland's Military Forces, 1634–1991* (Baltimore, MD: Maryland National Guard, 1991), 30–1; *Baltimore American,* May 15, 1861; Earl J. Coates, Michael McAfee, and Don Troiani, *Don Troiani's Regiments and Uniforms of the Civil War* (Mechanicsburg, PA: Stackpole Books, 2002), 6; William Worthington Goldsborough, *The Maryland Line in the Confederate States Army, 1861–1865* (Baltimore: Press of Guggenheim, Weil, 1900), 9–11; McHenry Howard, *Recollections of a Maryland Confederate Soldier and Staff Officer under Johnston* (Baltimore, Williams and Wilkins, 1914), 13–23; George Wilson Booth, *Personal Reminiscences of a Maryland Soldier in the War between the States, 1861–1865* (Baltimore: Press of Fleet, McGinley, 1898), 8–9.

13. *Baltimore American,* May 14 and 15, 1861.

14. Charles Camper and J. W. Kirkley, *Historical Record of the First Regiment Maryland Infantry* (Washington, DC: Gibson Brothers, 1871), 2–4; *Baltimore American,* May 16, 1861.

15. Scharf, *Chronicles of Baltimore,* 636.

16. *Baltimore American,* June 7, 1861.

17. Scharf, *Chronicles of Baltimore,* 617.

18. Heinrich Ewald Buchholtz, *Governors of Maryland from the Revolution to 1908* (Baltimore: Williams and Wilkins, 1908), 178–183.

19. *Baltimore American,* August 16 and 23, 1861.

20. *Baltimore American,* January 7, 1862. Also, in a bloodless coup of sorts, the Union Party removed the ex officio mayor, Charles J. Baker, a member of the secessionist-controlled Second Branch, who had served as ex officio since Brown's arrest in September. On January 6, 1862, the newly seated First Branch pointed out, rightly, how the city charter granted them the power to select the ex officio. Now dominated by Unionists, the First Branch appointed one of their own, John Lee Chapman,

to fill the mayor's office. The First Branch escorted Chapman there, demanding that Baker vacate immediately. A crowd formed, expecting a fight, but to everyone's surprise, he quietly acquiesced.

21. *Baltimore American,* June 18, 20, and 25, 1861.

22. Kevin Conley Ruffner, *Maryland's Blue and Gray: A Border State's Union and Confederate Junior Officer Corps* (Baton Rouge: Louisiana State University Press, 1997), 271; *Baltimore American,* December 11 and 12, 1861.

23. *Baltimore American,* January 15, 1862.

24. *Baltimore American,* October 2, 1861.

25. *Baltimore American,* June 27, 1861.

26. Charles Bowen to Augustus Bradford, June 4 and July 23, 1862, Adjutant General's papers, Record Group S935, Maryland State Archives, Annapolis, Maryland (hereafter MdSA).

27. J. E. Duryée, "Second Regiment, Maryland Volunteer Infantry," *Maryland Historical Magazine* 12, no. 1 (March 1917), 41–44. Duryée's accounts of his leadership of the Second Maryland and his subsequent resignation are highly suspect.

28. Edward Morony to Augustus Bradford, April 21, 1862; Charles Bowen to Augustus Bradford, June 4 and July 23, 1862; Andrew B. Brunner to Augustus Bradford, July 17, 1862; Adjutant General's papers, MdSA.

29. James Cooper to Augustus Bradford, April 19 and 20 and May 23, 1862; John Dix to Augustus Bradford, April 21, 1862; Dixon Miles to Augustus Bradford, May 23, 1862; James Deems to Augustus Bradford, May 14, 1862, Adjutant General's papers, MdSA.

30. Camper and Kirkley, *Historical Record of the First Regiment Maryland Infantry,* 27–28.

31. William B. Matchett, *Maryland and the Glorious Old Third in the War for the Union: Reminiscences in the Life of her "Militant" Chaplain and Major Samuel Kramer* (Washington, DC: T. J. Brashears, Printer, 1882), 16.

32. Undated letter to Augustus A. W. Bradford, Bradford papers, MdHS; *Baltimore American and Commercial Advertiser,* May 7, 1862.

33. Peter Cozzens, *Shenandoah 1862: Stonewall Jackson's Valley Campaign* (Chapel Hill: University of North Carolina Press, 2008), 307.

34. Scharf, *Chronicles of Baltimore,* 622–24; *Baltimore American,* May 26 and 27, 1862.

35. Augustus Bradford proclamation, Bradford papers, May 28, 1862, MdHS; William Schley proclamation, undated newspaper clipping, Bradford papers, May 31, 1862, MdHS; *Baltimore American,* June 11, 1862; William Schley to Augustus Bradford, June 7, 1862, Adjutant General's papers, MdSA.

36. *Baltimore American,* August 9, 1862.

37. Edward Schilling to friends, August 14, 1862, in Schilling, *My Three Years in the Volunteer Army of the United States of America, 1862–1865* (rpr. Baltimore, MD: Council of the Alleghenies, 1985), 2–3.

38. Frederick W. Wild, *Memoirs and History of Captain Frederick W. Alexander's Battery of United States Volunteers* (Baltimore, MD: Press of Maryland School For Boys, 1912), 9–12.

39. The Second Branch Councilmen suspected of Confederate sympathy and who resigned en masse were as follows: William Dean, Asa Higgins, Jesse Marden, John Wilson, William Swindell, Francis W. Alricks, Joseph Robb, Charles J. Baker, and Decatur H. Miller. Only Councilman James B. George Sr. (Fifth and Sixth Wards) remained.

40. *Baltimore American,* July 23 and 24, 1862; John Wool to Sarah Wool, July 26 and September 23, 1862, Wool papers, New York State Library, Albany, New York; Mitchell, ed., *Maryland Voices of the Civil War,* 209–210.

41. *Baltimore American,* August 4, 5, 6, and 7, 1862.

42. These recruits enlisted in Companies A-H, Fourth Maryland; Companies F and I, Sixth Maryland; and Companies A-H, Eighth Maryland. Muster rolls, Fourth, Sixth, and Eighth Maryland, Adjutant General's Papers, MdSA.

43. Wild, *Memoirs and History of Alexander's Battery,* 15; *Baltimore American,* October 6, 1862.

44. *Baltimore American,* August 12 and 19, 1862.

45. *Baltimore American,* August 2, 1862.

46. *Baltimore American,* September 1, 2, and 3, 1862.

47. *Baltimore American,* August 27 and September 9, 1862.

48. *Baltimore American,* October 16, 1862. The 20,621 names represented all fencible (males capable of military service) Baltimoreans, all men of military age. The city did not limit its drawing solely to those who served in the militia.

49. *Baltimore American,* October 29 and 30, and November 10, 1862.

50. "E. Shriver, "Detailed Report of the Proceedings of the Rendezvous for Drafted Men and Substitutes of the Western Shore of Maryland," Adjutant Generals Papers, MdSA; *Baltimore American,* November 12 and 13, 1862.

51. J. M. Sudsburg to A. W. Bradford, February 10, 1863; E. Kielmansegge to A. W. Bradford, January 26, 1863, Adjutant General's Papers, MdSA.

52. *Baltimore American,* June 17, 1863.

53. *Baltimore American,* June 17, 1863.

54. *Baltimore American,* June 16, 18, 19, and 20, 1863, and July 1, 1863.

55. *Baltimore American,* June 22, 1863.

56. Edward G. Longacre, *Regiment of Slaves: The 4th United States Colored Infantry, 1863–1866* (Mechanicsburg, PA: Stackpole Books, 2003), 1–7; *Baltimore American,* June 22, 1863.

57. G. W. Foster to William Cannon, June 24, 1863, Delaware Public Archives, Dover, Delaware (hereafter DPA).

58. Longacre, *Regiment of Slaves,* 11–3; *Baltimore American and Commercial Advertiser,* July 10, 1863.

59. Muster Roll, Fourth US Colored Troops, Adjutant Generals' Records, MdSA.

60. General Order 329, Series 1863, General E. D. Townsend, October 3 and 26, 1863, DPA.

61. Longacre, *A Regiment of Slaves,* 14; Charles Spencer Smith, *A History of the African Methodist Episcopal Church* (Philadelphia: D. M. Baxter, 1922), 51–53.

62. Matchett, *Maryland and the Glorious Old Third in the War for the Union,* 28.

63. US War Department, Inspector General's Office, *Murder of Lieutenant Eben White: Letter from the Chief Clerk of the War Department* (Washington DC: House Printing Office, 1874), 1–8.

64. D. B. Holmes to S. M. Bowman, April 5, 1864, and Joseph Perkins to S. M. Bowman, March 28, 1864, MdSA.

65. "Loyial Colard Men of Baltimore Citey" to Abraham Lincoln, August 20, 1864, Record Group 107 (Records of the Office of the Secretary of War), Entry 18 (Letters Received), National Archives and Records Administration, Washington, DC (hereafter NARA); Petition of William

Jackson to Abraham Lincoln, April 13, 1864, Record Group 94, Entry 360, Colored Troops Division, NARA; both in Jonathan W. White, ed., *African American Correspondence with Abraham Lincoln* (unpublished book manuscript in the possession of the author).

66. *Baltimore American,* January 14, 1864.

67. Maryland House of Delegates Bill, reprinted in *Baltimore American,* January 28, 1864.

68. *Baltimore American,* September 15, and October 8, 1863.

69. *Baltimore American,* March 14 and 24, and April 5, 1864.

70. Lemuel Allison Wilmer, J. H. Jarrett, and George F. W. Vernon, *History and Roster of Maryland Volunteers, War of 1861–1865* (Baltimore: Press of Guggenheim, Weil, 1898), 6–7.

71. Abraham Lincoln, April 18, 1864, in Roy Basler, ed., *The Collected Works of Abraham Lincoln* (New Brunswick, NJ: Rutgers University Press, 1955), 7:301–3.

72. *Baltimore American,* March 28 and April 19, 1864; *Philadelphia Daily Evening Bulletin,* April 19, 1864; Basler et. al., eds., *Collected Works of Abraham Lincoln,* 301–7.

73. James H. Rickard, *Service with Colored Troops in Burnside's Corps* (Providence, RI: Rhode Island Soldiers and Sailors Historical Society, 1894), 5, 15–16. Rickard included the *Baltimore American* article in his memoir.

74. *Baltimore American,* September 8, 9, 15, and 25, 1863.

75. *Baltimore American,* August 31, 1863.

76. *Baltimore American,* August 31, 1863.

77. *Baltimore American,* November 24, 1863.

78. *Baltimore American,* December 9, 10, 11, 15, and 16, 1863, and February 17, 1864. Mason's Island is presently called Theodore Roosevelt Island. It is part of the District of Columbia.

79. These statistics compare closely with other US cities. See Tyler Anbinder, "Which Poor Man's Fight? Immigrants and the Federal Conscription of 1863," *Civil War History* 52, no. 4 (December 2006): 349–50.

80. A. W. Bradford to Maryland Volunteers, December 26, 1863, Bradford papers, MdHS.

81. *Baltimore American,* January 25, 1864, and February 2 and 5, 1864.

82. *Baltimore American,* February 20, 1864.

83. Veteran Volunteer muster rolls, Second Maryland Infantry, N. T. Dushane to J. S. Berry, February 14, 1864, Adjutant Generals Papers, MdSA; *Baltimore American and Commercial Advertiser,* April 4, 1864.

84. N. L. Jeffries to A. W. Bradford, n.d., Adjutant Generals Papers, MdSA; *Baltimore American,* March 9, 1864.

85. *Baltimore American,* September 8, 9, 15, and 25, October 19, and November 30, 1863.

86. *Baltimore American,* May 4, 12, 14, 16, 17, 18, 19, and 24, 1864.

87. *Baltimore American,* June 7, 8, 10, 14, and 15, 1864.

88. *Baltimore American,* July 23, 25, and 26, 1864. Only the Second, Third, Fourth, Fifth, and Fourteenth Wards had filled their quotas. Under this call, volunteers could also enlist for two or three years and would be counted as two or three recruits, accordingly.

89. *Baltimore American,* October 19 and 31 and November 9 and 14, 1864.

90. *Baltimore American,* March 29 and 31, 1865.

91. *Baltimore American,* July 3 and 21, 1864; Corey S. Retter, *Union Executions, 1861–1865* (Morrisville, NC: Lulu Press, 2016), 159–60.

92. *Baltimore American,* September 16, 1864.

93. B. F. Taylor to A. W. Bradford, November 23, 1864; H. C. Woods to B. F. Taylor, December 22, 1864, and January 11, 1865; B. F. Taylor to S. Williams, January 6, 1865, referred to S. G. Griffin, January 7, 1865, H. B. Titus, January 7 and 11, 1865, R. Potter, January 10, 1865, J. Quay, January 10, 1865, O. Willcox, January 10, 1865, MdHS.

94. *Baltimore American,* January 26 and 28, February 15, and March 15, 1865.

95. *Baltimore American,* April 14 and 15, 1865.

96. Muster Rolls of the Maryland Volunteers, MdSA: Second, Fourth, Eighth, Ninth, Tenth, Eleventh, Twelfth, and Thirteenth Maryland Volunteer Infantry Regiments, Purnell Legion Infantry, Tyler Battalion Infantry, Fourth, Sixth, Tenth, Nineteenth, Thirtieth, and Thirty-Ninth U.S.C.I.

97. Specifically, the numbers are as follows: Baltimore's 1860 population (212,418), Maryland's 1860 population (687,049), Baltimore's estimated aggregate (17,000); Maryland's recorded aggregate (46,638).

98. Ernest A. McKay, *The Civil War and New York City* (Syracuse, NY: Syracuse University Press, 1990), 313.

99. Camper and Kirkley, *Historical Record of the First Regiment Maryland Infantry,* 217–18.

100. Wilmer, Jarrett, and Vernon, *History and Roster of the Maryland Volunteers,* 1:1.

"WHAT I WITNESSED WOULD ONLY MAKE YOU SICK"

Union Soldiers Confront the Dead at Antietam

BRIAN MATTHEW JORDAN

J ust two days after the Battle of Antietam, the photographer Alexander Gardner and his assistant James Gibson captured one of the most arresting images of the Civil War: a large federal burial party taking a much-needed respite from its macabre toil on David R. Miller's farm. Their muskets stacked, some men lean on shovels and spades; one slings a pick over his shoulder. The foreground is littered with splintered fence rails and human debris. Lifeless bodies—very likely the dead of the 124th Pennsylvania Volunteers, "raked" by a fierce rebel musketry from the West Woods—are arrayed in a neat row, awaiting their soon-to-be excavated graves. If inspected with care, this stereo negative—one of ninety-five images collected on the battlefield that autumn—yields some tantalizing clues as to the emotional toll levied by the inevitable postbattle errand. Somber and sallow-faced, the burial detail surveys the hellscape around them—appearing to oscillate between awe, horror, and disbelief. While some soldiers engage in conversation, one member of the crew points ahead—perhaps indicating the location of the next shallow trench into which bodies will be heaped. Seated on the ground, another man turns away from the carnage; still others knit their brows in seeming disgust.[1]

It has become axiomatic that the photographs of the Antietam dead—displayed that October in a public exhibit mounted in Mathew Brady's New York City gallery—were the first such images captured on an American battlefield.[2] But less appreciated and more significant is another novelty of the slaughter at Sharpsburg. Prior to its victories at South Mountain and Antietam, the Army of the Potomac had never wrested a battlefield from the enemy; as such, the possession "under arms" of these corpse-strewn fields provided many Union soldiers' first intimate encounter with the grim realities of death on a massive scale.[3] Taking cues from sensory history and histories of material culture, this essay examines how Union soldiers (and a few northern civilians) confronted the dead at Antietam.[4] As the sensory historian Adam Mack has pointed out, our narratives too often elide the ways in which the past was "immediately" felt and experienced by ordinary historical actors, though these raw feelings and emotions informed historical memories and stimulated future action.[5] Keenly aware that they were participating in history—though at pains to assimilate their place in the war as a whole—Union soldiers rummaged for meaning, living in the shadow of the dead. In the end, the assault that Antietam made on their senses—an assault that persisted six more weeks, as a listless Maj. Gen. George B. McClellan moored his Army of the Potomac in place—challenged and refined their ideas about the war and its conduct.

Union soldiers confronted a staggering spectacle on the Antietam battlefield after the shooting stopped. So surreal was the landscape that one brigade commander held, "If phantoms from the spirit world could ever come forth to bewilder mortals, sure never was there time or place or sight so seasonable." Men distrusted their eyes as they surveyed mangled bodies littering the field, the odor of burning animal flesh assaulting their nostrils and the death moans of wounded men drumming in their ears. "War has its glories," one Ohioan remarked, "but it has its ten thousand demons in these human tortures, that make the eye balls ache—the heart bleed—the lips palsy, and the brain reel." Indeed, the sensory overload exacted a physical toll. Cpl. Bernard F. Blakeslee reported that "many" soldiers detailed to the burial parties from his regiment, the newly formed Sixteenth Connecticut, became "sick" owing to the nature of their work. Similarly, twenty-four-year-old Maj. Rufus Dawes of the Sixth Wisconsin attributed a "severe attack of bilious sick-headache" to "the late terrible excitement and trying times." "We are encamped amid a dreadful stench of the half-buried thousands of men and horses on the battle field," he tellingly protested. Even Dawes' mount "trembled in fright" and was "wet with perspiration."[6]

The odors were truly most offending. Some men explained that while they did not mind *seeing* dead bodies, the "unsufferable stench" was quite another matter. "You can imagine how it must improve the air to have the bodies of men laying above the ground so long and then the dead Horses and Mules," explained one Massachusetts lieutenant in a letter to his wife. "Sometimes it is perfectly horrible."[7] Another Bay State volunteer objected that "almost everywhere carrion polluted the air." One regimental surgeon feared that the rank air was breeding "a pestilence" in his unit, which had been fortunate to see no action in the fight. "We must leave soon or we shall all die," one soldier echoed.

Meteorological conditions only exacerbated the foul smell, for the weather that September was "phenomenally hot." Temperatures in the mid-seventies (they climbed to an inopportune high of seventy-nine degrees Fahrenheit on the afternoon following the battle) hastened decomposition; in the humid evenings, the "low, dense fog" that blanketed the battlefield intensified the stench until it became "almost unendurable." A veteran of the 108th New York remembered that the scent of death was "thick" enough to be "cut in chunks."[8] First Lieutenant Samuel Fletcher, whose Massachusetts unit suffered 54 percent losses (only nine of the sixty-two men in his company emerged from their abortive stand in the West Woods), commented that "for several days," he "tasted the odor" of putrefying flesh. For that very reason, Joseph Ward and his comrades in the 106th Pennsylvania were unable to eat. "Even the food seemed tainted with the foul odor that enveloped us," he objected. "One had almost to dig one's nose into the ground to get a good breath."[9]

As historian Mark M. Smith has observed, the "stench" of battlefield death "constituted a very powerful form of meaning." Behavioral psychologists confirm that "the neuroanatomy of olfaction has a privileged and unique connection to the neural substrates of emotion and associative learning." Further, the "anatomical overlap between memory and smell" ensures that olfaction can "tap and retrieve far older memories than other sensory systems." Put simply, the men would never forget Antietam's offensive aroma. Their responses are all the more striking when we consider the normative smell-scape of the Civil War generation; these were men accustomed to dead pigs in alleys, fecal matter in the streets, and limited sanitation.[10]

Nor would the men forget what they had seen and heard. Antietam's carnage made clear the war's seemingly limitless capacity for human destruction. Men catalogued the many lifelike poses in which they encountered the dead: "with every rigid muscle strained in fierce agony," with "hands folded peacefully upon the bosom," "still clutching their guns," "hanging over a fence which they were climbing when the fatal shot" hit its target.[11] "It is an awful sight to go over the field after the excitement is over," one soldier remarked, "especially such a battle as last Wednesdays." Turkey buzzards circled ravenously over-head, eager for their "cadaverous feast." Clinging to life among the dead, the "wounded lay in all directions." One soldier catalogued the curses and prayers, the piteous pleas for water and supplications for medical care he overheard; unable to translate the battle's "raving agony" into neat or linear prose, he re-corded its auditory elements instead.

Decomposition was especially disconcerting. "I have seen, stretched along, in one straight line, ready for interment, at least a thousand blackened, bloated corpses with blood and gas protruding from every orifice," one regimental sur-geon sighed, "maggots holding high carnival over their heads."[12] George Noyes noted that the bodies of "our late antagonists" had turned "so absolutely black" that they could be easily mistaken for "a negro regiment." The irony was not lost on him; even so, the self-described "strong-hearted" soldier confessed that he had "gazed upon as much horror as I was able to bear."[13] James Voris agreed. His Thirty-Fourth Pennsylvania Volunteer Infantry tramped across the field on September 18, finding the dead putrefying "in heaps." He and his comrades "had to turn their heads and shut their eyes." "Oh," the young soldier remarked, "it was sickening." Rather than turn away, still other soldiers relied on alco-hol to dull their senses and manage their grief. "The bodies had become so offensive," one Ohioan reported, "that men could only endure it by being stag-gering drunk."[14]

Wincing, turning away, guzzling whiskey—these responses reassured men that they had not yet devolved into barbarism. While soldiers strove for the self-possession military discipline demanded, they feared growing desensitized to death and violence. Just weeks into his service, for example, one New York regimental surgeon wondered if it was already too late. "I pass over the putrify-ing bodies of the dead," he marveled, "and feel as little unconcerned as though they were two hundred pigs . . . whether I am indeed harder hearted or whether familiarity, ever so brief, with such scenes, tends to sear the better feelings, I know not; but certain it is, that I slept as soundly last night in the open air, and I could almost say under the same blanket with a dead man, as I ever did."[15]

A s they wandered the fields—in a real sense, the first battlefield visitors—soldiers endeavored to make sense of the fight that northern newspapers declared "a glorious victory." As historian Carol Reardon has noted, "a soldier's recollection of a battle began in his personal memory as scattered snippets of 'what happened to me.'" Such "snippets" demanded context and meaning. Over time, veterans filled in crucial gaps in their knowledge—or remedied their dim understanding of the larger operational picture—by consulting (and in many cases appropriating elements from) other survivor's published accounts. But those accounts were still years away. Most immediately, then, dead men helped to tell the tale of the battle. By evaluating the position, condition, and distribution of Antietam's casualties, soldiers attempted to piece together what the rush of adrenaline and their narrow vantage point had denied them: a coherent narrative of the engagement in which they had participated.[16]

For instance, men took note of which bodies had been riddled by musketry and which had been torn by shot and shell. "Heaps of rebel dead" mounded "behind stone walls" betrayed the rebel army's appropriation of fence lines as "breastworks." The concentration of the dead likewise revealed whether or not the enemy had prevailed at a certain point. Not unlike civilians back home, Civil War soldiers used the number of killed or wounded as a reliable index of a unit's courage and bravery in battle. Staggering losses betrayed stubborn stands. Wandering the fields, soldier spectators made their initial assessments about the contributions of particular outfits to the battle's outcome. The morning after the Battle of South Mountain, Maj. George H. Hildt of the Thirtieth Ohio brimmed with pride as he surveyed Wise's field at Fox's Gap, choked with dead North Carolinians. "Well satisfied with our work yesterday," he wrote.[17]

Close inspection of the enemy dead confirmed northern critiques of southern society and invited reflection on what was at stake in the war.[18] Dead rebels not surprisingly bore the marks of their character—and that of their treasonous rebellion. According to one commentator, they seemed "to have retained in death something of the last attitudes of their combative life." Wandering along the enemy lines, one of Duryée's Zouaves fixed his eyes on the corpse of a "young lad, of not more than fifteen years of age," whose "long curls" flowed "over his shoulders." Though his thighs had been "terribly mangled," he wore a "heavenly smile" that exposed "teeth of remarkable beauty." This prompted the New Yorker to suppose that the dead boy was "probably the pride of some aristocratic family, who has sent him willingly to the war." William Chamberlain, a medical inspector for the United States Sanitary Commission who traveled to the battlefield to organize the delivery of much-needed linens, blankets, bandages, and whiskey, "noticed that decomposition was proceeding much more rapidly among the Confederate dead than among ours," an incongruity he attributed to "the restricted use of salt" in southern rations. George Noyes confessed that the sight of the rebel dead provoked pangs of sympathy, even as he sanctimoniously crowed that the dead Confederates had merely reaped what they had sown. "So ends the brief madness which sent him hither to fight against a government he knew only by its blessings," Noyes mused as he gazed upon the decomposing body of a "young rebel officer." In his view, those who were willing to fight for a ghastly cause—those who were willing to wear "forever the Nessus shirt of slavery"—were fated for such a ghastly end.[19]

Soldiers and other spectators not only surveyed the location and condition of the dead but also took the time and effort to inventory the slain. Many historians have noted the statistical endeavors of Civil War veterans like William Freeman Fox, Thomas Leonard Livermore, and Frederick Henry Dyer, who assembled comprehensive, numbingly detailed registers of the dead that are still mined by scholars today. What has been less fully appreciated are the wartime origins of these postwar projects. The obsession with tallying the dead began as soon as the guns fell silent; such counts could render incontrovertible an army's claim to victory.[20] As the historian Patricia Cline Cohen has observed, in the mid-nineteenth century, "counting was presumed to advance knowledge," since "counting led to the most reliable and objective form of fact there was, the hard number."[21]

Quantification became especially important for the battle's veterans in the wake of the Maryland Campaign, when McClellan's failure to pursue the enemy into Virginia and a stubborn Confederate revisionism conspired to efface the decisiveness of the battlefield victories scored by the Army of the Potomac.[22] "In passing over the battle ground, which was now in our possession," one Ohio soldier was sure to point out, "it was evident that the loss of the rebels greatly exceeded our own." George Hildt made a careful count of the dead at Fox's Gap. "At one point 17 of their dead were lying touching each other," he wrote. "Their loss in that fight was five to one of ours." Three days later, the Ohioan was no less fastidious at Antietam, combing the fields opposite Burnside Bridge. Samuel Wheelock Fiske, whose Fourteenth Connecticut engaged the enemy at the Sunken Road, "counted nearly a thousand dead bodies of rebels lying still unburied in groves and cornfields, on hill-sides and in trenches." "The excitement of a battle comes in the day of it, but the horrors of it two or three days after," he reflected.[23]

In addition to statistics, men collected tangible objects. Battlefield relics made "tactile" an event that many soldiers described as ineffable; trophy-taking "confirm[ed] the victors' triumph" over the enemy.[24] "The whole field of battle was littered with abandoned caissons, cannon, rifles, swords, bayonets, dead animals, dead of both armies and accoutrements of the troops," one commentator observed, "and whilst burial parties were disposing of the human wreckage of the battle, other details were engaged in gathering the abandoned material enumerated." Company B of the Ninety-Third New York, for instance, was detailed to collect muskets discarded on the field; not far away, the Fourteenth Connecticut replenished its supply of haversacks and blankets.[25] Just as they had pondered the condition and arrangement of the dead, the men read and interpreted the physical detritus of battle in their efforts to piece together a narrative of the battle. "Some of their Regts must have left in a great hurry," Lt. Joseph W. Collingwood surmised, for "they left all their knapsacks, clothing, guns stores &c in large quantity." Samuel Fiske drew the same conclusion from the object-strewn fields. "Whole regiments threw away their overcoats and blankets and everything that encumbered them," he marveled, "and so with equipment and stores and ammunition and everything else."[26]

Not surprisingly, fields choked with the detritus of war invited scavenging and plunder. The catalogues of Sanitary Fairs and other public exhibitions provide partial inventories of items federal soldiers scavenged from dead bodies of their enemy: the caps of North Carolinians who died at South Mountain; the slouch hat of a Mississippi private felled at Antietam; a letter, bearing Confederate postage, addressed to the captain of the Sixteenth South Carolina; rifles, cartridge boxes, belt plates, and bayonet sheaths. Soldiers also boasted of their bounties in letters home. Collingwood, for one, "picked up a great many relics," including an overcoat worn by a soldier killed in battle. "I have got my chest & am going over the Battle field again [to] get some more," he vowed. In the weeks that followed, the lieutenant combed the fields on at least two more occasions. In October, the lieutenant sent home "a Button cut from a dead Rebels coat," assuring his wife, Rebecca, that she "need not be afraid of it." "Most of [their] officers are gentlemanly and intelligent," he cautioned, "but I never could find one yet who could define what their rights were except that the abolitionists wanted to steal all their niggers."[27]

Before long, soldiers encountered civilian competition in their pursuit of relics—powerful evidence that many loyal northerners apprehended the significance of the Antietam battle almost immediately. "The battlefield of Wednesday," one soldier reported, "is daily trampled by a small army of curiosity seekers from the West, North and East." The narrow roads leading into Sharpsburg were daily choked with carriages delivering civilians and aid workers to the battlefield. Within a week, these civilians had "pretty well cleared" away "all material evidence of the struggle," leaving only the few bodies that eluded the burial parties to testify to the fight. Many of these civilians felt, as Charles W. Loring explained, an urgent need "to see actual history, a battlefield, and veteran troops."[28]

One of the more famous visitors to the field was the prose poet Oliver Wendell Holmes Sr., who boarded a Maryland-bound locomotive upon receipt of the news that his namesake son, a captain in the Twentieth Massachusetts, had been wounded. After a frenetic search, Holmes located his son on a train; still, he felt the magnetic lure of the battlefield. "It was impossible to [return to Massachusetts] without seeing that," he declared. Hiring a hack driver to convey him to Sharpsburg, the Boston intellectual refused to return north without a souvenir. "I picked up a Rebel canteen, and one of our own," he began, "but there was something repulsive about the trodden and stained relics of the stale battle-field. It was like the table of some hideous orgy left uncleared, and one turned away disgusted from its broken fragments and muddy heel-taps." Ultimately, Holmes settled for "a bullet or two, a button, [and] a brass plate from a soldier's belt," together with "a letter which I picked up, directed to Richmond, Virginia, its seal unbroken."[29]

The elder Holmes was hardly alone in pondering the propriety of relic hunting, for many pondered "appropriate" conduct on a battlefield strewn with dead bodies. Even as his own morbid curiosity delivered him to the field, one Philadelphia spectator registered his "indignation" at the sight of civilians "plundering" the shot-ploughed ground, purloining discarded muskets and other souvenirs. "I expressed to many of them my opinion of such conduct, but men who will steal have no sense of shame," he insisted. Two years later, Lincoln's opponents tried to make political hay of the commander-in-chief's alleged lack of decorum during a postbattle visit to Antietam. Democratic newspapers reported that while touring the battlefield with General McClellan, the president asked his close friend and US Marshal Ward Hill Lamon—seated beside him in the ambulance conducting the presidential party across the field—to sing the minstrel tune "Picayune Butler." A pious McClellan objected, "'I would prefer to hear it some other place and time.'" The story reeked of raw political opportunism; by September, however, it had gained enough traction in the press to merit a reply from the administration. Lamon conceded that while in the ambulance he sang a "'little school boy song'" at the president's request, though not at the battle site. "The time was sixteen days after the battle," he protested. "Not a dead body had been seen during the whole trip, nor a grave that had not been rained on since it had been made." The manufactured controversy soon faded, though not before revealing the anxiety many northerners felt as they attempted to navigate life in a world of death.[30]

The Army of the Potomac bivouacked in close proximity to the battlefield for the next six weeks, which ensured that the sights and smells of Antietam lingered. Some civilian curiosity seekers visited with the encamped soldiers; their recollections further underscore the human effects of confronting Antietam's carnage. "Many [of the veterans] spoke of the scenes they saw [at Sharpsburg] with a shudder," one sightseer noted. "They could not throw off the impression made by the masses of wounded and dead; the wounded often lying neglected and helpless under the dead, sometimes crushed to death by the wheels of our own artillery." Neither, it seems, could the men of the Fourteenth Connecticut. The regiment conducted religious services on the Sunday after the battle. "Everyone wore a More Sober Face than I had before observed," Sgt. Benjamin Hirst recalled. A Massachusetts-born officer who fed his Twelfth Corps brigade into the Cornfield fight insisted that "neither time nor change" could "dim the remembrance" of carnage "too horrible to be real, and yet too real to forget."[31]

Still, confronting the war's realities sent no great wave of disillusionment crashing through the ranks; to the contrary, it seemed only to renew the army's resolve. "We see many sorrowfull sights," Collingwood remarked, "but the battle must be fought [and] victory must be ours. Rebellion must be put down at any price." Like Collingwood, Nathaniel Emerson Bright was once a devoted "McClellan man"; now, however, he rejected a war of conciliation. The dead of Antietam could not be permitted to have died in vain—a fate that seemed increasingly likely with each new day of inaction. "I am exceedingly desirous that something great be done this fall campaign," he wrote. "Unless something is done soon during this fall & the spring campaigns there does not seem to be much prospect that the war will be closed during Lincoln's administration, and if the latter does not take place why then all seems clouds and darkness." Fuming that the Army of the Potomac had failed to follow up on its victories, Charles McClenthen of the Twenty-Sixth New York was even more exacting. "Our present plans," he wrote of the enlisted ranks, "would admit of nothing less than the total annihilation of the whole rebel army, to be immediately followed by the collapse of that magnificent humbug, the so-called Confederacy."[32]

Ultimately, Antietam's aftermath proved a consequential moment in the life of the Army of the Potomac. As other scholars have argued, experiences between battles and behind the lines did as much as (if not more than) combat to shape soldiers' emerging understanding of the conflict.[33] "The war has just been recast," Frederick Law Olmsted vowed that November. "The cost of war had not been fairly counted—the horror of war had not been fairly seen . . . Now, in a moment of disappointment, depression, and mourning, the full cost was pondered, the full horror looked in the face." Equipped with this deeper, more capacious understanding of the war, Antietam's veterans braced themselves for the bloody work still ahead.[34]

NOTES

1. On the pioneering historical detective work that revealed the location of Gardner's photograph, see William Frassanito, *Antietam: The Photographic Legacy of America's Bloodiest Day* (New York: Charles Scribner's Sons, 1978), 144–45, 53. See also Robert M. Green, comp., *History of the One Hundred and Twenty-Fourth Regiment Pennsylvania Volunteers in the War of the Rebellion—1862–1863* (Philadelphia: Ware Bros., 1907), 33, 37. A vivid description of an Antietam burial trench is offered by Roland Bowen in Gregory A. Coco, ed., *From Ball's Bluff to Gettysburg . . . and Beyond: The Civil War Letters of Private Roland E. Bowen, 15th Massachusetts Infantry 1861–1864* (Gettysburg, PA: Thomas Publications, 1994).

2. Eleanor Jones Harvey, *The Civil War and American Art* (New Haven: Yale University Press, 2012), 76.

3. The novelty of sleeping upon arms on a battlefield seized from the enemy is described in a letter from New Jersey soldier Edmund English to his mother. "We camped last night on the ground we took from the enemy," he remarked, "I went after water last night and dead 'rebs' were everywhere." Edmund English to his mother, September 15, 1862, Edmund English Papers, Henry E. Huntington Library, San Marino, California. See also Charles S. McClenthen, *A Sketch of the Campaign in Virginia and Maryland, from Cedar Mountain to Antietam by a Soldier of the 26th N.Y.V.* (Syracuse: Masters & Lee, Printers, 1862), 33; *Gallipolis* [Ohio] *Journal,* October 30, 1862; Harvey Henderson Civil

War Diary, September 14, 1862, Huntington Library; James C. Voris to my dear sister, September 23, 1862, Miller Family Correspondence, box 1, Huntington Library. On the Maryland Campaign of 1862, see especially D. Scott Hartwig, *To Antietam Creek: The Maryland Campaign of 1862* (Baltimore: Johns Hopkins University Press, 2012); Richard Slotkin, *The Long Road to Antietam: How the Civil War Became a Revolution* (New York: Liveright, 2012); Joseph L. Harsh, *Taken at the Flood: Robert E. Lee and Confederate Strategy in the Maryland Campaign of 1862* (Kent, Ohio: Kent State University Press, 1999); and James V. Murfin, *The Gleam of Bayonets: The Battle of Antietam and Robert E. Lee's Maryland Campaign, September 1862* (Baton Rouge: Louisiana State University Press, 1965).

4. On sensory history and histories of material culture, see Mark M. Smith, "Producing Sense, Consuming Sense, Making Sense: Perils and Prospects for Sensory History," *Journal of Social History* 40 (Summer 2007): 841–58; Mark M. Smith, *The Smell of Battle, the Taste of Siege: A Sensory History of the Civil War* (New York: Oxford University Press, 2014); Richard Grassby, "Material Culture and Cultural History," *The Journal of Interdisciplinary History* 35, no. 4 (Spring 2005): 591–603; and Joan E. Cashin, ed., *War Matters: Material Culture in the Civil War Era* (Chapel Hill: University of North Carolina Press, 2018).

5. Adam Mack, *Sensing Chicago: Noisemakers, Strikebreakers, and Muckrakers* (Urbana: University of Illinois Press, 2015), 36. While no historical narrative can adequately convey the horror of the battle's aftermath, the surviving evidence nonetheless allows us to appreciate something of how individual historical actors felt, intuited, and made sense of the world around them.

6. "Battle of Hagerstown Heights," *Daily Cleveland* [Ohio] *Herald,* September 20, 1862; *Daily Ohio Statesman,* December 13, 1862; Bernard F. Blakeslee, *History of the Sixteenth Connecticut Volunteers* (Hartford: Case, Lockwood, & Brainard, Printers, 1875), 21; George H. Gordon, *A War Diary,* 4; Rufus R. Dawes, *Service with the Sixth Wisconsin Volunteers* (Marietta, OH: E. R. Alderman & Sons, 1890), 95, 99. On the hard-luck Sixteenth Connecticut, see also Lesley J. Gordon, *A Broken Regiment: The 16th Connecticut's Civil War* (Baton Rouge: Louisiana State University Press, 2014), and Scott Valentine, "Dark Memories after Antietam: Lt. Bernard Blakeslee's Desperate Fight against 'Soldier's Heart,'" *Military Images* 34, no. 1 (Winter 2016): 53–55.

7. Edmund English memoir, Edmund English Papers, Huntington Library; Joseph W. Collingwood to my dear wife, September 30, 1862, Joseph W. Collingwood Papers, box 3, Huntington Library; see also Daniel M. Holt to my dear wife, September 16, 1862, in James M. Greiner, Janet L. Coryell, and James R. Smither, eds., *A Surgeon's Civil War: The Letters & Diary of Daniel M. Holt, M.D.* (Kent, Ohio: Kent State University Press, 1994), 21; and Ransom Allen Perkins to dear friends, September 28, 1862, Ransom Allen Perkins Letters, Huntington Library.

8. Nathaniel Emerson Bright to dear brother Justin, September 29, 1862, Nathaniel Emerson Bright Papers, box 21, Huntington Library; Daniel Holt to my dear wife, September 25, 1862, in Greiner et al., eds., *A Surgeon's Civil War,* 28; Roland Bowen to Friend Guild, September 20, 1862, in Coco, ed., *From Ball's Bluff to Gettysburg,* 121. For a handy compendium of research on the campaign, including meteorological data, see Joseph L. Harsh, *Sounding the Shallows: A Confederate Companion for the Maryland Campaign of 1862* (Kent, Ohio: Kent State University Press, 2000), 20–23; *Pennsylvania at Antietam* (Harrisburg: Harrisburg Publishing Company, 1906), 164; Henry Rowan Brinkerhoff, *History of the Thirtieth Regiment Ohio Volunteer Infantry* (Columbus, OH: James W. Osgood, Printer, 1863), 47; George H. Washburn, *A Complete Military History and Record of the 108th Regiment N.Y. Vols.* (Rochester, NY: Press of E. R. Andrews, 1894), 26–27; "The Losses at Antietam," *Indiana* [Penn-

sylvania] *Weekly Messenger,* October 1, 1862. Joseph Collingwood reported in mid-October that "for the past two weeks it has been very warm, and dry, and very dusty." Joseph W. to Rebecca Collingwood, October 13, 1862, Joseph W. Collingwood Papers, box 3, Huntington Library.

9. Samuel Fletcher as quoted in Ted Alexander, "Destruction, Disease, and Death: The Battle of Antietam and the Sharpsburg Civilians," *Civil War Regiments* 6, no. 2 (1998): 164; Joseph Ripley Chandler Ward, *History of the One Hundred and Sixth Regiment Pennsylvania Volunteers* (Philadelphia: F. McManus, Jr., 1906), 116. Makeshift hospitals were equally rank; when describing one in Middletown that was packed to the overflowing with the wounded of South Mountain, William Gable of the Forty-Fifth Pennsylvania remarked, "There is a very bad smell." William Gable to dear mother and sister, October 9, 1862, William Gable Collection, Huntington Library.

10. Mark M. Smith, *The Smell of Battle, the Taste of Siege: A Sensory History of the Civil War* (New York: Oxford University Press, 2015), 83; Richard J. Stevenson, "The Forgotten Sense: Using Olfaction in a Museum Context: A Neuroscience Perspective," in *The Multisensory Museum: Cross Disciplinary Perspectives on Touch, Sound, Smell, Memory, and Space,* edited by Nina Levent and Alvaro Pascual-Leone (Lanham, MD: Rowman and Littlefield, 2014), 154; Rachel S. Herz, "The Role of Odor Evoked Memory in Psychological and Physiological Health," *Brain Sciences* (July 2016): 2.

11. *Daily Cleveland Herald,* September 20, 1862; "Incidents of the Battle of Antietam," [Concord] *New Hampshire Statesman,* October 4, 1862; Kilmer, "The Phenomena of Death in Battle," *Popular Science Monthly* 43 (June 1893); *Gallipolis* [Ohio] *Journal,* October 30, 1862; McClenthen, *A Sketch of the Campaign,* 43.

12. Joseph W. Collingwood to my dear wife, September 24, 1862, Joseph W. Collingwood Papers, box 3, Huntington Library; George Henry Gordon, *A War Diary of Events in the War of the Great Rebellion, 1863–1865* (Boston: James R. Osgood, 1882), 4; Ransom Allen Perkins to dear friends, September 28, 1862, Ransom Allen Perkins Letters, Huntington; McClenthen, *A Sketch of the Campaign,* 33; Daniel M. Holt to my dear wife, September 25, 1862, in Greiner et al., eds., *A Surgeon's Civil War,* 28; Oliver C. Bosbyshell, ed., *Pennsylvania at Antietam: Report of the Antietam Battlefield Memorial Commission* (Harrisburg: State Printer, 1906), 164.

13. George Freeman Noyes, *The Bivouac and The Battlefield: Or, Campaign Sketches in Virginia and Maryland* (New York: Harper and Brothers, 1864), 215–18. For another account of the blackened bodies of dead rebels, see Franklin Sawyer, *A Military History of the 8th Regiment Ohio Vol. Inf.* (Cleveland, OH: Fairbanks, 1881), 83.

14. James C. Voris to my dear sister, September 23, 1862, in Miller Family Correspondence, box 1, Huntington Library; Samuel Compton as quoted in Michael C. C. Adams, *Living Hell: The Dark Side of the Civil War* (Baltimore: Johns Hopkins University Press, 2014), 102. See also Report of W. M. Chamberlain, M.D., Sanitary Commission Circular no. 48, September 24, 1862, Huntington Library.

15. Daniel Holt as quoted in Greiner et al., eds., *A Surgeon's Civil War,* 21–22.

16. Luther Osborn diary, September 20, 1862, Huntington Library; Carol Reardon, "Writing Battle History: The Challenge of Memory," *Civil War History* 53, no. 3 (2007): 259. In an utterance typical of many soldiers, Joseph Collingwood explained to his wife that it was "impossible for anyone to give an account of the whole battle because it extended over so much ground." Collingwood to my dear wife, September 30, 1862, Joseph W. Collingwood Papers, box 3, Huntington Library.

17. "The 130th Pennsylvania Regiment Burying the Dead at Antietam," *Frank Leslie's Illustrated Newspaper,* October 18, 1862; "Battle of Hagerstown Heights," *Daily Cleveland Herald,* September 20,

1862; George Hildt to dear parents, September 22, 1862, George Hildt Papers, Ohio History Connection, Columbus.

18. Though a truce permitted the rebels to bury their dead, the work was done hastily at best—and in many cases not at all. For example, Columbus Chambers of the Eleventh Mississippi wrote that his comrades were given "the best burial possible upon such [an occasion as] Lee fell back to Va." As such, federal soldiers had plenty of opportunities to come face to face with the enemy. Columbus Chambers memoir [circa 1864], Columbus Chambers Reminiscences, Huntington Library.

19. George L. Kilmer, "The Phenomena of Death in Battle," *Popular Science Monthly* 43 (June 1893); Alfred Davenport, *Camp and Field Life of the Fifth New York Volunteer Infantry (Duryee Zouaves)* (New York: Dick and Fitzgerald, 1879), 317; Report of W. M. Chamberlain, M.D., Inspector, United States Sanitary Commission, published as Sanitary Commission Bulletin no. 48, September 24, 1862; Noyes, *Bivouac and The Battlefield*, 217.

20. On Fox, Livermore, and Dyer, see Mark E. Neely Jr., *The Civil War and the Limits of Destruction* (Cambridge, MA: Harvard University Press, 2007), and Drew Gilpin Faust, *This Republic of Suffering: Death and the American Civil War* (New York: Alfred A. Knopf, 2008).

21. Patricia Cline Cohen, *A Calculating People: The Spread of Numeracy in Early America* (New York: Routledge, 1999), 205.

22. Joseph W. Collingwood, for one, carped about early newspaper coverage of the Maryland Campaign. "It is shamefull," he commented, "to be so misrepresent[ed]." Collingwood to my dear wife, October 3, 1862, Joseph W. Collingwood Papers, box 3, Huntington Library. Regarded by generations of historians as a "stalemate," recent scholarship on Antietam has revealed that the battle was a decisive Union victory. After catching Lee's divided army off-guard and notching victories in the South Mountain passes on September 14, McClellan maneuvered Lee into a corner—with the Potomac River to his rear—at Sharpsburg. Indeed, the Rebels' strategic objective of resuming their northward thrust into Pennsylvania was thwarted before the battle began.

23. George Hildt to his parents, September 22, 1862, George Hildt Papers, Ohio History Connection; Samuel Wheelock Fiske, *Mr. Dunn Browne's Experiences in the Army* (Boston: Nichols and Noyes, 1866), 49.

24. Teresa Barnett, *Sacred Relics: Pieces of the Past in Nineteenth Century America* (Chicago: University of Chicago Press, 2013), 82. For recent work on the emotive power of relics, in addition to Barnett, see Peter S. Carmichael, "The Trophies of Victory and the Relics of Defeat: Returning Home in the Spring of 1865," in Joan E. Cashin, ed., *War Matters: Material Culture in the Civil War Era* (Chapel Hill: University of North Carolina Press, 2018).

25. Luther Osborn diary, September 19, 1862, in Luther Osborn Diaries, Huntington Library; Benjamin Hirst as quoted in Robert L. Bee, ed., *The Boys from Rockville: Civil War Narratives of Sgt. Benjamin Hirst, Company D, 14th Connecticut Volunteers* (Knoxville: University of Tennessee Press, 1998), 23.

26. *Catalogue of the Museum of Flags, Trophies, and Relics Relating to the Revolution, the War of 1812, the Mexican War, and the Present Rebellion . . . to Be Exhibited at New York, April 4, 1864* (New York: Charles O. Jones, Stationer and Printer, 1864), 45; Miles Clayton Huyette, *The Maryland Campaign and the Battle of Antietam* (Buffalo: n.p., 1915), 56; Joseph W. Collingwood to my dear wife, September 27, 1862, Joseph W. Collingwood Papers, box 3, Huntington; Fiske, *Mr. Dunn Browne's Experiences*, 50–51.

27. Joseph W. Collingwood to my dear wife, September 27, 1862, September 30, 1862, October 16, 1862, and October 21, 1862, Joseph W. Collingwood Papers, Box 3, Huntington Library.

28. "*Lowell* [Massachusetts] *Daily Citizen and News,* September 24, 1862; Loring, *A Trip to Antietam,* 145; "After the Battle," *Burlington* [Vermont] *Daily Times,* September 30, 1862.

29. Oliver Wendell Holmes, "My Hunt after the Captain," *Atlantic Monthly* (December 1862): 738–64. On Holmes Jr., in the Civil War, see also Stephen Budiansky, *Oliver Wendell Holmes: A Life in Law, War, and Ideas* (New York: W. W. Norton, 2019).

30. "*Lowell* [Massachusetts] *Daily Citizen and News,* September 24, 1862; Loring, *A Trip to Antietam,* 145; "After the Battle," *Burlington* [Vermont] *Daily Times,* September 30, 1862; A. J. Perkins to Ward Hill Lamon, September 10, 1864, and Ward Hill Lamon to A. J. Perkins, September 30, 1864, in Ward Hill Lamon Papers, Box 19, Huntington Library.

31. Edmund English memoir, Edmund English Papers, Huntington Library; Charles W. Loring, *A Trip to Antietam* (New York: The Continental Monthly, 1863), 155, copy in John Page Nicholson Collection, Huntington Library.

32. Joseph W. Collingwood to my dear wife, September 24, 1864, Joseph W. Collingwood Papers, box 3, Huntington Library; Nathaniel Emerson Bright to dear brother Sam, November 5, 1862, Nathaniel Emerson Bright Papers, box 21, Huntington Library; McClenthen, *A Sketch of the Campaign,* 43.

33. The time that yawned between military campaigns often proved more significant in effecting change than the battles themselves. See also Zachery A. Fry, *A Republic in the Ranks: Loyalty and Dissent in the Army of the Potomac* (Chapel Hill: University of North Carolina Press, 2020), and John J. Hennessy, "Evangelizing for Union, 1863: The Army of the Potomac, Its Enemies at Home, and a New Solidarity," *Journal of the Civil War Era* 4, no. 4 (December 2014): 533–58.

34. "What They Have to Do Who Stay at Home," United States Sanitary Commission Circular no. 50 (November 1862): 1.

CONFEDERATE INVASIONS OF MARYLAND

THOMAS G. CLEMENS

Maryland, perhaps more than any other Border State in the Civil War, was vital to the interests of both North and South. The strategic value of Maryland surrounding the District of Columbia was most critical, but also the Baltimore & Ohio Railroad and Pennsylvania Railroad were the only two east-west railroads in the northern United States. The railroad was an important asset for moving troops and supplies to the District, as was the Chesapeake & Ohio Canal, located almost entirely within Maryland, with its eastern terminus at Georgetown. Baltimore was the fourth largest city in the country, and one of the busiest ports as well. The value of the Chesapeake Bay as an invasion route was tempting, and might also have led to Delaware joining in any Maryland initiative. While the natural barrier of the Potomac River favored Union defensive abilities, even the brief loss of the Capital would have been disastrous for the Union cause.[1]

Thus Confederate military strategy was often focused on Maryland: threatening the Capital of the United States, using Maryland as a means to draw Union armies out of Virginia, creating panic in the North, and as a route for invading Pennsylvania. It also was the goal of the Confederate politicians that every slave state, including Maryland, *should* be a Confederate state. Whether that was a realistic goal is debatable, but Maryland was a critical factor in Confederate policy and strategy throughout the war.[2]

The delicate balance of luring Maryland into the Confederate fold and exercising extreme caution to avoid alienating Marylanders began soon after the war began. In May of 1861 Col. Thomas Jonathan (later known as Stonewall) Jackson was assigned to command Virginia troops gathered at Harpers Ferry. Although no fighting had yet occurred along the Potomac River, it was recognized as a de facto border between the Union and Confederacy. Jackson, concerned about the security of his post, was immediately struck by the impossibility of holding the town of Harpers Ferry because the dominant terrain feature, Maryland Heights, was in Maryland and if properly garrisoned, commanded the town. He thus informed his superior officer, Gen. Robert E. Lee, "I have finished reconnoitering the Maryland Heights, and have determined to fortify them at once, and hold them, as well as the Virginia Heights and the town, be the cost what it may." Lee, acutely aware of the potential hazard of an "invasion" of Maryland, and the risk of alienating sympathetic Marylanders, strongly advised against such an action, but Jackson ignored Lee's admonishment and placed Confederate pickets on Maryland Heights.[3] Thus the first actual "invasion" of Maryland was a brief occupation of a remote portion of the Potomac River bank in May of 1861.[4] More dramatic incursions would follow.

Shortly after the Battle of First Manassas or First Bull Run on July 21, 1861, Confederate president Jefferson Davis arrived in Fairfax in early October to discuss war plans. He discussed with his generals plans for an offensive north of the Potomac, consulting maps of the crossings points of the Potomac. Although no movements were made that fall, it is clear that an invasion of Maryland was part of Confederate strategy.[5]

Through the spring and early summer of 1862 Union general George B. McClellan's offensive operations against Richmond precluded implementation of Confederate war plans concerning Maryland. Only in August, when McClellan's Army of the Potomac was withdrawn to Washington, was there any opportunity for Lee to renew plans for invading Maryland. Following the stunning success of Lee's Army of Northern Virginia at Manassas, where during August 28–30 his army defeated a combined Union army commanded by Gen. John Pope, Lee returned to the strategy of invading Maryland. On September 3, 1862, Lee wrote to Davis, "The present seems to be the most propitious time since the commencement of the war for the Confederate army to enter Maryland."[6] Note that Lee was not asking permission, but was suggesting that moving into Maryland was an established goal of Confederate leaders. Lee added, "If it is ever desired to provide material aid to Maryland and afford her an opportunity to throwing off the oppression to which she is now subject, this would seem the most favorable."[7]

The following day Lee elaborated on his plans, writing again to Davis, "I wish therefore that if ex-Governor [of Maryland Enoch L.] Lowe can make it convenient, he would come to me at once, . . . I contemplate entering a part of the state with which Gov. Lowe is well acquainted, I think he could be of much service to me in many ways." Illustrating the view of Maryland as a stepping stone to Pennsylvania, Lee added, "Should the results of the expedition justify it, I propose to enter Pennsylvania, unless you should deem it unadvisable upon political or other grounds."[8]

Lee did move into Maryland. His advance troops crossed the Potomac River on September 4, 1862, and by September 7 the bulk of his army was assembled in Frederick. In crossing the river he cut the Chesapeake & Ohio Canal, rendering it inoperable for some time. At Frederick his troops destroyed the Baltimore & Ohio Railroad bridge over the Monocacy River and telegraph lines, further isolating Washington and Baltimore from the west. As he rested his troops for several days, Lee set his sights on Hagerstown and perhaps Pennsylvania.[9]

The Confederate incursion into Maryland caused great panic in Washington, DC, and Baltimore. Fear for the safety of the capital led to "removing money from the Treasury, contents from the arsenal, mobilizing War Department employees and plans for evacuating the president and cabinet."[10] Rev. Franklin Wilson speculated that "Baltimore will become a scene of confusion, anarchy, and perhaps a battle field." One Baltimore newspaper noted, "The present is full of danger and terror."[11]

The reaction in Maryland differed in that the Confederate army was usually met with sullen silence and little cooperation. Greater concern seemed to be expressed about protecting valuables than personal safety, as expressed by Anne Schaeffer, who "gathered small valuable articles" that she hid in pockets under her skirts. She also noted "the colored people are running in all directions."[12] In Frederick one southerner, after several unsuccessful attempts to buy food, wrote on September 6, "This part of Maryland did not welcome us warmly. I have long thought the State was a humbug."[13]

Although in disfavor by the Lincoln administration for his military actions and his political views, McClellan was chosen by President Abraham Lincoln to reorganize the various military elements in the capital and forge an army to confront Lee's invasion force. He quickly built an army from the remnants of forces in the city, adding approximately nineteen thousand soldiers recruited by President Lincoln's July 1 call for three hundred thousand more troops to bring the war to a "speedy and satisfactory conclusion."[14] The Army of the Potomac, numbering between seventy thousand and seventy-five thousand men, marched from Rockville on September 7 to pursue Lee. More troops joined McClellan on the march, bringing his numbers to about eighty-five thousand by September 17.[15]

Lincoln's appointment of McClellan was a bold move, for it faced strong opposition from his cabinet. Lincoln and General-in-Chief Henry Halleck directed McClellan to protect Baltimore and Washington, DC, and drive Lee's army from Maryland. McClellan proceeded with his hastily assembled force, guarding the Potomac River with his left and the National Road to Baltimore with his right. Every night McClellan circulated marching orders for the next day to the three wings. With little solid information about Lee's army or his intentions, McClellan moved forward cautiously, his intelligence about the size of Lee's army varying widely.[16]

Lee's army rested in Frederick while he addressed political and strategic concerns. Lee was well aware that many southern leaders believed Maryland would rise to support the southern army, and the Confederate government believed all slave states should join the Confederacy. To these leaders, Maryland seemed particularly disposed to joining the Confederacy because the electoral victory of John Breckinridge in the 1860 election indicated strong support for secession. The cultural ties to the South were evident, Baltimore was regarded as a southern city, and many of the prominent Baltimore families supported the Confederacy. In addition, the slave-based tobacco industry of eastern and southern Maryland, as well as of northeastern Virginia, shipped their crops from Baltimore. The Pratt Street riots in Baltimore the previous year encouraged these beliefs, and the forcible occupation of the city by Gen. Benjamin Butler, acting without orders, bolstered the idea of Lee entering Maryland as a liberator.[17]

Lee was aware that Confederate armies were invading neutral Kentucky and threatening Union armies in northern Mississippi. His incursion into Maryland was part of a 1,000-mile offensive by five separate Confederate armies: Gen. Braxton Bragg's army captured Richmond Kentucky on August 30, and General Van Dorn was moving to attack Corinth, Mississippi. With the war already five times longer than Lincoln's plan for a 90-day war, northern resources and morale were flagging. Confederate success in Maryland might have a cascading effect across the country to the Mississippi River and beyond. The pressure for success drove Lee to take enormous risks and push his army to the limits of exhaustion.

For a small state, Maryland was quite diverse in culture and politics, and much depended on what part of Maryland the Confederate army entered. Southern Maryland and the Eastern Shore were predominantly composed of descendants of English colonists and tied to a commercial agricultural economy driven by tobacco and slave labor. Baltimore was a hub of commercial shipping, railroads, and international trade. The Piedmont region and western Maryland were populated with many people of German descent, with smaller farms producing grain crops dependent on local markets and less slave ownership. Politically Baltimore and five counties had carried the state for John Breckinridge, the most pro-secession candidate in the 1860 election. Western Maryland embraced John Bell, the Constitutional Union candidate, reflecting a lukewarm support of secession.[18] The success of Breckinridge, who garnered only a plurality of less than 46 percent of the votes, was due to the splintering of the pro-Union vote primarily between Stephen Douglas and Bell, with the Republican candidate, Abraham Lincoln, receiving about 2.5 percent of the votes.[19]

In short, Lee had entered the part of Maryland least supportive of secession. He did so for strategic military reasons, but in an effort to placate Marylanders he issued a "Proclamation to Marylanders," assuring people that he was there to redress grievances against Marylanders by Union occupiers. He issued orders strictly prohibiting confiscation of goods from Maryland citizens and required his quartermasters to issue requisitions for all food and articles taken by the army. The hope that Maryland recruits would flock to Lee's army may have animated southern leaders, but Lee seems to have realized it was unlikely. Writing to President Jefferson Davis the night before the proclamation was read, Lee remarked, "Situated as Maryland is, I do not expect a general rising of the people on our behalf." The proclamation was read in Frederick by Col. Bradley T. Johnson, a Frederick resident commanding a brigade in Lee's army. If Lee had any hopes of his army being welcomed in Frederick, it is likely Johnson's local knowledge quashed that hope.[20] Also hindering Maryland recruitment was the fact that there was no Maryland infantry regiment in Lee's army for local volunteers to join. The First Maryland Infantry (Confederate) was recruited in the spring of 1861, but the regiment was disbanded in the summer of 1862. Another Maryland regiment was organizing, and would fight at Gettysburg in 1863, but that was no help in September of 1862.[21]

More important, politically, was Lee's letter of September 8. Lee encouraged Davis to open negotiations with the Lincoln administration regarding "the recognition of our independence." After listing the reasons why this was the time to do so, Lee added that if rejected, the northern people "at their coming elections" might punish the "party in power in the United States." This letter demonstrates that the Confederates understood the invasion of Maryland in 1862 offered the best opportunity so far to win southern independence. This expectation helps to explain why Lee took such risks during the campaign, and why he drove his army to the point of disintegration.[22]

Strategically, on September 9 Lee addressed a situation that threatened his plans. His presence in Maryland necessitated he move his supply line to the Shenandoah Valley. Union garrisons remaining in the lower (northern) valley, particularly Harpers Ferry, required his attention. After consultation with senior commanders Lee issued Special Order 191, which divided his army into several parts to neutralize the Union threat to his supply line and move west to secure the crossroads at Boonsboro and, eventually, Hagerstown. This order, which would perhaps become the most famous of the war, was copied and circulated that evening. Jackson moved out of Frederick the next morning, going west to approach Harpers Ferry from the northwest, while Gen. John Walker crossed back into Virginia to approach Harpers Ferry from the south and Gen. Lafayette McLaws led two divisions to take Maryland Heights overlooking Harpers Ferry and block the roads to the north and east. The rest of the army would be at Boonsboro, and the order designated there or Hagerstown for the army to reassemble on September 12.[23]

On the evening before Lee wrote Special Order 191, dividing his army, Union cavalry threatened his outposts east of Frederick, indicating the approach of McClellan's Army of the Potomac. Apparently unaware of this probe, Lee's troops departed Frederick on the 10th, the last elements, other than a rearguard of cavalry, leaving on the 11th. After assuming command, McClellan moved his army in three "wings," covering a broad front to protect the roads leading to Baltimore and Washington. Now he was closing in on Frederick as Lee left. Advance elements of the Union army drove Lee's rearguard from Frederick on September 12, and McClellan directed most of his troops to this important crossroads town on September 13. On that day, soldiers in the Twelfth Corps found a copy of Special Order 191 in a field near Frederick. It was quickly recognized for its value and made its way to McClellan by midday or shortly after.[24]

While the order didn't tell McClellan much he did not already know, it certainly solidified some of the intelligence he had received while discrediting other reports. He sought confirmation of it from his cavalry leader, Gen. Alfred Pleasonton, and before receiving it, wrote his orders for the next day, which were to attack Lee's scattered forces in hopes of catching the divided elements before they could combine. That same evening he ordered Gen. William Franklin to move through Crampton's Gap and drive off or defeat the Confederate force threatening Harpers Ferry from the north and rescue the surrounded Union garrison there. He also ordered portions of the Ninth Corps, part of Gen. Ambrose Burnside's wing, to seize Turner's Gap on the National Road, evidently preparing to move against the Confederates at Boonsboro.[25]

These attack orders precipitated the Battle of South Mountain, September 14, 1862. Fighting raged on South Mountain from Turner's Gap in the north to six miles south at Crampton's Gap. Confederate general Daniel H. Hill's troops held Turner's and Fox's Gaps and Lee hurriedly brought troops back from Hagerstown to bolster Hill's troops. By darkness more than 28,000 Union troops had assaulted the three gaps, ultimately defended by 18,000 Confederate soldiers. Casualties totaled over 2,500 Union soldiers and nearly 3,000 Confederate losses. More importantly, by nightfall two of the three gaps were in Union hands, with the Confederate position at Turner's Gap untenable. At 8 P.M. Lee issued orders for his army to return to Virginia and regroup.[26]

The order to leave Maryland was a critical turning point in the campaign. Until this point Lee, optimistic about success, held the initiative. The diversion to address the Harpers Ferry situation had led to a stinging defeat and a confused night retreat on the Boonsboro-Shepherdstown Turnpike to the closest Potomac River crossing at Shepherdstown, just seven miles away. From this point on Lee lost the initiative and was responding to McClellan's actions. Lee's campaign to invade the north and gain Maryland as an ally was now endangered, and the safety of his army was threatened. Yet Lee was not ready to abandon the campaign on which he, and the Confederacy, had so much at stake. Near dawn on September 15, as Lee made his way west to the Potomac River, he paused on a hilltop to peruse the surrounding terrain. While there he received word from Gen. "Stonewall" Jackson that the Harpers Ferry garrison would surrender that morning. Lee chose to gamble and ordered the troops with him to stop on the high bluffs on the west bank of Antietam Creek. He then ordered the troops under Jackson to join him there as soon as possible.[27]

Lee's position, near the town of Sharpsburg, was a strong one, situated on high ground facing Antietam Creek, and with only three bridges providing avenues of approach, the position could held by inferior numbers against a strong attacking force. He also had the use of interior lines, as the Hagerstown Turnpike intersected the Boonsboro Pike in Sharpsburg and allowed Lee to move troops from one end of his line to another with ease. The Hagerstown Pike also allowed Lee a road to Hagerstown, where he previously intended to move, and according to Lee's letters to Davis, potentially invade Pennsylvania. Although delayed by the Harpers Ferry operation, if Jackson's forces marched quickly to join him, Lee could still move north to Hagerstown, leaving McClellan's army to follow him.[28]

At dawn on the 15th McClellan ordered his troops forward in pursuit of Lee. By early afternoon it was apparent that Lee had halted in an advantageous position. With only a small number of troops available, and the daunting position assumed by Lee, McClellan could only order a cannonade across the creek. As more troops arrived McClellan distributed them to face the three bridges, and discovered two usable fords that provided access to the west bank of the creek. Whether this halt by Lee was an invitation to fight or simply a rearguard defense was not clear to McClellan that afternoon.[29]

Morning fog on September 16 prevented any observation until around 9 A.M. Once it was clear that Lee was still there, and had been reinforced by some of Jackson's troops, McClellan began planning an assault. Most intelligence reports still indicated to McClellan that he was outnumbered, and he proceeded cautiously to maneuver troops to negate the advantage of high ground and avoid a frontal assault across the narrow defile of the Turnpike Bridge. Although his exact plans were never clear, his general intent was to attack the left flank of Lee's line, as it was the most vulnerable. Success there would enable other attacks on the opposite flank or even against the center of Lee's line. Although it appears to have been unintentional, the troops sent on the afternoon and evening of the 16th to attack Lee's left flank achieved a position astride the Hagerstown Turnpike, negating Lee's ability to move north to elude McClellan.[30]

A sharp but small action occurred on the evening of September 16, and the opposing forces spent an uneasy night within earshot of each other. Dawn brought heavy fighting as Union forces surged toward the high ground opposite the small, whitewashed Dunker Church, the spiritual home of the local German Baptist Brethren adherents. A series of assaults and counter-assaults in this area through the morning hours ended in early afternoon with inconclusive results. Fighting also occurred near the center of Lee's line, and by mid-morning, as Lee shifted troops from his right flank to bolster his left, Union attacks began against Lee's right, focused on wresting Confederate control of the bridge there. Fighting continued throughout the day, with Lee artfully staving off several determined Union offensives and making famous such places as the Cornfield, Bloody Lane, and the iconic Burnside Bridge. The last-minute arrival of Lee's remaining troops, Gen. A. P. Hill's division, blunted the Union's final attack, and impending darkness ended the grisly conflict. By sundown the Federals had engaged roughly 55,000 soldiers and lost more than 12,400 men, killed, wounded, or missing. The embattled Confederates engaged roughly 38,000 men and suffered more than 10,300 casualties.[31]

This battle, nearly twelve hours of fighting, was, and remains today, the bloodiest single day in American history. The total casualties exceeded 23,000 men, greater than the total American in the Revolutionary War and the War of 1812 combined. Destructive as the fighting was for the soldiers, it was also deadly for the civilians whose farms were ruined and who were obliged to take care of the wounded, many of whom died from diseases resulting from the battle. Many houses were damaged or destroyed; those that survived were frequently sold or auctioned as the owners were financially devastated from battle damage or looting by both armies.[32]

During the night of September 17, as soldiers and medical assistants combed the field removing the wounded, both commanders pondered their next move. Lee, perhaps influenced by the disorderly and hasty retreat from South Mountain three days earlier, decided to remain on the field, contracting his lines and bringing up ammunition and stragglers to solidify his position. McClellan planned to renew his attacks, counting on reinforcements and ammunition resupply. Disappointed on both points, and ill with a fever during the night, he postponed the attacks until the 19th. No real fighting occurred on the 18th, but that night Lee quietly withdrew his army to the ford below Shepherdstown and his army crossed back into Virginia.[33]

Yet Lee was not ending his campaign for southern independence. He ordered his cavalry chief, Gen. J. E. B. Stuart, to secure the ford upstream at Williamsport, as Lee planned to reenter Maryland and strike at Hagerstown. Alerted to this movement of Confederate cavalry on the 19th, McClellan sent half his cavalry and a substantial force of infantry to Williamsport on the 20th. Stuart quickly withdrew.[34]

Pushing forward some cavalry and the Fifth Corps of his army on the 19th, McClellan met stern opposition at the Shepherdstown Ford from Lee's rearguard. Skirmishing on the 19th, and a Union reconnaissance in force on the 20th, were initially successful, but a determined counterattack by A. P. Hill's division forced a hasty withdrawal to the north bank of the Potomac. Both commanders abandoned their campaigns, and the second, and most important, Confederate invasion of Maryland was over. Lee's grand plans to sustain his army in the North, demoralize the northern public, and defeat a Union army on northern soil had ended in failure. Subsequent failures at Perryville, Kentucky, and Corinth, Mississippi, marked the ebbing of the high tide of the Confederacy.[35]

The fruits of victory rapidly spoiled for McClellan. Although directed to drive the Confederate army from Maryland, post-campaign critics soon disparaged his failure to destroy Lee's army. While Lee rested and replenished his depleted army in Virginia, Lincoln and some of his cabinet members insisted on further offensive operations against Lee by the damaged Army of the Potomac. Supply issues, and bitter arguments over them, soon worsened the situation. Rather than hailed as victor, McClellan was soon painted as a procrastinator.[36]

The most significant outcome of the Maryland Campaign of 1862 was unexpected. In July Lincoln had resolved to address the issue of slavery. The US Constitution limited his ability to free slaves, but Congress had passed two Confiscation Acts, allowing seizure of "property" being used by those in rebellion. Citing this authority, Lincoln wrote a proclamation freeing slaves only in territories and states in active rebellion. He had no authority to free slaves in Union states, such as Maryland, and cabinet members Edwin Stanton, Edward Bates, and Salmon P. Chase discouraged him from issuing anything until a Union victory. On September 22 Lincoln, following McClellan's victory, issued the preliminary announcement of the Emancipation Proclamation, allowing states that abandoned the Confederacy to rejoin the Union and maintain their slaves. To critics this was a largely symbolic act, but it was quite real to the millions of enslaved Americans who now saw Union soldiers as liberators. Where Union armies marched, freedom followed, as former slaves flocked to the shelter and protection of federal armies. It dismayed potential Confederate allies in Europe, where slavery had ended years ago, and changed the goal of the war from solely one to restore the Union to one to also end slavery in the

Confederate states. While the institution would not end completely until the passage of the Thirteenth Amendment in 1865, this was a major step that was made possible by the Union victory in Maryland.[37]

The failure of this invasion of Maryland, coupled with Confederate defeats in Kentucky and Mississippi, and the preliminary announcement of the Emancipation Proclamation, mark the Maryland Campaign of 1862 as the turning point of the Civil War.[38]

Following the Maryland Campaign, both armies returned to Virginia. A series of maneuvers led to a failed federal offensive in December at Fredericksburg, and in the spring of 1863 another Union plan to strike at Richmond and destroy Lee's army ended in the disastrous Union defeat at Chancellorsville. In the aftermath of this success, Lee again proposed to invade the North. At a strategy meeting in Richmond with President Davis and other leaders, they discussed sending Lee's army, or part of it, to relieve the isolated Mississippi town of Vicksburg, the last Confederate stronghold on the Mississippi River, or to reinforce Gen. Braxton Bragg's western army. Lee argued against it, stating that an invasion into the North would draw Union resources from the western theater of the war. He also argued that the southern coast would not be safe during the "sickly season," referring to yellow fever and its debilitating effects on northern troops. Lee again proposed a northern invasion to demoralize northerners and encourage a Union peace movement. His army had been revitalized and bolstered to approximately seventy thousand men. In mid-June 1863, Lee again led his army north to invade Maryland, and perhaps Pennsylvania. This movement, known as the Gettysburg Campaign, became the most famous in the war and resulted in its biggest battle.[39]

For this foray Lee chose to use the lower Shenandoah Valley to enter Maryland, rather than east of the Blue Ridge, as he had the previous year. Sending Gen. Richard Ewell's Second Corps of his army in advance, Lee followed with Gen. James Longstreet's First Corps, leaving A. P. Hill's Third Corps to convince Union commander Gen. Joseph Hooker that Lee was still in the vicinity of Fredericksburg. Ewell handily disposed of Union garrisons in the valley, chasing the forces of Gen. Robert Milroy and Gen. Dan Tyler toward the Potomac River and Harpers Ferry. The rest of the Confederate army soon followed.

After a stinging defeat at Chancellorsville, Union general Joseph Hooker's reputation and relationship with Lincoln declined precipitously. Hooker was briefly unaware of Lee's movement but soon saw this departure from Fredericksburg as an opportunity. He asked Lincoln and Gen. Henry Halleck for permission to attack Lee's rearguard and/or move toward Richmond. Lincoln and Halleck reminded Hooker of their orders to keep his army between Lee and both the capital and Harpers Ferry. Hooker marched his army north, keeping it between Lee and the capital in Washington, DC.[40]

Hooker's movements were hesitant, and he was reluctant to acknowledge Ewell's presence at Winchester and Martinsburg, while Lincoln and Halleck grew frustrated at Hooker's lethargy and confusion. Much of the contention stemmed from Halleck's tendency to give suggestions rather than orders and his concern for Harpers Ferry. Lee's army had reached the Potomac, and his advance forces were crossing into Maryland as Hooker strove to protect Washington and Harpers Ferry. After the humiliating defeat in 1862, much effort had been made to strengthen the defense of Harpers Ferry. Large cannon had been placed on Maryland Heights, and a stone fort was constructed there.

All of this came to head in late June as Hooker insisted the garrison at Harpers Ferry, approximately ten thousand men, be withdrawn and added to his army. This withdrawal would also require the evacuation or destruction of the public property there. Hooker included an ultimatum that if his request was denied, he would resign. Lincoln had lost confidence in Hooker, and so Halleck seized the opportunity and accepted Hooker's resignation. Gen. George G. Meade was ordered to take command of the Army of the Potomac.[41] Ironically, by order of General Meade, the garrison was subsequently withdrawn on June 29, the cannon dismounted and pushed over the side of the mountain, and the fort abandoned.[42]

The approach of Lee's army toward Maryland sparked a variety of actions from citizens north of the Potomac River. Most sources show that the Confederate army met with some curiosity and even support as they crossed the Potomac River. One rebel wrote of being greeted with large tables of food in Williamsport.[43] Governor Andrew Curtin of Pennsylvania again called to service thousands of men in "emergency" regiments to protect his state. Farmers and shopkeepers in the Washington and Frederick counties drove their animals into hiding and packed up goods from their stores and shipped them north. Remembering the devastation of 1862, many fled their homes, taking valuables with them.[44] Lee again issued orders forbidding offenses against civilians and their property, and specifying that only authorized officers could requisition property, with proper payment.[45]

This prohibition about property evidently did not include human property. Many slaves had escaped from owners and sought safety in both Union garrisons and in nearby free states. After the surrender of the Union garrison at Harpers Ferry in September 1862, a large number of "contrabands" were rounded up and sent southward into servitude.[46] Several hundred African Americans, some escaped slaves, others free Blacks, were rounded up and taken south into slavery. Capt. Andrew B. Wardlaw, a staff officer in Gen. A. P. Hill's Division, recorded in his diary on September 15 that "not less than 1,200 negroes were captured and restored to their owners." Most of these confiscations and kidnappings took place in Pennsylvania, as Lee was still hesitant to offend Marylanders, and certainly contributed to the bitterness of Pennsylvanians about the invasion.[47]

Preceded by cavalry, the first part of Lee's army to enter Maryland was Gen. Robert Rodes's Division of the Second Corps. Lee's forces crossed the Potomac at fords located at Williamsport and Shepherdstown and quickly moved north. Lee's intention was to follow the Cumberland Valley northeast toward the bridges over the Susquehanna River at Wrightsville and Harrisburg. With no real opposition, the Confederates steadily marched through southern Pennsylvania, the advance reaching the outskirts of Harrisburg and another column arriving to find the bridge at Wrightsville in flames.

While the advance skirmished with local militia, the Army of the Potomac approached from the south to disrupt Lee's plans. Hooker was replaced by Gen. George G. Meade, who quickly pushed into Maryland, securing Frederick from Confederate occupation and moving north to secure a supply depot at Westminster. Meade's right wing, moving along the eastern side of Catoctin Mountain through Mechanicstown (Thurmont) and Emmitsburg, soon encountered parts of Lee's forces near Gettysburg, where several roads intersected.

As fighting erupted, both commanders rushed troops to the town and struggled to secure the strategic high ground surrounding it. While the Confederates initially drove the Union forces through town, darkness prevented the loss of the most defensible terrain in the area. Meade quickly brought up the bulk of his army, while Lee's forces planned to attack the Union position.

Bloody fighting on July 2 and July 3 left both armies exhausted and damaged.[48] Lee, again recognizing his army needed to retreat, held the field on July 4, and started several long trains of wagons back into Maryland before ordering his battered army to march. Not only was Lee sending a train of ambulances and wagons containing wounded men, but also his normal trains of ammunition, food, and quartermaster wagons preceded the army's march. In addition to these trains, the Confederates had gathered a great deal of confiscated material, referred to as the "booty train," which would help sustain an army suffering limited resources.

Meade sent his cavalry to pursue and harass the Confederate retreat. The train of wounded took the westernmost route, which took them back into Maryland on the road into Hagerstown from Greencastle, Pennsylvania. Although not bothered by Union cavalry, some residents of Greencastle interfered with the wagons. The train continued and entered Hagerstown on July 5, making its way to Williamsport. Passage into Virginia was impossible as the pontoon bridge built by Lee's engineers had been destroyed, and recent rains had made the ford impassable. The wagon train of wounded parked in the lower part of town near the river, while the escorts and guards formed a semi-circular defense on the high ground around it.

This was the beginning of a series of small battles in Maryland that lasted from July 5 until July 14, when the Confederate army finally crossed the river into Virginia. Meade was soon in pursuit, traveling south along the eastern edge of Catoctin to protect Frederick and eastward from the Confederates. His cavalry pursued various wagon trains, and the retreating rebels clashed with Lee's forces in Hagerstown on July 6 and attacked the beleaguered forces at Williamsport that Lee was marching to join. Lee arrived and distributed his army downstream to cover Downsville and Falling Waters, where his engineers set to building a pontoon bridge. A long, low ridge paralleled the road from Hagerstown to Downsville, which was soon occupied by Confederate artillery and infantry, presenting an imposing front for Meade's men as they arrived on July 8–11. Meade then deployed his troops along the Hagerstown-Sharpsburg Pike centered at Jones' Crossroads, about three miles from the Downsville line. July 7 saw probing actions at St. James, midway between the two lines, and a running cavalry fight near Funkstown. A larger cavalry fight occurred at Boonsboro on July 8, as Stuart's cavalry bought time for Lee to reach and fortify the Williamsport-Downsville line. Emboldened by the arrival of Union infantry, an attack was launched by Gen. John Buford's Union cavalry division, supported by a Vermont infantry brigade, at Funkstown on July 10, resulting in the Confederates withdrawing westward and leaving the town in Union hands.[49]

By July 12, with Meade's entire army having taken position, a short skirmish cleared Hagerstown of remaining Confederates. The stage was set for a large-scale Union attack on the thinly held Confederate line. Lee expected an attack, and many in Meade's army did, too. No attack occurred that day, but with Hagerstown in Union hands, Lee was surrounded. He knew the pontoon bridge would soon be complete, and the river thus fordable, at Williamsport. A small cable ferry transporting wounded men to the Virginia shore was bringing supplies and ammunition on return trips to bolster Lee's defensive line.[50]

On the evening of July 12, Meade held a council of war with his generals to formulate a course of action. He resisted Halleck's urging to attack immediately, knowing Halleck had not seen the formidable defenses Lee had constructed. Meade's generals were divided in their counsel, with those opposed citing Lee's strong position and interior lines. The ultimate decision not to attack was bitterly criticized at the time by Halleck and Lincoln, and since by numerous historians. Yet, Meade, barely two weeks in command of the army and with a decisive win at Gettysburg, argued successfully that a loss in Maryland would negate the value of the win in Pennsylvania.[51]

While both armies held their positions on the 13th, the bridge at Falling Waters, constructed with timbers from several buildings in Williamsport, was completed. That night Lee retreated across the Potomac. When Meade realized the situation the next day, he sent a cavalry force forward; during a small but significant rearguard clash near Falling Waters, Gen. J. J. Pettigrew, who had commanded one of the three Confederate divisions during Pickett's Charge on July 3, was killed.

Few histories mention that both armies spent more time during the "Gettysburg Campaign" in Maryland than they did in Pennsylvania. Comparing this situation to 1862, when Lee's army reached the area around Williamsport on July 5–7, he was once again trapped with a river at his back. This time the river was impassable, and Meade's army arrived shortly afterward, trapping Lee against the swollen river. As in 1862, Lee was in a predicament that could end in disaster for his army and perhaps the Confederacy, but he again escaped, and saved his army after a failed campaign north of the Potomac River. Once again Lee's foray across the Potomac into Maryland ended in disaster, and the irreplaceable casualties lost weakened not only his army, but also the Confederacy, and hastened the end of the war.

The final invasion of Maryland by a Confederate army occurred not from the previous optimism, but rather desperation. By June 1864 a coordinated Union offensive operation had forced Lee's Army of Northern Virginia to defend the capital at Richmond, while another Union force commanded by Gen. David Hunter had driven deep into the Shenandoah Valley to threaten vital supply and transportation lines. Hunter's men had burned Governor John Letcher's home and the Virginia Military Institute in Lexington. Moving toward Lynchburg, this army under Gen. David Hunter posed a danger that could not be ignored. Lee, concerned for the safety of Richmond, at first detached a force under Gen. John Breckinridge (former vice president of the United States) to reinforce local troops defending Lynchburg.

Lee recognized that this force was inadequate, but again he gambled. Worried that detaching more troops would weaken his defenses, he initially resisted the suggestion by President Davis's military advisor, Gen. Braxton Bragg, that Breckinridge be reinforced. By June 12 Lee changed his mind and concocted a plan to cross the Potomac River into Maryland once more. This time he made no mention of influencing Marylanders to join the Confederacy; instead his intention was to invade Maryland and attack, or at least threaten, the US capital.[52]

Most of the troops defending Washington had been sent as replacements to the front near Richmond, and thus the capital was deemed vulnerable. At the least, a strike on Washington might draw Union forces back to defend it, relieving the pressure on the Richmond front. Lee thought the gamble viable and ordered Gen. Jubal Early to take the Second Corps of the Army of Northern Virginia westward to Lynchburg and attempt to drive off General Hunter's Union force, proceed down the Shenandoah Valley, and enter Maryland. He also planned for a Confederate Marylander, Gen. Bradley T. Johnson, to lead a cavalry raid to free Confederate prisoners at Point Lookout in St. Mary's County. There was also a plan for a Confederate naval force to cooperate in the attack on Point Lookout, but it never materialized.[53]

As hoped, Hunter retreated into West Virginia, away from what he believed a superior force, leaving the valley open to Early, who now commanded a small army of his own corps and Breckinridge's command, totaling roughly eighteen thousand men, a mere shadow of earlier invasion forces. With little opposition, Early marched north through the valley, encountering only a small force under Gen. Franz Sigel at Martinsburg and a small number of dismounted cavalry and other troops at Harpers Ferry. After the debacles in 1862 and 1863, the defenses of Harpers Ferry had been greatly increased, with more heavy guns placed on Maryland Heights and a strong line that connected the heights to nearby Fort Duncan on the Potomac River. Despite Sigel's repeated warnings, the high command of the Union armies discounted any real threat to Maryland.[54]

As Early expected, Sigel's force retreated, eventually making its way to Harpers Ferry to join the garrison on Maryland Heights. When the Confederates moved into Harpers Ferry, the Union garrison abandoned the town and moved to the nearly impregnable fortifications on Maryland Heights, where Union artillery forced Early to go upstream to cross the river, costing Early valuable time.

Early's cavalry led the way and crossed the Potomac at Shepherdstown, and by July 6 reached Hagerstown, county seat of Washington County, one of the largest towns in the state. Confederate general John McCausland's brigade dispersed a small Union cavalry force and took possession of the town. Enough advance warning had been issued that most of the stores were closed, livestock evacuated, and government animals taken northward. Unlike in previous invasions, demands were made upon the citizens of Hagerstown to furnish goods, supplies, and cash to the invaders. McCausland summoned the town treasurer (the mayor and some of the council having fled) and presented a written demand for $20,000 in Union currency and large amounts of clothing, threatening that he had orders to burn the town were the ransom not paid. Several banks financed the ransom, and though the clothing demand was not met, McCausland was persuaded not to burn the town. The ransom demand set the tone for this invasion of Maryland; the state was no longer treated as a potential ally. Despite this ransom demand, which was also levied against Middletown and Frederick, General Early issued strict orders preventing looting and pillage of private citizens.[55]

Early's infantry crossed the Potomac at Shepherdstown Ford on July 5 and 6 but never went near Hagerstown. Instead Early, fixated on Harpers Ferry, led his men along the river southward to test the Union defensive position. Through the afternoon of the 6th and all day on the 7th, Early tested the defenses at Maryland Heights, eventually declining to attack, and he moved on toward Frederick, his troops passing through Crampton's, Fox's, and Turner's Gaps. Early stated that while he could have taken the Heights (an optimistic claim), the cost to his army would have been too great.[56]

Confederate cavalry screened Early's advance to Frederick, and Early demanded Middletown pay a ransom of $5,000. He settled for an immediate payment of $1,500 and promise of the balance, but his forces moved on before that portion was paid. This pattern of ransoming towns was not an innovation of this particular campaign, and not necessarily in revenge for Union general David Hunter's destruction of the Virginia Military Institute in June. Over a year earlier Early had demanded a substantial ransom from York, Pennsylvania, during the Gettysburg Campaign.[57]

Early had marched from deep in the Shenandoah Valley to the Potomac River and into Maryland, virtually unopposed. For most of this time Union authorities believed he had returned to Richmond, and only belatedly did they realize he was within a few days' march of the undefended capital. A response to thwart this invasion was quickly organized, although the boundaries of several military districts and commanders led to complications. Baltimore & Ohio Railroad president John W. Garrett helped persuade Gen. Lew Wallace, commander of the Eighth Corps and the Middle Department, of the danger posed by Early's advance. Wallace had few troops at his disposal, and technically his command ended at the Monocacy River east of Frederick. Beyond the river, Gen. Max Weber at Harpers Ferry was in command, but with Early's army between them, there was no communication or coordination. Many of Wallace's troops, like the other troops in the area, were "one hundred day" men, recruited to serve as rear echelon troops for that period. He also had several regiments of the Potomac Home Brigade, Marylanders recruited specifically to garrison Maryland and combat partisans and raiders. Poorly armed and with little experience, they would be little match for Early's grizzled veterans.[58]

Finally responding to the increasingly fraught situation, late on July 5 Gen. U. S. Grant ordered the Third Division, Sixth Corps, commanded by Gen. James B. Ricketts, to leave the lines at Richmond, board transports on the James River, and steam to Washington. By July 9 Grant had agreed to send the other two divisions of the Sixth Corps to augment the defenses of the capital, and if possible destroy Early's force. He diverted the Nineteenth Corps, in route from New Orleans to reinforce the siege at Richmond, to Washington.

Lee's gamble was paying off, as the transfer of Union forces relieved the pressure on Richmond. Yet there was no guarantee that these Union troops would arrive in time to save Washington from an invasion.[59]

Wallace moved his untried troops, about 3,200 in number, to the western boundary of his command, gathering around Monocacy Junction, where the railroad spur line to Frederick branched off the B&O Railroad and continued to Harpers Ferry and further west. The railroad crossed the Monocacy River next to the Urbana Pike, which led to Washington. Just a couple miles north the National Road crossed the Monocacy at the Jug Bridge, and Wallace placed troops there. Wallace's men set about improving the defenses of the junction, which included two blockhouses. Wallace ordered troops across the river to scout Early's advance, and he evacuated supplies and Union soldiers from the hospitals in Frederick. Many civilians moved or hid valuables and supplies.[60]

After minor skirmishing with Union cavalry and artillery on July 7, and a more substantial contest west of Frederick on the 8th, Wallace ordered his forces to fall back behind the Monocacy that night. He was encouraged by the arrival of the vanguard of Ricketts's division, along with Ricketts himself. Together they deployed their troops to defend the roads to Baltimore and Washington, confident they could at least delay the Rebel force.

Early entered Frederick on the 9th and demanded a ransom of $200,000 from the city, a staggering sum for a city of eight thousand people.[61] After much haggling, the city council and mayor signed documents for "loans" from five banks in the city, demanding in return that all government property in town be spared. The deal was struck, and although the Confederates subsequently discovered much valuable government property in the town, they honored the bargain. After the war the banks demanded repayment, which the city paid by installments, and the loan was finally paid off in 1951, with principle and interest totaling about $600,000 in 1951 dollars.[62]

Later in July 1864 General McCausland's Confederates marched through Washington County, Maryland, to demand a ransom of Chambersburg, Pennsylvania. The demand was refused and the town was burned, demonstrating the threat, at least in this instance, was genuine.[63]

As these ransom negotiations in Frederick continued, Early and the army moved southeast of the city to take charge of the attack on the federal troops around Monocacy Junction. In a battle lasting most of the day, the Union troops put up a stubborn defense. After several failed efforts, the Confederates in late afternoon succeeded in crushing the left flank of the Union line below the Urbana Pike, causing a rapid retreat of the Federals toward the Baltimore Pike to the north. The Confederates also drove off the defenders of the Jug Bridge on the National Road, causing even more Union soldiers to retreat precipitously toward Baltimore. Casualties for the Confederates were heavy given the numbers engaged, overall estimated about 900 of roughly 14,000 men, with approximately 700 of those from Gen. John Gordon's division. The Union losses totaled 1,294 out of 7,500 men, mostly in Ricketts's division, with more than 500 captured. More important, Wallace had succeeded in his stated mission: delaying Early to protect the capital. Wallace rallied the survivors around the railroad depot in Monrovia, east of Frederick, and reported the situation to Halleck in Washington. Instead of thanks for the delaying action he had achieved, Halleck informed Wallace that he was being replaced as commander of the Eighth Corps.[64] After the war, Wallace was recognized for his stalwart actions at Monocacy by General Grant who, in his memoirs, wrote "General Wallace contributed on this occasion, by the defeat of troops under him, a greater benefit to the cause than often falls to the lot of a commander of an equal force to render by means of a victory."[65]

The Battle of Monocacy is often hailed as the delaying action that saved Washington, and perhaps rightly so, for it cost Early at least a full day. Yet Early spent a full day testing the defense of Maryland Heights before he moved on to Frederick. Had he moved immediately, Ricketts would not have arrived, and Early might well have brushed aside Wallace's rookies and attacked Washington before the rest of the Sixth Corps arrived. Washington was defended by only a small force of soldiers, many of them partially disabled, and untried recruits. Had not Gen. Max Weber and his Union troops successfully defended Harpers Ferry and delayed Early's army for more than a day, Washington might have been captured, and thus they deserve equal credit with Wallace in delaying Early's army.

The exhausted Confederates wasted little time celebrating their success. General Early had his army on the Urbana Pike/Georgetown Road the next morning, heading for Washington. Meeting only light resistance, the rebels reached the area of Gaithersburg and Rockville that night. The mid-July heat was oppressive, registering 92 degrees, and cooling very little at night. The dirt roads produced large clouds of dust and slowed the Confederate advance.[66]

The advance continued the next day, July 11, reaching the circle of forts located in the outskirts of Washington City. These forts, and the city itself, were almost devoid of troops. Many government workers were quickly armed and sent to defend the impressive forts on the northwest portion of the defenses. Occupying the northwest ring of forts of DeRussy, Stevens, Slocum, and Totten, and entrenchments was a motley collection of National Guard troops from Ohio, government workers, some Veteran Reserve troops (partially disabled veterans capable of light service), and some artillerymen, a few thousand in total. Through the evening of the 11th, Early's stragglers gathered north of Fort Stevens and camped, despite a harmless bombardment from the forts. Union pickets occupied the farm of Lincoln confidant Francis B. Blair.[67]

Not so fortunate was Silver Spring, the home of Francis Blair's son Montgomery Blair, postmaster general in Lincoln's cabinet, which was nearby. It was occupied by General Breckinridge, who knew Blair and protected his house, but it was later burned, circumstances unknown.[68] Also on the 12th, President Abraham Lincoln, along with his wife and Secretary of War Edwin Stanton, visited Fort Stevens. Lincoln was standing on the parapet observing the Confederate skirmishers when a nearby officer was wounded. Maj. Thomas Hyde, Seventh Maine Infantry, probably summed it up best: "Then a lot of people persuaded Mr. Lincoln to get down out of range, which he very reluctantly did."[69]

On the night of the 11th Early held a council with his subordinates to decide whether to attack the thinly held forts in their front, particularly Fort Stevens. An attack was agreed upon, but a dispatch from Gen. Bradley T. Johnson, now commanding a cavalry brigade, warned of Union reinforcements. Early scanned the Union works in the morning, feeling that he must attack or withdraw, but could not remain where he was. As he surveyed the forts early that morning, he saw them lined with troops, indicating that the other two divisions of the Sixth Corps had arrived. He recognized the forts were too strongly held to attack successfully and decided to retire across the Potomac. He kept up a skirmish through the day and ordered a retreat after dark. Early quickly moved his army west, and crossing at White's Ford on July 14, ending his threat to capture Washington. He put the best face on his actions, claiming he had frightened Lincoln and the citizens of Washington, reaped more than $220,000 in ransom; defeated Wallace; captured supplies, horses and prisoners; and retired successfully from Maryland.[70]

While Early focused on Washington, two other movements in Maryland took place. Confederate commanders discussed a mysterious plan for Gen. Bradley T. Johnson's cavalry brigade. Lee ordered Johnson to sweep across northern Maryland to disrupt railroads and communication, and then turn southward to cooperate with a Confederate naval force to capture the Union prison camp at Point Lookout, freeing several thousand Confederate prisoners there.[71] A naval force under Cdr. John Taylor Wood was organized to support Johnson's raid with an attack from the Chesapeake Bay, but before they set out a telegram from Davis alerted Wood the operation had been exposed, and Wood cancelled his expedition.[72] Johnson, who would later deem the mission "impossible," nevertheless attempted it. On July 9 he set out to cut the rail lines from Harrisburg and Philadelphia that connected to Baltimore so as to block Union reinforcements from getting to Washington.[73]

Johnson moved from Frederick across central Maryland to New Windsor, commandeering food and supplies in the town and burning the railroad station. At New Windsor he sent Col. Harry Gilmor, another Maryland cavalryman, to lead his advance. Gilmor commanded the First and Second Maryland Cavalry and led the combined unit to capture Westminster, driving out a small Union force. Johnson soon arrived and made demands on the town, but after destroying a portion of the railroad there, the cavalry moved on. After a brief rest, Gilmor arrived in Cockeysville early on July 10 and burned bridges on the Northern Central Railroad and the turnpike leading to York, Pennsylvania. These actions caused panic in Baltimore; streets were barricaded and volunteers were raised to protect the city. Word of the Confederate plan to liberate Point Lookout leaked, or was inferred, for precautions were taken to protect the prison camp there.[74]

Johnson soon arrived and split his command, sending Gilmor with 135 men to destroy the Philadelphia, Wilmington, and Baltimore Railroad bridge over the Gunpowder River while he and the bulk of the brigade rode to Point Lookout. Gilmor destroyed the bridge and captured a train bound for Philadelphia, along with Union general William B. Franklin. As his force returned east, exhaustion overcame most of his command, allowing Franklin to escape. Gilmor and his men struck out across Baltimore County, pausing in Pikesville, and by the 13th joined Johnson and the cavalry brigade near Poolesville.[75]

Johnson moved around Baltimore and sent a detail to burn the home of Governor Augustus W. Bradford, retaliating for the burning of Governor John

Letcher's home in Lexington, Virginia. Passing around the western suburbs of Baltimore, Johnson's brigade reached Beltsville on July 12, where he damaged the railroads and continued to Upper Marlboro, hoping to reach Point Lookout the next day. Here a courier from Early reached Johnson, with orders to rejoin the army, so Johnson rode north of Washington to meet Early at Silver Spring at midnight on the 12th.[76]

Of all the invasions of Maryland during the Civil War, Early's campaign is the most striking. Although having far fewer men than Lee in 1862 or 1863, he came closest to capturing Washington, DC, which, had he done so, would have had a significant impact on the outcome of the war. Had he captured the city, forcing Lincoln to flee or risk capture, the war might have continued into 1866 or beyond. Hostilities could have ended in the sort of negotiated separation Lee sought in 1862. Indisputably Maryland played an important role in the eastern theater of the Civil War. A valuable ally to either side, a source of provender and volunteers, a strategic location for disrupting rail and water transportation, a stepping stone to Pennsylvania and, for the Union, a ready source of Black men in 1863 for its army, Maryland was of great importance to both the Union and Confederacy. Because Maryland surrounded the nation's capital, it was vital that the state remained under Union control, despite its somewhat divided citizenry.

The repeated Confederate incursions into the state attest to Maryland's value to Confederate aspirations to become an independent nation. Yet all of these efforts ended, not just in failure, but in disasters as the invasions depleted southern manpower and resources for little gain, if any. The casualties incurred in these invasions could not be replaced, and thus accelerated the debilitation of Confederate armies and hastened the ultimate collapse of the Confederacy. Whatever the goals each invasion strove to attain, all ended in failure. This lack of success also dashed the hopes of those Marylanders who held out hope for Maryland's secession. The ragged and dilapidated appearance of Lee's army in 1862 dampened any enthusiasm on the part of Maryland citizens. Subsequent invasions displayed better uniforms but fainter hope for success. Those astute enough to recognize the temporary nature of the Confederate presence in Maryland recognized that any display of support would incur retaliation by Union authorities after the inevitable departure of southern forces. As Lee presciently predicted in September 1862, "Situated as Maryland is, I do not anticipate any general rising of the people in our behalf."[77]

NOTES

1. US Census Bureau 1860. At this time Brooklyn was a separate city from New York City; otherwise Baltimore would have been the third largest.

2. Joseph L. Harsh, *Confederate Tide Rising, Robert E. Lee and the Making of Southern Strategy, 1861–1862* (Kent, OH: Kent State University Press, 1998), 9–10.

3. US War Department, *War of the Rebellion, Official Records of the Union and Confederate Armies,* 128 vols. Government Printing Office: Washington, DC (all citations are from ser. 1), 2:809, 821.

4. Dennis E. Frye, *Harpers Ferry under Fire, a Border Town in the American Civil War* (Harpers Ferry, WV: Harpers Ferry Historical Association, 2012), 14–17.

5. The best summary of these plans is found in Harsh, *Confederate Tide Rising,* 27–31.

6. Clifford Dowdey and Louis H. Manarin, eds., *Lee's Wartime Papers* (New York: Virginia Civil War Commission, 1961), 292.

7. Dowdey and Manarin, *Lee's Wartime Papers,* 292–93.

8. Dowdey and Manarin, *Lee's Wartime Papers,* 294–95.

9. Joseph Harsh, *Taken at the Flood, Robert E. Lee and the Making of Southern Strategy, 1861–1862* (Kent, OH: Kent State University Press, 1999), 104–5, 121.

10. Thomas G. Clemens, *The Maryland Campaign of September 1862,* edited by Ezra Carman (El Dorado, CA: Savas Beatie, 2010), 1:130–31.

11. Rev. Franklin Wilson, Wilson papers, MSS 833, Maryland Center for History and Culture Library; *Baltimore American & Commercial Advertiser,* September 5, 1862.

12. "Schaeffer Diary, September 6," as cited in Charles W. Mitchell, ed., *Maryland Voices of the Civil War* (Baltimore: Johns Hopkins University Press, 2007), 309.

13. Ham Chamberlayne, *Ham Chamberlayne—A Virginian: Letters and Papers of an Artillery Officer in the War for Southern Independence 1861–1865* (Richmond: Dietz Printing, 1932), 132.

14. Roy P. Basler, ed., *The Collected Works of Abraham Lincoln* (New Brunswick, NJ: Rutgers University Press, 1953), 5:296–97.

15. Basler, *Collected Works of Abraham Lincoln,* 5:129–31; D. Scott Hartwig, *To Antietam Creek, the Maryland Campaign of September 1862* (Baltimore: Johns Hopkins University Press, 2012), 138–40.

16. See Clemens and Carman, *Maryland Campaign of September 1862,* vol. 1, chap. 4; and Hartwig, *To Antietam Creek,* chap. 5, for detailed studies of these events.

17. Harsh, *Taken at the Flood,* 48–49, 58.

18. US Census Bureau, *Agriculture of the United States in 1860, Compiled from the Original Returns of the Eighth Census* (Washington, DC: Government Printing Office, 1864); US Census Bureau, *Population of the United States in 1860, Compiled from the Original Returns of the Eighth Census* (Washington, DC: Government Printing Office, 1864); Lawrence M. Denton, *A Southern Star for Maryland: Maryland and the Secession Crisis* (Baltimore: Publishing Concepts, 1991), 29–38.

19. Charles W. Mitchell, "The Election of 1860 in Maryland," *Maryland Historical Magazine* 109, no. 3 (2014): 323.

20. Harsh, *Taken at the Flood,* 124–25, Dowdey and Manarin, *Wartime Papers,* 298.

21. Goldsborough, *The Maryland Line in the Confederate States Army 1861–1865* (Baltimore: Kelly Piet, 1869), 99–101.

22. Dowdey and Manarin, *Wartime Papers,* 301.

23. Harsh, *Taken at the Flood,* 145–67, has the most detailed discussion of this order.

24. Hartwig, *To Antietam Creek,* 282–83.

25. Hartwig, *To Antietam Creek,* 286–89; See also Steven R. Stotelmyer, *Too Useful to Sacrifice* (El Dorado, CA: Savas Beatie, 2019), chap. 1, "Fallacies Regarding the Lost Orders and the Maryland Campaign of 1862."

26. Carman, *Antietam,* vol. 1, chaps. 7 and 8; US War Department, *War of the Rebellion* vol. 51, pt. 2, 618–19.

27. Harsh, *Taken at the Flood,* 301–3.

28. Harsh, *Taken at the Flood,* 303–4, Lee to Davis, September 4, 1862, Dowdey and Manarin, *Wartime Papers,* 294.

29. Hartwig, *To Antietam Creek,* 489–90, 509–15.

30. These movements are a summation of Ezra Carman's manuscript, vol. 2, *Antietam,* as edited and annotated by the author.

31. Carman, *Antietam,* vol. 2. Casualty figures are from Carman, 2:601–12.

32. See Kathleen Ernst, *Too Afraid to Cry* (Mechanicsburg, PA: Stackpole Books, 1991).

33. Carman, *Antietam,* vol. 2, chap. 22.

34. Harsh, *Taken at the Flood,* 444–45, 448–52.

35. Carman, *Antietam,* vol. 3, *Shepherdstown Ford and Beyond,* chaps. 23 and 24.

36. Carman, *Antietam,* vol. 3, *Shepherdstown Ford and Beyond,* chaps. 25 and 26.

37. Stephen W. Sears, *Landscape Turned Red: The Battle of Antietam* (New Haven, CT: Ticknor & Fields) 1983, 43–45, 317–19, 334–35. Slavery in Maryland ended November 1, 1864, with the passage in 1864 of the new state constitution, which banned slavery in the state.

38. This argumnent is summarized from James McPherson, *Antietam: The Battle That Changed the Course of the Civil War* (New York: Oxford University Press, 2002).

39. Edwin B. Coddington, *The Gettysburg Campaign: A Study in Command* (Dayton, OH: Morningside Bookshop), 1983, 5–9; Dowdey and Manarin, *Wartime Papers,* 507–9, US War Department, *War of the Rebellion,* vol. 27, pt. 3, 869.

40. US War Department, *War of the Rebellion,* vol. 27, pt. 1, 30–31.

41. Details can be found in US War Department, *War of the Rebellion,* vol. 27, pt. 1, 46–61.

42. Dennis E. Frye, *Harpers Ferry under Fire,* 127–35.

43. Herman Schuricht, *Jenkins' Brigade in the Gettysburg Campaign* (Richmond, VA: Southern Historical Society Papers, 1896), 24:340; Mary Louise "Lutie" Kealhofer, a southern sympathizer, fondly remembered the Confederates passing through Hagerstown, and them being warmly greeted. Diary, courtesy of Washington County Historical Society, Hagerstown, MD.

44. Otho Nesbitt Diary, Washington County Historical Society, Hagerstown, MD.

45. US War Department, *War of the Rebellion,* vol. 27, pt. 3, 912–13.

46. Edward H. Phillips, *The Lower Shenandoah Valley in the Civil War: The Impact of the War on the Civilian Population and upon Civil Institutions* (Lynchburg, VA: H. E. Howard, 1993), 114; Lt. Channing Price of Gen. J. E. B. Stuart's staff, in a September 18, 1862, letter to his mother mentioned capturing "two thousand negroes and camp followers" at Harpers Ferry. See Robert J. Trout, *With Pen and Saber, the Letters and Diaries of Jeb Stuart's Staff Officers* (Mechanicsburg, PA: Stackpole Books), 101. See also Frye, *Harpers Ferry under Fire,* 102.

47. Wardlaw Diary, September 15, 1862, collection of the author. Confiscation detailed in Charles T. Alexander, "A Regular Slave Hunt," *North & South Magazine* 4, no. 7 (September 2001), 82–88. Specific sources noting the abduction of African Americans from Pennsylvania include *Mer-*

THOMAS G. CLEMENS

cersburg Journal, July 17, 1863; Charles Hartman Diary, Phillip Schaff Library, Lancaster Theological Seminary; and Jacob Hoke, *The Great Invasion of 1863* (New York: Thomas Yoseloff, 1863, quoted from 1959 ed.), 107–8.

48. Interestingly, on July 3 at Culp's Hill at Gettysburg, several Maryland Union regiments traded shots with Confederate Marylanders. Monuments honoring both sides are located within a few hundred yards.

49. For more details about these actions see Kent M. Brown, *Retreat from Gettysburg* (Chapel Hill: University of North Carolina Press, 2005), 9; and Eric J. Wittenberg, J. David Petruzzi, and Michael F. Nugent, *One Continuous Fight: The Retreat from Gettysburg and the Pursuit of Lee's Army of Northern Virginia, July 4–14, 1863* (El Dorado Hills, CA: Savas Beatie, 2008).

50. Dowdey and Manarin, *Wartime Papers,* 548.

51. Wittenberg, Petruzzi, and Nugent, *One Continuous Fight,* 258–61.

52. Jubal Anderson Early, *Autobiographical Sketch and Narrative of the War between the States, with Notes by R. H. Early* (New York: Konecky & Konecky, 1994), 371.

53. Early, *Autobiographical Sketch and Narrative;* Dowdey and Manarin, *Wartime Papers,* 806–8; *Official Records of the Union and Confederate Navies in the War of the Rebellion* (Washington, DC: US Naval War Records Office, 1894–1922), ser. 2, 5:467.

54. US War Department, *War of the Rebellion,* vol. 37, pt. 1, 175; pt. 2, 4.

55. Daniel C. Toomey, *The Civil War in Maryland* (Baltimore, MD: Toomey Press, 2004), 102; Stephen R. Bockmiller, *Follow the Money: The 1864 Confederate Ransom of Hagerstown, Maryland* (Mercersburg, PA: Mercersburg Printing, 2014), 13–22.

56. Early, *Autobiographical Sketch and Narrative,* 385; a handwritten copy of the original note is in the Washington County Historical Society, Hagerstown, MD.

57. US War Department, *War of the Rebellion,* vol. 27, pt. 2, 466; Richard R. Duncan, "Maryland's Reaction to Early's Raid in 1864: A Summer of Bitterness," *Maryland Historical Magazine* (Fall 1969): 252; "Account of Rebel Raid through Middletown Valley," *Valley Register,* July 22, 1864.

58. US War Department, *War of the Rebellion,* vol. 37, pt. 2, 17; *Atlas to Accompany the Official Records of the Union and Confederate Armies* (Washington, DC: Government Printing Office, 1891–5), Plate 169; Lew Wallace, *Lew Wallace, an Autobiography* (New York: Harper & Brothers Publishers, 1906), 2:699.

59. US War Department, *War of the Rebellion,* vol. 37, pt. 2, 7, 58–59, 119, 133–34, 136–37.

60. Spaulding, *Last Chance,* 52–53, B. Franklin Cooling, *Monocacy, the Battle That Saved Washington* (Shippensburg, PA: White Mane Publishing, 1997), 97.

61. Bockmiller, *Follow the Money,* 13–14, states there is no evidence to support the story of a misplaced zero allowing Hagerstown to pay ten times less than Frederick. He suggests it was the ease with which $20,000 was raised in Hagerstown that encouraged Early to demand a higher sum in Frederick.

62. Stan Goldberg, Special to the *Frederick News-Post,* March 22, 2015.

63. On the return through Maryland McCausland wanted to ransom Hancock, but Gilmor (and Bradley T. Johnson) objected and no demand was made. Harry Gilmor, *Four Years in the Saddle* (New York: Harper Brothers Publishing, 1866, 1997), 209–14; Timothy Ackinclose, *Sabres & Pistols, the Civil War Career of Colonel Harry Gilmor, C.S.A.* (Gettysburg, PA: Stan Clark Military Books), 1997, 128–37.

64. Spaulding, *Last Chance,* 141.

65. Ulysses S. Grant, *Personal Memoirs of U.S. Grant* (New York City: Charles L. Webster, 1885), 2:306.

66. Robert K. Krick, *Civil War Weather in Virginia* (Tuscaloosa: University of Alabama Press, 2007), 134.

67. Spaulding, *Last Chance,* 177–78.

68. Spaulding, *Last Chance,* 181.

69. Thomas W. Hyde, *Following the Greek Cross, or Memories of the Sixth Army Corps* (Boston: Houghton, Mifflin, 1894), 223.

70. Spaulding, *Last Chance,* 187–88, Early, 392–95.

71. In a letter to President Davis, Lee wrote; "I can devote to this purpose the whole of the Marylanders of this army, which would afford a sufficient number of men of excellent material and much experience, but I am at a loss where to find a proper leader. As he would command Maryland troops and operate upon Maryland soil it would be well that he should be a Marylander. Of those connected with this army I consider Col. Bradley T. Johnson the most suitable. He is bold and intelligent, ardent and true, and yet I am unable to say whether he possesses all the requisite qualities. Everything in an expedition of the kind would depend upon the leader." US War Department, *War of the Rebellion* vol. 37, pt. 1, 766–67.

72. US War Department, *War of the Rebellion* vol. 40, pt. 3, 761.

73. Spaulding, *Last Chance,* 144.

74. Spaulding, *Last Chance,* 149–52; Gilmor, *Four Years in the Saddle,* 190–91.

75. Gilmor, *Four Years in the Saddle,* 198–203.

76. Spaulding, *Last Chance,* 162–64. Chapter 9 is a splendid summary of these two raids and the efforts to thwart them.

77. US War Department, *War of the Rebellion,* vol. 19, pt. 1, 596.

ACHIEVING EMANCIPATION IN MARYLAND

JONATHAN W. WHITE

As a loyal state, Maryland was exempt from the provisions of the Emancipation Proclamation, which went into effect on January 1, 1863. Consequently, Republicans who hoped to bring freedom to the Border State's enslaved population had to do so through other means. In the spring of 1864 Maryland voters elected delegates to a constitutional convention to rewrite the fundamental law of the state. In order to accomplish their primary goal—which was to abolish slavery in Maryland—they had to enact other reforms as well. Most importantly, the delegates adopted provisions that allowed Maryland soldiers to vote in the field at the referendum. Though less radical than emancipation, the enfranchising of soldiers was an essential step in the path toward emancipation. Without the votes cast by the soldiers in the field, Maryland's new constitution would not have been ratified by the people, and legal freedom probably would not have been achieved in the state until the ratification of the Thirteenth Amendment in December 1865.

By the midpoint of the war, the slave system in Maryland had been significantly crippled, as thousands of enslaved men and women fled their masters and sought freedom in Washington, DC, or elsewhere.[1] But, warned one circuit judge in the state, Republican leaders should not be deceived by appearances. "It has been represented, that this State is becoming strongly union, and in favour of the emancipation of her slaves," wrote Judge Nicholas Brewer of Maryland's Second Judicial Circuit to Abraham Lincoln on October 31, 1863. "This I think is a great mistake. There is a great deal of bitter secession feeling every where in the State, but in the lower part of it, there is also a very strong pro-slavery feeling. The Slaveholders are exceedingly unwilling to part with their slaves and will use their utmost endeavours to prevent manumission in any form or at any time immediate or prospective."[2] Indeed, despite the handwriting on the wall, Democratic politicians and voters fought vigorously to protect their slave property by challenging the legitimacy of the new state constitution, which they saw as a document "intended to deprive them of their property and liberties."[3] They did so not by challenging the emancipation provisions but by contesting the sections of the constitution dealing with the elective franchise. If they could overturn the new voting qualifications that had been used to ratify the constitution—allowing soldiers to vote and disfranchising Marylanders of questionable loyalty—then they would be able to maintain the institution of slavery without having to argue explicitly in favor of it. By October 1864, preventing soldiers' votes from counting had become the last best hope of Maryland slaveholders to thwart the tide of freedom that was sweeping across the state. Indeed, when it became clear that the constitution had only passed because of the votes cast by soldiers, Democrats unleashed a full assault on soldier suffrage in both the judicial and executive branches of the state.

The process of enfranchising soldiers in Maryland is unique among the Union states. Some state legislatures simply passed laws that permitted soldiers to vote in the field. If a state's constitution required voters to cast their ballots in the ward or election district in which they lived (as did the Maryland constitution of 1851), then the states ratified constitutional amendments before passing the legislation.[4] In Maryland, however, Union soldiers were granted the right to vote by the new constitution, and Confederate soldiers and sympathizers were also disfranchised by it. A constitutional controversy arose because these new qualifications for suffrage were put into effect *before* the document was even ratified. In other words, soldiers were permitted to vote at the referendum and "disloyal" Marylanders were kept from voting on the new constitution's ratification. Maryland Republicans took this approach because they knew that this emancipationist document would not receive the consent of the people unless Confederate sympathizers were kept from the polls and Union soldiers had the polls taken to them.

Republicans defended their policies on ideological grounds, just as Republicans in other states had done. They insisted that Union soldiers deserved the full rights of citizenship, while rebels and Confederate sympathizers did not. "If Maryland is to be continued a loyal State she cannot afford to send to the battle-field so many of her trusty men, without securing to them the right of suffrage wherever they may be," argued the editors of one Cumberland paper. "They are fighting the enemy in the front with the bayonet, and they have a right to cast their ballots to keep down disloyalty at home."[5] This was a compelling political argument because it made Democrats seem unfriendly toward the soldiers for denying them the ballot. Simultaneously, it also made Democrats appear disloyal since they argued that rebels should be immediately forgiven and granted the privilege of electing the government they had just tried to destroy. The complication, of course, is that Democrats were often accused of disloyalty and consequently denied the ballot without much actual proof that they were disloyal.[6]

The debate over enfranchising soldiers in Maryland mirrored debates that had taken place in other Union states over the previous three years, but much more was at stake in the Maryland debate, for its outcome would determine the survival of slavery in the state. And this mattered greatly for the outcome of the war. As Lincoln explained in private correspondence with Maryland congressman John A. J. Creswell, he was "very anxious for emancipation to be effected in Maryland," and, "It needs not to be a secret, that I wish success to emancipation in Maryland. It would aid much to end the rebellion. Hence it is a matter of national consequence, in which every national man, may rightfully feel a deep interest."[7]

THE CONSTITUTIONAL CONVENTION

Following the state elections on November 4, 1863, Republicans (called Unconditional Unionists in Maryland during the war) held a strong majority in the state general assembly. Fifty-seven of the legislators were pledged to the Union and emancipation, eight more wanted a constitutional convention, ten Unionists were unpledged to a convention, and twenty-one Democrats wanted no constitutional change.[8] By a vote of 45 to 13 in the House of Delegates, and 17 to 2 in the Maryland Senate, the Unionist majority passed a resolution on February 3, 1864, calling for a constitutional convention to commence on April 27. When this resolution was submitted to the people of Maryland, they overwhelmingly supported holding a convention, casting 31,593 votes in favor of it and 19,524 against it.[9] At this referendum, were any voter challenged at the poll, he had to take an oath of allegiance to both the state and national governments, and every member elected to the convention was also required to take a similar oath. The convention was composed of ninety-six delegates, of whom sixty-one were in favor of immediate emancipation.[10]

Lincoln was thrilled to see the changes taking place in Maryland. On April 18, he delivered brief remarks at the opening of the Baltimore Sanitary Fair, congratulating Marylanders on their progress toward becoming a free state. "The world has never had a good definition of the word liberty, and the American people, just now, are much in want of one," he said. "We all declare for liberty; but in using the same *word* we do not all mean the same *thing*. With some the word liberty may mean for each man to do as he pleases with himself, and the product of his labor; while with others the same word may mean for some men to do as they please with other men, and the product of other men's are two, not only different, but incompatable things, called by the same name— liberty. And it follows that each of the things is, by the respective parties, called by two different and incompatable names—liberty and tyranny." He praised the people of Maryland for "recently . . . doing something to define liberty" in a way that would repudiate the slaveholders' understanding of the term.[11] Now the state constitutional convention had to get to work.

The convention opened on April 27. Within two weeks an order was adopted that the Committee on Elective Franchise and Qualification of Voters "inquire into the expediency of incorporating into the constitution an article extending the right of suffrage to soldiers, drafted or enlisted from this State into the service of the United States, and who may be out of this state . . . under such restrictions and regulations as may be deemed necessary to guard the purity of the ballot box." On May 22 the committee was also ordered to look into including a clause in the constitution "that every person who has in any manner aided in the present rebellion against the Government of the United States, ought to be forever disqualified and rendered incapable to hold or exercise within this State any office of profit or trust, civil or military, or to vote at any election hereafter to be held in this State."[12]

The committee submitted its majority report on August 9 and debate on the elective franchise began two days later. The report limited suffrage to white males at least twenty-one years old who had resided in the state for at least one year. Following the lead of many other Union states, the report stated that military and naval personnel were "entitled to vote wherever they may be." Criminals, bribers, and lunatics were excluded from the suffrage, and "no person who has at any time been in armed rebellion against the government of the United States or the lawful authorities thereof, or who has been in any way or manner in the service of the so-called 'Confederate States of America,' shall ever thereafter be entitled to vote . . . unless pardoned by the President of the United States." (This last provision was remarkable for giving the president control over the right of suffrage within the state.) Furthermore, the proposal required all elected officials to take an oath that they "had never, either directly or indirectly, by word, act or deed, given any aid, comfort or encouragement to those in rebellion against the government." The committee's minority report differed on several key points. First, it made no provision for soldiers to vote, and stated that military personnel from other states shall not "be considered as having acquired residence to vote because he has been" stationed in the state. Second, it proposed a prospective loyalty oath for office holders, making no mention of past loyalty.[13] The majority report, however, was the only one printed and distributed among the delegates.

Democratic members of the convention were highly critical of the majority report. Samuel H. Berry, a lawyer from Prince George's County, argued that it anticipated perpetual war and would bring about changes suited only for wartime but that would last into peacetime for decades. The proposals offered should not be part of the "organic law, setting forth organic principles for the government of the State," Berry stated, but mere "statutory provisions" passed by the general assembly. He also found the oath objectionable because it was not conclusive, meaning that even after taking it an election judge could still refuse to accept an elector's ballot. The soldier vote would thus "open a wide door for frauds in our elections, the extent of which is impossible to foretell" and is "dangerous to the institutions of our country" as soldiers from other states could carry elections in Maryland.[14]

Peregrine Davis, a farmer and former postmaster from Port Tobacco, Charles County, argued that requiring voters to swear an oath of past loyalty constituted an ex post facto law, which was expressly forbidden by Article I, Section 10 of the US Constitution. In response, he offered a proposal that the oath should require loyalty after January 1, 1865. Archibald Stirling, a lawyer and former city counselor of Baltimore City, disagreed, however, claiming that the state "has the right to define who shall vote within her limits." After some debate, the convention voted 48 to 12 against Davis's proposal. A voter would have to say, with a clear conscience, that he had never given aid, comfort, or support to the rebellion.[15]

Richard H. Edelen, a lawyer and former state's attorney from Charles County, challenged the disfranchisement of those who had supported the rebellion. Bringing up President Lincoln's December 1863 Proclamation of Amnesty and Reconstruction (which only required Confederates to take an oath of future loyalty), he suggested wiping out the rebel's offenses so that "he henceforth [may] occupy the position in regard to all political rights in the State or the country that he had before he took up arms." Perpetually depriving a citizen of the right to vote would be the highest "degree of punishment, short of taking a man's life," Edelen argued, and would make him "a mere cypher in the community where he lives, stripping him of every political right." If President Lincoln was willing to offer amnesty to those in rebellion, Edelen continued, then Maryland should follow the same course as the leader of the national government. Edelen accused Maryland Republicans of proposing to disfranchise rebels out of "a spirit of prejudice, or partisan hate." "Let bygones be bygones," he urged. "Let the dead past bury its dead. Let us, when this unhappy war shall come to an end, try to forget the past, and embark, if we can, upon a new era of happiness and prosperity."[16]

Such statements required answer. Henry Stockbridge of Baltimore City immediately rose from his seat to remind the Democrats that right "now we can almost hear the echo of the guns fired by natives of Maryland" at the loyal citizens of Maryland. Stockbridge, a native of Massachusetts and an advocate for equal rights for African Americans, had been elected to the legislature in 1863 and had framed and helped pass the law calling for the constitutional convention. He reminded his fellow delegates that rebellious Marylanders were robbing, plundering, and burning towns and villages with their "guns and bayonets directed at the hearts of peaceful, quite husbandmen about their daily avocations." Republicans merely wished to "brand such conduct as it deserves." Yet at such proposals "we are charged with malice, prejudice, partisan hate." Certainly this was not prejudice, declared Stockbridge, as prejudice is judgment before any action. The actions of these rebels, however, were "written in characters of fire and blood in every county of this State." Allowing rebels to come back and accomplish with the ballot what they had failed to do with the bullet would be unjust to all of the loyal citizens of Maryland who had been terrorized by the actions of the traitors. It would be "gross injustice" and "a wanton outrage" to allow those who "have done their utmost" and "staked their lives" to destroy the government to come back and exercise the full rights of citizens. "It is an act of justice, and not of prejudice, to exclude them from the right of voting," Stockbridge concluded.[17]

Archibald Stirling concurred and proceeded to rebut Edelen's remark about the president's proclamation of amnesty. Lincoln's offer of pardon was intended to get them to lay down their arms and had no bearing on whether or not a state would choose to re-enfranchise them. Furthermore, if these men could vote as soon as they returned to Maryland, they would be "a continual disturbing element in the community so long as they shall live."[18] In other words, disfranchising rebels, for Stirling, would be a just exercise of the state's power to preserve the peace.

As the discussion turned to the right of suffrage for Union soldiers, it was clear that no delegate could simply oppose permitting soldiers to vote—such a position would be distinctly unpatriotic and suggest Copperheadism and disloyalty. Thus, when Oliver Miller of Anne Arundel County—a Democrat who later would become Speaker of the House of Delegates and then a judge on the Maryland Court of Appeals—took the floor, he stated that he did not wish to deprive soldiers of any right to which they were entitled. He modestly supposed, however, that if he were "drafted and forced into the service," then he would not expect the state of Maryland to provide for him to vote. Such a policy, according to Miller, would violate constitutional liberty because a man "lays aside his civil rights and is placed under martial law" when he becomes a soldier. If soldiers were allowed to vote they would merely express the opinions of their commanding officers. When challenged on the issue, Miller could offer no sources or historical examples; he simply maintained that allowing soldiers to vote would annihilate "republican institutions and republican liberty; and if that hope is crushed out here, it dies upon the earth."[19]

Republican Joseph B. Pugh, a prominent businessman from Pennsylvania who had settled in Cecil County, rose to protest the idea that a man lays aside his civil or political rights when he becomes a soldier. "I believe the American citizen, when he becomes a soldier, is . . . the American citizen more nobly developed," declared Pugh. A citizen retains all of his rights when he puts on a uniform, but "is only in a position to express differently his rights as an American citizen, and to defend them as a soldier." Moreover, should the day arrive when the majority of the citizenry had to take up arms, there would "be nobody left to organize a constitutional form of government, because there will be nobody left who has not cast aside and shuffled off all his civil rights as a citizen."[20] Pugh then challenged the Democrats to prove that soldiers would not be at perfect liberty to vote as they pleased. American officers would never force their soldiers to vote a certain way, Pugh declared. And no American soldier would ever permit his officers to interfere with his exercise of the franchise.

Joseph M. Cushing, a merchant who sold books and stationery in Baltimore City, derided the Democrats for opposing "every single thing offered in this convention to support the government of the United States or the Union." Democratic opposition to these Republican measures, according to Cushing, was an open attack against the Union army. Cushing's pragmatism soon emerged, however. "There are more than votes enough in the army of the United States to change the whole destiny of this country; and they are Union men," he exclaimed. Even still, he could not fathom how Democrats wanted to disfranchise those "who have gone to the front to defend your institutions" while placing "the destinies of your land into the hands of the traitors that remain behind." Striking at what he believed was the heart of the issue, Cushing declared that the Democrats opposed permitting soldiers to vote because they knew "that every soldier from Maryland will vote for the prosecution of this war, for sustaining the government of this country, and for sustaining the principles of republican liberty of which the gentleman professes to be fond."[21]

Nearing the end of the debate on the elective franchise, Democrat Oliver Miller proposed a reasonable amendment to the constitution, that soldiers from other states who were stationed in Maryland would not have residency conferred upon them, and that Maryland soldiers would not lose their status as residents simply because they had been stationed elsewhere. Miller sought this provision to protect the sanctity of the ballot box in Maryland so that citizens of other states could not have a hand in setting Maryland's policies. The Republicans countered that Miller's proposition was unnecessary, however, and it was defeated by a partisan vote.[22]

The new constitution contained provisions for the taking of soldiers' votes at the referendum and the upcoming state and presidential elections. Polls were to be opened in every company of every Maryland regiment from 8 A.M. to 6 P.M., and the commissioned officers of each company were to act as judges of election. The judges were to collect the ballots and keep a record in poll books of who voted. Following the elections, they were to return the ballots and poll books to the governor. The constitution also disfranchised any person who had "at any time been in armed hostility" against the United States, or aided the rebels "in any manner," or advised any person to join the Confederacy, and it called upon the general assembly to enact a registry law to ensure that only qualified voters would be able to vote in the future. Finally, it required voters to take an oath of both past and future allegiance to the Union by which the voter swore "that I have never given any aid, countenance or support to those in armed hostility to the United States, that I have never expressed a desire for the triumph of" the Confederacy, and that "I will in all respects demean myself as a loyal citizen of the United States." The oath did not guarantee the right of an individual to vote, however. An election judge could charge a voter with perjury and deprive him of the ballot if he believed the voter was swearing falsely.[23]

The Democratic members of the convention had been powerless to stop the work of the majority, and they made sure to lodge their protests at the convention's close. When one delegate voted against the proposed constitution, he listed several "cardinal objections" to the final document. Among these were that "millions of dollars worth of property" were being "unjustly" taken from citizens, that the voice of the citizenry was being excluded from the polls, and that the federal system was being destroyed by the centralizing tendencies of the national government. Another Democrat contended that this constitution was "an attempt to subvert the present government of Maryland, as a revolution by usurpation." Finally, another declared that the new constitution permitted "a most unwarrantable seizure of property, and a wanton attack upon the rights of those in regard to whom we were sent here to afford protection for their persons, liberty, property, and every other political right."[24] The heart of their opposition was that this document would destroy slavery in their state.

The minority at the convention also issued a protest against ratification of the constitution, which they distributed among Maryland voters. In it they objected to abolition of slavery, the test oath, and that "the soldiers in the field and out of the State are to be allowed to vote on its adoption." They also circulated the written statements by US senator Reverdy Johnson and several other constitutional thinkers in the state that the convention did not have authority "to receive the soldiers' vote outside of the State on the question of the adoption or rejection of the new Constitution."[25]

THE REFERENDUM

The convention adjourned on September 6, with the constitution to be submitted to the people for ratification on October 12 and 13. Lincoln implored one Maryland Unionist "to go to work . . . for your Constitution, with all your energy. Try to impress other Unionists with its importance as a war measure, and don't let [it] fail! Don't let it fail!" He told Union general Lew Wallace "to be fair [in overseeing the referendum], but to give the benefit of all doubts to the emancipationists." Nevertheless, he and his administration were concerned about appearances. As Secretary of War Edwin M. Stanton explained to Wallace, "The President has set his heart on the abolition in that way [the upcoming referendum]; and mark, he don't want it to be said by anybody that the bayonet had anything to do with the election. He is a candidate for a second nomination. You understand?"[26]

Democrats, of course, were highly concerned about how the referendum would be conducted. Prior to the voting, George Vickers, a conservative Unionist from the Eastern Shore, wrote a letter to Unionist governor Augustus W. Bradford, voicing complaints about the proceedings of the constitutional convention and the document that it produced. Vickers challenged the extension of suffrage to the soldiers in the referendum because soldiers were not allowed to vote under the existing state constitution. The constitution of 1864, he maintained, "is but a skeleton, a form or plan, without vitality or energy. It requires the people to breathe into it life and power; till then it is a feather floating upon the breeze of popular opinion." Thus, prior to ratification, the provisions disfranchising some and enfranchising others were "inoperative and void." Vickers called on the governor to stop this injustice from taking place.[27]

Governor Bradford responded that the convention possessed the power to enact these provisions because the act of the legislature that called for the convention declared that the new constitution "shall be submitted 'at such time, in such manner, and *subject to such rules and regulations* as said convention may prescribe.'" Bradford concluded that he had no legal power to interfere; rather, if "any wrong has been perpetrated by the convention" then the state judiciary would be the proper branch of government to redress the injustice.[28]

Vickers replied that the convention had indeed overstepped its bounds. Considering the passage from which Bradford had quoted, Vickers suggested that Bradford should bear in mind the entire section of the bill calling for the convention, rather than just the clause that the governor had cited. "But when we read the whole section from which you quote, I find immediately following the words 'rules and regulations as said convention may prescribe,' these words, 'and the provisions hereinbefore contained for the *qualification of the voters* and the holding of the elections provided in the previous sections of this act, *shall be applicable to the election to be held under this section.*'" Vickers was certain that the qualifications for suffrage existing in the state could not be changed before the new constitution was ratified, and the "rules and regulations must be in accordance and not in conflict with the words that follow them." Vickers insisted that he had no reason to oppose enfranchising soldiers in theory, but he maintained that they would have to be given the vote legally and constitutionally. The method proposed by the convention clearly violated the basic principles of constitutional government, and Vickers would never support an unconstitutional measure just because it was patriotic. He further stated that Bradford's suggestion that disfranchised voters could seek redress through the courts was impractical. There would be many appeals to various judges and courts. This would lead to confusion and an array of conflicting decisions.[29]

Finally, Vickers reminded Bradford of the elections of 1863. In those elections Union general Robert C. Schenck, commander of the Middle Department, had issued orders to keep "evil-disposed persons" from voting in Maryland. Any suspicious persons "hanging about" the polls were to be arrested by the military, and any voters who might be of questionable loyalty would be ordered to take a loyalty oath. If they refused, they could be subject to arrest. Without such orders, Schenck believed, "we lose this State."[30]

Such military interference in the state election had made Bradford furious at the time, and in a letter to Lincoln he had declared that General Schenck's order was "justly obnoxious to the public sentiment of the State." Lincoln had replied that "in this struggle for the nation's life" some of these measures might be necessary to ensure the election of loyal candidates. Moreover, keeping the peace on election day and "prevent[ing] the persistently disloyal from voting" did not constitute "a just cause of offence to Maryland." Lincoln reminded Bradford that Gen. John A. Dix had used troops in a similar way "when your Excellency was elected Governor" in 1861.[31]

Lincoln revoked parts of Schenck's order stating that he "wish[ed] all loyal qualified voters in Maryland & elsewhere, to have the undisturbed previlege [sic] of voting at elections," but he insisted that the military must be present at the polls. In response, Bradford issued a proclamation on November 2, 1863, decrying such military interference in a loyal state. The use of the military was without justification, he said, because Maryland's loyalty had never faltered. Within the federal system, Bradford declared that the state had a right to protect its own ballot boxes. He called on the judges of elections, *in pursuance with the laws of Maryland,* to report to the state's attorney any soldiers posted near the polls. He also stated that the judges must uphold their own oaths as judges of election when determining who had a right to vote. General Schenck's order notwithstanding, Bradford declared that the judges of election should not administer the military's test oath for voters.[32]

The presence of Union troops at the Maryland election in 1863 led to a number of arrests as well as the suppression of Democratic turnout.[33] At the time, George Vickers sent three letters to Lincoln to state that the "outrages" conducted by the military had "shocked the moral sense of the people of Maryland."[34] In light of all of this—which had taken place just one year before—Vickers now asked Bradford whether it was "unreasonable to suppose that you would again address the judges of election to prevent a greater and more flagitious wrong than was attempted by the military order of General Schenck." If Schenck's order had been unconstitutional, Vickers suggested, then so were the actions of the convention. And if Schenck's order "was covertly designed to favor a certain political party, so is that of the convention." Vickers reminded Bradford that the constitution was "fraught with such momentous interests, having no parallel in our State, nor in any other State of the Union." It was here that Vickers finally struck at the heart of the matter. Slavery was at stake in this new constitution, and Vickers wanted it to "be fairly and honestly submitted to all the constitutional and legal voters of the State." If the referendum was fair, then all Marylanders would submit to the outcome, whatever it may be. But if the vote was "partial, limited, unfair; if party spirit is to be subserved, and not the public interest; if wrong and injustice prevail; if an unconstitutional oath is forced upon the people, and votes taken without the territorial limits of the State, then what respect can be paid to a constitution thus adopted, and what excitement and bitterness of feeling will not be engendered?"[35]

Governor Bradford professed surprise at the posture adopted by Vickers. He first countered Vickers's claim regarding the power of the convention in determining the "rules and regulations" for the referendum. Bradford understood the legislature as giving the convention broad powers to determine how the constitution would be submitted to the people, including the qualifications for voting.[36] The governor next questioned Vickers's assumption that the executive of the state was granted the power to "furnish a remedy . . . for the infraction of *political* rights, such as the right of franchise." Bradford proposed that since the people were the source of the power of the state and their representatives have been "duly delegated to ordain or alter their organic law," then the governor did not have the right to overrule that decision of the sovereign people.[37]

Finally, Bradford responded to the comparison of General Schenck's test oath and the oath imposed by the new constitution. He drew several distinctions between the two situations. "In the one a military commander arranges the form of an oath which he requires the judges of election in certain cases to administer, menaces them with arrest if they refuse, and sends a squad of soldiers to the polls to see that this order is enforced." Under Schenck's order the "judges were menaced with arrest for refusing to obey an unauthorized military order instead of the undisputed laws of the State." The constitutional convention, however, was called by the people. Bradford had opposed Schenck's order in 1863 because the military was attempting to interfere with the execution of the laws of the state.

Bradford knew that Vickers still believed that the convention's legitimacy was questionable and that it had usurped an unprecedented power. An important precedent did exist, however. In 1830 Virginia ratified a new state constitution that extended the franchise to those who did not own property; and though they could not vote under the existing constitution, nonproperty holders were allowed to vote in the referendum, undoubtedly providing the margin of victory. Invoking the advocacy of the Founders, Bradford pointed out that James Madison and John Marshall, among others, had supported ratification of the new constitution despite the new voter qualifications: "I hope and think that with such a precedent before us you will no longer press me to interpose the executive arm to arrest it upon the ground of its being a palpable violation of constitutional rights, 'having no parallel in our State or any other.'"[38]

On October 8, Bradford issued a circular to the judges of election stating that the election returns should distinctly show that the loyalty oath had been administered, and "that no military or other armed force had appeared at the place of voting and interfered with said election, unless under the call of the civil authorities as therein provided."[39] Nevertheless, Gen. Lew Wallace suppressed the Baltimore *Evening Post*, the only paper in the city that opposed ratification of the new state constitution and supported Lincoln's opponent, Gen. George B. McClellan, in the presidential election in November. The editor of the *Evening Post* complained that this suppression deprived the people of Baltimore "of the means of deciding intelligently upon the questions at issue and therefore makes the so called election a mockery."[40]

Lincoln publicly endorsed the work of the convention, both as a moral good and as a way of quickly ending the war and eradicating the possibility of future sectional conflicts. "I wish all men to be free," he wrote in a public letter to be read at a mass meeting in Baltimore on October 10. "I wish the material prosperity of the already free which I feel sure the extinction of slavery would bring. I wish to see, in process of disappearing, that only thing which ever could bring this nation to civil war." On October 12 and 13 the referendum was held for the new state constitution. In the final tally 30,174 ballots were cast in favor of the new constitution and 29,799 against it. Sixty-one blank ballots and thirty-three cast against the constitution by voters who had refused to take the oath were rejected from the final count. Maryland soldiers cast 2,633 votes in favor of the constitution and 263 votes against it. Thus, the soldiers supplied the slim 375-vote majority in favor of the constitution. After receiving the official returns from the election judges, Governor Bradford declared that the constitution would go into effect on November 1, 1864.[41]

Slaveholders in Maryland lamented the outcome. The Democratic State Central Committee charged that an election rife with voter suppression and fraud had "destroyed sacred rights of property without compensation."[42] And although the Border States had rejected such an offer from Lincoln in 1862, some slaveholders now vainly hoped that the federal government might compensate them for their financial losses.[43] Republicans, by contrast, celebrated the new constitution, for they understood that expanding freedom was essential to fully subduing the rebellion. "Maryland is now a free state and there is no party or power that can establish slavery within her territories," wrote one exuberant Baltimorean to Lincoln.[44] The Philadelphia *Inquirer* opined that Maryland soldiers "will be the subject of congratulation among the friends of human progress" for voting to end slavery in their state. "It will be a glory to the defenders of Maryland in the war against the Rebellion, that they not only fought for the security of the citizens of their State in the field, but that, by their votes, they secured the everlasting welfare of the Commonwealth through all time."[45]

From Lincoln's perspective, the emancipationist triumph in Maryland "was a victory worth double the number of electoral votes of the state because of its moral influence." He told journalist Noah Brooks, "I had rather have Maryland upon that issue than have a State twice its size upon the Presidential issue; it cleans up a piece of ground." To a delegation of Marylanders who visited the White House shortly after Lincoln's reelection in November, the president said that "the adoption of their free State constitution was a bigger thing than their part in the Presidential election." He could have won reelection without Maryland, but "the adoption of the constitution, being a good thing, could not be undone." The October referendum was, therefore, "a victory for the right worth a great deal more than their part in the Presidential election, although he thought well of that."[46]

African Americans in and around Maryland fully understood the momentous nature of what had just transpired. On the night of November 1, a large group of Black men and women gathered at the Fifteenth Street Presbyterian Church, an important Black church in Washington, DC, to express their enthusiasm for the constitutional change in Maryland. From the pulpit, the famous Black minister Henry Highland Garnet (an escaped slave from Maryland), urged the congregants to thank God, Lincoln, and the Union soldiers who had made this dream a reality. He warned the audience against speaking "harmful word[s] against the soldiers" because "when the fate of Maryland was trembling in the balance, the brave soldiery, who had met the fiery hail of lead and iron, who had stormed the breastworks and taken the rifle-pits, who were suffering and bleeding on the battle field, sent forth their votes, and by them decreed that henceforth 'My Maryland' was free." The crowd then took up a collection to assist sick and wounded Union soldiers while the choir sang "The Battle Cry of Freedom."[47]

A group of several hundred Black men and women who could not get into the church service made their way to the White House, singing songs and carrying torches and pro-Republican election campaign transparencies. In a report entitled "Light on a Dark Subject," journalist Noah Brooks described the scene. With "loud and repeated cheers" the gathering was able to summon the president to make an appearance. Lincoln looked upon the crowd and said, "I have to guess, my friends, the object of this call, which has taken me quite by surprise this evening." One of the Black men in the audience replied, "The emancipation of Maryland, sah." Upon hearing this, Lincoln told the assembly:

It is no secret that I have wished, and still do wish, mankind everywhere to be free. [Great cheering and cries of "God bless Abraham Lincoln."] And in the State of Maryland how great an advance has been made in this direction. It is difficult to realize that in that State, where human slavery existed for ages, ever since a period long before any here were born—by the action of her own citizens—the soil is made forever free. [Loud and long cheering.] I have no feeling of triumph over those who were opposed to this measure and who voted against it, but I do believe that it will result in good to the white race as well as to those who have been made free by this act of emancipation, and I hope that the time will soon come when all will see that the perpetuation of freedom for all in Maryland is best for the interests of all, though some may thereby be made to suffer tempo-rary pecuniary loss. And I hope that you, colored people, who have been emancipated, will use this great boon which has been given you to improve yourselves, both morally and intellectually; and now, good night.

Following the conclusion of Lincoln's remarks, the crowd cheered and "after some boggling about the order of march, the dark torchlighters gathered them-selves up, and hurrahing, disappeared in the darkness."[48]

LITIGATION

Bradford had maintained all along that, should problems arise in the election, the proper place to seek redress was in the courts, although the federal prose-cutor in Maryland correctly predicted that "the Governor, from my knowledge of him, will pay no respect to their mandate." Twelve days after the referendum, Samuel G. Miles, a voter from Baltimore, made an application to the Superior Court of Baltimore City for a writ of mandamus to be directed to Governor Bradford ordering him to exclude all votes cast outside of Maryland and to count all of the votes that had been rejected on account of the oath. Miles was a qualified voter under the existing constitution, but he had refused to take the oath required by the new constitution. Thus, when he attempted to cast his bal-lot "Against the Constitution" the election judges placed it in another box for rejected ballots. The ballot had been rejected, according to Miles, "*because* and *only because,* of" his refusal to take the oath of allegiance required by the new constitution. Miles averred that the soldiers who voted had not been required to take the oath, and that there was no evidence on their returns that they had (which Bradford's circular required). Therefore, Miles claimed that Bradford should not enumerate the returns from the military in the final tally.[49]

Miles challenged the soldier vote on constitutional grounds. His petition claimed that the new constitution could have no legal effect before it had been adopted by the people. Until then, the qualifications for voting ought to be found in the state's existing constitution. Since the new qualifications were responsible for the ratification of the constitution, "the entire instrument called the new Constitution is a nullity." The convention "had no authority to add new disqualifications unknown to the present Constitution, as it has affected to do by imposing a new oath to be taken." Furthermore, the convention had no right to authorize absentee balloting for the military. Even if such provisions were legitimate, Miles insisted that the oath ought to have been required of both soldiers and civilians. If the returns from the army did not show that the soldiers had taken the oath, then their votes should not be counted in the election.[50] (Although he could not have known it at the time, Miles had a valid point when he claimed that the oath should have been required of soldiers. Prior to the presidential election, less than a month after the referendum, a group of Maryland Confederates captured four Union soldiers. The Confederates took their prisoners' uniforms, as well as their Republican ballots, and confidently marched to the polls. Dressed in Union blue, they cast the Republican ballots without being administered the loyalty oath or having their qualifications questioned, "for of course no one could object to us after voting for Lincoln."[51])

Miles's opposition to the new qualifications for suffrage were not just about the principles undergirding the franchise or test oaths, however. The records preserved in the *Debates of the Constitutional Convention* indicate Miles's standing for filing his claim: "And your petitioner is advised that, as a qualified voter of this State, as hereinbefore stated, and as the owner of slaves in this State, he is entitled to demand of your honor a *mandamus* directed to the governor of the State, commanding him to do certain acts required by the constitution of the State and the laws passed in pursuance thereof, and without the doing of which your petitioner will be remediless in the premises" because "your petitioner will be deprived of his said slave property without any compensation" under the new constitution.[52] Samuel G. Miles's motivation in challenging the new qualifications of suffrage was grounded in the fact that he was losing his slave property, despite the reality that he had remained loyal to the Union.

The Superior Court of Baltimore City dismissed Miles's claim. An identical petition was similarly dismissed in the Circuit Court of Anne Arundel

County, as were two other analogous cases elsewhere in the state. All four cases were appealed to the Maryland Court of Appeals under the head of *Miles v. Bradford*. After arguments had commenced in the state's high court, Chief Justice Richard Johns Bowie and Associate Justice Brice John Goldsborough both recused themselves from the case because, "being themselves slaveholders, they had the same interest in the decision of the cause before them which the parties complainant in the cause had."[53] Thus, while the matter of qualifications for suffrage was the technical legal issue on the table, everyone recognized that this case was really about the perpetuation of slavery.

Ironically, Governor Bradford "declined to recognize the authority of the court to control his official action" and subsequently refused to appear at the trial. US Representative Henry Winter Davis and Henry Stockbridge, who had been a vocal proponent of soldier suffrage and emancipation at the constitutional convention, appeared on the governor's behalf and were admitted by the court as amici curiae to argue the governor's case. Davis first claimed that there was no precedent for a suit such as this and that the petitioner was suing for the entire public, not just the electorate. He further alleged that the judiciary could not interfere with the right of the people of Maryland to change their own organic law. Stockbridge argued that the convention was sovereign and "clothed with power to declare its own action" because it was "derived from the act of the people" and not simply the act of the legislature. Furthermore, the doctrine of separation of powers made it impossible for one branch of government to control another; nor did any branch of the government have the "power to obstruct or restrain the people in the legal expression of their will, or restrain the legal declaration of that will when the people have exercised it." Each department of the government operated within its own sphere, according to Stockbridge, and outside "its own peculiar sphere each is powerless." In other words, the judicial branch of the state had no means by which to compel the obedience of the executive. Finally, "political reasons alone, are enough to constrain the Judiciary to desist from any attempt to control the Executive." The time-honored doctrine of political questions, the appellee believed, should compel the judiciary to resist entering affairs related to elections.[54]

The Court of Appeals unanimously affirmed the lower court's dismissal of Miles's petition. Though the official records show that Bowie had recused himself from the case, he nevertheless delivered the opinion of the court. First, the chief justice quoted from the Maryland Declaration of Rights to point out that the powers vested in the various departments of the government "ought to be forever separate and distinct from each other, and no person exercising the functions of one of said departments, shall assume or discharge the duties of any other." Next, he determined that the governor's task of enumerating the soldiers' votes was a political power with which the judiciary could not interfere. Bowie quoted from Chief Justice Roger B. Taney's opinion in *Luther v. Borden* (1849), a strikingly similar situation in which dueling factions had fought over the legitimacy of constitutional reform in the state of Rhode Island—a reform that likewise dealt with the broadening of suffrage. Quoting Taney, Bowie wrote: "*The political department has always* determined whether the proposed Constitution or amendment was ratified or not by the people of the State, and the judicial power has followed its decision. Courts of law will not interfere with the exercise of high *discretionary* powers vested in the Chief Magistrate of the State." Taney had also stated that the judiciary was in no position to declare the qualifications for suffrage of the citizens of a state. How ironic that Taney would be used in support of emancipation—especially in light of the fact that Taney died on October 12, the first day of the referendum.[55]

While slavery never appeared in the court's opinion, it could not be severed from the Democrats' opposition to allowing Maryland soldiers to vote. Close scrutiny of the interests of those who challenged the soldier vote after the referendum is telling. Maryland slaveholders and those who were sympathetic to the institution actively sought a way to stop emancipation from taking place. Thus, the cause of preserving slavery became inextricably linked to opposition to permitting soldiers to vote and to disenfranchising Marylanders with southern sympathies. Slaveholders were incapable of altering the content of the new constitution, but if they could legally defeat the new qualifications for suffrage, then the referendum would be against the constitution, and slavery would still legally exist in the state.

Of the petitioners in the four suits that sought to nullify the new constitution, the names of two remain in the record: Ezekiel F. Chambers (former US senator and president of Washington College, who had been a prominent member of the constitutional convention) and Samuel G. Miles, both of Kent County. In 1860, Miles owned four slaves while Chambers owned fifty-one. One of Miles's counsel, Thomas S. Alexander, also was a slaveholder with three slaves. Of the three judges who immediately dismissed their petitions, none

owned any slaves. Finally, George Vickers, the governor's correspondent prior
to the referendum, owned twenty-eight. These numbers indicate a significant
interest in slavery. In 1860 most Maryland slaveowners owned only one slave;
half of the slaveowners owned fewer than three slaves; three-quarters of the
slaveholders owned fewer than eight; and 90 percent of the slaveowners owned
fewer than fifteen. Thus, Vickers's twenty-eight and Chambers's fifty-one were
substantial holdings. The median slaveholding was three enslaved. Although
the ostensible basis of Vickers's complaints had been suffrage, not emancipation, Vickers likely opposed the constitution on the grounds of suffrage because he knew that this was his only hope to stop the tidal wave of emancipation from crashing on his Eastern Shore estate. It was this outcome that these
slaveholders were desperately trying to avoid.[56]

In 1865 two other related cases reached the Maryland Court of Appeals;
one challenged the voter registration law that was passed that year, and the
second, *Anderson v. Baker*, sought to have the loyalty oath in the constitution
deemed an ex post facto law that punished those who had sympathized with
the rebels. The court upheld both the registry law and the oath. According to
the opinion of the court, the state possessed an "absolute, unqualified right" to
regulate the franchise. Furthermore, "citizenship and suffrage are by no means
inseparable; the latter is not one of those universal, inalienable rights"; and
because the right of suffrage was "the creature of organic law," it "may be mod-
ified or withdrawn by the sovereign authority which conferred it, without conflicting any punishment on those who are disqualified."[57]

CONCLUSION

The legal victories of the new constitution—its voting provisions and its ending of slavery—were complete. A month later, on November 8, 1864, the soldiers' ballots also contributed to a massive turnaround in the presidential election. In 1860, Lincoln had won only 2,294 votes of 92,142 cast in the state (2.5
percent). In 1864, however, he received 40,153 of the 72,892 votes cast (55.1 percent). Clearly the new qualifications for suffrage certainly had an impact on the
election. As one Maryland Republican informed the president, "Armed with
the powers conferred by the New Constitution, we have taken the precaution
to provide as far as possible against the introduction of votes obnoxious to it's
[sic] provisions."[58]

Sadly, however, Maryland slaveowners quickly found ways to undermine the emancipationist victory. Using an existing provision in the state's Black Codes, they instituted an apprenticeship system for Black children whose parents (the slave owners claimed), could not adequately provide for their offspring. This system permitted former slaveowners to use the court system to abuse their authority over newly emancipated slaves.[59] Moreover, within two years Maryland would again endure another constitutional convulsion. In 1867 the state ratified a new reactionary constitution that included neither a loyalty oath nor any provisions for soldiers to vote. Democrats quickly regained control of the state.[60] Thus, soldiers voting and the disenfranchisement of rebellious citizens proved short-lived though potent political experiments in Maryland history. Without them, there would have been no emancipation in the state prior to the Thirteenth Amendment.

NOTES

1. Jean H. Baker, *The Politics of Continuity: Maryland Political Parties from 1858 to 1870* (Baltimore: Johns Hopkins University Press, 1973), 104; Barbara Jeanne Fields, *Slavery and Freedom on the Middle Ground: Maryland during the Nineteenth Century* (London: Yale University Press, 1985), xii; Charles W. Mitchell, ed., *Maryland Voices of the Civil War* (Baltimore: Johns Hopkins University Press, 2007), chap. 10; Max Grivno, *Gleanings of Freedom: Free and Slave Labor along the Mason-Dixon Line* (Urbana: University of Illinois Press, 2011), 195–99; Kate Masur, *An Example for All the Land: Emancipation and the Struggle over Equality in Washington, D.C.* (Chapel Hill: University of North Carolina Press, 2010), 22–31.

2. Nicholas Brewer to Lincoln, October 31, 1863, Abraham Lincoln Papers, Manuscript Division, Library of Congress, Washington, DC; *The Biographical Cyclopedia of Representative Men of Maryland and [the] District of Columbia* (Baltimore: National Biographical Publishing, 1879), 65–66.

3. W. Kimmel and Joshua M. Bosley to Lincoln, October 8, 1864, Lincoln Papers.

4. Josiah Benton, *Voting in the Field: A Forgotten Chapter of the Civil War* (Boston: Plimpton Press, 1915), 7; Jonathan W. White, *Emancipation, the Union Army, and the Reelection of Abraham Lincoln* (Baton Rouge: Louisiana State University Press, 2014), chap. 1; Jonathan W. White, "Canvassing the Troops: The Federal Government and the Soldiers' Right to Vote," *Civil War History* 50 (September 2004): 290–316; Jonathan W. White, "Citizens and Soldiers: Party Competition and the Debate in Pennsylvania over Permitting Soldiers to Vote, 1861–64," *American Nineteenth Century History* 5 (Summer 2004): 47–70.

5. *Civilian and Telegraph* (Cumberland, MD), March 17, 1863.

6. See, for example, George Vickers to Lincoln, November 12, 28, 1863, both in RG 110 (Records of the Provost Marshal General's Buruea [Civil War]), Entry 40 (Records of the Central Office, 1862–1889, Correspondence and Reports Relating to Fraudulent Activities of Provost Marshals, Bounty

Agents, and Other Persons, 1863–1865), National Archives and Records Administration, Washington, DC (hereafter NARA).

7. Lincoln to John A. J. Creswell, March 7, 17, 1864, in Roy P. Basler, et al., eds., *The Collected Works of Abraham Lincoln*, 9 vols. (New Brunswick, N.J.: Rutgers University Press, 1953), 7:226–27, 251.

8. *Tribune Almanac and Political Register for 1864* (New York: Tribune Association, 1864), 63.

9. Charles Lewis Wagandt, *The Mighty Revolution: Negro Emancipation in Maryland, 1862–1864* (Baltimore: Johns Hopkins Press, 1964; reprinted Baltimore: Maryland Center for History and Culture, 2005), 219–20.

10. Benton, *Voting in the Field*, 234–35; *Tribune Almanac and Political Register for 1865* (New York: Tribune Association, 1865), 55; *Baltimore Sun,* April 27, 1864.

11. "Address at Sanitary Fair, Baltimore, Maryland," April 18, 1864, in Basler, *Collected Works of Lincoln,* 7:301–3.

12. William Blair Lord and Henry M. Parkhurst, eds., *The Debates of the Constitutional Convention of the State of Maryland,* 3 vols. (Annapolis: Richard P. Bayly, 1864), 1:70, 131.

13. Lord and Parkhurst, *Debates,* 2:1,193–94, 1:240–41. On loyalty oaths in the Civil War Era, see Harold M. Hyman, *Era of the Oath: Northern Loyalty Tests during the Civil War and Reconstruction* (Philadelphia: University of Pennsylvania Press, 1954).

14. Lord and Parkhurst, *Debates,* 2:1,266–67. For concerns about frauds that appeared in similar debates in other states, see White, "Citizens and Soldiers," 50–54, 59–64; White, "Canvassing the Troops," 293–98.

15. Lord and Parkhurst, *Debates,* 2:1,270–72.

16. Lord and Parkhurst, *Debates,* 2:1,272–74; *Biographical Cyclopedia,* 518; Lincoln, "Proclamation of Amnesty and Reconstruction," December 8, 1863, in Basler, *Collected Works of Lincoln,* 7:53–56.

17. Lord and Parkhurst, *Debates,* 2:1,274–75; *Biographical Cyclopedia,* 189–90.

18. Lord and Parkhurst, *Debates,* 2:1,275.

19. Lord and Parkhurst, *Debates,* 2:1,280–81; *Biographical Cyclopedia,* 580.

20. Lord and Parkhurst, *Debates,* 2:1,281–82; *Bel Air Aegis and Intelligencer,* September 7, 1877.

21. Lord and Parkhurst, *Debates,* 2:1,282–85; *Baltimore Sun,* November 24, 1902.

22. Lord and Parkhurst, *Debates,* 2:1,299–1,303.

23. Maryland Constitution, art. 1, sec. 2–4; and art. 12, sec. 8–16 (1864).

24. Lord and Parkhurst, *Debates,* 3:1,872–74.

25. Benton, *Voting in the Field,* 243–44.

26. Lincoln and Stanton quoted in Michael Burlingame, *Abraham Lincoln: A Life,* 2 vols. (Baltimore: Johns Hopkins University Press, 2008), 2:713–14.

27. George Vickers to Augustus Bradford, September 14, 1864, in Lord and Parkhurst, *Debates,* 3:1,904.

28. Augustus Bradford to George Vickers, September 19, 1864, in Lord and Parkhurst, *Debates,* 3:1,905–6 (emphasis is Bradford's).

29. Vickers to Bradford, September 27, 1864, in Lord and Parkhurst, *Debates,* 3:1,907–10 (emphasis is Vickers's).

30. *War of the Rebellion: A Compilation of the Official Records of the Union and Confederate Armies,* 128 vols. (Washington, DC: Government Printing Office, 1880–1901), ser. 1, vol. 29, pt. 2, 394–95; Robert Schenck to Edwin M. Stanton, November 1, 1863, Lincoln Papers.

31. Bradford to Lincoln, October 31, 1863, Montgomery Blair to Lincoln, November 1, 1863, both in Lincoln Papers; Lincoln to Bradford, November 2, 1863, in Basler, *Collected Works of Lincoln,* 5:555–58. On Bradford's election in 1861, see Mitchell, *Maryland Voices,* 145–47, 161–63, 251–52.

32. J. Thomas Scharf, *History of Maryland, from the Earliest Period to the Present,* 3 vols. (Baltimore: John B. Piet, 1879), 3:566–67; Thomas Swann to Lincoln, October 26, 1863; Schenck to Lincoln, November 2, 1863; Bradford to Lincoln, November 3, 1863; Nicholas Brewer to Lincoln, November 7, 1863, all in Lincoln Papers; Lincoln to Swann, October 27, 1863, in Basler, *Collected Works of Lincoln,* 6:542–43.

33. Charles L. Wagandt, "Election by Sword and Ballot: The Emancipationist Victory of 1863," *Maryland Historical Magazine* 59 (June 1964): 143–64; Court-Martial Case File MM-1277, General Court-Martial Case Files, RG 153 (Records of the Office of the Judge Advocate General [Army]), NARA; John W. Crisfield to Montgomery Blair, November 8, 1863; Nicholas Brewer to Lincoln, November 13, 1863; Thomas Franklin to Francis J. Keffer, November 21, 1863; Donn Piatt to Lincoln, November 27, 1863; Thomas G. Pratt to Edwin M. Stanton, November 28, 1863, brief of Daniel Clarke, December 1863, all in Lincoln Papers.

34. George Vickers to Lincoln, November 12, 27, 28, 1863, all in RG 110, Entry 40.

35. Vickers to Bradford, September 27, 1864, in Lord and Parkhurst, *Debates,* 3:1,910–11.

36. Lord and Parkhurst, *Debates,* 3:1,911.

37. Bradford to Vickers, October 3, 1864, in Lord and Parkhurst, *Debates,* 3:1,913.

38. Lord and Parkhurst, *Debates,* 3:1,912–14. It is surprising that Madison would have taken this view in 1830, since he consistently argued during his career that a constitution did not represent the sovereign will of the people until it had been ratified by the people. See Jeffry H. Morrison, "James Madison, Justice Scalia, and Constitutional Interpretation," *Perspectives on Political Science* 48 (2019): 3–6.

39. Bradford to the judges of the election, October 8, 1864, in Lord and Parkhurst, *Debates,* 3:1,915. The state also circulated instructions for holding elections in the field that were essentially copied from Ohio's 1863 soldier vote law. A copy is in the Benjamin Franklin Taylor Papers in the Maryland Center for History and Culture Library. For the report of a state official who took presidential ballots to the field, see Richard King to Augustus W. Bradford, November 11, 1864, Adjutant General's Papers (S395), Maryland State Archives (thanks to Tim Orr for making me aware of these two documents).

40. W. Kimmel and Joshua M. Bosley to Lincoln, October 8, 1864, Lincoln Papers; Harold Holzer, *Lincoln and the Power of the Press: The War for Public Opinion* (New York: Simon and Schuster, 2014), 508.

41. Lord and Parkhurst, *Debates,* 3:1,925–26; Lincoln to Henry W. Hoffman, October 10, 1864, in Basler, *Collected Works of Lincoln,* 8:41–42; Hoffman to Lincoln, October 15, 16, 17, 1864; Charles C. Fulton to Lincoln, October 17, 21, 1864, all in Lincoln Papers. A group of Democrats approached Governor Bradford and requested permission to inspect the ballots from the field. The governor acquiesced; following their inspection of the votes, Bradford discarded 290 soldier votes, 285 for the constitution and 5 against. See Lord and Parkhurst, *Debates,* 3:1,919–25.

42. *Bel Air Aegis and Intelligencer,* October 28, 1864.

43. Sarah A. Richards to Lincoln, November 18, 1864, Lincoln Papers.

44. Mitchell, *Maryland Voices*, 394–96, 436–37, 439; Thomas Webster to Lincoln, October 27, 30, 1864; Charles C. Fulton to Lincoln, October 29, 1864, all in Lincoln Papers.

45. *Philadelphia Inquirer* quoted in *Easton* (Maryland) *Gazette*, November 5, 1864.

46. Lincoln quoted in Burlingame, *Abraham Lincoln*, 2:715, 725–26.

47. *Washington Evening Star*, November 2, 1864; *Baltimore Sun*, November 3, 1864.

48. Michael Burlingame, ed., *Lincoln Observed: Civil War Dispatches of Noah Brooks* (Baltimore: Johns Hopkins University Press, 1998), 141–42.

49. William Price to Lincoln, October 24, 1864, Lincoln Papers; Lord and Parkhurst, *Debates*, 3:1,915–16; *Cincinnati Daily Enquirer*, October 25, 1864.

50. Miles v. Bradford, 22 *Maryland Reports* 172–78 (1864).

51. Harry Gilmor, *Four Years in the Saddle* (New York: Harper and Brothers, 1866), 272–75. On fraud and intimidation in the presidential election of 1864, see White, *Emancipation, the Union Army, and the Reelection of Abraham Lincoln*, chap. 4; William A. Blair, *With Malice toward Some: Treason and Loyalty in the Civil War Era* (Chapel Hill: University of North Carolina Press, 2014), chap. 7; Richard Franklin Bensel, *The American Ballot Box in the Mid-Nineteenth Century* (New York: Cambridge University Press, 2004).

52. Lord and Parkhurst, *Debates* 3:1,916.

53. Lord and Parkhurst, *Debates* 3:1,917.

54. *Miles v. Bradford*, 179–82.

55. *Miles v. Bradford*, 179–82; Jonathan W. White, *Abraham Lincoln and Treason in the Civil War: The Trials of John Merryman* (Baton Rouge: Louisiana State University Press, 2011), 110.

56. US Eighth Census, 1860, *Maryland Slave Schedule* (Washington, DC, 1864); Fields, *Slavery and Freedom*, 24–25; *Biographical Cyclopedia*, 97–98.

57. Anderson v. Baker, 23 *Maryland Reports* 531–33 (1865); Hardesty v. Taft, 23 *Maryland Reports* 512 (1865).

58. *Tribune Almanac and Political Register for 1865*, 55; Henry W. Hoffman to Lincoln, November 7, 1864, Lincoln Papers.

59. Mitchell, *Maryland Voices*, 7, 359–60, 396–99, 436, 441–53, 469.

60. Maryland, *Constitutional Revision Study Documents of the Constitutional Convention of Maryland* (Baltimore: King Brothers, 1968), chap. 15; Baker, *Politics of Continuity*, chap. 7.

MARYLAND'S
WOMEN AT WAR

ROBERT W. SCHOEBERLEIN

T he Civil War profoundly divided Maryland's women. Denied by social constraints and the spirit of their times to take up arms, they sought other means to express their political alignment.[1] Both Unionist and secessionist women alike supported the war effort in multiple ways that exceeded their traditional gender role boundaries. This chapter provides an overview of Maryland women's activities during the conflict and the immediate postwar period. Rather than focusing upon a notable few, whose stories have been related elsewhere, this narrative seeks to identify less celebrated women and their patterns of involvement.[2] Whereas Unionist women supported their cause mostly through caregiving and charitable work, their secessionist sisters engaged in similar activities, but also aided the Confederate army, becoming nonbattlefield participants in the war. The organizational skills required by these activities allowed both groups of women to conduct successful large-scale fund-raising fairs. The immediate postwar period witnessed the continued involvement of women regardless of their wartime political viewpoints.

The scarcity of primary resource material relating to women impedes a fuller understanding of their contributions. Most archival holdings overrepresent the papers of upper-class males and exclude the less socially prominent, as well as immigrant and minority women. Another limitation is that the research presented here is largely based upon the activities of Baltimoreans, simply because both more historical material and press coverage from the city have survived. Through study of these scarce primary resources along with insights derived from recent scholarship, a clearer image of women's roles begins to emerge from the home front setting of the divided citizenry in Civil War Maryland.

* * *

UNIONIST WOMEN'S ROLES

Individual and small-scale efforts, spontaneous in nature, characterized the relief work of Unionist women at the outbreak of the Civil War.[3] Nursing care, the making of clothing and other articles, and the provision of food and drink predominated. During the April 19, 1861, Pratt Street Riot in Baltimore, Anna Marley sheltered members of the Sixth Massachusetts Regimental band in her modest house, binding their wounds and feeding them.[4] Marley, as well as many other East Baltimore residents, opened their dwellings as safe havens to northern volunteers that day. In the riot's aftermath, Adeline Tyler, an Episcopalian deaconess and nurse, aided two injured Massachusetts volunteers for a month. In May 1861, as the first Maryland Union regiments formed, women gathered to sew haversacks and other useful articles in female circles formed in previous years to make clothing for the city's destitute. Sometimes women offered water to thirsty Union volunteers. A soldier noted, "In several places women, generally Negroes, came out with pails of water."[5] When wounded Massachusetts troops borne on stretchers passed through Baltimore's street en route to a hospital, citizens purchased oranges and other refreshments at a nearby city market and offered them to the men.[6] These spontaneous goodwill gestures of support continued throughout the war. A Connecticut volunteer stationed at Fort McHenry opined, "If the Secesh in Baltimore are the meanest . . . the union [people] are certainly the best and truest."[7]

Baltimoreans inaugurated their first formal relief efforts for US soldiers during June of 1861, when thirty-two men banded together to pledge their own funds and to create the Union Relief Association. While men initiated, administered, and financially sustained the effort, its inspiration was attributed to a "few [unnamed] benevolent ladies," who subsequently formed their own auxiliary. The association's initial task was to distribute bread and drinking water to every passing regiment on the march between city railroad stations. In September, the organizers opened the Union Relief Rooms, two warehouses that had been refitted with a kitchen and dining facilities to accommodate one thousand men. "One hundred and fifty thousand men were fed during the first year" and, by war's end . . . "[u]pwards of one million . . . soldiers, teamsters, refugees [newly released Union and Confederate prisoners of war], in addition to large numbers of disabled, discharged, and furloughed men, had been welcomed and relieved."[8]

The Ladies Union Relief Association, a formal auxiliary, was organized in October 1861. Mary Johnson, the fifty-nine-year-old wife of Reverdy Johnson, US senator from Maryland, served as its first head. The Ladies Association initially focused its activities at the Union Relief Rooms and, later, at the nearby National Hospital near the Camden Street Railroad Station.[9] Female volunteers played an integral role in the hospital's efforts by running the kitchen, assisting the nursing staff, constructing hospital garments, distributing reading and writing material, and occasionally organizing concerts and magic lantern shows. Annual reports of the association show that the women became increasingly proficient in their duties as time progressed, but success did not necessarily bring clinical detachment. Late in 1862, reflecting upon her ward experiences, association executive Sallie P. Cushing wrote: "It makes me so sad to go to the hospitals, and also see the soldiers going around on crutches—it is a melancholy sight, we will be a nation of cripples before this war is over."[10]

A separate German Ladies Union Relief Association, representing one of the largest ethnic groups in the city, was created as well. Many male German immigrants, some supporting both abolition and President Lincoln, volunteered for service with the newly organized Maryland regiments. German American women favored picnics, chorales, and concerts to raise funds for soldier aid.

Similar women's relief groups eventually formed in all areas of Baltimore, especially in proximity to the US military care facilities. These temporary hospitals were placed in prewar open spaces within the city, often in city parks or squares. Women from the surrounding neighborhoods, usually numbering from fifty to seventy-five individuals, supplemented the nursing efforts and made friendly visits. The East Baltimore branch, for example, focused its activities at the Patterson Park Hospital and provided refreshments to the soldiers getting off the train at the President Street Railroad Station.

Women's relief associations also organized elsewhere, with many important ones based in western Maryland. In August 1861, fifty women came together to initiate a Frederick City organization under Julia Bantz.[11] A Hagerstown association, led by Susan Harry, formed in November of that same year.[12] Smaller towns such as Middletown, Mechanicstown, Funkstown, and Boonsboro set up similar groups. These women provided invaluable service to the sick and wounded men in local encampments and hospitals, and on the nearby battlefields of South Mountain and Antietam.

Baltimore's African American women also were active in relief activities, but their work is not nearly as well documented. In 1863, with the initial recruitment of the US Colored Troops units, at least two groups did form. We know very little about the Colored Ladies Union Association other than the name of its president, Miss Mary A. Gibbs, daughter of Mary F. Gibbs, a middle-aged dressmaker, widow, and mother of nine.[13] The second group, the First Colored Christian Commission, counted Mrs. Annetta Jordon as one of its leaders.[14] Jordon, an educated and wealthy widow, previously had led the Dorcas Society of Baltimore's Bethel AME Church, an organization whose members constructed garments for the poor.[15] Both entities combined their efforts to host an 1864 Thanksgiving dinner for the African American soldiers at McKim's Mansion Hospital.[16]

Some women took their nursing skills to nearby battlefields. Jane Boswell Moore, a white, fifth-generation Baltimorean, was descended from a family line of women dedicated to nursing soldiers. In 1814, her great-grandmother assisted the wounded in the aftermath of the Battle of North Point.[17] With the onset of the Civil War, the 21-year-old Moore and her mother served as nurses at various battlefield hospitals surrounding Maryland. For four weeks after the Battle of Gettysburg, she toiled at a makeshift field hospital where she aided both the Union and Confederate wounded.[18] After the carnage of Petersburg, for two weeks she tended to the relief and suffering of African American soldiers. Many were Baltimore residents serving with the Thirty-Ninth US Colored Infantry Regiment.

Other women centered their attention on aiding the wives and dependents whom Maryland soldiers left behind.[19] Elizabeth Streeter, part of a husband and wife team that devoted their energies to war-related relief, was the first to see the need of supplemental support for families of Union soldiers. In November 1863, she assisted the organization and later presided over the Ladies Aid Society for the Relief of Soldiers' Families, which included in its efforts the relief of destitute female refugees. The society, funded by private and municipal sources, rented a house to accommodate these refugees, and its members, consisting of twenty-five women, visited the families of soldiers and distributed money, food, clothing, shoes, and fuel. Over 1,200 families were assisted. One association officer wrote, "Mrs. Streeter . . . did more than all of the rest of us together. I did not visit much. All of it was disagreeable work. Not nearly so satisfactory as going to the hospitals."[20]

Some women chose morale-building activities for soldiers. Elizabeth Graham, who had already organized and supervised the first kitchen at the National Hospital, pursued this work at the other Baltimore-based medical facilities until stricken by "camp fever" (typhus). After her recovery, she re-directed her energies toward organizing the Union Assemblies, an effort to promote friendships between the US officers and the Baltimore citizenry.[21] Military leaders and their wives or companions were the honored guests at a series of social events held in winter. The assemblies allowed for light-hearted diversion and social conversation between citizens and the regimental com-manders whose camps were situated throughout the city. The affairs, however, were unlike those in the prewar era: no fancy dresses and only modest fare of sandwiches and coffee.

Yet women did not confine themselves only to relief efforts, nursing work, and entertaining the troops. They organized and orchestrated patriotic activi-ties in Baltimore and elsewhere. Historian Jeanie Attie points out that "denied masculine means of political expression, women everywhere turned to public, symbolic ways of demonstrating their nationalism."[22] Flag presentations by women to Union volunteers from Maryland and elsewhere took place fre-quently during 1861 and afterward.[23] Thirty-four teenaged girls (representing the number of states in the Union before the war), each dressed in white with a red, white, and blue sash, added to the pageantry of some of these ceremonies. These participants were students known as "The Young Misses" from Balti-more's Eastern Female High School.[24]

On two separate occasions in August 1863, the city's African American community made flag presentations to the Fourth US Colored Troops, a regi-ment composed of many Baltimoreans. Ceremonies were held at Camp Birney, a segregated training facility located several blocks south of Druid Hill Park. A magnificent silk national flag (costing $75 in 1863; $1,230 in 2018 dollars) was given to the Fourth in a ceremony that included some three thousand African Americans joining their voices together in singing "John Brown's Body."[25]

In late August, a group calling itself "The Colored Ladies of Baltimore" bestowed a custom-made silk US flag in a program that included Baltimore's Bethel AME choir "sing[ing] some of their choicest pieces on the occasion."[26] Sixty-three-year-old Mary A. Prout headed the flag donation committee. The 1864 Baltimore City Directory lists her as a confectioner, but census sources also describe her as a "preceptor" and a "doctoress," a reference to her role as an educator and operator of a private primary school.[27] Prout was as well a skilled and dedicated fund-raiser. "During the early days of Bethel [Church], when it was poor and in debt, she was constantly devising ways and means of relieving it; now leading off in a festival; now an excursion; and now [walking] the streets with a subscription book."[28]

In what may be characterized as the ultimate transgressive act of patriotism, a few Maryland women disguised their gender in order to serve in the Union army. Historians DeAnne Blanton and Lauren M. Cook have documented about 250 cases of women soldiers serving during the Civil War, with at least six Marylanders donning Union uniforms. Two served as privates with the Second Maryland Cavalry until their discovery in August 1862.[29] Another pair joined the Second Maryland Infantry for six months before being detected.[30] Two more Marylanders saw service with the Signal Corps.[31] And seventeen-year-old Mary E. French, from the Hagerstown area, signed on with the Eighth West Virginia Infantry. After her gender was discovered, as she was being expelled from the regiment, she reportedly announced that she "would rather soldier, than eat."[32]

Maryland's Unionist women came forward immediately to aid the federal government in an unofficial, yet very essential, capacity. Hands-on nursing care to sick and wounded soldiers, relief aid to service members and their families, along with the organization of morale-building exercises, directly supported the war effort. A few, though officially barred from doing so, joined the Union military to shoulder a rifle and defend the US flag.

SECESSIONIST WOMEN'S ROLES

Maryland women provided overt and clandestine support to the Confederacy throughout the Civil War. They risked harassment, arrest, body searches, confinement, and banishment by the US military authorities. Even compassionate, humanitarian gestures by the women toward wounded Confederate soldiers might be met with a rebuke. During the summer of 1863, a wounded Confederate POW witnessed "a party of Baltimore ladies who were anxious to contribute to the well being of the [hospitalized] Confederate prisoners . . . [and] were driven from the sidewalk by a volley of decayed eggs hurled at them by the hospital guards."[33] Undeterred, the women continued to aid their husbands, lovers, sons, and brothers in gray. This support expanded after the cessation of hostilities to embrace the people of the war-torn South.

Like their Unionist counterparts, secessionist women called upon their domestic skills to aid and comfort the fighting men of the Confederacy. Small-scale, discrete efforts characterized the initial work of the women. They made clothing for soldiers, smuggled to the front correspondence and everything from buttons to blankets, along with providing nursing care. It is difficult to provide extensive detail of these activities since "the keeping of such records would be regarded as evidence . . . of treason."[34] As a result, the reminiscences of the women years later form the basis of the narrative.

Women in sewing circles met clandestinely in the evenings to work for the soldiers, and, later in the war, for the prisoners of war.[35] One participant remembered that "[w]e were often obliged to wear as bustles an entire suit of Confederate uniform, or 20 yards of gray cloth" to prevent its discovery by the Union authorities.[36] Apparently, this same spirit of devotion extended from foot soldier up to the chief executive. As a gift for Confederate president Jefferson Davis, one "noble-hearted lady of Baltimore" crafted an elaborate bed quilt featuring a large Confederate flag with the names of Davis's cabinet members and his main generals, though the US military confiscated it before it reached its intended recipient.[37] Rebecca Lloyd Shippen, one of Baltimore's "Monument Street Girls," recalled how the young women once put aside their needlework to set James Ryder Randall's stirring poem "My Maryland" to music. The song they produced, "Maryland, My Maryland," went on to become one of the most popular tunes of the Confederacy.[38]

But these efforts pale in comparison to those of Jane Claudia Johnson. Born and raised in North Carolina, Johnson returned to the South from Maryland to solicit funds to uniform and arm the First Maryland Infantry, CSA. She won accolades from the regiment after delivering to Harpers Ferry uniforms, equipment, tents, and five hundred rifles with ammunition. Gen. Bradley T. Johnson, her husband, recounted that she would "visit with the Maryland units in Virginia periodically throughout the entire war, serving as a courier between Gen. Joseph Johnston and Jefferson Davis and later providing the soldiers with a library and a church for their religious services."[39]

Relief work directed to Confederate POWs held in Maryland was another female project. After the Battle of Antietam in September 1862, a large number of POWs were transferred from the hospitals in Frederick to Fort McHenry in Baltimore for prisoner exchange purposes. "Many ladies greeted them at the [train] depot with baskets containing apples, cakes, sandwiches, etc."[40] Joanna Barry recalled making clothing for prisoners at Fort McHenry and Point Lookout.[41] In April 1862, a woman related that "I had the pleasure of helping to pack a large covered wagon of new clothing, eatables . . . and several hundred dollars" for the Confederate POWs in Baltimore at that time.[42]

A stream of secessionist women began arriving at the fort with additional food, drink, and other comforts. Within a few days, canteens, haversacks, and even officer uniforms began showing up, all items useful to the men after their parole. This practice was halted abruptly by US authorities.[43] Even so, monetary collections for Confederate POWs continued, with one totaling a generous $2,200.[44] As the war continued, the US military hoped to dampen similar citizen support for these men by further restricting access and other means, including, as we shall see, the outright arrest of those providing overt material aid.

Secessionist women presented flags to Maryland's and other Confederate army units early in the war. Whereas Unionist women could either make, or simply order, a national flag from one of Baltimore's several military supply businesses without any suspicion, secessionist women risked arrest for their participation in a clandestine enterprise. Sewing a flag necessitated the high skill level that might be found in an informal sewing circle.[45] Regimental flags often featured painted designs on silk, which required an experienced craftsperson willing to take on the order, despite the risk of arrest.[46] Then, once the flag was completed, the tricky task of smuggling the flag south presented its own perils. This task became increasingly difficult as those journeying through the federal lines endured searches by the Union military.

The flags made in Virginia by sisters Hettie and Jennie Cary, along with their cousin Constance Cary, are of special note. Though the siblings are better known for their connection to the "Maryland, My Maryland" song, they were part of the team that sewed the first Confederate battle flags. As cousin Constance recalled, "They were jaunty squares of scarlet crossed with dark blue edged in white, the cross bearing stars to indicate the number of the seceded states. We set our best stitches upon them, [and] edged [them] with golden fringes."[47]

Henrietta McLaughin, whose husband served in the Confederate navy, may have been the first Maryland woman to make a flag presentation. In early June 1861, she journeyed to Richmond to deliver a banner to the commander of the Baltimore Battalion.[48] In July 1861, Mrs. John James and Mrs. Pendleton gave a large fifteen-starred flag with "tassels and gold bullion" to the Parrett Guards of the Fifth Louisiana Regiment, a unit in which two sons of Mrs. James served.[49] A silk flag, featuring "a galaxy of eleven stars of pure white, and a single star merely circumscribed by a white outline" (this twelfth "aspiration" star to represent Maryland in hope that it still might secede), was sewn by a number of "patriotic young ladies" and presented to Capt. J. Lyle Clarke's Company.[50] The "Ladies of East Baltimore" smuggled a flag said to be worth $2,000 via the "underground railroad" (a secret network of southern sympathizers) to Richmond in January of 1862, for Captain Dorsey's Company of the First Maryland Regiment, CSA.[51]

Maryland's secessionist women also aided sick and wounded soldiers and provided nursing care to men on distant battlefields. Matilda Saunders, a woman in her mid-thirties, supervised "several war hospitals . . . and [also] conveyed quantities of medicine, food, and clothing from Baltimore homes to soldiers in the field."[52] She worked devotedly at temporary field hospitals at Antietam and Gettysburg, and the Confederate-run Receiving Hospital at Gordonsville, Virginia. She viewed these efforts as her life's highest achievement as her grave marker notes her service as a "devoted nurse" at these wartime locations.[53] Irene Orndorff, Dora Hoffman, and Euphemia Goldsborough, along with countless others, also nursed wounded Confederate prisoners at South Mountain, Frederick, and Gettysburg.[54]

SECESSIONIST WOMEN:
A FIFTH COLUMN ELEMENT

Maryland secessionist women, however, stepped outside the boundaries of these traditional, domestic roles from the beginning of the war by rejecting the authority of the male "Union occupiers," as they termed them. As suggested by historians LeeAnn Whites and Alecia Long, women in Union-occupied cities created a "second front" that can be perceived as an alternative form of military engagement.[55] Because Maryland never seceded, the state's secessionist women (as well as noncombatant men) are more accurately described as a "fifth column." A fifth column is a group within a country at war that is sympathetic to, or working for, its enemies, either in an overt or clandestine manner. Fifth column actions are usually performed behind the lines of combat. In this case secessionist women actively assisted the enemy from behind the lines.

Documentary evidence from 1861 suggests that the US military was deeply concerned that the Confederate army might enter Maryland and, in combination with an insurrectionary force (read fifth column) within Baltimore, cut the state off and perhaps even capture Washington. Anxious federal and Baltimore city officials were well aware of the danger.[56] As the authorities suspected that many of the wealthiest citizens of the Baltimore favored the Confederacy, the funding available to arm such a fifth column force would have been ample. Searches for caches of arms stored in private homes continued throughout the war.[57]

Secessionist women proved themselves to be a threat to the Union cause on many levels and for a variety of reasons. Patricia Dockman Anderson's study of 109 US military arrests of secessionist women in Baltimore reveals the scope of Confederate activities in which they participated. Anderson divided these into two broad categories: those arrested under an array of "disloyal" activities and those whose actions warranted the more serious charge of treason or the equally serious charge of violating the rules of war.[58] The latter category often resulted in a prison sentence.

A further analysis of the arrests included in Anderson's study provides additional insights.[59] The charge of disloyalty was the most prevalent, with "Southern sympathizer" appearing most often as the general descriptor. These women represented all social classes, and the majority of incidents in which they participated appears to have been spontaneous or a reaction to comments by a Unionist.[60] The simple display of a secessionist red and white emblem or utterance of a verbal slur against the Union or a Union soldier might lead to detainment or temporary confinement.

Verbal and physical assaults by women on US troops, though unreported in newspapers, did occur. Unionist Samuel Harrison of Baltimore noted in his diary that "the [US] soldiers are not only assaulted . . . with insulting words & gestures, but the grossest acts are committed, sufficient to enrage any man."[61] In one entry, he recounted a house search of a suspected secessionist where a Mrs. McCoy stepped forward from among a crowd of women gathered outside to intentionally interfere "and abused the officers saying all manner of taunting things."[62] Writing of a local street known for its "notorious treasonable demonstrations," Harrison reflected that the women who resided there "in some instances have forgotten ordinary decency [and] have actually cursed the soldiers aloud as they passed."[63] Lastly, a Mrs. Whitney, an acquaintance of Harrison, described to him an incident she witnessed while shopping where a Union "officer came in [to the store] wiping his face with a handkerchief & said a *lady* had that moment spit in his face upon the street."[64] How best to react to such disrespectful and defiant public acts seemed to bedevil the US military administrators for the duration of the war.[65]

The second most frequent reason for arrest was acting as a courier for mail to and from the Confederacy. As Claudia Floyd has noted, "Confederate women in Baltimore created a subterranean network of intelligence that stretched across Maryland and down through the Shenandoah Valley of Virginia."[66] Baltimore resident Mary E. Sawyer was charged with "violation of the laws of war" and sentenced to two years in prison for carrying mail south. Sawyer, while confined, appealed to President Lincoln and was allowed to go south and join her husband, who served in the Confederate army.[67] Evidence of this statewide network of women is apparent from several sources. Seventeen-year-old Sallie Pollock, from western Maryland, attempted to deliver secret messages throughout the Shenandoah Valley in Virginia, only to be arrested and sent to the penitentiary in Pittsburg for several months.[68]

The third most frequent reason for arrest was the charge of providing aid and comfort to the enemy. What actually constituted aid or comfort appears to have been open to interpretation by US military authorities. Offering whiskey and food to Confederate POWs passing on a Baltimore street resulted in the arrest of Mary O'Keefe and Bridget Jennings.[69] A December 1863 US military raid at a Baltimore boarding house netted a large quantity of contraband goods that included "about one thousand letters . . . [and] nearly one bushel of Confederate military buttons." Eighteen men and women were arrested, but only three were temporarily detained. Battlefield nurse Matilda Saunders was one of them; the sole woman, she was banished to the South for the duration of the war, a fate of many other women caught with contraband.[70] However, Saunders had been lucky up to this time. She had made six or seven previous clandestine supply trips back and forth to the Confederacy without being detected.

Though arrests for outright spying were numerically insignificant, the case of Catherine V. Baxley stands out. Baxley, a thirty-three-year-old Baltimore County resident, merchant's wife, and Virginia native, was arrested for disloyalty in December 1861. The federal government later charged her with being a spy for the Confederacy after she returned from Richmond with concealed letters, including a commission signed by Jefferson Davis. While jailed, she bragged to her captors that "some five months ago she had sent some 200 guns to the Southern army," though later she recanted her claim.[71] "Baxley remained defiant in her cell in the Old Capitol Prison [in Washington, DC] where she soon became known for her temper, foul language, and giving a guard a black eye."[72] Appealing to Secretary of War Edwin Stanton for her release, she criticized the North's "women-imprisoning process" by holding that "the Southern man ... has too exalted an opinion of woman, her attributes and her mission to treat her other than as a woman." Her appeal did not help her case, but in June, Baxley was released and sent south for the duration of the war.

Maryland's secessionist women expanded beyond their traditional domestic sphere from the earliest days of the war. In addition to their expected role as caregivers, they actively worked against the US government by embracing activities to benefit the Confederate cause. Provisioning its soldiers, gathering and dispersing intelligence southward, and even spying, were all weapons they used against the Union. While a Maryland woman serving in the Confederate armed forces has yet to be identified, Maryland's secessionist women acted as part of a fifth column to demoralize Union soldiers and undermine the US military administration within the state.

FUND-RAISING FAIRS

Unionist and secessionist women each held a large and successful fund-raising fair, though the latter one took place after the war in 1866. An examination of both events adds insights into the women's motivations and their organizational prowess.

Fund-raising fairs in Baltimore had long been a staple in the schedule of annual city events. In one of the earliest recorded, held in 1827, Baltimoreans raised $1,600 to help alleviate the sufferings of children during the Greek War of Independence.[73] Most early Baltimore fairs appear to have been orchestrated by women to benefit their own church congregations. However, this soon changed at the onset of the Civil War. The demands of the current conflict and the immediate postwar era, however, enlarged the focus of such events to include the care of soldiers and their dependents, war orphans, veterans, and the destitute population of the South.

THE US FAIR FOR SOLDIER RELIEF
(BALTIMORE SANITARY FAIR)

The 1864 Baltimore Sanitary Fair provided a large-scale means for Unionist women to combine their benevolent and patriotic impulses.[74] Other cities across the Union, such as Chicago and Boston, had successfully produced such events. Proceeds from urban fairs had swelled the coffers of the US Christian and the US Sanitary Commissions, the two major national relief organizations for the Union armed forces. Both entities had Maryland-based committees with local agents who provided coordinated aid to both Union encampments and regional battlefields.

The idea of holding a Maryland fair to raise funds for these organizations first arose in Baltimore in the fall of 1863. Two members of the Ladies Union Relief Association, Ann Bowen and Fanny Turnbull, are credited with the initial promotion of the event. Bowen, a thirty-six-year-old recording secretary and "a South Carolinian & yet a very strong Union Person," proposed the idea.[75] Her spouse, a Unitarian minister, served as chaplain of the National Hospital where he "devote[d] all his leisure time, in fact all his time to the soldiers."[76] Harriet Hyatt, a native Marylander and battlefield nurse who was active in the US Christian Commission's local branch, is also counted as a founding fair organizer.

A series of women's organizational meetings held in Baltimore occurred in December 1863. No minutes have survived, so only scant details of the proceedings are available. At a second gathering of county women on December 10, the group adopted three recommendations that appeared in the *Baltimore American and Commercial Advertiser:* that Maryland counties and towns set up committees to define and organize local participation in the Baltimore Fair, that the event be held during Easter week 1864 (it was later scheduled to begin on April 19), and that a list of items wanted for sale at the fair be made up so that the public might be solicited for donations. Though men were encouraged to assist in gathering the articles, they had no active involvement in these initial organizational steps. By the third meeting on December 19, seventy-six women had banded together to shape and promote the relief fair.[77]

Members of the fair's committee came primarily from white, upper middle class, merchant households in the Baltimore area. Wives of lawyers composed the second-largest group. A sample of more than half of the women revealed their median age to be forty-five years. Most were Maryland-born; however, a few came from other states, both North and South, and one was foreign-born. African American women were barred from participation. The names of only two single women appeared on the committee.[78]

The organizers embraced promotion and fund-raising measures used by earlier Sanitary Fairs. Popular appeals generated widespread publicity and built momentum. Fair solicitations ranged from circular leaflets to newspaper advertisements. In December, thousands of circulars went out to newspapers and individuals, requesting "[f]ancy articles" but "even an ironing-holder, quilted of old calico will be acceptable to us."[79]

The women issued direct written appeals. Ann Bowen wrote to William Whittingham, Maryland's Episcopal bishop and a staunch Unionist, to request six of his autographs and photographs to be raffled at the fair. When his pictures did not arrive, she asked if he would sit for his portrait, explaining that "in my ardent zeal for the cause which you love so much, I dare to do [what] at other times would simply be impertinence."[80] Augusta Shoemaker addressed a businessman in a more temperate tone: "The women of Maryland, intend holding a fair . . . and I now write to ask for a contribution. . . . I ought not to be surprised at an unfavorable response . . . but nevertheless think it my duty, to make every exertion in every way to further this object."[81]

Items for sale and monetary donations soon began flowing into the fair's offices. Women involved in relief activities at military hospitals around Baltimore gathered to prepare items for their respective display tables. "The Ladies of these societies . . . meet weekly . . . at an early hour in the evening and go to work in earnest—some in cutting out clothes, silks and other goods . . . others, preparing the work, and many diligently engaged in plying the needle."[82] Money, along with random gifts of goods such as bolts of cloth or china, was soon forthcoming.

Publications served as fund-raising supplements to the organizing effort. Almira Hart Lincoln Phelps, the driving force behind one project, solicited short stories and poetry from noted authors and personalities throughout the Union. The persistence of the fair's corresponding secretary was formidable. On one occasion, having received a check in lieu of a manuscript, she respectfully expressed shock and remarked that "it deemed like asking for bread and receiving a stone."[83] Phelps, a seventy-one-year-old former school headmistress and noted author in her own right, was the editor of *Our Country—In Its Relations to The Past, Present and Future: A National Book*. This volume, dedicated "to the Mothers, Wives and Sisters of the Loyal States," contained material that celebrated the Union as well as two essays that advocated a wider sphere for women.

From the beginning, the fair's organizers had guarded expectations for the overall financial success of their event, and they faced competition from other cities holding similar events. The New York Metropolitan Fair partially overlapped Baltimore's, while Philadelphia's gathering was slated for just weeks later in June. There were three other cautionary factors. Committee members feared that the women's household responsibilities, combined with the scarcity of goods in a wartime economy, would keep women from extending themselves. Thinking of the tasks involved, the organizers worried that "many domestic women may hesitate . . . their own domestic duties demand all their attention; and that, moreover they have nothing to spare in these 'hard times.'"[84] As one woman confided to her spouse: "[the fair] is a secondary consideration with me I assure you. I must first attend to home duties & all that calls upon me here. Whatever I can do that will not interfere in the least with them will be cheerfully done."[85]

Anxiety over the possible lack of female participation brought the active solicitation of men to supplement the cause. "Lady officers were at first selected, but as the enterprise appeared too formidable for their unassisted labors, it was agreed that a number of gentlemen should be chosen" to provide aid.[86] Men were appointed to the positions of treasurer and secretary; the committee on finance was all male. A parallel men's committee arose featuring its own president and managers. Though no meeting minutes of this auxiliary exist to provide a deeper insight into their activities, they likely solicited funding and donations, as had been the case in similar fairs elsewhere. Men also acted as floor traffic managers throughout the run of the fair and provided assistance within the New England kitchen, the fair's restaurant.[87] While the role of the men in the restaurant cannot be determined, it may have pertained to some of the fair's most special guests: the recently released Union prisoners of war brought in from the city's military hospitals. Their emaciated condition, on daily view within the restaurant, was a stark reminder of the importance of relief efforts. The kitchen staff, "fed and comforted . . . those martyrs to our great cause, and monuments of Rebel inhumanity."[88]

The women also feared that the organizations that would benefit from the fair's proceeds might not elicit sympathy from all loyal Marylanders. The financial allegiance of many might rest more with local soldier relief efforts—those geared specifically to Maryland volunteers and their families, rather than with the seemingly impersonal bureaucratic agencies outside the state. Referring to the Sanitary Commission, historian Lori Ginzberg observes that "people were suspicious of an organization that seemed to absorb enormous amounts of money and still cried out for more."[89]

The greatest danger to the success of the fair was the division of Maryland's citizenry into Unionist and secessionist factions. Southern counties with large secessionist populations, namely St. Mary's, Charles, Somerset, Caroline, Wicomico, and Queen Anne's, sent no official delegations. As the Eastern Shore diarist Samuel Harrison wrote, "Sentiment in this state is so divided—and so many of those who are accustomed to spend money are disloyal . . . it can not be reasonably expected that this fair should produce near as much as it would [if] this state [was] united in sentiment."[90] On the eve of the fair, the *Baltimore Clipper* made a dire prediction: "It is not expected that the proceeds of this fair will equal those of the Northern cities . . . whose society is not thronged with enemies of the Government."[91]

Acting on a resolution of the Baltimore city council, Mayor John Chapman issued a proclamation asking businesses to close at noon on April 18; most complied. Pupils at the city's public schools likewise enjoyed a half-day off. The frenetic pace of city life came virtually to a standstill as a large military parade with over three thousand soldiers commenced at 2 P.M. Starting at Monument Square, the column, nearly a mile long, wended its way through the heart of the business district as the Eighth New York and Second US Artillery bands played for an estimated thirty thousand persons lining the streets. A second parade featuring three thousand newly enlisted African American soldiers followed later that day.[92]

At the invitation of the female organizers, President Lincoln agreed to preside over the opening ceremonies at the fair. Lincoln, with an entourage of political leaders in tow, toured the site afterward. The president's appearance in Baltimore held symbolic importance for city Unionists. For loyal citizens it offered both a chance to display their devotion to the man who embodied the Union and to cast off doubts about Baltimore's political sympathies. By opening the Maryland fair, Lincoln had the opportunity to express his confidence in the city's loyalty to the Union.

The fair's site, the Maryland Institute in the heart of Baltimore's downtown, appeared at its peak of splendor on the night of Lincoln's visit. A thousand flickering gas lamps brightly lit up the great hall's rectangular space and in the center, just behind the speaker's platform, stood the Floral Temple. Trimmed with wreaths, evergreens, and flowers of every color, the octagonal, domed structure rose over thirty feet. Inside the temple, a cascading fountain held varieties of fragrant water flowers in its basin. At either end of the building stood large ornamental arches draped with national flags, surmounted by jets of gaslight. The remaining space, around the perimeter and in the center, housed lavish display tables arranged by the organizers. With red, white, and blue a favored color scheme, US flags, carved eagles, framed portraits of Union heroes, and evergreens predominated. Suspended above the Baltimore County tables, opposite the main entrance, an allegorical depiction of "the Goddess of Liberty" vied for the fair-goer's attention.

For the more culturally inclined, and those whose wallets escaped the temptations of the main hall, a fee-for-admission fine arts gallery on the third floor featured paintings culled from local and northern private collections, with subjects ranging from the poetic to the patriotic. Yet, amid the gold-leaf frames of the tasteful room, the prominent display of a large silk US flag served as a reminder of a secondary purpose of the event: Maryland's Unionists sought to expunge the memory of the 1861 Baltimore Riot by replacing it with an outpouring of Unionist devotion on its third anniversary. Embroidered in the flag's field were the words "April 19th, 1864—May the Union and Friendship of the Future obliterate the anguish of the Past." The flag's seamstress, Christie Johnson, offered an explanation of her work: "We have wrought this field in needle-work in weaving paternal love with every silken thread, and writing out our fidelity to the whole Union, with every stitch," she said.[93] Miss Johnson later presented the flag to the people of Massachusetts.

The attendance of ordinary Marylanders ultimately determined the overall success of the two-week event. Despite the apparent solidarity of the state's Unionist population, the Maryland fair can be termed only a modest financial success compared with similar events in the North during 1864. The net proceeds were just over $80,000.[94] In contrast, the New York and Philadelphia fairs each cleared over $1,000,000. However, those cities had more than double the population of Baltimore, according to the 1860 US Census.[95] (New York City and Brooklyn combined contained over one million residents.) Yet, when compared to all similar soldier relief fairs, the Maryland total was respectable. Competition for donations from other cities clearly affected Baltimore's net result, but the economic realities of a city in wartime and divisions among Maryland's citizens were probably the largest factors in limiting the financial success of the Baltimore fair.[96]

Maryland Unionists, nonetheless, regarded their efforts as successful. At the closing ceremonies on May 2, Governor Augustus Bradford stated that "success is not to be estimated merely by its financial results, but by the wholesome moral influences it has exerted . . . it has brought together loyal women . . .

and served to show that American patriotism is confined to no climate, nor indigenous to any particular soil."The press singled out the organizers and participants for compliments. The *Baltimore American* lauded "the noble women of Maryland who have labored so long and so well . . . [they] deserve all praise and honor."[97]

Unfortunately, few primary documents exist to assess the women's own perception of their efforts. A reminiscence by Elizabeth Blanchard Randall provides a rare, illuminating example. Randall, who supervised the Anne Arundel County effort, spent several days away from her husband, children, and other responsibilities in order to prepare her stands. Upon his arrival in Baltimore on April 24, her husband "found her very happy as she had been the whole week taking charge of two tables."[98] Evidently, Mrs. Randall received both the approval and encouragement of her spouse for her soldier relief activities. With her husband apparently supportive of her volunteer work in Annapolis, she recalled years later, "He insisted on my taking part in an immense fair to raise funds for the Sanitary commission, to which the Ann Arundel table, of which I had the management, was able to contribute $1000."[99] Elizabeth Blanchard Randall's reluctance to take credit for her actions may stem from the fact that she was writing a complimentary life sketch of her deceased husband, an accomplished Maryland politician. Yet, even in her modest and limited comments, one can detect the pride of her accomplishment at the fair.

The Maryland Fair did succeed in fostering a benevolent patriotic spirit among the state's loyal populace. Even before the event ended, Baltimore's African American community expressed interest in holding a similar fair for the sake of their sons in uniform. "We have heard them express impatience at being held in dependence on their white brethren, in this matter," the *New Era* reported.[100]

The "Colored State Union Fair," as it was known, was held in late November 1864. While the identities of the committee members are unknown, it is likely that key individuals belonged to the Bethel AME Church. Its prewar congregation of approximately 1,400 made it the third largest of Baltimore's Black churches; it had hosted soldier recruitment meetings and sent several companies of its congregants into the army.[101] Bethel's lecture hall, just a few blocks from the Maryland Institute, hosted the fair.

Notices for the Colored Fair appeared in several of the Baltimore newspapers in mid-November 1864. Solicitations for goods and donations from the public to benefit sick and wounded soldiers stipulated that the proceeds would be distributed to the men "without distinction of color." On November 17, Frederick Douglass, in Baltimore as part of a lecture tour, spoke at Bethel with proceeds from the admission fees for his lecture earmarked for the fair's coffers. African American women's societies and church circles prepared their handiwork and coordinated and ran their fair tables. Meals were provided by a "New England Kitchen," likely modeled on those in previous Sanitary Fairs.[102] While no detailed description or report related to the event seems to have survived, the enterprise netted $1,827.34 for soldier relief.[103]

In summary, the women of Maryland's Sanitary Fairs were barred from the formal political process but managed nevertheless to adapt their traditional domestic skills to meet a large-scale organizational challenge and make a profound statement of moral and benevolent import in a time of crisis—a public act of no small measure. The fairs unleashed the charitable impulse of women unto different pathways and gave rise "to a spate of new and newly defined causes, most of which were tied to a domestically defined identity," in the postwar era.[104] Enhanced societal and political roles for women lay years ahead in the lives of their granddaughters, but in their own era, their soldier relief fairs were a triumph of women's spirit and ability.

IMMEDIATE POSTWAR EFFORTS

By the winter of 1865, a Ladies' Shenandoah Relief Association had formed in Hagerstown, Maryland, the state's fourth largest city and a Unionist stronghold. Though the women supposedly "comprise[d] all political shades," more research needs to be done to verify the accuracy of this statement.[105] Large numbers of refugees from the devastated Shenandoah Valley came across the federal lines to seek aid. Hagerstown women requested contributions of "money, food, hats, bonnets, shoes and any kind of substantial clothing (new or second-hand)."[106]

In the last year of the war, Unionist women shifted their focus toward disabled veterans and the orphans of deceased soldiers.[107] In the spring of 1865, a women's group called the Maryland Disabled Soldiers Relief Association formed to explore the prospect of founding a home for disabled, white Union servicemen. With some funding from Baltimore City and the dissolved Baltimore branch of the US Christian Commission, a building was secured and the Maryland Disabled Soldier's Home opened in the fall of 1865. Private donations and fund-raising fairs supplemented the coffers.[108] Between twenty and seventy men resided at the facility at certain points in time. The female managers ran the facility in a businesslike manner and enforced strict rules for acceptable behavior, with temperance at the top of the list. Men who did not comply were removed. The federal government soon established its own facilities for disabled soldiers, and the inhabitants of the home were transferred elsewhere. By 1871 the facility had closed down.[109]

Discussion about the founding of an orphanage for the children of white Union soldiers began in 1864 and in January 1865; fifteen women petitioned the Maryland General Assembly for funding for a Union Orphan Asylum to be located in Baltimore. Initial funding came from a combination of state, municipal, and private sources. The orphanage, "under the management of ladies exclusively," opened in November 1865. The asylum housed as many as ninety children, with roughly equal numbers of girls and boys. All attended city public schools, with four-fifths at the primary level. Religious instruction was provided once a week.[110]

The Shelter for Orphans of Colored Soldiers and Friendless Colored Children was another enterprise initiated by women, many of whom had been involved previously in soldier relief work. White women formed the officers and the board of managers, with some white men acting as "counsellers." The unexpended funds from three disbanded local Unionist relief organizations provided some seed money to enable the purchase of a building that opened in May 1867. Prominent African Americans, such as businessman Isaac Myers and the Reverend J. H. Brice, along with sixty-five other community members, gave early funding support.[111] The children lived in a family-like setting under the supervision of a matron and received daily educational instruction. A female volunteer taught basic sewing lessons. All residents attended worship services as well as Sunday school. African American organizations and individuals provided continued significant financial backing, moral support, and the material goods to keep the institution in operation. In September of 1867, contributions from the community alone underwrote the entire month's operating expenses.[112] Congregants from the Sharp Street, Orchard Street, and Bethel churches gave Sunday offerings and held fund-raising fairs. Even individuals of limited means in the large Baltimore African American community gave what they could. For example, Serena Johnson, possibly a former slave, offered the orphans a simple gift of crackers and rice.[113]

Unable for obvious reasons to mount a fair during the war, the Southern Relief Fair of 1866 provided a large-scale vehicle for secessionist women to showcase their philanthropic impulses and to celebrate their devotion to the conquered Confederacy and its impoverished people.[114] Baltimoreans were well aware of the financial circumstances of the South. The city hosted a branch of the American Union Commission, an organization founded in 1864 to aid the poor and destitute people in the conquered areas of the war-ravaged Confederacy.

The prospect of holding a fair to raise funds for destitute southerners first arose in Baltimore during the fall of 1865. No particular individual or individuals were recognized by the press as promoting the initial idea. The *Baltimore Sun* simply stated that "[v]arious means of procuring relief for the suffering poor in the South have been devised by those in more favored sections and among our own citizens. . . . It is understood that the ladies of Baltimore, of earnest and benevolent sympathies, have the matter in hand."[115]

A series of organizational meetings, held in private homes, began in February 1866. Sixty-six-year-old Jane Howard, wife of Gen. Benjamin Chew Howard, was elected to serve as president. Her spouse had been a key figure in Democratic Party politics, losing to Augustus Bradford, the Unionist candidate, in Maryland's 1861 gubernatorial election. Annie Thomas, 46, a Virginian by birth, and Elizabeth Key Howard, 62, the daughter of Francis Scott Key, served as vice presidents. The latter two women are distinguished from the other executive committee members in that their spouses had been arrested and detained by US military authorities for disloyalty in 1861.[116] All six of Mrs. Howard's sons, incidentally, wore the Confederate gray serving as line officers or in the medical corps.

Minutes from the planning meetings provide valuable insight into the challenges the women confronted. As was the case with the 1864 Sanitary Fair, the managers sought the aid of men as an "advisory committee" to assist them in their efforts. Three men formed the finance committee. About twenty men, in their role as auxiliary managers, acted as both soliciting and collecting agents for funds and goods on behalf of the women. However, one incident clearly demonstrates that the ladies did not heed all male advice. When a gentleman's letter was read before the women that suggested "that the M[arylan]d Fair should be held in N. Y. as there was much active sympathy there & it would be very much more profitable than if held in Balt[imore]" it was "rejected with derision."[117]

Unlike their Unionist sisters, they declined to engage in direct solicitation of contributions from individuals. A suggestion to form a women's committee to solicit contributions was raised, quickly opposed, and the matter referred to the auxiliary managers, the men.[118] The women instead limited themselves to the production of five thousand circulars, sending a portion to the local press and various newspapers in New York, Philadelphia, and St. Louis.[119] Printed appeals also were mailed to prominent businesses in Baltimore to solicit contributions of goods or monetary donations.

As the number of interested women grew, it became necessary to formalize the organization and secure a permanent meeting place. In an irony appreciated by many Baltimoreans, the ladies leased the building that had once housed the Union Club, the gathering place for Baltimore's Unionist gentlemen during the war. The large building also served as an additional collection point and temporary storage for items earmarked for the fair. Donations poured in from sympathetic citizens in Boston, New York, Philadelphia, Chicago, St. Louis, Richmond, Charleston, Great Britain, and elsewhere.

By early March 1866, 316 women had banded together to shape the Relief Fair. Though a full, demographic study has yet to be undertaken, the constituency of the fair's officers and managers appears to have been drawn primarily from white, wealthy households of the Baltimore area. A handful of well-to-do German immigrant women were also included. Not a single woman officer connected with Baltimore's 1864 US Sanitary Fair served as a manager in this endeavor. Apparently wartime allegiances were still too raw to allow any consultation with their sisters who had experience with a large-scale event. Describing the fair's committee, the *Baltimore American* newspaper stated, "We do not find the name of a single loyal lady, nor among its gentleman managers and . . . we find . . . that the great mass . . . have been, and still are, active and persistent in the sentiment of disloyalty."[120] Spouses of at least six of the managers had spent time incarcerated at either in Fort McHenry or Fort Warren on suspicion of disloyalty.[121] Among the general managers, two women had been arrested and detained. Mary Norris had been placed under arrest in 1862 for holding "disloyal correspondence," and Bessie Perrine was confined temporarily in 1864 for being a "southern sympathizer."[122]

In contrast to the opening day of the 1864 Sanitary Fair, the Relief Fair's opening day did not create a holiday-like atmosphere in the city. No municipal closures occurred, nor did a grand parade mark that day. The Relief Fair witnessed the attendance of no prominent Washington officials. Also noticeably absent was any delegation from Baltimore City or the Maryland State government. The doors of the grand salon of the Maryland Institute merely swung open to the public at 7 P.M., and "in a very short time" an estimated five thousand individuals swarmed into the hall, filling it "not only to overflowing, but packing it to a jam and almost to suffocation."[123]

Attendees observed a highly decorated fair site. Flickering gas lamps illuminated the great hall—"the blaze of light which fell on the whole scene added additional luster and beauty, and exhibited the article on sale to the very best advantage."[124] Two lines of display tables ran along the length of the side walls, while the center of the hall featured a grand floral temple, special booths, arbors, and grottoes. Festooned drapery, evergreen boughs, flowers, and house plants characterized the general decoration of the tables. Most items for sale consisted of women's needlework, baked goods, and items for home decoration.

As the *Baltimore Gazette* reported, "Stretched across the centre of the hall is the star-spangled banner [a US flag], and at the end of the hall, the same emblems are festooned."[125] This overt nod to national patriotism and to the Union was tempered by what no other city newspaper described explicitly. On many of the fifty-seven display tables, either for sale or for raffle, could be found portraits of the military heroes of the Confederacy. Paintings, prints, and photographs of Robert E. Lee, Stonewall Jackson, and Joseph E. Johnston, to name a few, could be found throughout the hall. Less than one year before, Baltimore's secessionists could have been arrested by the US provost marshall for displaying or even possessing such images. Thus the process of restoring the Union, while remembering the past, had begun in Maryland.

Other activities, displays, and vendors offered light-hearted diversions. Several fortune tellers tempted the slowly milling crowds with their mystical powers. "The young ladies in charge do not profess to be versed in astrologic wisdom . . . but do contend . . . that they can read the future with as much accuracy as those who 'talk with the stars.'"[126] Items related to the much-venerated "Father of Our Country," George Washington, seemed to be of universal popularity. Fairgoers, for ten cents a turn, could momentarily seat themselves upon a "chair . . . used by [the General] when he was living in Alexandria." For the dry-throated, present-day young Rebekahs proffered refreshments of iced lemonade or cold mineral water for purchase at "Jacob's Well." Famished fairgoers could buy either a slice of cake at one of the tables (with the chance of possibly discovering a genuine gold ring baked inside) or else enjoy an ice cream, sandwich, or hot meal in the lunchroom, whose female managers assured that everything would "be served up in the style equal to Delmonico['s]."[127] Lastly, a fine arts gallery featured paintings and engravings either borrowed temporarily, or donated outright for sale, from local private collections and elsewhere.

The attendance of Marylanders themselves, and their willingness to open their wallets and purses to an event that supported a recent enemy, ultimately determined the overall success of the eleven-day event. The railroads and steamship companies offered reduced rates to Baltimore, facilitating attendance. Local newspapers reported immense crowds during the entire length of the fair's run. By April 7, in just five days, the gross receipts totaled over $60,000. By the April 13 closing, over $100,000 had been raised, mostly from Baltimoreans. Yet the Relief Fair organizers still possessed many unsold items. In a worthy-of-note, entrepreneurial stroke of genius, the managers removed the goods from the hall and placed them back at their clubhouse, whereupon they conducted a mini-fair until most goods were liquidated. In comparison, the 1864 Sanitary Fair managers auctioned off their remaining donated goods, achieving only a fraction of their actual worth, for a final amount raised of about $86,000. The Relief Fair women ultimately grossed about $160,000.[128]

The Southern Relief Fair could be termed a great success when compared to similar efforts. Donations from other cities and the lack of competition from other such fund-raising ventures no doubt helped assure financial success.[129] The press singled out the organizers and participants for their participation. The *Baltimore Gazette* opined, "[The ladies] have been constant in their attendance and unwearied in their attentions . . . [t]he Fair women of Baltimore have crowned themselves with laurels, well deserved in many ways. In justice to purchasers, however, it must be said that their liberality made the task of the saleswomen an easy one."[130] The *Baltimore Sun* expressed the sentiment that the outcome of the event "must gratify the hearts of all who acknowledge a common brotherhood among men, and especially among fellow countrymen."[131]

Yet the fair also revealed continuing political divisions. The *Baltimore American*, a moderate Unionist paper during the conflict, refused to report on the Relief Fair, giving the following reason:

If there had been any attempt made, or any desire evinced, to secure the participation of the Union people of the city or State in this Fair, it would have been promptly responded to by them and heartily seconded by the [*Baltimore*] *American*. On the contrary, there has been a persistent effort to make [the fair] a grand disloyal demonstration.

It appears that prominent wartime Unionists did not play a role in organizing the Relief Fair. Some, as evidenced by donor lists, did contribute money or goods for sale, though it cannot be determined in what numbers they frequented the fair's site.[132]

In conclusion, the Southern Relief Fair gave Baltimore's secessionist women their most spectacular means to express their devotion to the people of the South. Channeling their energies, the women successfully mobilized thousands of fellow Marylanders, as well as sympathetic out-of-state parties, behind the cause of assisting the destitute of the former Confederacy.[133] Remarkably, they achieved their organizational task in just over two months, as Baltimore, for some eleven days, witnessed an influx of citizens united in their desire to celebrate the Lost Cause. However, the old wounds brought on by the sectional strife had yet to heal.

The Southern Relief Association, with Jane Howard as its head, continued to bring aid to the people of the former Confederacy. A state appropriation helped to assist them in their efforts. The women organized a four-day fair at the Maryland Institute in the winter of 1868, consisting of "music, tableaux, suppers and other entertainments."[134] The association hoped to raise one-third of the amount of $140,000 netted by its previous 1866 affair. However, the January event did not attract the same numbers, especially since a snowstorm occurred on opening night.[135] The final amount realized did not appear in the *Baltimore Sun*.

In addition, the Southern Industrial Association of Maryland arose soon after the war's end. "This Association is designed to give employment to the ladies of the Southern States . . . who are obliged to rely on the labors of their own hands (sewing skills) for support."[136] Though part of a network that sprang up in many Confederate and Border States, as well as New York, New Jersey, and Pennsylvania, a clear description of this Maryland-based group's activities remains elusive.[137] Ellen M. Harrison, the wife of a Methodist minister, served as its president. Harrison became a manager of several different charities during the 1870s. In 1868, a Maryland state legislature appropriation of $10,000 aided the women in their efforts.[138] The association voluntarily dissolved, due to dwindling interest by its members and the public, in 1871.[139]

In February 1867, a committee of women founded the Ladies Depository, an entity formed to help alleviate "the continued and increasing destitution of the South."[140] Its mission would later expand to embrace female southern refugees living in Baltimore. Ellen M. Harrison presided over the organization. Opening a Baltimore retail establishment under the supervision of Matilda Saunders, the depository provided an outlet for southern women to sell their needlework and knitted products plus other items, such as drawings, paintings, and handmade wax flowers.[141] It also took custom orders for what it termed family work, which may be interpreted as everyday clothing. In its first fourteen months, the store sold $9,000 worth of articles that included garments for women and children.[142] In 1873, the depository reported that it had assisted one hundred local women and untold numbers in the South, and that the organization prospered.[143] The store would continue in business until about 1879.[144]

In the ensuing decades, Maryland's secessionist women continued their efforts to offer assistance in multiple ways. Claudia Floyd noted that the "'manly deeds' that Baltimore's [secessionist] women performed in the Civil War were replaced after the conflict by more traditional female services: honoring the dead, offering material and emotional support for the veterans and their families, and shaping the historical memory that perpetuated their particular culture of war."[145]

CONCLUSION

Maryland women, both Unionist and secessionist, drew upon their domestic skills to support the physical well-being and morale of Union and Confederate soldiers, respectively, throughout the Civil War. The socially acceptable, traditional women's roles of making garments, preparing food, and providing nursing assistance were an extension of their prior domestic and charitable work. Though barred from the political process, they expressed their devotion to their respective political alignments in multiple and somewhat different ways. The Unionist women, through the organization of patriotic and supportive activities, buttressed the martial spirit of Union soldiers and civilians alike. Secessionist women, as nonbattlefield participants in support of an alien government, provided it with both intelligence and material aid and undermined the morale of US troops and the Unionist population. The nature of their wartime activities allowed the women to place demands upon men, stretched the boundaries of their traditional domestic sphere, and provided them with the confidence that empowered them to found charitable organizations in the immediate postwar era.

NOTES

1. Some Maryland women, disguised as men, did serve with Union military units. See DeAnne Blanton and Lauren M. Cook, *They Fought Like Demons: Women Soldiers in the American Civil War* (Baton Rouge: Louisiana State University Press, 2002).

2. See Claudia Floyd, *Maryland Women in the Civil War: Unionists, Rebels, Slaves & Spies* (Charleston, SC: History Press, 2013). Floyd includes extensive narratives on Harriet Tubman, Anna Ella Carroll, and Hetty Cary.

3. Some content in this section appears in Robert W. Schoeberlein, "A Record of Heroism": Baltimore's Unionist Women in the Civil War, *Maryland Historical Magazine* 109, no. 2 (Summer 2014), 189–201. New material has been added.

4. Frank Leslie, *Heroic Incidents of the Civil War in America* (New York: Frank Leslie, 1862), 58–59; Pamphlets on the Civil War, 1861–1865, 1862; ProQuest Civil War Era.

5. Rice C. Bull, *Soldiering: The Civil War Diary of Rice C. Bull* (San Rafael, CA: Presidio Press, 1977), 7.

6. *Boston Herald,* May 12, 1862, 2.

7. William Carey Walker, *History of the Eighteenth Regiment Connecticut Volunteers in the War for The Union* (Norwich, CT: "Published by The Committee," 1885), 29.

8. Frank Booth Goodrich, *The Tribute Book: A Record of Munificence, Self-Sacrifice, Patriotism of the American People during the War for the Union* (New York: Derby & Miller, 1865), 424.

9. The National Hospital employed the Sisters of Charity as nurses. Mostly Irish American women served as the matrons. (See MSA SC 5963-11-1, muster roll of the US General Hospital, National Hotel, Camden Street, Baltimore, MD, March–April 1862, Maryland State Archives.)

10. Sallie P. Cushing to "Dear Aunt," November 2, 1862, Josephine C. Morris Papers, MS. 190, Maryland Center for History and Culture, Baltimore, MD.

11. *The Frederick Examiner,* August 21, 1861, and October 2, 1861.

12. *The Herald of Freedom & Torch Light* (Hagerstown, MD), December 11, 1861.

13. *Baltimore Sun,* November 26, 1864. See also US Census for 1860.

14. *Baltimore Sun,* November 22, 1864, and US Census for 1860.

15. Benjamin T. Tanner, *An Apology for African Methodism* (Baltimore: n.p., 1867), 466–67.

16. Other coordinators included Henrietta Toomey, the wife of a barber, and Julia Greatfield, a twenty-eight-year-old unmarried dressmaker's daughter.

17. *Baltimore Sun,* March 14, 1898.

18. United States Christian Commission, *Second Report of the Committee of Maryland* (Baltimore: Printed by James Young, 1863), 104–5.

19. Though the Maryland General Assembly set aside some funding to aid dependents of Maryland Union soldiers, the small monthly payments, averaging $6 to $7, proved inadequate for many.

20. Clara Turner to "My Dear Cousins," June 14, 1864, The Samuel E. and Clara Turner Papers, 1861–1865, Special Collections & College Archives, Musselman Library, Gettysburg College, Gettysburg, PA.

21. *Baltimore Sun,* October 24, 1920.

22. Jeanie Attie, "Warwork and the Crisis of Domesticity in the North, " in Catherine Clinton and Nina Silber, *Divided Houses: Gender and the Civil War* (New York: Oxford University Press, 1992), 254.

23. See 1861 examples in the *Baltimore American,* July 24, September 28; *Baltimore Clipper,* July 11, 22, 25, 26; *Baltimore Sun,* November 6.

24. *Baltimore Sun,* June 28, 1862.

25. Data derived from the Economic History Association website (EH.Net), accessed September 7, 2019, www.measuringworth.com/calculators/uscompare/relativevalue.php; *New-York Daily Tribune,* August 17, 1863.

26. *Baltimore Sun,* August 22, 1863.

27. Bishop Daniel Alexander Payne, DD, LLD, *Recollections of Seventy Years* (Nashville, TN: Publishing House of the A. M. E. Sunday School Union, 1888), 224, https://docsouth.unc.edu/church/payne70/payne.html.

28. Tanner, *An Apology for African Methodism,* 445–46. Other women mentioned include Mary Jane Cephas, a porter's wife, Mary Jane Hill, a dressmaker, and Elizabeth Cox and Sarah Crane, whose husbands worked as waiters.

29. Blanton and Cook, *They Fought Like Demons,* 113.

30. Blanton and Cook, *They Fought Like Demons,* 54–55.

31. Blanton and Cook, *They Fought Like Demons,* 50.

32. *Baltimore Sun,* March 26, 1864.

33. Henry B. Shepherd, *Narrative of Prison Life at Baltimore and Johnson's Island, Ohio* (Baltimore: Commercial Ptg. & Sta. Co., 1917), 7.

34. Laura Lee Davidson, "The Services of the Women of Maryland to the Confederate States," *Confederate Veteran* 28, no. 9 (September 1920), 333.

35. "Fashionable Baltimore during the Civil War," Amy D'Arcy Wetmore, *Baltimore Sun,* July 21, 1907.

36. "Fashionable Baltimore during the Civil War," Amy D'Arcy Wetmore, *Baltimore Sun,* July 28, 1907.

37. *Southern Recorder* (Milledgeville, GA), September 2, 1862.

38. Charles W. Mitchell, *Maryland Voices of the Civil War* (Baltimore: Johns Hopkins University Press, 2007), 136–37. Shippen claimed to have taken the song to the Miller & Beacham music store to have it published. Constance Cary Harrison (Mrs. Burton Harrison), in her *Recollections Grave and Gay* (New York: Charles Scribner's Sons, 1911), claimed that Jennie Cary selected the tune (see page 57).

39. Bradley T. Johnson, "Memoir of Jane C. Johnson," *Southern Historical Society Papers* (Richmond, VA, 1901), 29:33–42.

40. *Baltimore Sun,* October 13, 1862.

41. Claudia Floyd, "Baltimore's Confederate Women: Perpetuating a Culture of War," *Maryland Historical Society Magazine* 106, no. 1 (Spring 2011), 47. See the 1860 Census for name spelling: "John Anna" in other sources.

42. *Southern Confederacy* (Atlanta, GA), June 10, 1862.

43. *Daily Dispatch* (Richmond, VA), October 28, 1862.

44. *Baltimore Sun,* April 2, 1862; also August 23, 1861, and March 28, 1862.

45. The flag presented to Capt. J. Lyle Clark's company was made by women; see the *Baltimore Sun,* July 10, 1861.

46. A regimental flag was expensive and complicated to produce. More deluxe models featured hand-painted imagery and lettering on heavy-gauge silk with gold wire thread forming the fringe.

47. Constance Cary Harrison, "Virginia Scenes in '61," in Robert Underwood Johnson and Clarence Clough Buel, *Battles and Leaders of the Civil War* (New York: Century, 1887–1888), 1:161–62.

48. *Richmond Enquirer* (Richmond, VA), June 11, 1861.

49. *The Daily Dispatch,* July 29, 1861.

50. *Baltimore Sun,* July 10, 1861.

51. *Richmond Enquirer,* February 28, 1862.

52. *Confederate Veteran* 28, no. 9 (1920), 334.

53. See findagrave.com, accessed June 27, 2019, www.findagrave.com/memorial/63088751/matilda -saunders.

54. *Baltimore Sun,* March 8, 1901.

55. Claudia Floyd, "Baltimore Women: Perpetuating a Culture of War," *Maryland Historical Magazine* 106, no. 1 (Spring 2011), 38. See also LeeAnn Whites and Alecia Long, eds., *Occupied Women: Gender, Military Occupation, and the American Civil War* (Baton Rouge: Louisiana State University Press, 2009), 9–10.

56. William Henry Hurlburt, *General McClellan and the Conduct of the War* (New York: Sheldon, 1864), 117–23; Stephen Sears, *Civil War Papers of George B. McClellan: Selected Correspondence, 1860–65* (New York: Ticknor & Fields, 1989), 95–6, 100, 102; Moran Dix and John Adams Dix, *Memoirs of John Adams Dix* (New York: Harper & Brothers, 1883), 24–34.

57. *Baltimore Sun,* July 3, 1863.

58. Patricia Dockman Anderson, "'Traitorous Demoiselles': Women Imprisoned in Baltimore, 1861–1865," paper presented at the Southern Historical Association Conference, Baltimore, MD, October 28, 2011, 3.

59. See arrest list in Anderson, "Traitorous Demoiselles."

60. Anderson, "Traitorous Demoiselles," 9.

61. Samuel A. Harrison journal, July 17, 1861, entry, MS. 432.1, Maryland Center for History and Culture Library, Baltimore, MD.

62. Samuel A. Harrison journal, October 18, 1861, entry.

63. Samuel A. Harrison journal, October 19, 1861, entry.

64. Samuel A. Harrison journal, July 17, 1861, entry.

65. See Anderson, "Traitorous Demoiselles," 12, and Floyd, "Baltimore's Confederate Women," 43, regarding General Robert E. Schenck's command in Baltimore.

66. Floyd, "Baltimore's Confederate Women," 39.

67. Anderson, "Traitorous Demoiselles," 7; Thomas Lowry, *Confederate Heroines: 120 Southern Women Convicted by Union Military Justice* (Baton Rouge: Louisiana State University Press, 2006), 64–71; *Baltimore Sun,* April 25, 1864, August 15, 1864.

68. H. Donald Winkler, *Stealing Secrets: How a Few Daring Women Deceived Generals, Impacted Battles, and Altered the Course of the Civil War* (Naperville, IL: Cumberland House, 2010), 294. See also *Union Provost Marshals' File of Papers Relating to Individual Civilians, 1861–1867,* Microfilm publication M0345, 300 rolls, War Department Collection of Confederate Records, Record Group 109, National Records and Archives Administration, Washington, DC.

69. Anderson, "Traitorous Demoiselles," 10; *Baltimore Sun,* July 14, 1863.

70. Anderson, "Traitorous Demoiselles," 11; *Baltimore Sun,* December 28, 1863.

71. *The War of the Rebellion: A Compilation of the Official Records of the Union and Confederate Armies* (Washington, DC: US Government Printing Office, 1897), ser. 2, vol. 2, Cases of Mrs. C. V. Baxley and Septimus Brown, 1,315–21.

72. Floyd, "Baltimore's Confederate Women," 43.

73. Beverly Gordon, *Bazaars and Fair Ladies: The History of the American Fundraising Fair* (Knoxville: University of Tennessee Press, 1998), 37.

74. Most of the content of this section was published previously in Robert W. Schoeberlein, "A Fair to Remember: Maryland Women in Aid of the Union," *Maryland Historical Magazine* 90, no. 4 (Winter 1995): 467–88. The article has been condensed for inclusion in this chapter.

75. Ann Bowen's mother was Caroline Howard Oilman (1794–1888), a native of Boston who settled in Charleston, SC, where her Unitarian husband presided over that city's Second Independent Church.

76. *Dictionary of American Biography,* under the auspices of the American Council of Learned Societies, Allen Johnson, ed. (New York, Scribners, 1928–36, 7:298). Charles J. Bowen, the rector of Baltimore's Second Independent Church, had resigned his position to enlist as a full-time military chaplain.

77. A list of organizers' names appeared in the *Baltimore American and Commercial Advertiser,* December 18, 1863 (hereafter the *Baltimore American*). I used this list to compile demographic information on the women. The combination of an 1863–1864 Baltimore Directory search, plus information garnered from the 1860 US Census, revealed the socioeconomic identity of two-thirds of the fair's initial organizers.

78. Elizabeth Bradford, the Maryland governor's wife and later the fair committee chair, would visit soldiers at Camp Tyler. Mary Pancoast already served as the treasurer of the Ladies Union Relief Association. Both Sarah Ball and Sarah Applegarth had nursed wounded soldiers on western Maryland battlefields.

79. *Baltimore American,* February 5, 1864.

80. Mrs. C. J. Bowen to Bishop William Whittingham, February 23, 1864, Vertical File, F. Garner Ranney Archives, Maryland Episcopal Diocese, Baltimore, MD.

81. Augusta C. E. Shoemaker to A. J. Lewis, April 9, 1864, Shoemaker Family Papers, MS. 1973, Maryland Center for History and Culture Library.

82. *Baltimore American,* February 12, 1864.

83. Mrs. A. H. L. Phelps to Bishop William Whittingham, December 21, 1863, Unindexed Correspondent's File, F. Garner Ranney Archives, Maryland Episcopal Diocese.

84. *Baltimore American,* December 22, 1863.

85. H. H. Williams to "Dear Husband," February 27, 1864, Archer-Stump-Williams Family Papers, MS. 1948, Maryland Center for History and Culture Library.

86. *United States Christian Commission, Third Report for the Committee of Maryland* (Baltimore: James Young, 1864), 192.

87. A review of the meeting minutes in the Union Club Record Books (MS. 855, Maryland Center for History and Culture) revealed no mention of the Maryland Fair. See issues of "The New Era," the souvenir Fair newspapers (especially from April 20–22, 1864), for insights into the roles of men.

88. *Baltimore American,* May 2, 1864.

89. Lori D. Ginzberg, *Women and the Work of Benevolence* (New Haven: Yale University Press, 1990), 167.

90. Harrison Collection, April 20, 1864, diary entry, MS. 432, Maryland Center for History and Culture Library.

91. *Baltimore Clipper,* April 18, 1864.

92. *The New Era,* April 26, 1864.

93. *The New Era,* April 26, 1864.

94. *US Christian Commission: Third Report,* 195; and Charles J. Stille, *History of the Sanitary Commission* (Philadelphia: J. B. Lippincott, 1866), 548.

95. In contrast, the New York and Philadelphia fairs each cleared over a million dollars. However, over a million people inhabited the New York City and Brooklyn area alone; Philadelphia's population total was more than double than that of Baltimore's of 212,418.

96. Chicago's fair in December 1863 "netted between $86,000 and $100,000"; Boston's, held in the state whose militia first answered Lincoln's call to put down the rebellion, garnered but $146,000. Both Illinois and Massachusetts possessed larger and much less philosophically divided populations.

97. *Baltimore American,* May 2, 1864.

98. Diary of Alexander Randall, April 24, 1864, entry, Alexander Randall Diaries, MS. 652, Maryland Center for History and Culture Library.

99. Life-sketch of Alexander Randall by Elizabeth Blanchard Randall, Blanchard-Randall-Philpot Papers, MS. 2824, MdHS.

100. *New Era,* April 26, 1864.

101. Rev. A. W. Wayman, D.D., *My Recollections of African M.E. Ministers, or Forty Years' Experience in the African Methodist Episcopal Church* (Philadelphia: A.M.E. Book Rooms, 1881), 88–89.

102. See M 1384–1 and M 1387–1, Bethel African Methodist Episcopal Church Collection, MSA SC 2562, Maryland State Archives, for proceeds of New England kitchen.

103. *Baltimore American,* January 7, 1865. The final tally was $1,827.34.

104. Gordon. *Bazaars and Fair Ladies: The History of the American Fundraising Fair,* 106.

105. *Aegis & Intelligencer* (Bel Air, MD), March 3, 1865.

106. *Aegis & Intelligencer,* March 3, 1865.

107. The Unionist content of this section was published previously in Robert W. Schoeberlein, "A Record of Heroism": Baltimore's Unionist Women in the Civil War, *Maryland Historical Magazine* 109, no. 2 (Summer 2014): 196, 200.

108. *Aegis & Intelligencer,* October 26, 1866. A three-day fair was held at the New Assembly Rooms.

109. Maryland Soldiers Managers Record Book, MS. 569, Maryland Center for History and Culture Library.

110. Union Orphan Asylum Record Book, MS. 857, Maryland Center for History and Culture Library. A review of entries reveals the names and activities of the women.

111. See the *First Annual Report of the Shelter for Orphans of Colored Soldiers and Friendless Colored Children* (Baltimore: Daugherty, Maguire & Wright, 1868) and *Second Annual Report . . . Colored Children* (Baltimore: n.p., 1869).

112. *Second Annual Report . . . Colored Children,* 4.

113. *Fourth Annual Report of the Shelter for Orphans of Colored Soldiers and Friendless Colored Children* (Baltimore: n.p., 1871), 13.

114. The content of this section is derived from an unpublished paper by Robert W. Schoeberlein entitled "Secessionist Women and the Southern Relief Fair of 1866" delivered at the Southern Historical Association Conference, Baltimore, October 28, 2011.

115. *Baltimore Sun,* February 13, 1866.

116. J. Hanson Thomas and Charles Howard were arrested by US military authorities during the summer of 1861; see the *Baltimore Sun,* September 14, 1861, and July 2, 1861, respectively.

117. Report book, March 14, 1866, entry, Frick Family Collection, MS. 2703, Maryland Center for History and Culture Library, Baltimore, MD.

118. Report book, February 19, February 21, and March 5, 1866.

119. Report book, March 2, 1866.

120. *Baltimore American,* April 6, 1866.

121. The husbands of Mrs. J. Hanson Thomas, Mrs. Charles Howard, Mrs. T. Parkin Scott, Mrs. George Wm. Brown, Mrs. Wm. Gatchill and Mrs. Charles Pitts.

122. Anderson, "Traitorous Demoiselles," arrest list, March 2, 1862, and July 12, 1864.

123. *Baltimore Gazette,* April 3, 1866. Five thousand people appeared to be the maximum capacity for the Maryland Institute; the same number visited the 1864 Sanitary Fair.

124. *Baltimore Gazette,* April 3, 1866.

125. *Baltimore Gazette,* April 3, 1866.

126. *Baltimore Gazette,* April 4, 1866.

127. *Baltimore Gazette,* April 2, 1866. Delmonico's, of New York City, was a nationally famous restaurant.

128. *Baltimore Sun,* December 16, 1867. The newspaper reported the final netted amount as $141,102.

129. Competition with other cities had always been a concern with wartime Sanitary Fairs.

130. *Baltimore Gazette,* April 11, 1866.

131. *Baltimore Sun,* April 14, 1866.

132. Samuel M. Shoemaker, one of the auxiliary managers of the 1864 Sanitary Fair, donated a prize turkey; Senator Sprague, who visited the Sanitary Fair with President Lincoln, made a monetary gift.

133. The example of Maryland likely prompted Missouri, another border state, to host its own relief fair. The St. Louis Grand Southern Relief Fair held in October 1866 raised approximately $150,000 and Baltimoreans gave generously to this cause. See the *St. Louis Republic* (St. Louis, MO), April 19, 1903.

134. *Aegis & Intelligencer,* January 10, 1868; *Baltimore Sun,* December 30, 1867.

135. *Baltimore Sun,* January 15, 1868.

136. Davidson, "The Services of the Women of Maryland to the Confederate States," *Confederate Veteran* 28, no. 9 (September 1920), 336.

137. It was known more broadly as the Ladies Industrial Association. The South Carolina group supported a workshop where destitute women were employed in the making of garments. See the *Daily Phoenix* (Columbia, SC), November 28, December 20, 1866, and June 9, 1868.

138. *Laws of Maryland,* chap. 290, 498–99.

139. *Baltimore Sun,* March 10, 1871.

140. *Baltimore Sun,* February 7, 1867, and April 4, 1868. A brief article in the *Baltimore Sun* of January 11, 1872, seems to imply that the depository was possibly an adjunct activity of the Southern Relief Association.

141. *Baltimore Sun,* April 18, 1867.

142. *Baltimore Sun,* April 4, 1868.

143. *Baltimore Sun,* February 1873.

144. The year of 1879 is the final listing for the depository found within the Baltimore City directories.

145. Floyd, "Baltimore's Confederate Women," 39.

THE FAILED PROMISE OF RECONSTRUCTION

SHARITA JACOBS-THOMPSON

hortly after President Abraham Lincoln issued the Emancipation Proclamation, Emily Saunders Plummer gathered her five children. She fled the Woodlawn plantation in Ellicott Mills, where she was a slave of the Thompson family. Some Black Marylanders had misconstrued Lincoln's proclamation as a universal declaration of freedom extended to the state. So assured was Plummer of the federal government's capacity and willingness to destroy the state's "peculiar institution" that she encouraged her nineteen-year-old son, Henry Vinton Plummer, to abscond after the passage of the District of Columbia's Emancipation Act. The following year, she prepared to strike out with the other children in an effort to make the Emancipation Proclamation a reality.

She made her way to Baltimore, where she was subsequently arrested and jailed when a Black man serving as their guide "misled and robbed [them] of $5.00 and a bundle of clothing."[1] Plummer and her children would have joined the more than twenty-five thousand free Blacks already residing in Baltimore City if she had evaded capture. However, local officials swiftly disabused her of the notion that freedom was within reach. They exhibited a willingness to uphold state laws and slaveowners' property rights when they reduced her and her children to a new unfree status by placing them in a Baltimore jail.

Her master, Col. Gilbert Livingston Thompson—apparently made aware of her arrest and confinement—arrived at the jail "brandishing hands filled with stones" and threatened to have her whipped. Maryland laws regarding slavery remained intact, and Thompson had a legal right to reclaim his slaves. Still, a state law stipulated that owners must pay all fees associated with "apprehending, imprisoning, and advertising" for fugitives. Thompson lacked the necessary funds to retrieve his "property." As a result, Plummer and her children "escaped the stones that were in his hands and the murder that was in his heart."[2]

Importantly, she was able to use her cooking skills to defray the legal cost and other expenses related to her family's confinement.[3] This spared all of them an extended stay in jail or possibly being sold. After approximately sixty days, the Orphans' Court discharged Plummer and her children.[4] Her husband, Adam Plummer, who also received word of her imprisonment, had prepared to take custody of his family upon their release. In December of 1863, Adam and Emily Plummer, along with their five children left the city on the Baltimore & Ohio Railroad and headed toward Prince George's County, Maryland. Emily Plummer and the children settled with Adam Plummer and began their lives on Riversdale plantation, where he was still a slave for the Calvert family. Emily Plummer and her children were now free, but her husband remained enslaved until the new state constitution—which was narrowly approved by 263 votes—went into effect on November 1, 1864. After emancipation in Maryland, Adam Plummer continued to work on the same plantation. Initially, his income was not solely used to secure the day-to-day necessities for his family. He saved and borrowed money to support his son Henry Vinton Plummer's passage to the Deep South. Adam Plummer tasked his son with retrieving his sister, Sarah Miranda Plummer, who was sold shortly before the outbreak of the Civil War. In 1866, Sarah Miranda and Henry Vinton Plummer left New Orleans and rejoined the family in Maryland.[5]

While the Plummer family continued to confront challenges after the war, they were also able to thrive and build a legacy. Adam and Emily Plummer purchased land and secured education for their children. Their children supported and created local institutions that served their community, and in addition, they became politically active. Hence, this Prince George's County family's wartime and postwar experiences are instructive. They provide us with a lens to understand the transition from slavery to freedom and the process of Reconstruction in Maryland.

Using the Bureau of Refugees, Freedmen, and Abandoned Lands (Freedman's Bureau) records, local newspapers, and national and state legislative records, this chapter examines one of the most turbulent periods in the nation's history. It suggests that Maryland was able to direct "Reconstruction" largely unfettered by congressional mandates. The state remained in the Union and internally emancipated its enslaved population. Therefore, Maryland precluded the federal government from instituting policies put in place in the states of the former Confederacy. Furthermore, when the move toward reconciliation permeated the country, the federal government was even more willing to invoke a laissez-faire policy toward the state.[6] The ability of Maryland planters and state and local legislators to manipulate the federal apparatus meant that freed people's experiences were less influenced by policies that briefly shaped freedom in the Deep South.

Ultimately, by the time redemption, conciliation, and abject repression of Black Americans defined the postbellum period in the former states of the Confederacy, Marylanders had already experimented, tinkered with, and fine-tuned the system that would continue to define race relations in this nation until the modern civil rights movement of the 1950s and 1960s. Therefore, it is crucial to examine Maryland and investigate its transitional period, focusing on the complexity of a state that used its Union loyalty as a pretext to demand that the federal government allow it to self-Reconstruct.

By the end of 1864, Maryland's Reconstruction process was underway. The state's Union Party wielded significant power. They used that political power to call for the convening of a constitutional convention. That April, delegates met in Annapolis to draft a new constitution that, among other provisions, emancipated the state's more than eighty-seven thousand slaves.[7] Some Unionists also used the opportunity to support loyalty oaths that disenfranchised ex-Confederate soldiers and Confederate sympathizers and stipulate that the slave-holding regions could no longer use disenfranchised Black people to their political advantage.[8] Still, they had no plan to implement laws to create citizenship rights for the state's Black population. One Democrat even chided Unionists whom he deemed only supported Black Marylanders "up to a certain point."[9]

For their part, delegates representing the planter class arrived at the convention ready to denounce efforts to destroy the state's peculiar institution. Unable to do so, they sought concessions for the loss of political power and slave labor. Delegates moved to compensate slaveholders for their "property" by voting for provisions that provided funds for assessing how much a slave was worth based on age, gender, and physical condition.[10] According to Daniel Clarke of Prince George's County, this information would assist "those persons who have sustained losses of property by reason of the invasion of the State by the public enemy."[11] The amendment failed by a vote of 34 to 17.

With compensation for slave owners unlikely, these delegates moved to strengthen and institute laws that would benefit planters' immediate needs. These laws allowed slaveholders to control freed people's labor and bind Black children to white planters. Delegate Isaac Jones of Somerset County sought to expand the apprenticeship system. He submitted an amendment that would "provide by law for all negroes manumitted by the new Constitution, to be placed in the condition of apprentices to their owners, males until they are twenty-one years old, and females until they are eighteen."[12] A vote of thirty-one to nineteen defeated this amendment. Delegates representing the largest slaveholding counties cast the majority of those nineteen affirmative votes.

Clarke and other delegates representing the largest slaveholding counties were the most vocal proponents of legislation that sought to control the labor of Black Marylanders, diminish their population in the state, and prevent them from participating in the political system as voters. He proposed an amendment that would prohibit "free blacks and free mulatto" from settling in the state after adopting the new constitution and void existing labor contracts with the same. Clarke also agitated for funding to colonize freed people elsewhere.[13] On the subject of extending the franchise to Black Marylanders, Clarke concluded, "If they are allowed to come here, and men, for party political purposes, succeed in giving them the elective franchise . . . white men of Maryland [will] become virtually enslaved by the [N]egro vote."[14] He argued that in counties like his own, with significant Black populations, Black men would be able to influence and indeed shape local and state politics. However, according to the historian Eric Foner, "No thought was given to expanding the Unionist base by allowing the black 20 percent of Maryland's population to vote."[15] At the convention, support for Black suffrage was practically nonexistent. Even more radical Unionists did not propose voting rights for freed people.[16]

The following year, Abraham Lincoln's assassination on April 15, 1865, would further heighten tensions between the North and the South and leave the business of postwar Reconstruction in the hands of his successor, Andrew Johnson. Shortly after being sworn in, Johnson was outlining his plan of Reconstruction and beginning to appoint provisional governors in the former Confederate states. Concurrently, in Maryland, the division between the radical Unionists and conservative Unionists became apparent. The ties that bound Maryland's Union Party had significantly unraveled. The party was deeply divided, particularly over the issue of disfranchising white citizens of the state by using the loyalty oath. This led to the "high-level defections" of prominent Unionists such as "Governor Thomas Swann, former Postmaster General Montgomery Blair, and United States Senator Reverdy Johnson." It was not long before these politicians "began seeking deals with Democrats."[17]

By early 1866, President Johnson and congressional Republicans' struggle over Reconstruction had taken center stage. Republicans wrestled power away from Johnson and proposed to divide the Confederate states into five military districts and compel them to hold state constitutional conventions. In Maryland, the alliance of Unionists that had been forged by war was no more. Democrats were regaining power, and Maryland was poised to return to its prewar political order. They—thanks to their alliance with the conservative Unionists—regained control of the statehouse. Therefore those who had supported secession and had been wedded to the maintenance of institutionalized slavery would begin to play a decisive role in Maryland's "Reconstruction" process. The expedient return of Democrats to political power impacted postwar policies. Hence, "a recalcitrant slaveholder class and a resurgent Democratic Party, bolstered by pervasive anti-Black racism and violence, worked quickly to recreate conditions approximating slavery."[18]

For their part, Maryland's remaining Unionists, who had lost significant power, did not disappear from the political landscape. They used the state's redemption as a rallying cry. They agitated for and indeed challenged congressional Republicans to intercede in Maryland's affairs. Ironically, they lobbied to extend military Reconstruction to the state. In 1866, United States congressman Francis Thomas, an Unconditional Unionist, urged his colleagues to "reconstruct" Maryland."[19] And United States senator John A. J. Creswell, from Cecil County, suggested that the federal government consider his state with the late rebellious ones. He surmised that this would grant power to the Freedmen's Bureau and allow them to play a more direct role in reconstructing the state.[20] Those Maryland Unionists had the difficult task of convincing Congress to intervene in the state's Reconstruction process. Indeed, Congress threatened to and occasionally launched investigations, but they ultimately resisted the call from "citizens of Maryland praying for a republican form of government."[21]

To be fair, some Unionists summoned the support of Congress when they effectively lost power. Immediately after the war, Maryland remaining loyal to the Union and emancipating its enslaved population without congressional mandates held currency for them. Therefore, Unionists initially suggested that the state could handle its internal affairs without federal oversight. They were suddenly cured of their aversion to the federal government playing a role in their state's Reconstruction after Democrats were in control.

Once the Democrats dominated the general assembly, they proposed convening a constitutional convention, the second in three years. On May 8, 1867, thirty-seven farmers, forty-five lawyers, and a planter were in attendance at its opening in Annapolis. Former Confederate soldier John F. Lee arrived to represent the county that the Plummer family called home. Democrats were determined to repeal the law concerning loyalty oaths. They also sought to reject the Fourteenth Amendment, affirm that state's rights superseded federal authority, and reapportion representation to benefit regions with large numbers of disenfranchised Blacks and deny "negro" enfranchisement.[22] State delegates used the convention to denounce congressional efforts to extend the vote to Black men in the former Confederacy. Governor Thomas Swann, who broke with the Unionists and aligned with the Democrats, condemned the federal government's objective of enfranchising Black men in the former Confederacy.[23] He attacked what he perceived as schemes to extend universal male suffrage to Maryland.[24]

Black male suffrage in Maryland was now a dead issue, certainly for a white population invested in denying them any measure of civil and political rights. This did not dissuade Black people from organizing and preparing to take full advantage of these essential rights. Black men were aware that while they were being denied participation in Maryland's 1867 constitutional convention, their counterparts in the former Confederacy were voting to determine if their state would convene a convention. They were also being elected as delegates and playing a pivotal role in rewriting their state constitutions.[25] Black Marylanders were also keenly aware that residing in a redeemed state would make it increasingly difficult for them to receive relief from the federal government, particularly from the Freedmen's Bureau.

The Freedmen's Bureau, established in the War Department in 1865, was tasked with providing supervision and management of confiscated and abandoned lands as well as providing provisions, clothing, and fuel to refugees and freedmen from rebel states or territory embraced in the operations of the army. It was to operate during the war and one year after that. In 1866, a congressional act extended the Freedmen's Bureau's life for two years. It expanded its responsibilities to include building schools, overseeing hospitals, supervising labor contracts, and investigating racially motivated incidents. In Maryland, the Freedmen's Bureau activities were limited largely to assisting in the construction of schools and with veteran's claims and administering justice. However, agents would find it difficult to impact the latter since Maryland had every intention of exercising its civil functions without interference from the federal government. State representatives argued, and some Bureau agents agreed, that Maryland was supposed to have these civil functions in full force. The federal government's early efforts to respect the state's sovereignty, coupled with the diminishing political power of the Unionists, meant that Black Marylanders would struggle to define the terms of freedom for themselves. Maryland Blacks were vulnerable, particularly as they forced the issue of enfranchising Black men, challenged the state's Black Codes, exercised a degree of mobility, and fought to establish new labor arrangements.

Like many newly freed people, Adam Plummer remained on the Riversdale plantation, where he labored as a foreman. By 1868, he was in the process of purchasing ten acres of land in Prince George's County. B. F. Guy sold the property to Plummer but had no intention of honoring their agreement. Guy addressed the concerns of white residents, who were angered by this transaction, by assuring them that he would reacquire the land before it was paid off. He routinely sent notes to the Plummer household requesting payments toward the $1,000 purchase price. These impromptu demands were challenging for the Plummer family, although Adam Plummer's wife and children contributed to the household income. To Guy's surprise, the Plummer family's ability to pool their meager earnings made it possible for them to pay off the deed before the eighteen-month deadline. More importantly, they did so before Guy was able to carry out his scheme to have them develop the land and summarily repossess it.[26]

Securing land for cultivation was paramount to freed people. Those unable to obtain it desired the ability to negotiate for their labor and the labor of their offspring, void contracts with landowners who were unaware, or who refused to acknowledge, that slavery had come to an end, and exercise the mobility necessary to seek opportunities in other parts of the state. Besides distributing abandoned and confiscated land in the former Confederacy, a crucial component of the Freedmen's Bureau function was working out new labor arrangements between former slaves and masters. They played a pivotal role in supervising the drafting and execution of labor contracts. However, the limited scope of the Freedmen's Bureau duties in Maryland meant that they would be far less instrumental in this regard. It did not take long for Maryland's Black residents to recognize the limits of the federal government's reach.

A few examples prove the point. In September of 1865, Samuel Brown attempted to commence labor negotiations with Thomas Allaby of Anne Arundel County. When Brown, who was previously employed by the federal government, suggested that they seek a federal official's counsel, Allaby flew into a rage. He assaulted Brown with a brick to the head and "cut him with an axe and cowhided him." Brown escaped and sought legal redress from the justice of the peace located in Annapolis. He failed to find a local justice who would accept his testimony; therefore, his request to "issue a warrant for Allaby's arrest" was denied.[27]

That same year, Jacob Giles's appealed to federal officials to aid him in "remov[ing] his family to Washington" from Prince George's County. He sought to retrieve his wife Lucy and two children from Richard Hardisty, who refused to relinquish them. Before emancipation in Maryland, Hardisty owned one of Giles's children, and he claimed they both were contracted to him for one year. Hardisty also argued that Lucy willingly entered into a labor agreement with him. Lucy possibly agreed to work for Hardisty in order to remain with her children.

Giles also requested assistance in the matter of his son William, who contracted with the sister of George Hardisty for $10 per month. William fled after being whipped, and George Hardisty accused him of breaching a contract and requested a "writ of arrest." The teenager was ordered, by Magistrate Joshua T. Clarke, to return to the plantation and "stay the year." Upon hearing the order, Jacob Giles requested "permission to speak." Deeming himself justified in preventing Jacob Giles from addressing the matter before the magistrate, Hardisty commenced beating him "in the most violent manner." When Clarke refused to detain Jacob Giles, Hardisty enlisted Justice of the Peace George A. Mitchell to make the arrest. Jacob Giles was promptly committed to jail, where he remained for four weeks. A sympathetic Clarke secured Jacob Giles's freedom and directed him to address his complaint to the Freedmen's Bureau as he determined "in this, I have done all that I can do under the law here" regarding Giles retrieving his family.[28]

The Freedmen's Bureau was not always successful in mediating the terms of labor contracts between ex-slaves and ex-masters to the satisfaction of newly freed people. This did not preclude Black Marylanders from appealing to them and demanding that the federal government disrupt the state's apprenticeship system. This proved to be an even more difficult task because "even written contracts to labor, including the names of each member of a family, have proved insufficient to protect from apprenticeship those whose age alone brought them within the scope of the law; and it has often happened that the children taken were the mainstay of aged parents, whose best years had been spent in unrequited toil for their masters."[29] The federal government was also aware that some Maryland planters were using the law to compel the parents' labor because they were unwilling to part with their children. Black children as young as eight months old were apprenticed to their former masters, even as their parents complained and protested these bindings. The Freedmen's Bureau received numerous complaints from families who were denied their children and endured threats of violence and physical attacks for daring to challenge these bindings.[30]

For example, in 1864, Rindy Allen claimed that her son was illegally apprenticed by Joseph Hall, of Prince Frederick County, who whipped the boy and provided him with very little food and clothing. After her protest, Allen was arrested and charged for enticing her son to leave. In June of 1866, bureau agents investigated a complaint in Calvert County regarding the illegal apprenticeship of Basil Crowdy's three children, who had been bound by Mr. R. D. Sollay since 1864. When Crowdy and his wife protested these bindings, Constable A. O. Buckmunslin struck Crowdy's wife in the face for being "obdurate." Joseph Prout of Calvert County was holding Dennis Smith's children despite protest by him and his wife. It was reported that Prout assaulted Smith's wife, presumably because she challenged his right to her children.

The apprenticeship system was, not surprisingly, most pervasive in the former slaveholding southern counties of Maryland, where plantation owners commandeered the children of freed people, some by brute force. One Freedmen's Bureau report estimated that "six hundred cases of unjust apprenticing in Calvert and almost as many in Anne Arundel"[31] had come to the federal government's attention. The report indicated that "a few days after the emancipation constitution went into effect, it was the practice to take the children on a farm before the orphans' court and have them apprenticed to former owners."[32]

When federal officials confronted apprenticeships, state representatives summarily rebuked them. Governor Augustus Bradford complained that the federal government was trampling on the rights of a loyal state.[33] In response, the Freedmen's Bureau was forced to adopt alternative methods to address the issue. To circumvent Democrats, who were in control of the state legislature, agents depended on judges like Hugh Lennox Bond to issue writs of habeas corpus so that Black parents could retrieve their children. Judge Bond, a Baltimorean who had advocated for the enlistment of Black men in the Union army and championed Black suffrage, would also collaborate with the Freedmen's Bureau to free Black children from apprenticeships.

Democrats, furious at Judge Bond's cooperation with the Freedmen's Bureau, sought to remove him from the Baltimore criminal court. In 1867, the Maryland General Assembly successfully diminished his power to intervene with apprenticeships. They passed "a law restraining Judge Bond's power to issue writs of Habeas Corpus." With this decision, Freedmen's Bureau superintendent William Van Derlip conceded that "the law is undoubtedly unconstitutional, but our hands are tied, for, though Judge Bond might issue the writ, the sheriff would not serve it, the master would not obey it, and the Judge could not enforce it." Judge Bond's intervention did play a significant role in preventing new apprenticeships. However, it was exceedingly more challenging to aid children already apprenticed. Although the Freedmen's Bureau made progress destabilizing the state's apprenticeship system, Black parents still struggled to reclaim their children. In some cases, federal officials declined to intervene at all, deeming it better for the child to remain with white landowners.[34]

Freedmen's Bureau agents also had to contend with Maryland judges who sought to enforce antebellum criminal codes and sell the labor of newly freed people. In 1864, the state legislature supposedly outlawed this practice. Yet, two years later, freed people convicted of committing minor infractions "were sentenced to be sold in the state on giving eight days' notice."[35] For instance, in March of 1866, Theodore Waters was charged with "taking and carrying away one pig." That April, state officials charged River Smith and Benjamin McCall with stealing tobacco from John Howard. Colonel Skinner's alleged crime was taking a beehive from the property of Stephen Stanforth. Judge William H. Tuck of Calvert County denied these men a jury trial and resolved to imprison and eventually sell them.[36]

By the time Judge Tuck sentenced these men, Congress had passed the Civil Rights Act of 1866, overriding President Andrew Johnson's veto. The bill extended citizenship rights and provided for full and equal benefits of all laws to Black people. Importantly, it protected their right to give evidence. Judge D. R. Magruder's desire to test the constitutionality of the act compelled him to deny "negro testimony" and order "four negroes-two men and two women" convicted of larceny auctioned off in front of the Annapolis courthouse. An elderly freedman purchased himself for $37. The brother of another man purchased him at the auction for $35. The two women had their labor sold for one year; $37 was collected for one freedwoman, and the other one's labor went for $25.[37]

The Freedmen's Bureau deemed these legal decisions an insult to the letter and spirit of the Civil Rights Act. They seized the opportunity to hold judges who levied them accountable for such violations. Federal officials sought indictments—and at times secured them—for judges who refused to permit Black people to testify. Even so, these legal proceedings were mostly "insufficient to change practice."[38] Freedmen's Bureau agents operating in Maryland encountered these formidable judges determined to uphold even the most outdated state laws. One agent lamented that Judge Magruder was so committed to maintaining autonomy from the federal government that "on the subject of States' Rights . . . he searches the statute books to find laws sustaining them."[39]

On December 17, 1867, the United States House of Representatives Committee on the Judiciary resolved to authorize the continuation of inquiries regarding public affairs in Maryland. One of the main issues they sought to address was the alleged "sale of colored persons in the State of Maryland as punishment for crime." Congressman Charles E. Phelps, a former Unconditional Unionist serving Maryland's Third District as a member of the Conservative Party, was outraged by these investigations of a "State in full relations with the Government of the United States." He went on to accuse his party rivals of holding hearings on the matter without a Maryland member of Congress present. Phelps denounced the proceedings and condemned them as "impeachment and trial summarily consolidated" that questioned the state's "integrity."[40] Congressman Francis Thomas, also of Maryland, interrupted Phelps' attempt to prolong the point. He argued that they were engaged in a "matter of much graver importance than this question touching the condition of public affairs in Maryland," specifically President Johnson's impeachment. Phelps, however, continued to protest any further congressional investigation into this matter. He declared that sixty days after the Judiciary Committee was notified of these sentencings, the General Assembly of Maryland repealed the code—a code that they supposedly addressed three years earlier.[41] While the state legislature again attended to the law, Maryland Democrats wanted to make it clear that their action was not the result of the views of Congress.

Federal authorities continued to receive complaints about the treatment of Black Marylanders, particularly regarding labor. Unscrupulous practices by labor brokers reached federal agents. These brokers convinced Black people to take up work throughout Maryland with the promise of "$12 a month, quarters and rations." Freed people accused them of forcing laborers to reimburse farmers for transportation costs, misleading them about their destination and the type of work they would perform, and even taking them against their will to labor outside of the United States.[42] For instance, the Freedmen's Bureau inquired about the practices of Oliver Wood, a labor broker in Washington, DC, accused of forcing freedmen onto ships bound for Haiti and Guano Island (where they would dig bat dung, a valuable fertilizer). These inquiries yielded no known intervention on behalf of these freedmen. The Freedmen's Bureau's decision to not intervene may have been self-serving. They were pursuing measures to remove poor, unemployed, and underemployed Black people from the nation's capital. Wood primarily recruited Black men living in the city, among them numerous Black Marylanders.[43]

Despite the federal government's inability (and at times unwillingness) to protect freed people, members of the Black community still lobbied for redress. The scores of accounts that reached Freedmen's Bureau agents revealed the extent of outrages committed against freed people. In February of 1866, former United States Colored Infantryman Essex Barbour reported that ex-rebel soldiers in St. Mary's County assaulted him. Barbour stated that these former rebels physically attacked Black people at will, but Black men associated with the Union army were their primary targets.[44] One month later, reports of burning schoolhouses throughout the state and the destruction of colored churches, which also served as centers of learning, reached the federal government. The situation became so tense that some white Marylanders called for the establishment of military courts to address the attacks on Black institutions and the violence against freed people. Ultimately the federal government conceded that they would have to depend on local and state authorities to mete out justice equitably. Even Freedmen's Bureau official Seldon Clark concluded that white Marylanders were able to heap abuses on "negroes" chiefly due to their "powerlessness to secure legal redress" as "cases of personal assault were numerous; [but] the punishment of any assailant, if white, was unknown."[45]

It was also common for white Marylanders to respond violently to freed people who displayed any degree of political agency. Democrats, at least temporarily, settled the issue of extending the franchise to Black Marylanders when they rewrote the state's constitution in 1867. Additionally, they used the convention to voice their opposition to granting voting rights to Black men in the former Confederacy. Much to their disappointment, not only did Congress enfranchise Black men in the former Confederacy, but they also crafted a constitutional amendment that removed race as a barrier to voting.

Despite the objections of the Maryland General Assembly, which was dominated by Democrats who unanimously rejected the legislation, on February 3, 1870, the Fifteenth Amendment to the United States Constitution was ratified. Black Marylanders celebrated this occasion by organizing a series of events. On March 30, 1870, freed people in Baltimore held "a grand demonstration and civic procession in honor of the ratification of the fifteenth amendment to the federal constitution." White Marylanders responded by roundly criticizing such displays of thanksgiving. They accused freed people of having "nightly parade[s]" where participants hurled "insulting mottoes and indecent harangues"[46]

Immediately after the celebration ended, freed people got down to business. In May 1870, Arthur Smith was appointed chairman of a committee that assembled in Baltimore. Overcome by emotion, he "expressed his gratification at the honor conferred as it was the first time in his life he had been called to preside over a political meeting."[47] At the meeting, those in attendance lauded congressional Republicans for extending the vote to the Border States. Religious and community leaders expressed their gratitude by urging Black men to support the party of Abraham Lincoln.[48]

While the state Republican Party was slow to endorse extending the franchise to Black men, they planned to benefit from their participation in state and local elections. The party played an integral role in registering thirty-five thousand out of thirty-nine thousand eligible Black voters. These efforts prompted one Charles County politician to lament, "The Republican Party is straining every nerve to get the [Black] vote. The Democratic Party is standing by with its hands folded. Once joining the Republican Party, the negro will stay in it for years."[49]

Anticipating proceedings fraught with problems, federal officials attempted to provide oversight for the 1870 elections. Fearful of the Republican "machine," state Democrats flexed their political muscle and rejected the federal government's offer to assist on election day. Those who protested argued that "there was no more justification than law for Federal interference"[50] in Maryland's elections because state and local officials would protect the "colored" man as he cast his vote for the first time.[51]

Maryland Democrats, however, diligently worked to diminish the vote of these newly enfranchised Black men. With the federal government tending to civil matters in the former Confederacy, Black men residing in Maryland were contending with schemes that threatened to weaken their newly acquired voting rights. After vetting candidates, Black men in Maryland prepared themselves to travel to local polling places to cast their votes as the dominant political party devised schemes to eliminate them as part of a voting bloc.

For example, freed people had to stave off allegations of illegal registrations. One newspaper account stated that "between sixty and eighty colored men are registered as residing in dwellings occupied exclusively by whites and one hundred and fifty names of colored men are assigned to residences the occupants of which state that no such persons reside there."[52] State officials also alleged that over two hundred Black men had registered to vote in Washington, DC, during the previous election, and now they appeared on Maryland's registry books. State officials validated such claims by placing alleged violators under arrest and threatening them with confinement in a Maryland jail for "not less than five or more than ten years."[53] They declared that "nineteen colored men" had already been charged and were serving time for violating the law.[54] Ironically, Democrats who had once struggled to abolish the state's registry law, casting it as partisan legislation used to disenfranchise white men, successfully employed it to stifle the political aspirations of freedmen.

Democrats prepared further assaults against the Black vote by passing legislation to prevent freedmen convicted of a felony from participating in elections. This law was problematic for Black men charged with a crime for violating laws related to slavery. In December of 1870, Judge Daniel Magruder of the Circuit Court of Calvert County ruled that "colored men" convicted of a felony before the fifteenth amendment was adopted "were entitled to vote."[55] With a firm understanding of the tactics employed by Democrats to skirt national legislation, Republicans as far away as Milwaukee celebrated this victory. They concluded, "This decision is noteworthy as a formal recognition by the Democrats of Maryland of the validity of the 15th amendment."[56]

By and large, Black men cast their votes for Republicans. For their part, Democrats seemed astonished by their inability to sway freedmen. In the 1870 election, a noticeable number of Democrats running in counties with large Black populations confronted serious challenges. An editorial in the *St. Mary's Beacon* attributed some of the losses by Democratic candidates to the party's inability to convince Black voters that "the interest of the black race of our county was identical with our own."

Although Black men supported Republicans, which kept them competitive in local and state elections, the party was reluctant to run Black candidates. Comparatively, twenty-two Black men from the former Confederacy served in the United States Congress representing states such as neighboring Virginia, South Carolina, Mississippi, North Carolina, Alabama, Georgia, Florida, and Louisiana. A much higher number served in state and local governments. Maryland served as a counterpoint to such political progress. Some suggested that Black men held no meaningful place in Maryland politics, but this claim is a bit of an overstatement.[57]

On September 6, 1872, the *Baltimore Sun* reported that Henry Vinton Plummer was elected to be part of a delegation "to represent the county in the congressional convention." Eleven days later, this former slave traveled to Laurel, Maryland, to represent the county where he, his siblings, and his parents first experienced freedom.[58] Four years later, Plummer attended another Republican convention in Frederick, Maryland. As delegates spent time debating the issue of credentials, he took the opportunity to support the nomination of James A. Gary for delegate-at-large. Plummer boldly declared that he primarily endorsed Gary because he had "never spoken against negro suffrage," like other party members. For their part, Black Americans were keenly aware that their position in the party was tenuous. Black men often experienced resistance to their political participation. While the national efforts to grant Black men the franchise were indeed necessary and critical, the Black vote meant little without additional federal protection and the extension of other citizenship rights. If granted, Black men such as Henry Vinton Plummer may have been able to participate not only as voters and Republican delegates but also as local, state, and national officeholders.

By the time Henry Vinton Plummer articulated his concerns about members of the Republican Party attempting to exclude Black Americans, his father had built the family home on those ten acres of land. His sister, Sarah Miranda Plummer had founded St. Paul Baptist Church, and another sister, Nellie Plummer, was preparing to enter Wayland Seminary as its first female student and a classmate of Booker T. Washington. Black Marylanders were taking advantage of opportunities offered by organizations like the Baltimore Association for the Moral and Educational Improvement of the Colored People, which established educational facilities as early as 1864. They were also spearheading efforts to build schools and supply them with teachers. Freed people were appearing on plantations, in the middle of the night, and retrieving their children from their former masters. In parts of the state where labor was scarce, Black people successfully negotiated for more favorable working conditions. To be sure, the "ugly violence [against freed people] continued for years. Black people [in Maryland] did not cease to be scorned, rebuked, and persecuted, but they did cease to be slaves."⁵⁹ Therefore, as freed people, they seized every opportunity to better their circumstances.

By the end of 1866, Black Marylanders were confronting the reality that Reconstruction had come to an abrupt conclusion in the state. The Union Party's rule had come to an end, the state was redeemed, federal intervention was largely thwarted, and freed people were surviving freedom without adequate federal protections. The experience of inhabiting a loyal state with all its rights reserved during "self-Reconstruction" provided crucial lessons for the state's Black population. As their counterparts in the former Confederacy grappled with the consequences of the federal government's withdrawal, Black Marylanders—such as the Plummer family—had long been engaged in the arduous task of attempting to define and shape freedom for themselves.

NOTES

1. Nellie Arnold Plummer, *Out of the Depths: Or, the Triumph of the Cross* (New York: G. K. Hall, 1997), 83; "I think I shall never be comfortable again . . .: The Family during Slavery," Smithsonian Anacostia Community Museum, accessed January 1, 2017, https://anacostia.si.edu/exhibits/Plummer/Docs/Family_Slavery.pdf; "The Plummer Diary," Smithsonian Anacostia Community Museum, accessed January 1, 2017, https://anacostia.si.edu/exhibits/Plummer/Docs/PlummerMSS_FastWeb.pdf.

2. Plummer, *Out of the Depths*, 83.

3. On Black women using food as a tool to barter, see Psyche A. Williams-Forson, *Building Houses Out of Chicken Legs: Black Women, Food, and Power* (Chapel Hill: University of North Carolina Press, 2006).

4. *Baltimore City Jail Records,* Runaway Dockets, 1854–1864, MSA C2065–1 2/72/4/21, Maryland State Archives, Annapolis, Maryland. General Assembly (Laws), 1802, MdHR 820898–3, 2/2/6/10, 51. In 1802, the Maryland General Assembly passed a law stipulating that owners had sixty days from the time of a runaway advertisement to pay all legal costs related to apprehending, advertising, and imprisoning said slave. If they failed to do so, the jailer sold their slave. Jenny Masur, "Emily Plummer Going Home in Prince George's County," in *Heroes of the Underground Railroad around Washington, DC* (Charleston, SC: History Press, 2019).

5. "I think I shall never be comfortable again . . .: The Family during Slavery."

6. Eric Foner, *Reconstruction: America's Unfinished Revolution* (New York: Harper & Row Publishers, 1988), 271–80.

7. James Warner Harry, *The Maryland Constitution of 1851*, Johns Hopkins University Studies in Historical and Political Science, edited by J. M. Vincent, J. H. Hollander, and W. W. Willoughby, ser. 20, nos. 7–8 (Baltimore: Johns Hopkins Press, 1902). Article 3, Section 43 of this constitution forbid the passage of "any law abolishing the relation of master or slave, as it now exists in this State."

8. Edward Otis Hinkley, *The Constitution of the State of Maryland. Reported and Adopted by the Convention of Delegates Assembled at the City of Annapolis, April 27th, 1864, and Submitted to and Ratified by the People on the 12th and 13th Days of October, 1864* (Baltimore: John Murphy, 1864). In 1862, the United States Congress determined that an oath should be administered to "every person elected or appointed to any office of honor or profit under the Government of the United States" that pledged allegiance, that they had not borne arms against the United States or given aid, countenance, counsel, or encouragement to the persons engaged in armed hostility. The Maryland State Constitution of 1864 (Article1, Section 4) contained a loyalty oath allowing judges of elections to administer to any person attempting to vote an "oath or affirmation" that they had not given "any aid, countenance or support to those hostile to the United States."

9. Maryland Constitutional Convention, *The Debates of the Constitutional Convention of the State of Maryland [1864]* (Annapolis, MD: R. P. Bayly, 1864), 2:1,052, 1,067.

10. Maryland Constitutional Convention, *Proceedings of the Maryland State Constitutional Convention of Maryland to Frame a New Constitution, Commenced at Annapolis, April 27, 1864* (Annapolis, MD: R. P. Bayly, 1864), 333.

11. Maryland Constitutional Convention, *Proceedings of the Maryland State Constitutional Convention,* 404–5.

12. Maryland Constitutional Convention, *Proceedings of the Maryland State Constitutional Convention,* 838.

13. Maryland Constitutional Convention, *Proceedings of the Maryland State Constitutional Convention,* 79.

14. Maryland Constitutional Convention, *Debates of the Constitutional Convention,* 1:1,255.

15. Foner, *Reconstruction,* 41.

16. Richard P. Fuke, *Imperfect Equality: African Americans and the Confines of White Racial Attitudes in Post-Emancipation Maryland* (New York: Fordham University Press, 1999), 148.

17. Barbara J. Fields, *Slavery and Freedom on the Middle Ground: Maryland during the Nineteenth Century* (New Haven: Yale University Press, 1984), 135.

18. Laura Savarese, "The Freedmen's Bureau in Maryland: An Early Experiment in Legal Aid" (2019). *Student Scholarship Papers,* 134, https://digitalcommons.law.yale.edu/student_papers/134.

19. *Baltimore American,* December 4, 1866.

20. On the process of self-reconstruction in Maryland, see Edward Myers, *The Self-Reconstruction of Maryland* (Baltimore: Johns Hopkins Press, 1909).

21. *Congressional Globe,* 40th Cong., 2nd Sess., 230–31 (1867).

22. The Fourteenth Amendment passed, and it extended citizenship rights, prohibited states from depriving its citizens of due process and equal protection, reduced representation if adult male citizens of the state were not allowed to vote, barred those who engaged in rebellion or insurrection from holding office, and denied compensation for emancipated slaves to disloyal owners.

23. *Message of Governor Swann, to the General Assembly of Maryland, at Its Regular Session, 1867* (Annapolis: Maryland State Archives, 1867).

24. For seminal works on wartime and post-Civil War Maryland politics also see Charles L. Wagandt, *The Mighty Revolution: Negro Emancipation in Maryland 1862–1864* (Baltimore: Johns Hopkins University Press, 1964); Jean H. Baker, *The Politics of Continuity: Maryland Political Parties 1858–1870* (Baltimore: Johns Hopkins University Press, 1973).

25. See Dennis Patrick Halpin, *A Brotherhood of Liberty: Black Reconstruction and Its Legacies in Baltimore, 1865–1920* (Philadelphia: University of Pennsylvania Press, 2019) for a discussion on Blacks organizing politically in Baltimore post-Civil War.

26. "I think I shall never be comfortable again . . . The Family during Slavery."

27. Records of the Assistant Commissioner of the District of Columbia, Bureau of Refugees, Freedmen and Abandoned Lands, 1865–1869, "Miscellaneous Reports and Lists," Microfilm Publication M1055 Roll 21, National Archives, Washington, DC.

28. Records of the Assistant Commissioner of the District of Columbia, Bureau of Refugees, Freedmen and Abandoned Lands, 1865–1869, "Miscellaneous Reports and Lists."

29. *Report of the Assistant Commissioner of the Freedmen's Bureau: Summary Report of the District of Columbia* by Brevet Brigadier General John Eaton Jr., Assistant Commissioner" (Washington, DC: National Archives, December 1865), 158.

30. Fukes, *Imperfect Equality,* 78. Union general Lew Wallace placed newly freed Blacks in the state under special military protection, which ordered that courts cease to apprentice Black children and take the testimony of Black parents regarding the apprenticing of their children. Also see documents in Charles W. Mitchell, ed., "Freedom?," in *Maryland Voices of the Civil War* (Baltimore: Johns Hopkins University Press, 2007).

31. 39th Congress 1st Session House of Representatives, misc. doc. no. 50, *Protection of Emancipated Slaves and Freedmen,* February 26, 1866.

32. 39th Congress 1st Session House of Representatives, misc. doc. no. 50, *Protection of Emancipated Slaves and Freedmen.*

33. Fields, *Slavery and Freedom on the Middle Ground,* 150–52.

34. Tera Hunters, *To 'Joy My Freedom: Southern Black Women's Lives and Labors after the Civil War* (Cambridge, MA: Harvard University Press, 1997). She asserts that some American Missionary Association agents desired for Black-orphaned children to remain with white families, avoiding the "outside influences" of their Black family. Deborah Gray White, *Ar'n't I a Woman?: Female Slaves in the Plantation South* (New York: W. W. Norton, 1999), 162. White argues that Black women interpreted freedom as an opportunity to mother their children.

35. Records of the Assistant Commissioner of the District of Columbia, Bureau of Refugees, Freedmen and Abandoned Lands, 1865–1869, "Miscellaneous Reports and Lists."

36. Records of the Assistant Commissioner of the District of Columbia, Bureau of Refugees, Freedmen and Abandoned Lands, 1865–1869, "Miscellaneous Reports and Lists."

37. *Daily National Intelligencer,* December 25, 1866.

38. Savarese, "Freedmen's Bureau in Maryland," 134.

39. Records of the Assistant Commissioner for the District of Columbia Bureau of Refugees, Freedmen, and Abandoned Lands 1865–1869, Microfilm Publication M1055, Roll 21, "Report of Bvt. Major W. L. Vanderlip to W. W. Rogers, December 19, 1866," National Archives, Washington, DC. There is much evidence to suggest that local authorities also employed flogging as a punishment for minor infractions.

40. Congressional Globe, 40th Cong., 2nd Sess., 230–31 (December 17, 1867).

41. Congressional Globe, 40th Cong., 2nd Sess., 230 (December 17, 1867).

42. "Affidavit of a Former Employee of a Maryland Labor Broker and Lewis W. Bruning, September 25, 1865," Unregistered Letters Received, ser. 457, DC Assistant Commissioner, Bureau of Refugees, Freedmen, & Abandoned Lands, Record Group 105, National Archives, Washington, DC; Oliver Wood to Maj. Gen. Howard, September 4, 1865, Unregistered Letters Received, ser. 457, DC Assistant Commissioner, Bureau of Refugees, Freedmen, & Abandoned Lands, Record Group 105, National Archives Washington, DC.

43. "Affidavit of a Former Employee"; Oliver Wood to Maj. Gen. Howard.

44. Records of the Assistant Commissioner for the District of Columbia, Bureau of Refugees, Freedmen and Abandoned Lands, 1865–1869, "Miscellaneous Reports and Lists."

45. "Report of the Assistant Commissioner of the Freedmen's Bureau: Summary Report of the District of Columbia by Brevet Brigadier General John Eaton Jr., Assistant Commissioner [December 1865]," 157.

46. *Baltimore Sun,* November 7, 1870.

47. *Baltimore Sun,* March 30, 1870, and May 5, 1870.

48. *Baltimore Sun,* May 5, 1870.

49. *Port Tobacco Times and Charles County Advertiser,* September 2, 1870.

50. *Baltimore Sun,* October 10, 1870.

51. *Baltimore Sun,* November 8, 1870.

52. *Baltimore Sun,* November 8, 1870.

53. *Baltimore Sun,* November 8, 1870.

54. *Baltimore Sun,* November 7, 1870.

55. *Milwaukee Sentinel,* December 2, 1870.

56. *Milwaukee Sentinel,* December 2, 1870.

57. Jeffrey Brackett, *The Progress of Colored Men in Maryland* (Baltimore: Johns Hopkins University, 1890); Bianca P. Floyd, *Records, and Recollections: Early Black History in Prince George's County Maryland* (Maryland-National Capital Park and Planning Commission, Department of Parks and Recreation, Prince George's County, History Division, January 1989), 62.

58. *The Baltimore Sun,* May 5, 1872.

59. Fields, *Slavery and Freedom on the Middle Ground,* 130.

"F—K THE CONFEDERACY"

The Strange Career of Civil War Memory in Maryland after 1865

ROBERT J. COOK

More than 150 years after the end of the Civil War, African Americans in Maryland wreaked a measure of revenge on their adversaries. In the early hours of August 16, 2017, contractors removed three Confederate monuments and a statue of Chief Justice Roger B. Taney, architect of the US Supreme Court's 1857 *Dred Scott* ruling that denied the citizenship of African Americans, from their locations across Baltimore. The city's Democratic Black mayor, Catherine Pugh, justified her decision to take down the monuments on the grounds of public safety. Just four days earlier violence had erupted in neighboring Virginia, when far-right activists rallied in Charlottesville to defend a statue of Confederate general Robert E. Lee that had been scheduled for removal. One antifascist demonstrator, Heather Heyer, was mown down by a car, and two state troopers died when their helicopter crashed while they monitored her killer's escape. "We all are seeing lessons via the media of uprisings and violence," announced Pugh the morning after the statues had been hauled away, "and violence is not what we need in our city."[1] Evidence abounded, however, that the monuments' removal had more to do with contemporary racial struggles than a simple desire to preserve the public peace. Mayor Pugh herself asked rhetorically why a memorial to Taney existed: "Why does someone like that even deserve a statue? Why should people have to feel that kind of pain every day?"[2] On the forlorn empty pedestal of the Lee-Jackson Monument in Wyman Park Dell, fresh slogans appeared announcing local Blacks' blunt refutation of their state's racist past. "F—k the Confederacy," read one of them. "Black lives matter," asserted another.[3]

The removal of the Baltimore statues provided vivid proof of the Civil War's lingering grip on Maryland, a border slave state that had remained within the Union. Unsurprisingly, the war's mnemonic impact was greatest in the half century after 1865. It was felt primarily by those Unionists and Confederates who had lived through it. Their determination to hold onto the receding past fed ongoing party battles in the state as the organization most closely associated with Union victory, the Republican Party, lost political ground to its Democratic rival in large part because the majority of Marylanders, even the Unionists among them, had precious little sympathy for the national Republican Party's Reconstruction-era commitment to Black equality under the law. Confederate and Union veterans and their immediate kinsfolk contributed to a rash of monument building in public places across the state in the late nineteenth and early twentieth centuries, and they enlisted considerable community support for commemorative activities. But by 1915 the wartime generation was passing away quickly and with it went the vigorous collective memories of the veterans on both sides. For the next fifty years, traces of the Civil War struggle remained embedded in the South's Lost Cause and a bland reconciliatory narrative of the contest. Only when the modern civil rights movement stirred local and national awareness that the Civil War was, in racial terms, unfinished business did growing numbers of Marylanders begin to realize that the inert stones of the past concealed a remarkable amount of ideological ballast.

Civil War memories were at their most vivid in the immediate aftermath of the bloodletting—in part because they were directly linked to contemporary political struggles arising out of the conflict. Many Union veterans in the state vehemently opposed President Andrew Johnson's lenient Reconstruction policy for the defeated South because they believed it would surrender the fruits of their military service and enable the rapid return of discredited ex-Confederates to political power. In order to prevent their enemies from winning the peace, they insisted on drawing the line between those who had been loyal to the United States in the war and those who had sought to destroy it. That line, they insisted, should apply to the dead as well as the living.

In 1867 Union veterans in Maryland began joining a new national organization, the Grand Army of the Republic (GAR), committed to defending the United States against its enemies and to a concomitant remembrance of the Union cause. The Grand Army men's deep suspicion of the defeated "rebels" manifested itself in several ways, but none more strongly than in their opposition to burying the Confederate dead in the country's new national cemeteries. Speaking in the predominantly Unionist town of Frederick in September 1867 shortly after Andrew Johnson had attended a reconciliation-themed dedication ceremony at nearby Antietam National Cemetery, the local GAR commander condemned the "insult offered to our loyal dead, by burrying thoes [*sic*] who fell in trying to break up our country, by their side."[4] Early the following year his outraged comrades urged the state's governor, conservative Unionist Thomas Swann, to ask "Congress to prevent the desecration of Antietam Cemetery by the interring therein of the Traitors who fell in battle on the soil of Maryland."[5] Although the state legislature, exemplifying Maryland's position as a divided Border State, had initially favored the co-interment of Union and Confederate corpses at Antietam, the opposition of Union veterans in Maryland and beyond to this reconciliatory gesture ensured that fallen Confederates in the state would be buried not in any of the country's new US cemeteries but in separate plots in local graveyards like Hagerstown's Washington Cemetery.[6]

In critical state elections in 1867, however, white-supremacist Democrats triumphed over their opponents with the assistance of conservative Unionists who, hostile to the racial revolution portended by Union victory and the abolition of slavery in the state, opposed congressional Republicans' mounting support for adult Black male suffrage. This watershed political triumph sealed the early and decisive defeat of war-born Republicanism in Maryland and laid the foundations for the development of a racially segregated society that consigned newly liberated African Americans to the status of second-class citizens. Their power restored, Maryland Democrats frequently privileged former Confederates in the distribution of high offices such as attorney general.[7] Their victory, however, did not signal an end to the Civil War's influence on the state.

By the time they reached middle age, large numbers of Maryland's Civil War veterans were casting their minds back to the days of their youth. "The old times, and old army experiences crowd up till if they were men," wrote one ex-Federal in 1887, "I could have a corps to muster in. And they take possession of me till I want to talk right out."[8] And talk about the war to one another they increasingly did, often in veterans' groups whose discussions consolidated certain memories and filtered out others. They also helped to raise monuments, spoke in public about their respective causes, and urged younger Marylanders not to forget the sacrifices of the wartime generation. A small minority wrote about their experiences in the great conflict and published the results in journals, local newspapers, and book-length recollections. By the 1890s the state was awash with Civil War memories that reflected not only the divisions of the past but also the consensual pressures of the difficult present.

During the quarter century after Appomattox this veteran-led output of war memories generated two dominant historical narratives in Maryland: first, a defiant Lost Cause narrative constructed by southern sympathizers who had left the state in the early 1860s to fight for the Confederacy and, second, an initially robust account of the Union cause that lauded patriotic citizen-soldiers for saving the Republic from its domestic foes and finally bringing about the destruction of slavery in the United States.

While their attachment to themes such as the valor of southern soldiers, the virtuousness of their principles, and the beneficence of slavery was shared by many Confederate veterans and their female kin in other states, Maryland "rebels" also embraced the South's Lost Cause for reasons closely connected to their distinctive wartime experience. Postbellum efforts to remember a minority of Marylanders' commitment to the Confederacy were led by Bradley Tyler Johnson, a college-educated lawyer who had edited a secessionist newspaper in Frederick and left the state for Dixie in the spring of 1861. Although disappointed not to lead the newly organized Maryland Line two years later, he temporarily commanded a full brigade of Virginia troops at Second Bull Run and was appointed a brigadier general before squandering something of his reputation when his unit was routed by federal forces in 1864. After the war Johnson practiced law and Democratic politics in Richmond, Virginia, but spent much of his time defending the actions of Maryland Confederates from fellow southerners as well as local Unionists. Initially, like the Virginian Jubal A. Early (another leading proponent of the Lost Cause with whom he corresponded frequently), his chief aim in honoring the Confederacy was to rebut Unionist claims that he and his defeated comrades should be treated "as unconvicted rebels" worthy only of "dishonored graves."[9] But Johnson also struggled to combat sneers from fellow southerners, rooted specifically in his state's failure to secede and to rise up subsequently against Yankee tyranny when Lee's Army of Northern Virginia raided into the state in the fall of 1862. Confederate Marylanders, he contended, were the bravest of the brave precisely because they had had to overcome enormous hardships to fight for southern independence.

Johnson helped to create two important institutional vehicles for Confederate veterans' memory. In 1871 he organized the Society of the Army and Navy of the Confederate States in the State of Maryland, an outgrowth of the Loudon Park Memorial Association established by Confederate servicemen in Baltimore to reinter and honor Confederate soldiers who had died in federal custody at nearby Fort McHenry. Nine years later, by which time he had relocated to Baltimore, Johnson founded the Association of the Maryland Line to complement the society's activities.[10] In November 1886 he articulated his views on the Lost Cause in a speech delivered to a joint meeting of these two Confederate memorialization groups. He was, he said, often asked why he did not let the Confederate dead rest in peace. "My answer is," he responded, "the cause of the Confederate States was the cause of civil liberty, under constitutional forms, on this continent." There would, he added, be no such thing as a Lost Cause "as long as freemen all over the world love liberty long and struggle for it, and if need be fight for it; and they will respect the people who dared, at such great cost, to stand in defense of it against overwhelming odds and irresistible force."[11] This partisan description of the proslavery Confederates' liberation struggle was echoed in the writings of other prominent "rebel" veterans, including Henry Kyd Douglas and George Wilson Booth, who contributed full-blown memoirs to the state's burgeoning Lost Cause canon, and William W. Goldsborough, who penned a detailed and predictably laudatory account of the Maryland Line.

By the late 1880s Bradley Johnson and his allies, determined that the modern South should be built on the foundations of the old, had largely succeeded in their aim of restoring honor and respect to Maryland Confederates. More than that, they had already done much to fabricate a false historical narrative of wartime Marylanders as, in Johnson's words, "intensely Southern, with all their hearts."[12] As was the case in Kentucky, another divided border slave state that had not seceded and provided more troops to the Union than the Confederacy, the political predominance of the Democratic Party and the opposition of a majority of local Unionists to racial equality enabled Maryland to embrace the Lost Cause with a far tighter grasp than it had ever extended to the Confederacy itself.[13] In 1888 the state's Democrat-controlled legislature voted funds to enable the Maryland Line Association to create a Confederate Soldiers Home in Pikesville.[14] No similar facility was ever set up for local Union veterans, in part because those veterans were granted relatively generous pensions by the US government in 1890.

The regular commemoration of Confederate Memorial Day every May revealed the growing reach of the Lost Cause. Baltimore developed rapidly after the Civil War, but social and economic change was no barrier to memorializing the Confederacy—even in a racially and ethnically diverse city that had not been a mainstay of "rebel" support in the state during the Civil War. Veterans and supportive womenfolk congregated at the Confederate cemetery in Loudon Park to watch young girls lay flowers on the graves of fallen southern heroes and hear speeches lauding the heroism of the past. "Our resistless troops knew no defeat," intoned one orator. "Our great chieftains well knew the heroic character and reliability of their troops, who uniformly stood like a stone wall to unflinchingly meet victory or death."[15]

Commemorative rituals intended to disseminate veneration for the Lost Cause across the generations were complemented by the construction of monuments that were, essentially, messages from the Jim Crow present to the uncertain future. Perhaps surprisingly, when the Society of the Army and Navy first mooted construction of a stone tribute to Confederate servicemen, the idea was not well received by all Maryland "rebels." Opposing the Baltimore city council's decision to allow the monument to be located in Eutaw Place, southern veteran Charles T. Crane wrote an open letter to the city's mayor, Ferdinand C. Latrobe, reminding him that Maryland had never left the Union and asserting that nothing should be done to stir old hatreds. "I am unwilling," he wrote, "to see erected in the public streets of this city a monument to a dead idea, but which will be a standing menace, and a source of bitterness not only to a great number of the citizens of Baltimore and Maryland, but to a great number of the people of the United States."[16] Although Crane's views probably did little to influence the mayor's subsequent decision to veto the monument (he was a well-known supporter of Blue-Gray reconciliation), they were not shared by all his old comrades and their allies. Aided by the efforts of well-to-do white women belonging to local Ladies' Memorial Associations and most notably, after its formation in 1894, the United Daughters of the Confederacy (UDC), pro-Confederate Marylanders pressed ahead with their commemorative activities. The Daughters achieved a major coup in early 1899 when, fifteen months after the unveiling of a statue to Roger Taney in Baltimore's elite Mount Vernon Place district, the city council backed the construction of a Confederate Soldiers' and Sailors' monument.[17] The resulting memorial was dedicated in May 1903, with many aging "rebels" carrying faded battle flags in attendance.[18]

These and other pro-southern monuments were built during a period of heightened tensions over the place of African Americans in Maryland society. The election of a Republican governor at a time of churning social change in

1895, accomplished with the assistance of Black votes, impelled Old Guard Democrats like Arthur Pue Gorman—restored to power in 1901—to follow recent efforts by Deep South states like Mississippi to construct a Jim Crow society. Gorman asked John Prentiss Poe, dean of the state university law school, to draft an amendment to the Maryland constitution disfranchising Black voters. Poe's handiwork gave the vote to any adult male whose grandfather had voted before passage of the Fifteenth Amendment and enabled registrars to turn away prospective voters who could not demonstrate a "reasonable" understanding of the constitution.[19] The proposal encountered fierce opposition from African Americans, some of whom conjured memories of the Civil War to bolster their case. It was condemned, for example, by local Black Methodists who convened for their annual conference in Washington, DC, in March 1904. The Poe amendment, they announced, was "class legislation" that ran counter to the republican views "so eloquently stated by our greatest commoner in his Gettusburg [sic] address when he prayed for the preservation of a government by the people, for the people, and of the people."[20] The amendment was eventually rejected by the electorate in part because some leading Democrats feared its impact on illiterate white voters. But the trend toward racial segregation in the state under the Democrats continued in the early twentieth century, the consolidation of an unequal society assisted by the growth of an openly racist Lost Cause culture that glorified the imagined virtues of the aborted Confederacy.

African American Methodists' attempt to enlist the support of Abraham Lincoln against disfranchisement indicated the persistence of Civil War memories running counter to the Lost Cause in Maryland. Blacks were always the staunchest proponents of an emancipation-focused Unionist narrative that found meaning in the war as a moment of racial liberation and national renewal in which they had played an active part. During the early years of Reconstruction Black leaders asserted the demonstrable loyalty of slaves and Colored Troops to the Union as leverage in their struggle for the suffrage. At Maryland's racially integrated Republican convention in May 1867, Alfred Handy, an African American tailor from Baltimore, pressed his white co-partisans to fulfill the fragile racial promise of Union military victory. "We demand of the Radical Republican Union Party," he said, "that when they shall have gotten into power that they will stand by their colored brethren—that they will not forget the assistance we tendered them in their hour of greatest need."[21]

Maryland Blacks continued to mark their loyalty to the Union after the Democrats' political victory in 1867 by regularly celebrating Lincoln's Birthday and Emancipation Day in their principal communities in Baltimore, in southern Maryland, and on the Eastern Shore.[22] While African American veterans were generally poorer than their white counterparts and likely to die at an earlier age than the latter, many of them resolutely demonstrated their patriotism and manhood by joining all-Black GAR posts like Logan, Lincoln, and Ellsworth in Baltimore, Sheridan in Annapolis, and Brown in Cambridge.[23] In the 1880s the Baltimore posts sponsored an annual September pilgrimage to Gettysburg, the nation's chief Union shrine, to mark the anniversary of the preliminary emancipation proclamation.[24] Not every Black visitor to the battlefield went there to venerate the Union cause. Baltimore's middle-class Black press, keen to disseminate notions of uplift and respectability at a time of deteriorating race relations, was quick to criticize any reports of rowdy behavior by the excited trippers.[25] But the presence of thousands of African American tourists on the famous battlefield bore witness to the fact that Maryland Blacks in the late nineteenth century had no intention of relinquishing Civil War memories to their oppressors.

This was especially true of the Black veterans and their kin who participated enthusiastically in national Memorial Day exercises every May. In some Eastern Shore towns like Centerville, these rituals were dominated by African Americans.[26] In places where Blacks participated with whites, the day's events were often marked by none-too-subtle racial distinctions. In Baltimore parades Black veterans normally marched behind their white comrades and then made their way separately to Black cemeteries in the city that were the main repositories for deceased Colored Troops. However, clad as they were in the blue uniform of the United States, their very public performance of loyalty to the Republic announced their uncompromising defiance of white claims to racial superiority.

Most white Unionists fostered a distinctive narrative of the Civil War that highlighted their own contribution to national salvation. This stirring account of the wartime patriotism and courage of Marylanders in the 1860s did not ignore the subject of Black emancipation entirely. The theme was a relatively commonplace one in Memorial Day and monument dedication texts composed by some of the aging soldiers. "Thank God no slave repines where now our banners wave in this broad land," rejoiced one member of the John F. Reynolds GAR post in Frederick. "And none again will ever wish to forge the chain that binds indurance [*sic*] vile upon man, whate'er his color, race or class."[27] However, in contrast to their Black comrades and many white ex-Federals in the

North East and upper Midwest, white Union veterans in the state normally rel-
egated emancipation to a secondary place in the narrative and did not connect
it to the waning contemporary fight for racial equality. J. Polk Racine, a soldier
from Easton in the Fifth Maryland Infantry who had seen combat at Antietam and in the trenches around Petersburg, was one of the few white Union
veterans in the state to write a full-blown memoir of his wartime service. Like
many of his comrades, Racine deplored slavery (mainly because of its deleteri-
ous impact on whites) and welcomed its demise. But his book, published for a
local readership in 1894, made no mention of the contribution of US Colored
Troops to the Federals' decisive breakthrough at Petersburg and, tellingly, was
sprinkled with evidence of the past and present racial prejudices of Maryland
Unionists. He remembered, for example, that shortly before the Battle of Antietam his comrades had amused themselves by tossing a young "nigger" in a
rotten blanket—an episode that had culminated in the boy's death as a result of
a broken neck.[28] He also recalled seeing inebriated Union soldiers kill a "poor
half-witted darkey" when they occupied Richmond at the end of the war.[29]

It was in their support for monuments and performance of loyalty to the
Republic that white Union veterans made their most significant contributions
to Civil War remembrance in Maryland. While many of these ex-Federals
bemoaned the Democrats' return to power in the late 1860s, they continued to
demand recognition of their wartime service to the Union from the state and
national governments. Over time their hatred of "rebels" tended to dissipate.
Racine described the Confederates as "a brave and gallant foe, well worthy our
steel."[30] But their growing willingness to articulate reconciliatory sentiments
(which was partly a consequence of their limited influence in a predominantly
Democratic state) did not moderate their determination to be remembered for
posterity.

Benjamin Franklin Taylor is a case in point. A colonel from Towson who
served in the Second Maryland Infantry that fought on the Union side at
Antietam, Taylor nurtured ties with many of his former comrades throughout
his postwar career and in the early twentieth century was elected president
of the state's Union Veterans' Association.[31] A Republican in politics, he was
a prime mover in efforts to remember the Union cause in a state that was
largely controlled by a party with little interest in paying homage to the sixty-
two thousand white and Black Marylanders who had once fought to save the
United States from destruction. It was often a difficult struggle. Union veterans

required support from ex-Confederates in the state legislature to secure modest public funding for five regimental monuments at Gettysburg. At a dedication ceremony on the battlefield attended by white veterans and two companies of Black militiamen from Baltimore in October 1888, Elihu Emory Jackson, the state's Democratic governor who hailed from a family of southern sympathizers, declined to hail Unionists' defense of the country.[32] The governor wished, he said, "that time will crumble all monuments to dust in this country ere we shall witness another day like this one. These monuments commemorate the deeds the mention of which to-day opens afresh the wounds in the hearts of thousands of widows and orphans."[33]

Although Taylor certainly shared the view of one of his former comrades that Maryland Unionists could "look back with pride to the service they rendered the country in its hour of peril," he joined the majority of former Federals in supporting the idea of reconciliation with ex-Confederates, especially after witnessing the support afforded by a number of leading southerners to the United States in its war against Spain in 1898.[34] Five years later, speaking at a ceremony to dedicate a state monument to all Maryland soldiers who had participated in the extensive military operations around Chattanooga, Tennessee, in 1863, he paid tribute to those southerners who "took up arms to vindicate what, for them, was a righteous cause." Added Taylor, "To say who was right or who was wrong . . . would be invidious and out of place." The war was over, he concluded, "The questions that caused it, the questions it involved, of the nation's power have long since been settled and one who would seek to revive them would not be taken seriously."[35]

Broadly consensual views like this accorded well with a waxing national mood of North-South reconciliation at the turn of the century. This trend toward consensus, sentimentality, and forgetting has been ably documented by historians such as Nina Silber and David Blight and facilitated the growth of a racially segregated society in the United States by marginalizing memories of the Civil War as a patriotic war for the Union fought against the nation's southern enemies by Blacks as well as whites.[36] In Maryland reconciliation was assisted by the conservatism of most Unionists, the durability of white supremacy, and the state's own fractured Civil War experience. These factors certainly contributed to the efforts of state leaders to fashion a usable reconciliatory past by providing funds to build single monuments honoring both Maryland Unionists and Confederates at Antietam as well as Chattanooga. Although these monuments were accepted and sometimes enthusiastically endorsed by aging soldiers like Benjamin Taylor, they did not halt efforts by former Unionists or Confederates to commemorate their respective causes. Federal veterans belatedly secured state funding for a Union Soldiers' and Sailors' monument dedicated in Baltimore's Druid Hill Park in 1909, while local UDC members raised funds to build a monument to Confederate women in the same city in 1917. By this date, however, memories of the Civil War had begun to loosen their grip on the state. The wartime generation was passing away rapidly, and most younger Marylanders, regardless of their racial, ethnic, and socioeconomic background, had more pressing matters than the issues of the distant past to attend to in the challenging present.

In the half century after the First World War Marylanders lived in the shadow of two dominant historical narratives of the Civil War. The first, a reconciliatory account of the conflict which depicted it as a tragic and essentially white brothers' war in which brave American men on both sides had fought for grand principles like freedom and self-government, subsumed the fading Unionist narrative that, in the early years of Reconstruction, had assisted the cause of equal rights for African Americans. At the National Park Service-owned battlefield at Antietam in September 1937 President Franklin D. Roosevelt spoke the language of North-South reconciliation by applauding the courage of soldiers on both sides in what he pointedly called "the war Between the States," by giving thanks that the Union cause had been successful, and by dismissing Reconstruction as a barrier to national unity.[37]

The second dominant narrative of the Civil War in twentieth-century Maryland, that of the Lost Cause, was actively sustained not only by southern heritage groups like the UDC and the Sons of the Confederacy but also by white-supremacist Democrats keen to defend racial segregation against internal and external attack. Black newspapers like the *Baltimore Afro-American* provided the chief opposition to the Lost Cause tradition, for example by opposing the state's participation in a UDC-sponsored effort to memorialize Heyward Shepherd in Harpers Ferry, West Virginia. Shepherd, an African American, had been killed in John Brown's abolitionist raid on the town in 1859 and was therefore deemed by Lost Cause advocates to personify both Black loyalty to the supposedly beneficent proslavery regime and Black victimhood in the face of irresponsible political radicalism.[38] But in the conservative racial climate of the 1920s and 1930s, Black leaders struggled to persuade Maryland whites, certainly those living in rural strongholds like southern Maryland and the Eastern Shore, that the state had not been a natural Confederate stronghold forced to remain in the Union by the actions of a tyrannical Union government. Faced with growing evidence of Black assertiveness, epitomized by the efforts of Baltimore-based lawyers Thurgood Marshall and Charles Hamilton Houston to force integration of the University of Maryland law school, the Democrat-controlled legislature in Annapolis signaled its contempt for the incipient civil rights movement by making "Maryland, My Maryland!," a rabidly anti-Yankee poem, the official state song in April 1939.[39]

More keenly aware of the contested nature of Civil War memory than most Americans in the 1960s, Maryland state officials adhered steadfastly to a reconciliatory narrative of the conflict during the centennial observances of that troubled decade. Fearing the kind of adverse publicity that had accompanied an overcommercialized reenactment of the First Battle of Bull Run in Virginia in July 1961, the state centennial commission refused to support a similar event at Antietam sponsored by Hagerstown-based organizers the following year. Instead, the commission followed national policy by encouraging "honest research" into the Civil War in the expectation that this would "heal old wounds" and provide "better understanding of the causes that led to conflict."[40] Among its limited accomplishments was the placement of a commemorative plaque in the state house. Unveiled in October 1964, the plaque marked "the centennial of that great struggle between the citizens of the temporarily divided nation in the 1860s." Continuing the dual Confederate/Unionist heritage approach that had informed the construction of joint monuments at Chattanooga and Antietam, it also declared that the centennial commission "did not attempt to decide who was right and who was wrong, or to make decisions on other controversial issues" and described the soldiers on both sides as trying "to do their duty as they saw it."[41] While this statement appeared unproblematic to many people in the light of the state's divided history as well as the national centennial commission's desire to foster public unity in the midst of the Cold War, it ignored the view of Black Marylanders that the slavery issue had imparted a moral dimension to the late conflict that the burgeoning civil rights movement was proceeding to uncover.

Twenty-first-century controversy over the meaning of Civil War statues and emblems has its roots in the race-inflected culture wars unleashed by opposition to the civil rights movement in the 1950s and 1960s. White supremacists, angered by rising Black militancy and the prospect of open accommodations legislation, embraced the Confederate battle flag as a symbol of resistance to racial integration. When Alabama governor George Wallace, an ardent segregationist, launched his campaign to win the Democratic primary in Maryland in 1964, he was greeted at his motel near Baltimore by enthusiastic supporters, many of them teenagers waving battle flags.[42] Three days later he spoke to a gathering of conservative women at a local restaurant and denounced the comprehensive civil rights bill pending in Congress for its likely destruction of "the neighborhood schools in Maryland." The "well-dressed" women responded "with Rebel yells and distributed Confederate bills."[43] The governor went on to carry seventeen counties and win 43 percent of the primary vote.[44] He was especially popular in areas like southern Maryland, the Eastern Shore, and Baltimore and Anne Arundel counties, where opposition to the desegregation of public facilities was strongest.

Alert to the linkages between modern-day and historic racism, Maryland Blacks and their liberal white allies in the Washington suburbs moved to condemn contemporary evidence of support for the Lost Cause. Howard A. Denis, a white state senator from Montgomery County, denounced "Maryland, My Maryland!" as "a hate song" in 1980 and attempted to have it scrapped by holding a statewide contest to replace it.[45] Although his maneuver failed, it indicated a new mood of assertiveness on the part of antiracists—a mood that was facilitated by the growth of a large African American middle class in the city of Baltimore and Prince George's County and the growing influence of confident Black politicians at the state and local levels. These developments ensured that when Maryland officials began planning for the Civil War sesquicentennial, they could not ignore Black concerns. Bill Pencek, the state's director of heritage tourism, declared in 2009 that forthcoming events would "highlight diverse viewpoints on the war, a departure from centennial observances that mainly honored Confederate veterans."[46]

Maryland Blacks redoubled their efforts to excise physical evidence of the state's Lost Cause past after the well-intentioned sesquicentennial—their efforts galvanized by the murderous events in Charlottesville and President Donald Trump's open contempt for people of color. As well as demanding the removal of Confederate statues, they insisted that a clear line must be drawn between the Confederate and the Union causes. In May 2019 Adrienne Jones, the first African American Speaker of the state House of Delegates, urged the removal of the old centennial plaque from the capitol in Annapolis. "History clearly tells us there was a right and a wrong side of the Civil War," she contended, "I believe it is our duty to ensure truth in history for what it is, not what some may have wished it to be."[47] The sentiment would have been music to the ears of many Marylanders, Black and white, in the 1860s. At long last, the days of the Lost Cause in this predominantly Unionist state looked to be numbered.

NOTES

1. "Baltimore Hauls Away Four Confederate Monuments after Overnight Removal," *Washington Post*, August 16, 2017.

2. "Baltimore mayor on Confederate statues: Why should people have to feel that pain every day? *Guardian*, August 22, 2017.

3. "Baltimore Hauls Away," *Washington Post*, August 16, 2017.

4. Minutes of September 25, 1867, vol. 1 ("General Orders and Minutes"), box 1, GAR Post No. 2 (Frederick, MD), Grand Army of the Republic Collection, 1863–1901, Historical Society of Frederick County.

5. Minutes of January 8, 1868, vol. 1 ("General Orders and Minutes").

6. For an account of how the dead on both sides obstructed sectional reconciliation see especially John R. Neff, *Honoring the Civil War Dead: Commemoration and the Problem of Reconciliation* (Lawrence: University Press of Kansas, 2005).

7. Benjamin F. Taylor to Lloyd Lowndes, November 9, 1895, box 2, Benjamin F. Taylor Collection, MS 2197, Maryland Center for History and Culture Library, Baltimore, MD.

8. William H. (Sivel) Mathews to Taylor, December 5, 1887, box 1, Taylor Collection, MS 2197.

9. Bradley T. Johnson, *Address Delivered by Gen. Bradley T. Johnson, Before the Society of the Army and Navy of the Confederate States in the State of Maryland, and the Association of the Maryland Line, at Maryland Hall, Baltimore, MD, on Tuesday, November 16, 1886* (Baltimore: Andrew J. Conlon, n.d.), 2.

10. Thomas E. Will, "Bradley T. Johnson's Lost Cause: Maryland's Confederate Identity in the New South," *Maryland Historical Magazine* 94 (Spring 1999): 9.

11. Johnson, "Address," 1.

12. Quoted in Will, "Bradley T. Johnson's Lost Cause," 14.

13. On Kentucky's rapid transition from a wartime Unionist state to a postwar Confederate one, see especially Anne E. Marshall, *Creating a Confederate Kentucky: The Lost Cause and Civil War Memory in a Border State* (Chapel Hill: University of North Carolina Press, 2010).

14. Robert J. Brugger, *Maryland: A Middle Temperament 1634–1980* (Baltimore: Johns Hopkins University Press in association with the Maryland Center for History and Culture, 1988), 393.

15. "The Lost Cause Not Forgotten," undated press clipping [c.1900], scrapbook 2, box 1, Benjamin F. Taylor Collection, MS 1863, Maryland Center for History and Culture Library, Baltimore, MD.

16. "The Proposed Confederate Monument," *Baltimore Sun*, March 27, 1880.

17. Baltimore's Civil Rights Heritage, "Baltimore's Confederate Memory & Monuments," accessed August 5, 2019, https://baltimoreheritage.github.io/civil-rights-heritage/confederate-memory/.

18. Baltimore's Civil Rights Heritage, "Baltimore's Confederate Memory & Monuments."

19. Brugger, *Maryland,* 420.

20. Resolutions of the Washington Annual Conference of the Methodist Episcopal Church on the Negro Disfranchisement bill and the Separate Car Law of Maryland," March 16, 1904, folder 27, box 3, Edwin Warfield Collection, Maryland Center for History and Culture Library, Baltimore, MD.

21. Quoted in Jean H. Baker, *The Politics of Continuity: Maryland Political Parties from 1858 to 1870* (Baltimore: Johns Hopkins University Press, 1973), 179.

22. "Lincoln, Still Lives," *Baltimore Afro-American,* February 15, 1896.

23. For a full listing of GAR posts in Maryland see Grand Army of the Republic (GAR) Records Index, https://suvcw.org/garrecords/garcat/garcatalog.htm. All-Black posts in the state are identified in Barbara A. Gannon, *The Won Cause: Black and White Comradeship in the Grand Army of the Republic* (Chapel Hill: University of North Carolina Press, 2011), 204. On the difficult lives of Black Union veterans after the war see Donald R. Shaffer, *After the Glory: The Struggle of Black Civil War Veterans* (Lawrence: University Press of Kansas, 2004).

24. Jim Weeks, *Gettysburg: Memory, Market, and an American Shrine* (Princeton: Princeton University Press, 2003), 94.

25. Weeks, *Gettysburg,* 95–96.

26. "In Carroll County," unidentified and undated newspaper clipping, scrapbook 3, box 1, Taylor Collection, MS 1863.

27. Minutes of May 30, 1889, vol. 2 ("Minutes"), box 1, John F. Reynolds Post No. 2 (Frederick, MD), Grand Army of the Republic Collection, 1863–1901, Historical Society of Frederick County.

28. J. Polk Racine, *Recollections of a Veteran. Or Four Years in Dixie* (1894; repr. [Easton?]: Bicentennial Commission of Cecil County, 1987), 25.

29. Racine, *Recollections of a Veteran,* 157.

30. Racine, *Recollections of a Veteran,* 151.

31. "Banquet of Union Veterans," unidentified newspaper clipping [1900], scrapbook 2, box 1, Taylor Collection, MS 1863.

32. "Maryland Day on Gettysburg Field," *Baltimore Sun,* October 25, 1888.

33. *Report of the State of Maryland Gettysburg Monument Commission to His Excellency E. E. Jackson, Governor of Maryland, June 17th, 1891* (Baltimore: William K. Boyle & Son, 1891), 78.

34. J. E. Duryee to Taylor, June 22, 1886, box 1, Taylor Collection, MS 2197.

35. *Chattanooga News,* October 9, 1903, clipping in scrapbook 5, box 2, Taylor Collection, MS 1863.

36. Nina Silber, *The Romance of Reunion: Northerners and the South, 1865–1900* (Chapel Hill: University of North Carolina Press, 1993) and "Reunion and Reconciliation, Reviewed and Reconsideration," *Journal of American History* 103 (June 2016): 59–83; David W. Blight, *Race and Reunion: The Civil War in American Memory* (Cambridge, MA: Belknap Press of Harvard University Press, 2001). As Silber makes clear in her 2016 article, "reunion" and "reconciliation" are treated distinctively by some historians of Civil War memory, most notably by Caroline E. Janney in *Remembering the Civil War: Reunion and the Limits of Reconciliation* (Chapel Hill: University of North Carolina

Press, 2013). Janney argues that, while reunion was achieved by the defeat of the Confederacy in 1865, reconciliation was an uneven political and cultural process that remained incomplete well into the twentieth century. Of course Maryland, like the other border slave states, did not need to be reunited with the United States because it never seceded. However, as this essay demonstrates, state officials and ordinary citizens, especially Civil War veterans and their female kin, contributed significantly to intersectional *and* intrastate reconciliation during the late nineteenth century.

37. Franklin D. Roosevelt, "We Are Not Only Acting But Also Thinking in National Terms," Address at Antietam Battlefield, September 17, 1937, in *The Public Papers and Addresses of Franklin D. Roosevelt: 1937, The Constitution Prevails* (London: Macmillan, 1941), 357–58.

38. David K. Graham, *Loyalty on the Line: Civil War Maryland in American Memory* (Athens: University of Georgia Press, 2018), 149–50.

39. Graham, *Loyalty on the Line*, 150–56. Maryland repealed this state song in 2021.

40. Graham, *Loyalty on the Line*, 161.

41. "Maryland's First Black House Speaker Calls for Confederate Plaque to Be Removed from State Capitol," *The Hill*, accessed July 17, 2019, https://thehill.com/homenews/state-watch/445341-marylands-first-black-house-speaker-calls-for-confederate-plaque-to-be.

42. "Wallace Opens Maryland Drive," *New York Times*, May 9, 1964.

43. "Wallace Draws Wild Applause from Women Conservatives," *Washington Post*, May 12, 1964.

44. Brugger, *Maryland*, 611.

45. Graham, *Loyalty on the Line*, 169.

46. "Unity Goal as Modern South Marks Civil War's 150th," *San Diego Union-Tribune*, August 13, 2009.

47. "Maryland's First Black House Speaker," *The Hill*.

CONTRIBUTORS

JEAN H. BAKER is professor emerita at Goucher College and the Bennett-Hartwood Professor of History. She is the author of ten books, including *Mary Todd Lincoln: A Biography; James Buchanan (The American Presidents, #15); Sisters: The Lives of America's Suffragists,* and *Margaret Sanger: A Life of Passion.* Her most recent book is *Building America: The Life of Benjamin Henry Latrobe.*

RICHARD BELL is professor of history at the University of Maryland. He is the author of *Stolen: Five Free Boys Kidnapped into Slavery and Their Astonishing Odyssey Home* and *We Shall Be No More: Suicide and Self-Government in the Newly United States.* He has held major research fellowships at Yale, Cambridge, and the Library of Congress and is the recipient of the National Endowment of the Humanities Public Scholar award. He serves as a Trustee of the Maryland Center for History and Culture.

THOMAS G. CLEMENS received his doctorate in history education from George Mason University, where he studied under noted Civil War historian Dr. Joseph L. Harsh. Following a thirty-four-year career at Hagerstown Community College, he retired as professor emeritus in 2012. He edited and annotated General Ezra A. Carman's manuscript, *The Maryland Campaign of September 1862,* in addition to numerous articles and several monographs. Clemens is a founding member and current president of Save Historic Antietam Foundation Inc., a nonprofit historic preservation organization. He is an NPS-certified Antietam Battlefield Guide.

ROBERT COOK is emeritus professor of American history at the University of Sussex, UK. He is the author of several books on the memory of the Civil War, including *Troubled Commemoration: The American Civil War Centennial, 1961–1965,* and *Civil War Memories: Contesting the Past in the United States since 1865.*

MARTHA S. JONES is the Society of Black Alumni Presidential Professor and professor of history at The Johns Hopkins University. She is a legal and cultural historian whose work examines how Black Americans have shaped the story of American democracy. Professor Jones is the author of *Vanguard: How Black Women Broke Barriers, Won the Vote, and Insisted on Equality for All* (2020), winner of the *Los Angeles Times* 2020 Book Prize for history, and *Birthright Citizens: A History of Race and Rights in Antebellum America* (2018), winner of the Organization of American Historians Liberty Legacy Award for the best book in civil rights history, the American Historical Association Littleton-Griswold Prize for the best book in American legal history, and the American Society for Legal History John Phillip Reid book award for the best book in Anglo-American legal history. Jones is also the author of *All Bound Up Together: The Woman Question in African American Public Culture 1830–1900* (2007) and a coeditor of *Toward an Intellectual History of Black Women* (2015). Jones holds a PhD in history from Columbia University and a JD from the CUNY School of Law. Prior to her academic career, she was a public interest litigator in New York City, recognized for her work as Charles H. Revson Fellow on the Future of the City of New York at Columbia University.

BRIAN MATTHEW JORDAN is associate professor and chair of the department of history at Sam Houston State University. His books include *Marching Home: Union Veterans and Their Unending Civil War*, which was a finalist for the Pulitzer Prize in History; *The War Went On: Reconsidering the Lives of Civil War Veterans* (coedited with Evan C. Rothera); and *A Thousand May Fall: Life, Death, and Survival in the Union Army*.

JESSICA MILLWARD is an associate professor in the department of history and Core Faculty member of African American Studies at UC Irvine. Her first book was *Finding Charity's Folk: Enslaved and Free Black Women in Maryland*. Millward has published in the *Journal of African American History*, the *Journal of Women's History*, *Frontiers*, *Souls*, the *Women's History Review*, *The Chronicle of Higher Education*, *The Feministwire.com* and *The Conversation.com*. She is currently working on a book-length project that discusses African American women's experiences with sexual assault and intimate partner violence in the late nineteenth century.

CONTRIBUTORS

CHARLES W. MITCHELL is the editor of *Maryland Voices of the Civil War*, winner of the 2009 Founders Award from the American Civil War Museum, and the author of *Travels Through American History in the Mid-Atlantic: A Guide for All Ages*, winner of the 2016 Lowell Thomas Gold Award from the Society of American Travel Writers. Both titles are published by Johns Hopkins University Press. Mitchell's research focuses on the effects of the Civil War on civilians. In 2018 he was selected as a Baltimore Historian-Scholar for his contributions to the history of Maryland. Mr. Mitchell serves on the Advisory Council of the National Civil War Museum and as a Trustee of the Maryland Center for History and Culture. He holds degrees from Penn State University and the University of Maryland.

TIMOTHY J. ORR is associate professor of history at Old Dominion University in Norfolk, Virginia. He is the author of several essays about the Army of the Potomac, editor of *Last to Leave the Field: The Life and Letters of First Sergeant Ambrose Henry Hayward*, and coauthor of *Never Call Me a Hero: A Legendary American Dive-Bomber Pilot Remembers the Battle of Midway*. For eight years, Orr was a seasonal park ranger at Gettysburg National Military Park. His television appearances include *Who Do You Think You Are?* (TLC), *Battle of Midway: The True Story* (Smithsonian Channel), and *The Greatest Events of World War II in Colour* (Netflix).

ROBERT W. SCHOEBERLEIN is employed by the Maryland State Archives and is presently the Acting Baltimore City Archivist. His research and publications have focused mostly on Civil War–era social history and reform movements in twentieth-century mental health care. Dr. Schoeberlein is a Trustee of the Maryland Center for History and Culture, where he chairs its Library Committee and is a member of its Publications Committee. He holds a PhD from the University of Maryland.

SHARITA JACOBS-THOMPSON is professor of history in the Social Sciences Department at Prince George's Community College and a program consultant in Washington, DC. Jacobs-Thompson is a former Assistant Professor of Civil War Era Studies and Africana Studies at Gettysburg College.

331

FRANK TOWERS is professor of history at the University of Calgary. He is author of *The Urban South and the Coming of the Civil War* and coeditor of three books: *Remaking North American Sovereignty: Towards a Continental History of State Transformation in the 1860s; Confederate Cities: The Urban South during the Civil War Era;* and *The Old South's Modern Worlds: Slavery, Region, and Nation in the Age of Progress.*

JONATHAN W. WHITE is associate professor of American studies at Christopher Newport University. He is the author or editor of ten books, including *Abraham Lincoln and Treason in the Civil War,* and *Emancipation, the Union Army, and the Reelection of Abraham Lincoln,* which was a finalist for both the Lincoln Prize and Jefferson Davis Prize, a "best book" in *Civil War Monitor,* and the winner of the Abraham Lincoln Institute's 2015 book prize. He serves as vice chair of The Lincoln Forum and on the boards of the Abraham Lincoln Association, the Abraham Lincoln Institute, and the John L. Nau III Center for Civil War History at the University of Virginia, as well as the Ford's Theatre Advisory Council. His recent books include *Midnight in America: Darkness, Sleep, and Dreams during the Civil War,* selected as a "best book" by *Civil War Monitor;* and *"Our Little Monitor": The Greatest Invention of the Civil War,* coauthored with Anna Gibson Holloway.

FRANK WILLIAMS is the founding chair of The Lincoln Forum and President of The Ulysses S. Grant Presidential Library and Association. He is the retired Chief Justice of the Rhode Island Supreme Court and the author or editor of more than twenty books and many articles.

INDEX

Morgan, Jennifer, 51
Morgan, Margaret, 28
Morris, William, 143
Mudd, Samuel A., 154
Murray, Anna, 21
Murray, Pauli, 36
Myers, Isaac, 279

Nannie, Queen, 55
National Hospital, 262–63, 272
National Road, 212, 215, 227–28
Navy (Confederate), 224, 230
Navy (Union), 118, 129, 153, 182
Neely, Mark, 152, 154
Nevins, Allan, 96
New England, 20, 35, 84
New Jersey, 84, 284
New Orleans, 16, 23–24, 226
New York, 46, 92–93, 96–97, 130, 167, 197–98, 201, 204, 284
New York City, 28–29, 63, 100, 140, 142, 146, 174, 186, 188, 195, 273, 276, 281
New York Times, 116
New York Tribune, 27, 96, 116
Newbern, 166–67
Niles, Hezekiah, 23–24
Nineth Corps, 8–9, 166–67
Norris, Mary, 281
North Carolina, 94, 121, 129, 166, 199, 201, 266, 307
North Point, Battle of, 263
Noyes, George, 198, 200
nursing. *See under* women's participation in the Civil War

Ogle, Samuel, 49
Ohio, 65–66, 84, 91, 115, 121, 196, 199–200, 229
Ohio River, 100
Olmsted, Frederick Law, 204
Oregon, 96
Orndorff, Irene, 268
orphanages, 279
O'Keefe, Mary, 270

Paludan, Phillip Shaw, 161
Pancoast, Mary, 289n78
Parker, Rachel, 6, 16, 35–36
Peace Party, 165
Pearce, James, 89
Pelosi, Nancy, ix
Pencek, Bill, 324
Pennington, J. W. C., 46
Pennsylvania, 5, 16–18, 22, 28–30, 36, 91, 98, 110–11, 116–17, 123, 162, 168, 197, 209, 211, 216, 219–224, 226–27, 230–31, 284
People's Contest, A (Paludan), 161
Perine, David, 67
Perrine, Bessie, 281
Perkins, Joseph G., 178
Petersburg, Battle of, 9, 187, 263, 320
Phelps, Almira Hart Lincoln, 273
Phelps, Charles E., 303
Philadelphia, 26, 29, 63, 98, 100, 111, 140, 142, 174, 182, 186, 230, 249, 273, 276, 281
photography, 195–96
Pickett's Charge, 223
Pierce, Franklin, 95
Piet, John P., 90
Pinkerton, Allan, 98–99, 140–41
Pittsburgh, 26, 140, 270
plantations, 18, 26–28, 49, 56, 152–53, 176–77, 293–94, 299, 307–8
Pleasonton, Alfred, 215
Plummer, Emily Saunders, 293–94, 298–99
Plummer, Henry Vinton, 294, 307
Poe amendment, 318
Point Lookout, 12, 151, 224, 230, 266
police, 32, 110–11, 113, 115–16, 118, 123, 130, 182, 184
Pollock, Sallie, 270
popular sovereignty, 86
populism, 126–27, 131
Potomac River, 10, 151, 168, 175, 209–212, 215, 218–225, 229
Pratt Street Riot, 2, 5, 8, 108–131, 161–62, 181, 212, 261, 276
Prigg v. Pennsylvania, 28